"Father Hogan's argument is an exercise in exact thinking. That, in itself, is a prime desideratum. Right ethics is impossible without correct logic. But the question has not merely dialectic value. Several years ago, MacSwiney made the hunger-strike a vital problem, and now again it acquires great practical importance because of Gandhi's similar strategy for compelling a great empire to do justice. 'There ought to be a law' that no one be permitted to discuss the question without having first undergone the mental discipline involved in the study of an argument, as close as that to which Father Hogan treats us."

REV. JAMES M. GILLIS, C.S.P.,
Editor, *The Catholic World*.

* * *

"Father Hogan's interesting and informing pamphlet is a valuable contribution to a subject which has been widely discussed. Even the opponents of hunger-strike must concede that Father Hogan's arguments are intelligently, forcefully and illuminatingly stated, and are, therefore, most pertinent to any study of that subject."

The Brooklyn Tablet.

* * *

"Father Hogan's brochure on the morality of hunger-strike is both timely and interesting. Indeed it has a special news value, for the hunger-strike, so dramatically brought to the notice of the whole world by MacSwiney, is, as Father Hogan points out, an appeal, not to mercy but to justice, essentially a protest against injustice, and, as such, patriotic men are still resorting to it.

"There is a great deal of misunderstanding concerning hunger-strike, principally because its essential elements have not been presented by any other writer in the clear manner that Father Hogan has done."

The Catholic News (New York).

* * *

"The conciseness, accuracy and clearness of Father Hogan's excellent treatise on the Morality of Hunger-Strike should commend it to every reader of ethical subjects in this country and abroad. Thank God, someone with ability has finally discussed this ethical question in all its details and ramifications.

"As far as I am concerned, and, I feel sure, as far as all others interested in the question are concerned, the matter has been settled definitely by Father Hogan once and for all. With unerring logic he points out the defects of those who would summarily dismiss every hunger-striker as a suicide.

"The author's treatment of supposed parallelism must prove disconcerting to those who offer so-called parallels in justification of their conclusions.

"I sincerely hope that Father Hogan's discussion of hunger-strike will receive the wide audience that its merits deserve."

REV. EDWARD LODGE CURRAN, LL.B., Ph.D.,
    President, International Catholic Truth Society and Editor of *Truth*.

Imprimi Potest

FRANCIS X. BYRNES, S.J.,
  Vice-Provincial, Maryland-New York Province

Nihil Obstat

ARTHUR J. SCANLAN, S.T.D.,
  Censor Librorum

Imprimatur

† PATRICK CARDINAL HAYES,
  Archbishop of New York

Second Edition of Ten Thousand Copies

Reprinted in part from THE IRISH WORLD of May 20, 1933.

This publication is intended for private circulation only.

In

Bond and Token

of

Abiding Friendship

the author dedicates these pages

to

John Stephen Burke

Papal Chamberlain

Philanthropist and Scholar

OTHER PUBLICATIONS BY THE SAME AUTHOR

I. Vocational

* "The Priesthood — How Holy!"

II. Apologetical

* "Darrow versus Chesterton"
* "Clarence Darrow's Gospel of Lawlessness"
* "Clarence Darrow Champion of Unbelief"
  "Lord Bacon versus Scholastic Philosophy"

III. Labor Organization

"Loyal to the Union, Just to All"
"Educate the Rank and File"

IV. Theologico-Scientific

"Bacon and Newman Bar God from Science"

* Supplied by The International Catholic Truth Society, 407 Bergen Street, Brooklyn, N. Y.

Printed by St. Peter's College Press
144 Grand Street
Jersey City, N. J.

THE ECCLESIASTICAL REVIEW
on
MORALITY OF HUNGER-STRIKE

Rev. Michael Hogan, S. J.

"TRUTH CRUSHED TO EARTH SHALL RISE AGAIN:
"THE ETERNAL YEARS OF GOD ARE HERS."
BRYANT—"THE BATTLEFIELD."

ST. PETER'S COLLEGE PRESS
JERSEY CITY, NEW JERSEY

Contents

Introductory Comments by the Author 10-13

Chapter One
HUNGER-STRIKE DEFINED AND EXPLAINED 14-16

Chapter Two
HUNGER-STRIKE IS ESSENTIALLY A PROTEST AGAINST INJUSTICE 17-25

Chapter Three
THE QUESTION STATED 26-29

Chapter Four
THE SOURCES OF MORALITY 30-32

Chapter Five
THE END OR INTENTION 33-37

Chapter Six
THE ESSENTIAL MEANS—THE ACTION ITSELF 38-40

Chapter Seven
THE CIRCUMSTANCES 41-44

Chapter Eight
FIFTH COMMANDMENT NEGATIVE AND POSITIVE 45-47

Chapter Nine
SELF-KILLING INTENDED AND UNINTENDED 48-50

Chapter Ten
"IT LOOKS LIKE SUICIDE" 51-53

Chapter Eleven
THE VALUE OF HUMAN LIFE 54-56

Chapter Twelve
GOD'S DOMINION OVER HUMAN LIFE 57-59

Chapter Thirteen
WHETHER HUNGER-STRIKE UNTIL DEATH IS OR IS NOT SUICIDE 60-63

Chapter Fourteen
WHETHER HUNGER-STRIKE UNTIL DEATH IS EVER LAWFUL 64-76

242.51
H714e

8869

Chapter Fifteen
SOME OBJECTORS AND THEIR OBJECTIONS — FR. TANQUEREY, S.S. 77-93

Chapter Sixteen
SOME OBJECTORS AND THEIR OBJECTIONS — FR. WOUTERS, C.SS.R. 94-98

Chapter Seventeen
SOME OBJECTORS AND THEIR OBJECTIONS — FR. MERKELBACH, O.P. 99-100

Chapter Eighteen
SOME OBJECTORS AND THEIR OBJECTIONS — FR. DAMAN, C.SS.R. 101-105

Chapter Nineteen
SOME OBJECTORS AND THEIR OBJECTIONS — FR. VERMEERSCH, S.J. 106-110

Chapter Twenty
SOME OBJECTORS AND THEIR OBJECTIONS — AN IRISH "PROFESSOR OF MORALS" 111-122

Chapter Twenty One
SOME OBJECTORS AND THEIR OBJECTIONS — LA "CIVILTA CATTOLICA," ROME, ITALY 123-182

Chapter Twenty Two
SOME OBJECTORS AND THEIR OBJECTIONS — "THE EXAMINER," BOMBAY, INDIA 183-262

Chapter Twenty Three
THE CHURCH AND THE QUESTION OF HUNGER-STRIKE 263-270

Chapter Twenty Four
ACTIONS OF IRISH HUNGER-STRIKERS MORE THAN LAWFUL 271-311

Appendix A
COMPLETE TEXT OF "A PROFESSOR OF MORALS IN AN IRISH ECCLESIASTICAL COLLEGE" 312-314

Appendix B
COMPLETE TEXT OF "THE CASE OF THE MAYOR OF CORK—A MUCH DISCUSSED QUESTION" 315-322

Appendix C
COMPLETE TEXT OF "THE ETHICS OF HUNGER-STRIKING. A POST-FACTUM SURVEY" 323-336

Index
NAMES OF PERSONS AND SUBJECTS OCCURRING IN THE TEXT 337-349

Introductory Comments by the Author

QUESTION ASKED AND "THE REVIEW'S" ANSWER

UNDER the title "Morality of the Hunger-Strike" the January number of The Ecclesiastical Review contained a communication and reply likely to prove interesting and instructive alike to students and professors of Moral Theology. Here is the communication:

> "To the Editor, The Ecclesiastical Review":
>
> "Do you know whether or not there is any manual "of Moral Theology taught in seminaries which treats "the question of death brought on by wilful fast? It "cannot be said that the question needs no teaching, 'being so clear of itself, because contradictory asser-"tions about the question have found their way into "Catholic reviews. On the other hand, to say that the "Church keeps silence and avoids committing herself, "out of consideration for some political or national "party, would be an insult to the fearless Church of "the Apostles and of the Martyrs." (January 1933).

The foregoing communication was published anonymously. Its author, however, was evidently a Catholic Priest, who, thirteen years after the controversy about the morality of the MacSwiney hunger-strike, was still unaware that hunger-strike is essentially a protest against injustice – not merely "death brought on by wilful fast." He evidently meant to inquire about hunger-strike. And his unfamiliarity with the essentials of hunger-strike is shared by ninety-nine per cent of the Catholic Clergy. How few of them seem to be aware (1) that no hunger-striker unto death intends his own death, either as an end or as means; (2) that no act of refusing food until death is ever evil from itself – intrinsically evil; and (3) that, therefore, the determining factor of the lawfulness or unlawfulness of every hunger-strike is the proportion or disproportion of the good effect to the life sacrificed to obtain it. The theology of hunger-strike was not known to the Clergy when MacSwiney died, nor is it known to them now, thirteen years later. As a gauge of the American Clergy's knowledge – that is to say, lack of knowledge – of the theology of hunger-strike, we might take the answer given by "The Ecclesiastical Review" to the foregoing inquiry.

The citation just given is made up of (1) an inquiry, (2) an assertion and (3) an implication. Let us consider each in turn. The inquiry is "whether there is **any manual** of Moral Theology taught in seminaries which treats the question of death brought on by wilful fast." To this question **The Ecclesiastical Review** gave the following answer:

> "Assurance is given that the manuals of Moral The-
> "ology do not pass over in silence the problem of the
> "morality of the hunger-strike. Tanquerey – Synopsis
> "Theologiae Moralis et Pastoralis – briefly yet adequ-
> "ately treats the subject, to name one widely used
> "manual."

THE INQUIRY, THE ANSWER

It seems well to point out that the inquiry **is not about hunger-strike at all**, but only about "**death brought on by wilful fast.**" Not every death brought on by wilful fast is hunger-strike. Again the inquiry is whether there is **any manual** of Moral Theology taught in seminaries, which treats the question. The answer of **The Review** is that **all or most** of the manuals treat it. If, when The Review said that "the manuals of Moral Theology do not pass over in silence the problem of hunger-strike," it was speaking only for one or two manuals – those of Fr. Tanquerey and Fr. Wouters – it should rather have said: "**Not all** the manuals of Moral Theology pass over in silence the problem of hunger-strike." But instead of speaking for one or two or a few manuals, The Review speaks for all or practically all manuals of Moral Theology. "**The Manuals of Moral Theology**" etc.

In proof of its assertion, as well as in disproof of its correspondent's main contention – that theology maintains silence regarding death brought on by wilful fast – The Review makes answer that "**Tanquerey treats the subject briefly yet adequately.**" And, in a letter to the present writer, the Reverend Editor of The Review likewise states that "**the last edition of Wouters' 'Manuale' discusses that problem.**"

Supposing, for the sake of discussion –"dato sed non concesso"– that **the assertion of The Review** regarding Fr. Tanquerey's Synopsis, and the other assertion of the Reverend Editor regarding Fr. Wouters' Manuale, correspond to the facts of the case; supposing that both Fr. Tanquerey and Fr. Wouters **do treat the question** under consideration, does that justify the assertion of The Review that "the manuals" of Moral Theology do not pass over that question in silence? The manuals of Ethics and Moral Theology, within whose scope the subject in question lies, **number more than one hundred.** If, of that number, two, and only two, treat a question, is it true to say that **the manuals** treat it? "The manuals" means **manuals in general.**

NOT TREATED BY ANY THEOLOGIAN

But, unfortunately, it must be pointed out, in addition, that neither Fr. Tanquerey nor Fr. Wouters discusses hunger-strike at all. Nay more. In studying the present question, the present writer has had occasion to examine practically every extant manual of Ethics and Moral Theology, and can therefore assert, from personal knowledge, that not a single one among them discusses the specific question of hunger-strike. Nor, with the exception of Fr. Tanquerey, is there one among them who even mentions hunger-strike expressly.

FR. TANQUEREY ALL TOO BRIEF

The Ecclesiastical Review says that Fr. Tanquerey "briefly yet adequately treats the subject." Certainly the brevity of Fr. Tanquerey's treatment leaves nothing to be desired in that respect. One small paragraph of eight and one-half lines contains that author's entire treatment of the morality of hunger-strike – that troublesome question which, only twelve years ago, in the case of Mayor MacSwiney of Cork, called forth more than one hundred pieces of controversy from Archbishops, Bishops and Priests, some of whom were then, while others had previously been, professors of Moral Theology. Fr. Patrick Gannon, S.J., Professor of Dogmatic Theology, writing on the MacSwiney case, in The Tablet (London) of November 20, 1920, called it "a vexed question that is exercising the best casuists of the Church," and expressed the hope "that a solution will result from their endeavours." A writer in the Catholic Columbian (October, 1920) said that "there will always be two opinions on the question of hunger-strike." And Monsignor Belford, of Brooklyn, N. Y., wrote in his Nativity Mentor that "it might be necessary for the Church to decide it."

Was it, then, to be supposed that the myriad assertions and denials, accusations, denunciations and rejoinders, all the violent clashing of rival theological opinions, could be harmonized, and the many partisan and bitterly contentious minds and hearts that produced them be set at rest by the single paragraph of Fr. Tanquerey or any other theologian? Theology has no thermometer or micrometer or magic talisman wherewith to automatically reconcile apparent contradictions, or decide the merits of conflicting claims.

Even the most elementary discussion of any subject needs a definition of that subject and usually begins with it. Not so the discussion of hunger-strike. In a hundred magazine articles, its "pros" and "cons" were discussed with vehemence by hierarchy and clergy. But not a single one of the parties to the controversy defined or attempted to define hunger-strike. Did they know accurately what hunger-strike is? Judging from what the great majority wrote about it, they did not.

TWO CONSPIRACIES AGAINST THE TRUE DOCTRINE

Two types of conspiracy are responsible for still leaving the morality of hunger-strike until death a question-mark for all Catholics – clergy as well as laity. The one is a conspiracy of deliberate equivocation, the other a conspiracy of deliberate silence. Professors of Morals are very largely responsible for both. Their lectures and publications have been, and continue to be, full of the unmistakable silence, while the meagre compositions on hunger-strike, published under their names, are full of the unmistakable equivocation. These are grave charges, but they are fully substantiated in the pages that follow.

--- MACSWINEY'S PHILOSOPHY ---

"Let the cultivation of a brave, high spirit be our great task. It will make each man's soul an unassailable fortress. Armies may fail, but it resists forever."

"We all recognize that great virtue of mind and heart that keeps a man unconquerable above every power of brute strength. I call it moral force."

"A true soldier of liberty will always remember that self-restraint is the great attribute that separates man from the brute; that retaliation is the vicious resource of the tyrant and the slave; that magnanimity is the splendor of manhood."

Chapter One

HUNGER-STRIKE DEFINED AND EXPLAINED

HUNGER STRIKE—
ANY REFUSAL OF ALL NECESSARY FOOD, INTENDING TO CONTINUE IT, IN PROTEST AGAINST INJUSTICE.

ALL REFUSALS MORALLY ONE REFUSAL

Note I. Whether the refusals of all necessary food be **few or many**, the entire hunger-strike is **morally a single act**, having the same **essential** morality as if it had been only a single refusal. The several refusals are made **a unit by the single, unrevoked intention to continue.** For this reason the morality of any single refusal does not change as the hunger-strike progresses. The entire morality of his hunger-strike is contracted by the hunger-striker the **very first instant that he decides on his course**, and even before he has yet actually refused a single meal.

Note II. Hence refusal of food when death is **near** has no essentially different morality than refusal when death is **remote**. Neither have **very many** refusals an essentially different morality from fewer. A hunger-strike consisting of refusal of **only a single meal** would have the same essential morality as the MacSwiney hunger-strike of seventy-four days, and **the first and almost harmless** refusal the same essential morality as **the last, fatal** one.

"of **all necessary food**,"
that is to say, of all nutriment **necessary for preserving life**. This does not include water, for water is not considered nutritious. It were useless to inquire whether **a morsel** of food taken each day, or sustenance **injected** into the alimentary tract, or into the blood-stream, would prevent a prolonged fast from being hunger-strike. An infinity of such unpractical questions might be asked regarding any case of morals. 'Twere like asking the **precise moment** when a lamb ceases to be a lamb and becomes a sheep. Practical questions cannot and need not use the infinitesimal system of Mathematics for their solution. At all events, partial self-starvation in protest against injustice, and causing premature death, even though it might be suicide, **would not be hunger-strike.**

On Morality of Hunger-Strike

"**intending** to prolong it"

I. This intention may be either
   (A) Limited—for a specified number of days, or
   (B) Unlimited—until death

The hunger-strike of Mahatma Gandhi, begun March 3, 1939, in protest against the autocratic rule of Thakove Saheb of Raykot, was intended until death. He said:

"He who urged me to undertake this fast will give "me strength to go through with it, **if it is his will I** "**should still live** for a while on this earth to carry on "my self-chosen mission to humanity."

His hunger-strike immediately preceding was **for a stipulated length of three weeks**. His yet earlier hunger-strike, begun September 20, 1932, was **also intended until death**. He wrote to Prime Minister McDonald:

"I have to resist your decision with my life. The only "way I can do so is by declaring **a perpetual fast until** "**death from food of any kind**."

ACTUAL CONTINUANCE NOT ESSENTIAL

II. **Actual death is not essential** to hunger-strike. Otherwise every hunger-striker must die of hunger. But Mahatma Gandhi, and many others, are still alive notwithstanding their **several** hunger-strikes.

III. The **intention to continue** the refusal of all necessary food, whether for a limited period or until death, **is essential**. This intention, conceived prior to every actual refusal of food, **remains unaltered**, because unrevoked (virtual), until either discontinuance or death.

IV. This intention to refuse all food, either for a specified period or until death, **is never absolute**. It is **always conditioned** by some circumstance extrinsic or intrinsic to the hunger-striker. His mind is "I intend to fast for this number of days, or I intend to fast until death, **unless** the injustice against which I am protesting be redressed, or **unless** someone having authority over me bids me to desist, or **unless** my family and friends dissuade me from continuing, or **unless** constancy to continue fails me, or **unless**," etc., etc. And since several "unlesses" may operate conjointly to move the hunger-striker from his original purpose, **the continuance of the hunger-strike is never antecedently certain**. Therefore the **death** of the hunger-striker is **never antecedently certain**, even when he at first intends to continue until death. It can never be more than probable. This very pivotal consideration has been entirely ignored by every one of those who wrote against hunger-strike. They all assumed, without

3. Finally, the connection, for instance, between an act of profound bowing and obsequious submission is morally necessary. It is **morally impossible** that the act of prostrating oneself at the feet of another **should not mean submission**, or that the cry "long live the king" **should not mean loyalty**. And, similarly, it is morally necessary that hunger-strike should mean protest against injustice, and **morally impossible that it should not mean such protest**.

The necessity with which some actions produce their effects is **absolute**, because the relation of such actions to their effects is **essential**, and all essential relations are **absolutely immutable**, because **the essences so related are absolutely immutable**, like the Divine Essence which is their exemplar. It is **absolutely necessary**, for instance, that every act of comparing should have for its effect a judgment of identity or diversity, **and absolutely impossible that it should not**.

The actions of physical agents, on the contrary, not being immediately founded **on the divine essence, but rather on the divine decrees, have not an essential but only a natural** relation to their effects, and they, therefore, produce these effects **not with absolute but only with physical necessity**. A stone thrown into the air must fall to the ground, **not with absolute** necessity but only with **physical necessity**, which, though **ordinarily immutable**, in accordance with the Divine Wisdom that instituted it, is **absolutely subject to exceptions**, as the exercise of Divine Providence may require.

Lastly, the **moral** necessity with which definite human actions produce definite effects, originated, not in **divine** institution, as in the cases of absolute and physical necessity, but in **human institution**, afterwards sanctioned by the convention of immemorial usage.

Of conventional causes operating with necessity according to conventional laws, **language furnishes a familiar example**. It had its origin in the need that human beings have of communicating with one another by external signs. Theologians tell us that the Angels need no external signs in order to communicate their ideas one to another – that they **merely will to do so and 'tis done**. But the need is universal among humans, at least on this side of Eternity. And so, the laws of language operate **with conventional necessity**. If, in regulating motor-traffic at street crossings, the word "stop" were to mean "go" for some of the drivers, the consequences could only be disastrous. If, when the military commander gave the order to "halt," the rank and file understood it to mean "charge," this too must inevitably spell disaster. The "confusion of tongues" at the building of the Tower of Babel, has ever since been proverbial.

Thus we see the need of conventional forms of expression that are **fixed** and **immutable** and **universally accepted**. Human intercourse depends on them. And thus, for instance, each color in the rainbow spectrum has its distinguishing name, fixed and irrevocable. The color which is first, and lowest in order of vibrations, is called "red"; the next is called "orange"; the next "yellow," and so on. And the term "red," or its equivalent in other languages, designates that specific color for all men, for all time. At the original institution of names, the opposite convention might have been adopted. There is no compelling reason why our "North" could not then have been called "South," and "South" "North," nor why the color which was actually called "green" could not have been called "yellow," and **vice versa**. But whatever might be said about original possibility of the opposite, that individual color **was actually** called "green," "green" has been its name ever since, and "green" will continue to be its name until the end.

PROTEST WITH CONVENTIONAL NECESSITY

And, for similar reasons, the **fixed** and **irrevocably accepted** signification of **protest against injustice has attached to hunger-strike for nearly two thousand years.** In his "Social History of Ancient Ireland," the scholarly Dr. Joyce gives the following account of hunger-strike as practised in ancient Ireland:

"In some cases a curious custom came into play – the "plaintiff 'fasted on' the defendant. It was done in this "way. The plaintiff, having served due notice, went to "the house of the defendant, and, sitting before the "door, **remained there without food.** It may be inferred "that the debtor generally yielded. It was considered "**outrageously disgraceful** for a defendant not to sub-"mit to it. **Hereditary custom,** backed by public opinion, "was so overwhelmingly strong that resistance was "hardly ever resorted to. It is pretty evident that the "man who refused to abide by the custom not only in-"curred personal danger but lost **all character,** and was "subject to something like what we now call **a universal** "**boycott,** which, in those days, no man could bear. He "had, in fact, to fly and become a sort of outlaw.

"Fasting as a mode of enforcing a right is men-"tioned in the tripartite and other lives of St. Patrick, "and Patrick himself, as related in these, **fasted against** "**several persons to compel them to do justice.**

"This institution of fasting on a debtor is still widely "diffused in the East. Our books do not give us much "information about the Irish institution, but it is evi-"dently identical with the Eastern custom."

(Part I, Chap. VIII.)

PRACTISED BY HIERARCHY AND CLERGY

It is worthy of particular notice that among those who practised hunger-strike in ancient Ireland were many archbishops, bishops and priests, some of whom afterwards became canonized saints. In addition to St. Patrick himself, may be mentioned St. Caimin of Inishcaltra, St. Ailbe of Emly, St. Enda of Aran More, St. Malachy of Armagh, St. Deelan of Waterford, St. Lugith, St. Ruadah, St. Brendan, St. Adamnan, St. Comgall.

PRACTISED BY SEVERAL SAINTS TOGETHER

And it may be further remarked that these and other holy men sometimes practised hunger-strike together, by way of cooperative protest against injustice. Dr. Douglas Hyde, in his "Literary History of Ireland," gives the following account of one such cooperative protest.

> "Another instance of the clergy fasting upon a lay ruler was that of the notorious Raghallach (Reilly), King of Connacht, who made his Queen jealous by his infidelity, and committed other crimes. The story is thus recorded by Keating:
>
> "'The scandal of that evil deed soon spread throughout all the land, and the saints of Ireland were sorrowful by reason thereof. St. Fechine of Tobar (West Meath) came in person to Raghallach to reprehend him, and many saints came in his company, to aid him in inducing the prince to discontinue his criminal amour. But Raghallach despised their exhortations. Thereupon they fasted against him'." (page 233)

AND BY "THE TWELVE APOSTLES OF IRELAND"

And again Dr. Hyde narrates a further instance of organized fasting against Diarmud, the High King:

> "Upon this we are told that Ruadhan made his way to Brendan of Birr, and thence to the so-called twelve apostles of Ireland, and they all followed the King and came to Tara, and they fasted upon the king." (pp. 196, 229)

The "twelve apostles of Ireland" here mentioned were St. Ciaran of Clonmacnoise, St. Ciaran of Saigher, St. Brendan of Birr, St. Brendan of Clonfert, St. Columba, St. Columkille, St. Mobhi, St. Senanus, St. Ninnidh, St. Lasserian, St. Rodan, and St. Kenneth.

And the Rev. Louis Gougaud, O.S.B., in an article published in "The Irish Ecclesiastical Record," seven years before Mayor MacSwiney's hunger-strike, concludes with these words:

> "With the practice of an interested asceticism we may compare a legal institution of ancient Ireland – the procedure of fasting. Having exhausted all legal

"means to conquer the resistance of a powerful debtor, his creditor had only one means of constraint left to him – that of standing before the door of the debtor and **refusing to take nourishment till the debt had been paid.** If the debtor allowed the person fasting **to die of hunger, he was responsible for his death, and had to pay his family a considerable indemnity** in addition to the original debt. This was called fasting against or on a person." (1913, Vol. 1, page 231.)

IRELAND'S ANCIENT REGARD FOR JUSTICE

Such unimpeachable authorities as Dr. Joyce and Dr. Hyde testify, moreover, that "the whole tenor of ancient Irish Literature shows the great respect which the ancient Irish entertained for justice," and that they were "a law-abiding public," without any compelling sanction except the popular verdict. Their testimony has a direct bearing on the legal procedure of "fasting" as a means to secure justice. That law, as written in the Brehon Code, (1,113) runs thus:

"Notice precedes every distress (i.e. legal seizure of debtor's property by creditor) in the case of inferior grades, except it be by persons of distinction or upon persons of distinction. 'Fasting' precedes distress in their case. He who does not give a pledge to fasting is an evader of all. He who disregards all things shall not be paid by God or man. **He who refuses to cede what should be accorded to fasting, the judgment upon him, according to the Brehons, is that he pay double the thing for which he was fasted upon.**"

Thus, according to this law, a debtor who refused to satisfy the claim of a hunger-striking creditor could not himself obtain a legal judgment against any of his own debtors – "shall not be paid by God or man." Furthermore, if the debtor remained obstinate, and the creditor persisted in his hunger-strike even until death, in that case **the debtor was held responsible for the creditor's death, and was obliged to pay an indemnity to his relatives.**

* * * * *

LONG INSTITUTED, RECOGNIZED, PRACTISED

The way is now prepared for the proof of our thesis that hunger-strike is essentially and therefore always – not accidentally and therefore only sometimes – a protest against injustice. In syllogistic form the proof runs thus:

Major Proposition –

That action is **essentially a protest against injustice** which (1) was originally instituted as such; (2) has always been recognized as such; and (3) commonly practised as such for more than fifteen hundred years, up to the present time.

Minor Proposition –

But hunger-strike, (1) was originally instituted as a protest against injustice; (2) it has always been recognized as such; and (3) has been commonly practised as such for more than fifteen hundred years, up to the present time.

Conclusion –

Therefore hunger-strike is **essentially** a protest against injustice.

The **major** proposition of this syllogism merely enumerates qualities sufficient that an act be **essentially** a protest against injustice. Proof of the **minor** proposition has been already given in substance.

ALWAYS PROTEST AGAINST INJUSTICE ONLY

1. The words themselves of the **Law of Fasting**, together with the history of its original institution and ancient practice – both of which are given above – prove conclusively that hunger-strike was originally instituted as a protest against injustice.

2. When and where and by whom, **in times ancient or modern**, was hunger-strike regarded as not being a protest against injustice, but rather as a protest against **intemperance** or **profanity** or **immorality**, or as an appeal to **patriotism** or **sectarianism** or **charity**? When Mahatma Gandhi, dean of hunger-strikers, began one of his hunger-strikes on September 20th, 1932, **did anyone**, in any part of the civilized world, **fail to understand what precisely it meant? Was there anyone who judged it to be an act of worship of some Hindoo deity**, or an **act of expiation** for the crimes of transmigrated souls, or an **act of public thanksgiving and rejoicing**, for the prospective national independence of the Mahatma's countrymen? No! There was **no such misunderstanding anywhere** regarding Gandhi's hunger-strike. The world at large understood it to be **exactly what it is by its nature – a protest against injustice –** the injustice of dooming "the depressed classes" to perpetual depression, through segregation, separate electorates, etc.

That **protest** is expressed in Gandhi's own words, in his letter of August 18, 1932, from Yeravda Central Prison, to Prime Minister MacDonald.

"I have read the British Government's decision on "the representation of the minorities. I have to resist "**your decision with my life.** The only way I can do so "**is by declaring a perpetual fast until death, from food** "**of any kind**" . . .

"This fast will cease if, during its progress, the "British Government, on its own motion, or under pres-"sure of public opinion, revise their decision, and with-"draw their scheme of communal electorates for the "depressed classes."

Here we find, expressed in the hunger-striker's own words, all the essential elements of hunger-strike. First, there is a **real injustice** – segregation of the "untouchables;" secondly, there is refusal of all **food in protest** against it; thirdly, there is the intention to continue the refusal **until death;** fourthly, that intention is not absolute, but only hypothetical – unless the British Government **"revise their decision and withdraw their scheme."**

PRACTISED FOR FIFTEEN HUNDRED YEARS

From St. Patrick, who repeatedly practised hunger-strike in the fifth century, to Mahatma Gandhi who has repeatedly practised it in this twentieth century, is a period of **fifteen hundred years. Nor was the practice inaugurated at the coming of St. Patrick to Ireland. Even in the time of the Druids, justice was a sacred thing in Ireland, and hunger-strike a favorite means of vindicating it.**

Again, in the biographies of Irish saints of the seventh, eighth, ninth, and tenth centuries, hunger-strike is frequently recorded **as a common practice** not only of the laity but also of the **clergy, bishops and archbishops. Thirteen of the clergy,** every one of whom was afterwards placed on the calendar of canonized Saints, **fasted together** against Diarmuid, last of the High Kings to reside at Tara.

Contemporaneously with its practice in Ireland, hunger-strike **was also practised in some eastern countries. Professor Joyce,** who wrote in 1903, testifies that "this institution of fasting on a debtor **is still widely diffused in the East."** "Our books," he continues, "do not give us much information about the Irish institution, but it is evidently **identical with the eastern custom."** That hunger-strike prevailed extensively in British India in recent times is evident from the fact that it was **abolished there by penal statute as recently as the year 1861.**

TWENTIETH CENTURY HUNGER-STRIKES

The following further instances of hunger-strike, recently practised, and **always as a protest against injustice,** may be mentioned in conclusion. Twenty years ago, ten thousand **Irish Republican prisoners** went on hunger-strike together, in protest against their unjust imprisonment. Thousands of them fasted an entire month, and hundreds of them for forty days. Only a few years since, **one hundred and ten German** political prisoners went on hunger-strike at **Lichtenburg, Saxony,** in protest against the German Government's refusal to reconsider the sentences imposed on them for participation in the proletariat riots. It was in protest against their unlawful arrest and imprisonment that, in October, 1920, **MacSwiney, Fitzgerald and Murphy,** and subsequently **O'Sullivan and Barry,** died from uninterrupted hunger-strike. In February, 1930, **Richard Stewart, rug merchant** of Warren, Ohio, fasted thirty days in protest against arrest and imprisonment. In September, 1933, **Harrison Sasaki,** Mexican pugilist, went on hunger-strike to recover his purse for a bout with Arturo Scheckels of Belgium. At Nanking, China, in 1934, **Paul Noulens fasted twenty-six days, and his wife eighteen days,** in protest against sentences of life imprisonment for Communist plotting.

On August 21st, 1936, **three hundred coal miners** at Eichenau, in Polish Upper Silesia, went on a hunger-strike inside the mines, to recover their **unpaid wages.** In February, 1934, five members of the Irish Republican Army – Barry, Kearney, O'Neill, Cornelius Crowley and Michael Crowley began a hunger-strike in Cork Jail because they were not treated as political prisoners.

About the same time, **Professor Kraus,** of City College, New York City, went on a hunger-strike in protest against anti-Semitic agitation in Central Europe, and **Mahatma Gandhi** went through another of his several hunger-strikes, in protest against the English Government's maltreatment of the "untouchables." In July of last year, one hundred convicts in the **Alcatraz Prison** of California conducted a hunger-strike, the grievance of which was not stated in the Public Press. And as if in sympathy with their sequestered brethren in the western institution, nine long-term convicts in the **Old Eastern Penitentiary**, Philadelphia, Pa., staged a hunger-strike for more than a week in protest against the overcrowded condition of the prison cells. In March of this year **Anthony Esposito,** a prisoner in **The Tombs** (New York City) awaiting trial on two first-degree murder indictments, went on a hunger-strike. Finally, **forty-three German and Italian sailors** are now (April, 1941) on hunger-strike at East Boston Immigration Station, in protest against their detention following the surprise seizure of their long tied up vessels by the Government of the United States.

In the conscientious objectors' camp at Avalon, Md., **Corbett Bishop** of West New York, N. J., was on hunger-strike during the entire month of July, 1942, and **Mahatma Gandhi** has just now concluded his seventeenth hunger-strike (of twenty-one days' duration) **in protest against the arrest and** imprisonment of himself and several other leaders of the Indian Nationalist Party by the English Government.

We respectfully submit that the reasons embodied in the foregoing proof, establish, conclusively and beyond challenge, that hunger-strike is **essentially a protest against injustice**.

TYPICAL CASE OF "TWO EFFECTS"

The intimate bearing of this truth on the morality of hunger-strike is very evident. Hunger-strike is a typical case of "two effects," (duplex effectus") sometimes called **"indirect voluntary"** because the agent does not direct his action to produce the ill effect, but only to produce the good effect. Now since the same act of refusing food, which is exclusively directed by the hunger-striker to producing the good effect of protest against injustice, essentially, and therefore **always**, tends to produce the ill effect of his own physical weakness, the act would be unlawful if it did not tend to produce the good effect of protest, **essentially**, and therefore **always** – not merely accidentally and therefore only occasionally. If the ill effect is certain, the good effect must also be certain – unless indeed the probable good effect is very great and the certain ill effect is very small.

――――――――― MACSWINEY'S PHILOSOPHY ―――――――――

"Where now are the empires of antiquity? The peoples have endured; the empires perished. And the nations of the earth in this day will survive in posterity, when the empires that now contend for mastery are gathered into the dust, with all dead bad things."

"One armed man cannot resist a multitude, nor one army conquer countless legions. But not all the armies of all the Empires of the Earth can crush the spirit of one true man."

"You miss the significance of the philosopher completely when you take him for a theorist. The theorist propounds a view to which he must convert the world; the philosopher has a rule of life to immediately put in practice."

Chapter Three

THE QUESTION STATED

GOOD EFFECT PROTEST. ILL EFFECT DEATH

The question of hunger-strike is not as complicated as is generally supposed. It is clearly a case of an **omission** producing two effects ("**duplex effectus**"), the one good, the other ill. The **essential** good effect of hunger-strike is **protest against injustice**. Its essential **ill effect** is the **certain physical debility, and possible death of the hunger-striker**. We purposely say "ill" effect rather than "evil" effect. It will be here shown, **to a certainty**, that the "ill" effect of hunger-strike is not **intrinsically evil**. If it were, it would be forbidden **on its own account**, and so the action producing it could not be placed, no matter how much good besides might result from it. We shall therefore continue to call it the "ill" effect, and not the "evil" effect, to prevent its being inadvertently mistaken for something **intrinsically evil**. Moreover, **this ill effect is not intended, but only permitted**, and therefore lacks the chief requisite for moral evil. To avoid confusion of terminology we shall refrain from calling it "**indirectly voluntary**," that is to say, inseparable from another effect **directly voluntary**. "**Merely tolerated**" expresses the will of the agent towards effects indirectly voluntary, even better than the term "**permitted**."

ILL EFFECT OFTEN INSEPARABLE FROM GOOD

There are innumerable human actions and omissions that produce a **good** effect and at the same time **an ill effect inseparable** from the good effect. The good effect cannot be produced without, at the same time, producing the ill effect. If it could, the agent would be, in conscience, obliged to omit the ill result. But there are many cases in which this is not morally possible. In all such cases, the ill effect is **merely tolerated** on account of the good effect, so much so, that the human action which produced the ill effect, would be forbidden, were it not for the good effect which the action also produces.

An example will make the principle clearer. Suppose that a large business block in the heart of a city takes fire. The firemen play several streams of water on the burning building. The water extinguishes the fire, but, at the same time, destroys great quantities of stock merchandise – clothing, hardware, groceries. Strictly speaking, the firemen do not intend to destroy the merchandise. They are bound in conscience to do everything they can, in the circumstances, to save it. But their first care must be **to save the building**, and prevent the conflagration from spreading to other buildings. To do this the loss of the **merchandise**, and other lesser losses, must be disregarded. They are unable to save the building and save its contents, and so they proceed to save the building, even if, to do so, they are compelled to ruin much that is valuable within the building. Aside from saving the building, or some other result proportionately good, it would be manifestly unlawful for the firemen to deluge the merchandise with water. If the burning building were in the open country instead, where no other buildings would be in danger, and if the merchandise were of much greater value than the building, and well protected against fire by asbestos covering, then the firemen would be obliged to allow the building to burn to the ground rather than save it by destroying the merchandise.

ACT WITH ILL EFFECT SOMETIMES LAWFUL

This example shows, first, that it is sometimes lawful to place an action having an ill effect, and second, that certain conditions must be fulfilled in order that such action may be lawful. The conditions are the following:

1. The ill effect **must not be intended**, either as **end** or as **means**.
2. The means (the action itself) must be either **good** or **indifferent**;
3. The good effect **must be proportioned to the ill effect**.

WHY ABOVE CONDITIONS ARE NECESSARY?

It may now be asked why must the several conditions just mentioned be verified in order that an action may be lawful which has an ill effect inseparably attaching to the good effect on account of which the action is performed? And, **in the first place**, why must the sole intention of the agent be to produce the good effect? Why may not the agent intend the ill effect, either as an **end** or as a **means**? Because if any grave evil effect were **intended** – either as an end or as a means – the entire action would thereby become evil, in accordance with the principle just enunciated: – "malum ex quocumque defectu." **Secondly**, why must the means – the action itself – be either good or indifferent – not intrinsically evil? Because if the action be intrinsically bad – bad in itself – **no intention** and **circumstances**, however good, can remove this intrinsic evil. It is evil and forbidden on **its own account**. There can be no justification for perjury or blasphemy. Thirdly, why must the good effect be **proportionate** to the ill effect? Because it is **for the sake of the good effect** that the ill effect is **tolerated**, and an ill effect that is **very great**, cannot be **tolerated** for the sake of a good effect that is **very small**.

WHY ARE ABOVE CONDITIONS SUFFICIENT?

It has already been said that if all the foregoing conditions are fulfilled, an action, even when it also produces an ill effect, is nevertheless lawful. All theologians are agreed on this, and Reason itself recommends it. For, otherwise the vast majority of human actions would be forbidden, since the vast majority of human actions, or at least very many of them, while **primarily attaining some good result**, have some ill effect or other, in some way, attaching to them. And so life would be intolerable if each person, before every action, were to feel obliged to eliminate every possibility of every ill result of such action. It would make all action practically impossible.

Now hunger-strike is another such action — another case of an action having two effects — the good effect, **a protest against injustice**, the ill effect, the **diminished strength and possible death** of the hunger-striker. When therefore it is asked whether hunger-strike is lawful or not, it is asked whether the conditions mentioned above are verified or not —(1) whether or not the ill effect is **intended, either as end or as means**; (2) whether or not the action is evil in itself — intrinsically evil; and (3) whether or not the good effect is proportioned to the ill effect.

CASES ONLY APPARENTLY DIFFERENT

For a clearer and more accurate understanding of the question, two different cases of hunger-strike until death may be distinguished:

First — the case of one who **internally** decides on hunger-strike until death, and **externally** refuses a meal or two or three, but afterwards desists from all further refusals.

Second — the case of another who, in the same determination, persistently continues to refuse food, and finally dies in consequence.

Now it should be carefully noted that the two foregoing cases, entirely different in their actual results, differ nowise in **their ethical character**. If the hunger-strikes were unlawful, the sin attaching to them would be contracted in both cases, and would be **essentially the same sin**. The intention of refusing all food until death in protest against **proportionate injustice** constitutes the entire essence of hunger-strike as regards its morality. And thus is eliminated the doubt as to whether the question considers **only the first refusal, or only the last, fatal refusal, or the entire series of refusals.** Supposing always the **intention of refusing food until death,** the essential morality is the same for the first and only refusal, the last fatal refusal, and the whole series of refusals until death.

IS IT SUICIDE? IF NOT IS IT EVER LAWFUL?

Two main considerations are involved in the question of hunger-strike until death – first, **whether it is suicide or not,** and, **secondly,** supposing that it is not suicide, **whether it is ever lawful.** The lawfulness of any hunger-strike does not follow as an inference from the assured conclusion that it is not suicide. Without being suicide, it may be **objectively suicidal,** and therefore **objectively** unlawful. Whenever the injustice is either **entirely imaginary,** or **trivial** in comparison with the life sacrificed in protest against it, the act of refusing food until death is **objectively suicidal.** But cases have happened in which the person refusing the food **thinks otherwise** – thinks that there is a **real injustice,** when in reality there is **none,** or thinks that the injustice is **grave,** when in reality it is not. Is such a person a suicide? Certainly not! He does not intend his own death. His action is not placed **in order** to kill himself, but in order to **protest** against what he falsely judges to be a proportionate injustice. Is his action **objectively suicidal?** It certainly is. It holds the **matter** of suicide, but lacks the **intention,** the **form,** which makes every human action morally what it is, and without which no action has any moral character atall. No one is judged to be a suicide because he kills himself by swallowing bichloride of mercury, thinking it to be bicarbonate of soda. Such action is **suicidal** but **not suicide.**

And so, while insisting that **no hunger-strike is ever suicide,** and may sometimes be lawful, **we are not defending the lawfulness** of every chimerical hunger-strike fitfully undertaken on account of any imaginary injustice. **We are defending only a hunger-strike intended until death, in protest against an injustice so grave that the benefit resulting from that protest is proportionate to the life sacrificed in order that justice may be vindicated.**

MACSWINEY'S PHILOSOPHY

"An idea that you hold as true is not to be professed only where it is proclaimed. Wherever your path lies, it will cross you, and you must glory in it or deny it."

Chapter Four

THE SOURCES OF MORALITY

MORALITY IS THE GOOD OR EVIL OF ACTS

"Morality," in the **popular though narrower** sense, is the observance of the Sixth Commandment, whose violation is called by the opposite name of "immorality." But in the **strict, theological** sense, "morality" signifies either the observance or violation of any moral precept. Theology speaks of the "morality" of an **unlawful** as well as lawful act, of an act according or contrary to the **First or Second or Third** Commandment as well as the Sixth.

When, therefore, the theologian speaks of the "morality" of an action, he means either its lawfulness or unlawfulness – its good or its evil character. This technical meaning of the word "morality" should be borne well in mind. In the following pages, the term "morality" will be used indiscriminately to designate either **the good or the evil** of human actions.

HAD FROM END, MEANS AND CIRCUMSTANCES

It is a fundamental principle of Moral Theology that every action, good and evil, derives its total morality from the aggregate of three distinct sources – from **end, means and circumstances** – (1) the end which the agent aims to attain; (2) the means he uses, namely the action itself; and finally (3) the circumstances in which the action is placed. This moral truth is astonishingly well known even to the uneducated. They understand that one person may give alms to the poor with the **intention** of relieving their distress, another to acquire a reputation for benevolence, a third to secure their votes on election day. They understand that, independently of all intentions and all circumstances, some actions (prayers, almsgiving, etc.) are good in themselves, and others evil in themselves (blasphemy, theft, etc.). They understand too that blasphemy becomes a still greater sin by the circumstance that it is done **in a church,** and that the sin of theft is aggravated by the circumstance that the person whose property was stolen happens to be a beggar, that the stolen property (a chalice) was especially consecrated to God's service. "Good, bad or indifferent" is an expression frequently on the popular lips.

END IS THING INTENDED. ACTION IS MEANS

Every human action is placed with some intention or other, and in some circumstances or other. But the mind may, for the moment, disregard the intention and the circumstances, and consider only the action itself – the thing done. This is what is meant by an action "in the abstract." Now it is only in the abstract that any human actions are indifferent – neither good nor evil. Every individual action is either good or evil. It is good if all the sources of its morality – end, means and circumstances – are good; it is evil if any one of these several sources of morality be evil. "Bonum ex integra causa; malum ex quocumque defectu." Evil in any one of the "sources" is "the leaven that corrupteth the whole mass." Moral Theology, therefore, asks three and only three questions about any human action – (1) What is done – the action itself; (2) Why it is done – the end or intention; and (3) How it is done – the circumstances. The action and its circumstances form an inseparable unit, and correspond to a substance and its accidents in the physical order. They are often extrinsic to the agent, whereas the end or intention is always in the mind and will of the agent. The action of killing a priest, by prolonged torture, in order to persecute the Church, furnishes an example of all three sources of morality. The deadly torture is the action or means; that it was prolonged, and that its victim was a priest, are circumstances; that it was to persecute the Church is the end or intention.

GOOD ACTIONS EVIL FROM CIRCUMSTANCES

These important principles may be further illustrated by yet other examples. To nurse the sick is an action that is intrinsically good, yet it becomes evil instead when it is done entirely through pride or vain glory, or any other unworthy motive. So too, prayer is an intrinsically good act, and yet if a servant should deliberately spend in prayer the time assigned for doing her master's work, or a father the time required to provide for his children, such prayer would be a crime rather than an act of virtue. In the first example, the action, intrinsically good, was vitiated by the evil intention of the agent; in the second case, the action intrinsically good, was made evil by evil circumstances.

ACTIONS EVIL FROM THEIR OWN NATURE

On the other hand, there are actions which, **independently of any purpose** on the part of the agent, and independently of any **circumstances** in which the actions may be placed, are **intrinsically bad,** and therefore can never be lawful. Such, for instance, is the act of telling a lie. In the words of Dr. Butler's catechism, "no lie can be lawful or innocent, and no motive, however good, can excuse a lie, because a lie is always sinful and bad in itself."

ACTIONS IN THEMSELVES INDIFFERENT

Finally, midway, as it were, between these two extreme classes of actions, there is a third class which, **intrinsically, and aside from the intention of the agent and the circumstances** of their placing, are neither good nor bad. Such actions are called **indifferent.** Examples of indifferent action would be the act of walking, of reading, of speaking. All such actions, intrinsically indifferent, become good when performed with the right intention and in right circumstances, evil if either the intention or the circumstances be evil. "Bonum ex integra causa; malum ex quocumque defectu."

It will not be a loss to consider separately each one of the three sources of morality already mentioned. Much of the false reasoning and prevalent misconception regarding the morality of hunger-striking has come from failure to grasp with accuracy the meaning of the moral principles involved, and the correct method of their application. Both must be done by all who would hope to understand the theology of hunger-strike.

MACSWINEY'S PHILOSOPHY

"It is only in the light of a perfect ideal that we can come near to perfection."

"If we are to be fit for the heroic tomorrow, we must arise and be men today."

"When men revolt against an established evil, it is their loyalty to the outraged truth we honor. We do not extol a rebel who rebels for rebellion's sake."

"He will be the best patriot and the best soldier, who is the best friend and the best citizen. One cannot be an honest man in one sphere and a scoundrel in another."

Chapter Five

THE END OR INTENTION

EXACT MEANING OF "INTENTION" NOT KNOWN

Many will also find it difficult to understand that the hunger-striker does not intend his own death. This is because they do not accurately grasp the meaning of "intention." The several acts of the will with regard to its object are (1) Desire; (2) Intention; (3) Election (of means to attain it); (4) Use of means (execution); (5) Possession. Desire is a mere longing for the object without even thinking how it may be possessed. **Intention is a tending towards means to possess it.** Election is a choice of certain means rather than others. Execution is the making use of the means chosen. Possession is the fruition of the object of desire, intention, election and execution. Intention, therefore, adds to mere desire the idea of striving to possess the thing desired. Hence our English word "tension."

Now many, not understanding these distinctions, fail to see that a person may **desire** his death, **hope** for it, **pray** for it, **rejoice** in it when it comes, and still not **intend it**. Over and above all the desiring and hoping and praying and rejoicing, intention implies the consideration of means – more or less violent – to bring about death. On the other hand, the mere desire does nothing, takes no means to hasten death, and moreover, may be for supernatural reasons. St. Paul had a "desire to be dissolved and to be with Christ." (Phil. 1.23.) The same must be said of hope. And the prayers and the rejoicing may be in entire conformity with God's will. Hence it could be altogether lawful for a hunger-striker, or any one else, to desire his own death, to hope and pray for it, and when it came unintended, lawful to rejoice in it. During the MacSwiney hunger-strike, the English Government received warnings from many sources against allowing him to die. The French paper Le Matin said: "It is an act of sincere friendship to cry out to our allies while it is yet time: 'Don't make martyrs'." From the very first hour of the Lord Mayor's detention, it was entirely lawful for him to **desire** and **hope** and **pray** that the English Government might be impolitic enough to allow him to die. And when they did so, it was entirely lawful for him, in his last hour, to sing his "nunc dimittis"

– to rejoice in his own death, both because it spelled the end of his long drawn out death-agony and added another glorious name to the long list of his country's martyrs.

INTENTION CHIEF SOURCE OF MORALITY

Like every abstract word, the word "intention" is intangible, evasive, half unintelligible. And yet it is **chiefly from the intention** that all moral actions derive their morality. The intention is the **substantial form** constituting every individual human action either morally good or morally bad. The action itself together with the circumstances, are the **matter** – in themselves undetermined to either good or evil – of every good and evil act. Action and circumstances correspond to the materials – wood, iron, cloth, leather, etc.– on which the mechanic works; to the particular **shape** which he gives these materials – table, drill, overcoat, shoes – corresponds the **intention** in moral actions. Since, therefore, the intention is the determining element, **the moral form** of every action both good and evil, it follows that, apart from the intention of the agent, no action could ever be either good or evil. No man is found guilty of murder because, accidentally and without any deliberate intention, he happened to kill a fellow man, nor is anyone convicted of theft merely because he unintentionally took into his possession the valuable belongings of someone else.

END GOOD, ACTION GOOD. END EVIL, ACTION EVIL

It may therefore be inferred as a corollary from the foregoing, that whenever the intention is good, **the action cannot be evil**, and on the contrary, whenever the intention is evil, the action can never be good – **must always be evil**. Nay more, though the good action intended be never placed, **the merit** of it is, notwithstanding, acquired by **the good intention alone**. The Lord said to Abraham: (Genesis, xxii, 16): "Because thou hast done this thing, and hast not spared thy only begotten son for my sake, I will bless thee, and I will multiply thy seed as the stars of heaven, and as the sand that is by the seashore." And, similarly, the guilt of an evil action is always incurred by **its evil intention, even when the evil action itself is never placed**. In the Sermon on the Mount, Christ said: "Whosoever shall look on a woman to lust after her, hath already committed adultery with her in his heart." (Matthew, v, 28.) True, the man or woman is not indicted in our courts of civil justice, for merely **intending** to commit murder or robbery, because civil authority has no jurisdiction over merely internal acts of intellect or will. But the law of Conscience has authority over internal as well as external acts, and returns a verdict of "guilty" against the person **who only intends** murder or burglary, as well as it does against the actual murderer or the actual burglar. **The will to commit the crime is sufficient for the guilt.**

For suicide then, one must (1) **intentionally** take one's own life, and (2) must, moreover, do it **on one's own authority.** God, the Giver of life, might, if He chose to do so, authorize any one to take his own life, and it is probable too that the civil government has the right to authorize a criminal under just sentence of death to execute that death sentence on himself.

Neither good nor evil is possible, therefore, independently of intention. The good must be intended if it is to be good at all, and the evil must be intended if it is to be evil at all. And this is the place to answer an objection or two.

Obj. I   If neither good nor evil be possible independently of intention, is it not incorrect to speak of an action as "good in itself" or "evil in itself"? Does not the "in itself" mean independently of intention and circumstances?

Ans.   The objection fails to distinguish **material or fundamental** good and evil, from **formal** good and evil. When an action is said to be "good in itself" or "evil in itself," it is only **material or fundamental** and **not formal** good or evil that is meant. Action "good in itself" means only **good materials,** (prayer, almsgiving, adoration) which, **placed in good circumstances, a good intention makes into formally good acts.** Similarly, action "evil in itself" signifies only **evil materials,** (blasphemy, lies, theft), which an **evil intention** makes into **formally evil acts.**

Obj. II   It has already been said that if any one of the three sources of morality, is it not evil, the entire action is evil. How then can it be said that if the intention be good, the action cannot be evil, notwithstanding evil object and circumstances.

Ans.   If the intention be good, as is supposed, then the evil in the object or circumstances, **has not been recognized.** For if the evil had been recognized, the intention could no longer be said to be good, – it could not be said that the evil in the object was not intended. The action was placed in good faith by one having an erroneous conscience. It has just been said that the action and circumstances are only **materials,** to be made **formally good** or evil by a good or evil intention.

SUBJECT AND OBJECT OF INTENTION

To understand what precisely is meant by "intention," it will help to consider that its immediate **subject is the will of the person** who "intends," and its object, something to be attained by an action. Intention itself is **a movement of the will towards means to attain some object.** The object is not the intention, but something to be attained by the intention – something moving the will to tend to it, and moreover specifying that intention. It is the "finis operantis" – not the operans nor the operatio. And as the object is either **ultimate** or **proximate**, according as it is intended for its own sake or only as a means to attain some further object, so the corresponding intentions are ultimate and proximate respectively. Furthermore, since the attaining an object always necessitates the use of some means, every ultimate intention calls for a proximate intention corresponding. They are correlated.

ONE ACTION TWO INSEPARABLE EFFECTS

But most important in discussing the morality of hunger-strike is the distinction between intending **a thing itself** and intending **its inseparable adjunct**, desirable or otherwise. The firemen intend to extinguish the fire, but not to destroy the merchandise by water. The drug addict intends the soothing derived from the opiate, but not the sickness which he knows to be inseparable from it. The highwayman intends the crime of robbery, but not the death which he knows must inevitably follow from depriving his victim of the bare necessities of life. In each of these examples, there is a **main effect**, which is itself intended **explicitly and directly**, and a **secondary effect**, which is **not intended but only permitted** – because the main effect cannot be attained without it.

"Aliud est esse permissum, aliud esse volitum" says Suarez (De Volunt. et Liber. 1. IV. 8). And Rev. Timothy Brosnahan, S.J., in his "Adversaria in Ethicam," says: "It is one thing not to preserve one's life and "quite another to destroy it. If an action is placed, "which, of its nature, is destructive of human life, and "the destruction of life is **intended as an end, and the** "**action as its means**, then the killing is direct. But if "an action, of its nature deathly, be, at the same time, "essentially ordained to produce some other effect, then "the killing is only indirect, provided the death was not "intended.

(Page 171.)

ONE INTENDED, THE OTHER ONLY TOLERATED

The distinction then between an effect which is itself intended, and another effect inseparable from it, **but only tolerated**, is a clear, concise and complete answer to another seemingly serious difficulty against the lawfulness of hunger-striking. The sincere inquirer who found it difficult to understand how a deliberate action inevitably causing the death of the agent, could be anything short of evil in itself, now finds it equally difficult to understand how it can be truly said that the agent **does not intend** his own death when he deliberately places an action which he knows **must inevitably cause his death**. How can it be said that a man does not intend his own death, when he deliberately places a revolver against his own head, and discharges its contents into his own brain? Here is their objection presented in syllogistic form:

Major Prop. Whoever deliberately places an action, intends every effect which he knows must follow inevitably from that action.

Minor Prop. But the hunger-striker deliberately refuses all food, knowing that his own death must inevitably result.

Conclusion Therefore the hunger-striker intends his own death.

This difficulty is solved by the distinction already given between direct and indirect killing. It will be answered more fully in another place – when the intention of the hunger-striker is considered.

Another ground for the suspicion that Mayor MacSwiney intended his own death, is derived from his own words to the Bishop of Cork, when His Lordship visited him in Brixton prison. "My death," he said, "will be an example and an appeal to our young men to make every sacrifice for Ireland." Is not this a plain statement of MacSwiney's intention that his own death should be a **means** to further inspire his countrymen? We shall see.

MACSWINEY'S PHILOSOPHY

"It is the distinguishing glory of our soldiers of the forlorn hope that the defeats of common men were for them but incentives to further battle. They knew that they stood for the Truth, against which nothing can prevail."

Chapter Six

THE ESSENTIAL MEANS – THE ACTION ITSELF

ACTS THEMSELVES GOOD, BAD, INDIFFERENT

Every human action must be placed for **some end or other** and **in some circumstances or other**, and its adequate morality, good or evil, is constituted by the combined character of **the action itself, the end for which** it is placed, and **the circumstances in which** it is placed. All three constituents are **inseparably involved** in the morality of every action.

But though inseparable in constituting the morality of every action, these factors may be, indeed must be, examined and judged separately before a verdict about the aggregate morality of the action can be arrived at. And so the moralist disregards, for the moment, the end and circumstances, and **considers only the action itself.** He finds that some actions are **always good**, intrinsically good, as for example an act of **adoration**, and that other actions are **always evil**, intrinsically evil, as for instance an act of **blasphemy**. The moralist also finds that there are yet other actions which, aside from end and circumstances, are **neither good nor evil**, but rather **indifferent.** Such are acts of walking, reading, singing, and the like. And so we have actions **good in themselves**, actions **evil in themselves**, and actions **indifferent in themselves**, always bearing in mind that "in themselves" means aside from end and circumstances.

ACTS MORAL FROM THEIR OBJECTS – EFFECTS

Now it will be asked why are some actions good (fundamentally) and other actions evil (fundamentally), independently of every end and circumstances. **On account of God's infinite perfections**, acts of **adoring** Him are always **in accord with right reason**, and acts of **blaspheming** Him are always **contrary to right reason.** Again, **to tell the truth** is always conformed to right reason, and to tell a lie is always contrary to right reason. In general, some actions are always good because the **objects which they attain are always good**, and, contrarywise, some actions are always evil because the **objects which they attain are always evil.**

Since we are here dealing with the rock-bottom foundations of all morality, **it is all-important that the exact** meaning of the term "object" in this context should be well understood and remembered. The term "object" and its correlative term, "subject," must always be the bane of philosopher and theologian. Like the word "thing," they are both of such restricted connotation that they apply to almost everything, and so mean almost nothing. We have (1) the disloyal subject; (2) the subject of a discourse; (3) the thinking subject; (4) the subject seeking, in contradistinction with the thing sought. So too we have (1) the object in simple opposition to the subject; (2) the object in the mind of the agent, synonymous with purpose, aim and intention; and (3) object meaning any effect which any action produces or may produce. Agents have their objects or objectives (finis operantis), and actions too have their objects or objectives (finis operis), sometimes identical with the object or objective of the agent, but sometimes different from it. In every case of accidental shooting, the action is the discharging of the gun. The death of the victim is the object of the action, but it is by no means the object of the agent. Thus we see that, independently of any object or purpose in the mind of the agent, every action has an object of its own – its conatural effect. This is either material or formal. The material object of every action is the thing in which or on which the action produces its effect. The human body is the material object of medical treatments. The formal object is some aspect or other under which the action attains that material object. The formal object of medical treatments is the same human body, to be restored to health. And it is from that formal object or conatural effect that every action derives its intrinsic morality – its intrinsic good or evil. That is exactly what is meant by the ethical principle that "actions are specified by their formal objects," namely by the effects which they produce. "By their fruits you shall know them!" "Handsome is that handsome does!" Lawful is that lawful does, and evil is that evil does! Actions receive their morality – intrinsic morality – from their formal objects.

"TWO EFFECTS" OR "INDIRECT VOLUNTARY"

Let no one try to understand the morality of hunger-strike without first grasping the exact meaning of the terms "direct voluntary" and "indirect voluntary," sometimes called "voluntary in itself" and "voluntary in its cause." These terms have wrought untold mischief, chiefly on account of the indefiniteness of the word "direct," with its twelve or more different meanings. We submit each of the following propositions for separate and orderly consideration.

1. **Voluntary** means wished, willed, wanted.
2. **Actions** are either
    (a) **simply voluntary**, e.g. reading, walking, etc.,
    or
    (b) **simply involuntary**, e.g. breathing, pulsation.
3. **Effects** of actions are **called** (denominated) **voluntary** when **produced by voluntary actions**.
4. **Effects** of voluntary actions are **never called simply** "voluntary" as the actions which produce them are.
5. **Effects** of voluntary actions are either called "voluntary in themselves" or "voluntary only in their causes," according as the agent **intends** or **does not** intend them.
6. **Agents are continually placing good actions, intending only their good effects.**
7. But frequently the action produces **not only the good effect** which the agent intends, but also **an inseparable ill effect**, which he does not intend, but must tolerate for the sake of the good effect. Firemen do not intend to destroy merchandise with water.
8. The good effect **intended** is called **"direct voluntary"** or **"voluntary in itself."**
9. The ill effect, **not intended**, but merely tolerated, is called **"indirect voluntary"** or **"voluntary in its cause."**

The doctrine regarding "indirect voluntary" asks the following question and furnishes the following answer:

10. Question: **"When is an action lawful even though producing an ill effect?"**
    Answer: "An action producing an ill effect is lawful provided (1) the ill effect is not intended, nor (2) the action itself intrinsically evil, nor (3) proportion of good effect wanting."
11. The principle contained in that answer excludes:
    (1) An evil end (intention); (2) Evil means – the action itself; (3) **Evil circumstance** – disproportion of good.

MACSWINEY'S PHILOSOPHY

"The end of freedom is to realize the salvation and happiness of all peoples – to make the world, and not any selfish corner of it, a more beautiful dwelling-place for men."

Chapter Seven

THE CIRCUMSTANCES

CIRCUMSTANCES ADD MORALITY TO ACTIONS

Circumstances belong to actions and modify them. "Circumstances alter cases." The action itself may be likened to the skeleton or framework of a structure, the circumstances, to such superadded parts as complete the structure. What a circumstance is, and how it attaches to an action and modifies it, will be made clearer by an example or two.

On October 1, 1939, in St. Vincent's Hospital, New York, Dr. Clarence Payne Howley operated on the President of Mexico for appendicitis. Here the combination of action itself, intention and circumstances, is exhibited in one and the same act. The action itself is the act of making an incision, removing the inflamed appendix and lastly suturing the wound. Nothing more is included within the action, considered in itself. The primary intention is to improve the health of the patient, though several other worthy intentions, such, for instance, as to get further experience in surgery, or to gain a livelihood, may exist concomitantly with it.

It is a **circumstance** that the surgeon happens to be Dr. Howley rather than Dr. Poole, and the patient President Calles rather than Pancho Villa; that the operation was performed at St. Vincent's Hospital and not at Bellevue; that it was in October 1939 rather than 1839 or 1999; that the operation was performed skillfully rather than crudely; that it was performed with most modern instruments and safeguards against infection, instead of the insufficient equipment of half a century ago. All these superadded considerations are "circumstances" attending the action. They are, by no means, in no sense, the action itself, nor any part of the action itself. Whenever the action is considered "in itself" these superadded considerations must be left out.

Again, the engineer on a fast express, disregarding "slow down" and "stop" signals, runs his train into an open switch or telescopes another train, causing the death of several passengers. Here again the separate moralities of action itself, intention and circumstances, combine to constitute the total morality of the engineer's single act. The **action itself** is his deliberate omission to shut off the steam from the engine and apply the air-brakes. It includes nothing besides. Wrongly judging that he could safely disregard the signals, the engineer's **intention** was to make up the time he had previously lost, and bring his train "on time" into the Terminal Station. That the omission to "slow down" and "stop" was **at night and not during the day;** that it happened on the Pennsylvania Railroad and **not on the Baltimore and Ohio** or New York Central; that it happened **near Pittsburgh** and not near Philadelphia; that it happened to be **this particular engineer and train, rather than another** engineer and another train – of these several considerations, no one is any part of the **omission itself.** They are, all of them, **circumstances** connected with the omission, and nothing more.

CIRCUMSTANCE IS A COMPLETING ADJUNCT

The word "circumstance," as its etymology (circumstans) indicates, means "adjunct," "accidental determination or modification." And as, in the physical order, accidents supervene on their substances already substantially complete, bringing them a yet further **accidental** completeness, so, in the moral order, circumstances attach themselves, as it were, to human actions already morally and essentially complete from their objects, and give them a **superadded morality.**

CIRCUMSTANCES ARE MORAL ACCIDENTS

Indeed the parallel between **accidents** in the physical order and **circumstances,** in the moral order, is very complete. The number of **different species of physical accidents** is practically the same as that of **moral circumstances, and** even the **names** of the different species, though not given for exactly the same reasons or with the same meaning, are sometimes **the** same for both orders. All physical accidents belong to some one of nine classes called **categories.** Each physical accident is either a **quantity, a quality, a relation,** an **action,** a **passion** (being acted upon) a **place,** a **time,** a **posture** or an **equipment.**

And similarly, in the moral order, every circumstance belongs to some one of the seven following classes:

1. **The person who –**
   To punsh **criminals** is lawful for **public officials,** and even obligatory on them. It would be **unlawful for a private citizen.** Sexual transgression between **unmarried** persons is **fornication;** between persons **married** is **adultery;** between **blood relations** is **incest.**

2. **The thing which –**
   To steal a **consecrated** chalice is a greater sin than if it had not been consecrated. To steal a **large sum** of money is a greater sin than to steal a smaller sum.

3. **The place where –**
   Irreverence **in a place of worship** is a greater sin than it is elsewhere, a greater sin **in public** than in private.

4. **The reason why –** *
   The prayer of the Publican in the Temple was acceptable to God, **because he intended to humble himself**; that of the Pharisee was not, **because he intended only to exalt himself.**

5. **The time when –**
   The good or evil of an action is increased as the action is committed on the Sabboth, or sustained for **a longer period** – the **quantity of the action.**

6. **'The way how –**
   It is unlawful to eat or drink **immoderately,** lawful and praiseworthy to do so with moderation, unlawful to kill another, and still more so to do it **by torture.**

7. **By what means –**
   To strike a person **with a crucifix** is a greater sin than to do so with a stick. It is a sin to tell a lie, but a greater sin **to confirm it by an oath.**

NOT ALL CIRCUMSTANCES ADD MORALITY

It must not be concluded, however, that **every circumstance attaching to an action must always modify its morality.** It is a circumstance that the act of shooting a person to death was done **with a repeating rifle and at long range,** and not by an automatic revolver at close range; that poisoning was by **strychnine and not by arsenic;** that jubilee visits were made to **certain churches rather than to others;** that an alms was given to a **blind** man rather than to a **cripple.** All these different modifiers of actions are circumstances – the first and second referring to the **means by which,** the third to the **place where,** and the last to the **person who.** But none of them changes, in any way, the moral character of the actions to which they belong. Hence, some circumstances though present, **do not modify** the morality of their actions.

*Since **end, means** and **circumstances** are set down as separate sources of morality, it is likely to be supposed that the end or intention (why) **is not a circumstance. This is not so.** A circumstance is anything that modifies, **in any way,** the object or its corresponding action, and the intention does this. And because it does so in a very special way, **and to a greater extent than any of the other circumstances,** it is said to be a **separate** source of morality – a sort of second object.

CIRCUMSTANCE MAY CHANGE MORAL SPECIES

Of the circumstances that **do** modify the morality of an **action**, some change its **moral species** – make it an entirely different kind of action, while others **merely vary it within the same species**. The act of stealing is **theft** and nothing more, whether the watch stolen be an Ingersol or a Hamilton. But, while to steal one hundred dollars is simply a sin of theft, to steal a consecrated chalice – even when its currency value is only one hundred dollars – besides being a sin of theft is also a sin of **sacrilege**. The greater value of the Hamilton watch is a merely **aggravating** circumstance – **a greater theft**, whereas the consecrated character of the chalice makes the sin of stealing it **a different species** of sin. The consecration is a **specifying** circumstance.

"Circumstance" may therefore be defined as **an accident modifying the morality of an action** – because of special **agent** or special **object** or special **intention** or special **time** or special **place** or special **manner** or special **means**. It is a "**source**" of morality for the same reason that object and intention are. Like them, the circumstances just enumerated are capable of making the action to which they pertain, **conformed to right reason or difformed from it**.

MACSWINEY'S PHILOSOPHY

"The liberty for which we strive today is a sacred thing, inseparably entwined with that spiritual liberty for which the Saviour of men died. Death for it is akin to the sacrifice of Calvary."

Let us, with the old high confidence, blend the old high courtesy of the Gael. Let us grow big with our cause."

"We may reach the mountaintops in aspiring to the stars."

Chapter Eight

FIFTH COMMANDMENT NEGATIVE AND POSITIVE

FORBIDS ALWAYS. COMMANDS SOMETIMES

Every precept is either **negative or positive** – either forbids something – "thou shalt not kill, steal, lie" – or commands something – "keep holy the sabbath day; honor thy father and thy mother." "Avoid evil and do good" is a summary of the whole law. The double precept which it enunciates, includes within its scope every obligation. It is, in reality, two precepts rather than one.

The negative precept – to avoid evil – is obligatory **at all times**, and can **never admit an exception** for any reason whatever, or in any circumstances whatever. **Evil is never to be done under any pretext.** God Himself could not permit it, could never dispense from the obligation of avoiding it. "Avoid all evil at all times" is a fuller wording of the negative precept. "Thou salt **never** worship false Gods, never blaspheme, never hate, etc.

The other – **the positive precept to do good** – is just as obligating as the negative precept, in the sense that **it is just as unlawful to disobey it.** It differs, however, from the negative precept in that **it does not oblige at all times.** The positive precept does not say "do good at all times," but "do good sometimes." Every precept divine and human **must be reasonable**, and it would be unreasonable to oblige a person **to do good at all times.** It would be morally impossible to fulfill such a precept, and no one is obligated to the impossible. ("Ad impossibilia nemo tenetur.") The positive precept is not "keep every day holy," but "keep holy the sabbath day"; not "honor thy father and thy mother at all times," but "honor thy father and thy mother **at suitable times – when the occasion calls for it.**"

EXPRESSLY FORBIDS. IMPLIES COMMAND

In form, the Fifth Commandment is altogether negative. It merely forbids – tells what **is not** to be done. In **substance**, however, it is **both negative and positive**. While **explicitly** saying what is not to be done, **it implicity** says what is to be done.

There are two **entirely different** ways in which human life may be destroyed. A person may be killed either by positive violence – shooting, poisoning, etc.– or by **withholding the means by which life is preserved** – sleep, food, warmth. Both of these kinds of killing are forbidden by the Fifth Commandment.

We are here concerned with the Fifth Commandment, **only inasmuch as it forbids the killing oneself**. In this respect, the Commandment says: "Never aim **to destroy** your own life by any **positive act**. Moreover, **preserve** your life in **ordinary circumstances, and by ordinary means**." Accordingly, we are not obligated to preserve our lives **by extraordinary means, nor in extraordinary circumstances**. Not only are we not obligated by the Fifth Commandment to preserve our lives by **all possible means** and **in all conceivable circumstances**, but we are, **in some circumstances, obliged to the opposite**, and **in others, recommended and exhorted** to it. If you are given a choice between committing sin and being put to death, you are evidently obliged to choose death. You are **forbidden, in this case, to save your life**. If the State commands you to do something which you forsee will entail your inevitable death, you are again forbidden to preserve your life by disregarding the command. Finally, when a proportionate benefit accrues to another from sacrificing your life, you are **allowed** and **recommended** and **exhorted** to do so. That is **not taking** your own life **but giving it**. And Christ Himself points to it as the most perfect act that man is capable of. "Greater love than this no man hath, that a man lay down his life for his friends." (John, xv, 13); "He that loses his life for my sake shall find it." (Matt. xvi, 25.)

DESTRUCTION FORBIDDEN. SACRIFICE PRAISED

If this patent theological principle, which there is no room to dispute, were borne well in mind; if it were well remembered that there are circumstances in which one is **not obliged to even the ordinary means** to preserve life, and yet other circumstances in which it is **even forbidden** to preserve one's own life, **the phantom of suicide** that, in the minds of many, attaches to hunger-strike would be dispelled. Failure to grasp this distinction between the **negative** precept of **not destroying** one's own life by positive act, and the **positive** precept of **preserving** it, is the cardinal reason why many still consider hunger-strike suicide. They identify the **refusal to preserve life** with the intended destroying of it. And so they speak of Mayor MacSwiney as "that poor deluded man," "deluded enthusiast" and such like, when, in reality, the delusion is all their own. It cannot be repeated too often that God's dominion over human life forbids only its wanton destruction. It by no means forbids, it permits, recommends, glorifies the unselfish, heroic sacrifices of that life in any good cause.

And this is the universally received interpretation of the Fifth Commandment among the greatest Catholic theologians.

THE WORDS OF SUAREZ

"The precept of self-preservation," says **Suarez**, "really includes two precepts – one negative, which "binds ever and always, namely, not to take one's own "life, the other positive, namely to take steps to pre- "serve life and avoid death, which does not always "bind, but often can be neglected, not only to observe "a civil law but also in the interest of friendship or for "other honorable reasons."

("De Legibus," Book III, Chap. 30, No. 1)

THE WORDS OF LESSIUS

"Though one may never slay oneself directly," writes Lessius, "it is not commanded that a person "shall always endeavour to preserve his life. This is "confirmed by the fact that if a person in extreme "necessity had only food offered to idols, he might ab- "stain from eating it, and choose rather to die. And if "two are placed in extreme necessity, one may lawfully "yield to the other the bread by which he could pre- "serve his life, and allow himself to die, for he had a "just reason for not eating, namely the duty of charity "toward his neighbour."

("De Justitia et Jure," Book II, Chap. IX, nn. 27-29)

THE WORDS OF ST. ALPHONSUS

"It is never lawful to kill oneself **directly and inten- "tionally**. It is, however, sometimes lawful to kill one- "self **indirectly**, that is, to do or omit something from "which death is certain to result. This is because the "precept to preserve one's own life is affirmative, and "so is not always binding, but may be disregarded for "a good reason. A Carthusian monk, even when a meat "diet is the only food that can sustain him through- "out a deadly illness, may lawfully and laudably refuse "it. He, with good reason, sacrifices his own life for the "common good of his Order."

("Theologia Moralis," De Quinto Praecepto, No. 366)

— MACSWINEY'S PHILOSOPHY —

"Freedom is an individual right that is inalienable. One man alone may vindicate it, and because that one man has never failed, it has never died."

Chapter Nine

SELF-KILLING INTENDED AND UNINTENDED

The Fifth Commandment is the negative precept—"thou shalt not kill." Killing, morally considered, is, like every other moral act, made up of the **material element**—the mere physical action of destroying human life—and the **formal element**—the intention to do so. It has already been said that the intention is the **substantial form**, constituting human actions either good or evil, and without which they could be neither the one nor the other. Apart from the **intention to kill**, no act of killing can ever contract the guilt of murder.

DIRECT SELF-KILLING ON ONE'S OWN IMPULSE

For the guilt of murder then, the **intention to kill** is necessary, and for the guilt of suicide the **intention to kill oneself**. But not every intended killing of self is suicide. Civil authority sentenced Socrates to die by drinking poison. He intentionally caused his own death, **but not on his own authority**. He merely carried out the mandate of the State, and hence his intended self-killing was not suicide. Suicide is "intended self-killing on one's own authority." This is an **essential**, and **not a merely descriptive** definition of suicide. If any one of the elements that make up that definition be lacking, the self-killing, may or may not be otherwise unlawful, but it is not suicide. Too much emphasis cannot be laid on the necessity of thoroughly understanding the definition. The first and principal inquiry is **whether hunger-strike until death is suicide or not**, and it were idle to begin the inquiry without first understanding well **just what suicide is**.

A clearer understanding of the act of suicide and its definition will be obtained by considering the suicide's mind and heart. He is tired of his earthly existence, though this state of soul is not the exclusive lot of the suicide. Job, a model of holy patience, tells us that his soul was weary of his life. (Job, x, 1). Solomon, amid all his wisdom, said he was weary of his life when he saw that all things under the sun were evil, vanity and vexation of spirit. St. Paul, who told the Corinthians that he gladly gloried in his infirmities that the power of Christ might dwell in him, (ii, xii, 9), also told them that tribulation pressed him out of measure beyond his strength, so that he was "weary of life." (ii, 1, 8).

THE SUICIDE IS ESSENTIALLY A COWARD

It is not the being weary of life then that is the distinctive mark of the suicide. Soldier, saint, **and indeed all humanity** besides, share it with him. "Through many tribulations we must enter into the Kingdom of God." (Acts, xiv, 21). The essential difference is that soldier, saint and all others, **however weary of life, are still willing to endure the weariness patiently, whereas the suicide is not.** Soldier and saint are men of **courage; the suicide is, before all else, a coward.** He is easily recognized by his cowardly refusal to carry the burdens of life any longer or any farther. A soldier, in the best sense of that word – the sense in which Washington was a soldier – is a brave, courageous man, fearless of hardships, danger, death, for God, for country, for any noble cause. The suicide has neither God nor country nor cause. He recognizes no Creator's dominion over his life; no Redeemer's agony and death to elevate and sanctify his own; no apostolic mission to perpetuate, save that of Judas who "hanged himself with a halter." The soldier's devotion to his righteous cause, like the affection of Evangeline, "hopes and endures and is patient." The suicide has no righteous cause, and hence no devotion, no hope, no endurance, no patience. The soldier, weary of the camp, the heat, the cold, the hunger, the thirst, the drill, the march, the battle, has yet the courage to hope and suffer and wait for the merited triumph that will turn his sorrow into joy. The suicide is unwilling to hope or suffer or wait. He wants the end of his suffering and wants it **now.**

MOST SELFISH END BY MOST SELFISH MEANS

And even in choosing **means** to attain the inglorious end he sets before himself, the suicide is **still consistent with himself,** and still in contrast with the soldier. He is the same coward in his choice of **means** that he is in his choice of end. Of the several roads at his disposal for journeying to his own premature death, he invariably chooses the easiest – the shortest – the smoothest. He wants no uphill journeying, no "nitor in adversum." The world has had myriad suicides, but not a single one of them has ever been known to bring about or even attempt his own death by burning in a slow fire, or by deliberate exposure to freezing temperature, or by entirely dispensing with food or drink or sleep. The soldier cheerfully accepts the fortunes of war, even when they are misfortunes. The suicide wants either to live the upholstered life or not live at all. And he insists on the upholstering, even in the way he kills himself. Diligently selecting end and means that will entail what he believes **the very minimum of suffering**, he turns on the gas or pulls the trigger or takes the fatal plunge or drinks the deadly draught. He intentionally destroys his own life, **and does so on his own impulse.**

> "Our time is fix'd; and all our days are number'd;
> "How long, how short, we know not; this we know,
> "Duty requires we calmly wait the summons,
> "Nor dare to stir till Heaven shall give permission;
> "Like sentries that must keep their destined stand,
> "And wait th' appointed hour, **till they're relieved.**
> "Those only are the Brave who keep their ground,
> "And keep it to the last. To run away
> "Is but a Coward's trick: to run away
> "From this World's ills, that, at the very worst,
> "Will soon blow o'er, thinking to mend ourselves
> "By boldly vent'ring on a World unknown,
> "And plunging headlong in the dark! 'tis mad:
> "No Frenzy half so desperate as this."

MacSWINEY SOLDIER OR SUICIDE – WHICH?

Here are two sharply contrasting types to one of which Lord Mayor MacSwiney must be assigned. He belongs either to the one class or the other. Were his the traits that characterize the soldier, or were they rather those of the suicide? He was no admixure of both. His character was no colorless blend of these or any other remotest extremes. He was either a brave man – the bravest of the brave – or a craven coward. That he deliberately refused all food, certain that it must inevitably result in his own death, is beyond dispute. To deny this would be as impossible as it is unnecessary. But did he or did he not **intend** his own death? If he did, he is a suicide, and all the patriotism the world ever knew or ever will know, all the benefits that Ireland could ever derive from his life or from his cheerful sacrifice of it, cannot save him from the **crime** and the **guilt** and the **ignominy** of suicide. But if, on the contrary, **he did not intend his own death**, then, all the subtle fallacies, all the foul misrepresentations, that the friends of despotic England – the enemies of sore afflicted Ireland – can evolve from their inner consciousness, will never establish Terence MacSwiney a suicide. Our answer to the question will be given in a later chapter.

Chapter Ten

"IT LOOKS LIKE SUICIDE"

IT LOOKS LIKE SUICIDE BUT ISN'T

The popular theology is inconsistent, and sometimes prone to cry "suicide" on little provocation. The greatest theologians readily allow the sailor fighting a just war, to sink his ship and go down with it, and the soldier to dynamite his fortress and go up with it, in order to prevent either from becoming the property of the enemy. But, in the same circumstances, the popular theology will forbid hunger-strike, as being nothing short of **suicide**. This is unreasonable. **In the first place, both soldier and sailor place actions** which are, **from their very nature,** destructive of their own lives, **and are foreseen to be so**. The hunger-striker on the contrary places **no external action at all**. His hunger-strike is only **an internal act of refusal to act**. Secondly, the formal object of the soldier's and sailor's action is their own **sudden and violent deaths**. The death of the hunger-striker is **neither sudden nor violent**. **The manner** in which death comes to the hunger-striker is **slow and almost imperceptible**. In this it is farther removed from a violent and **approaches nearer to a natural death**. And the **intention** of soldier, sailor and hunger-striker is **exactly the same**. On what count then are the actions of soldier and sailor lauded, and the act of the hunger-striker reprobated? Why does the **merely negative** position of omitting to take food, and its formal object – a nearly natural, **probable death** – "look like suicide," and why does **the positive act** of exploding the dynamite, and whose formal object is **sudden, certain and violent death** of soldier or sailor, not "look like suicide"?

By the common consent of all moral theologians, every one of the following actions is lawful, though every one of them **borders on the domain of suicide, and so looks like it**:

1. A criminal condemned to the death of starvation, may **lawfully refuse food given to him secretly.**

2. A beggar may give to another in extreme necessity, his last morsel of food, **even when he is himself dying of hunger.**

3. A Carthusian monk, when, for the saving of his life, a meat food is supposed to be indispensable, would neither be bound to abstain from meat, on the

grounds that his rule forbids it, **nor obliged to use meat in order to preserve his life. He may lawfully refuse the only food that for him is food at all,** in order to promote religious discipline and mortification in his Community.

4. The garrison of a city under siege may, **even when dying of hunger, lawfully refuse the food offered by the besiegers on condition of surrender.**

5. A soldier may attempt a **hopeless** attack on the enemy, **even in the face of certain death.**

6. And the same must be said of every Pastor of souls, when there is question of caring for his flock – on the battlefield, amid pestilence, and in any other situation **that involves the inevitable sacrifice of his own life.** He too is **not only permitted but obligated** to make the sacrifice.

7. A garrison may **lawfully** blow up a fortification, and a ship's crew may **lawfully** sink their vessel, in order that the enemy may not come into possession of them, **even when they clearly understand that there is no possibility of saving their own lives.**

8. It is lawful for any private citizen to deliberately thrust himself in front of an assassin, and receive the deadly dagger or bullet that was intended for the President, the Governor, the Lord Mayor, or any other important official.

9. If your friend is **unjustly** condemned to death, **it is lawful for you to offer and give your life in place of his.**

10. One may lawfully leap from the window of a burning building **to certain death below,** in order to escape the more prolonged and more acute suffering of certain **death by fire.**

11. In a shipwreck, any one may **lawfully** and laudably surrender to another, the boat, the plank, the lifepreserver – anything and everything that holds out even a last slender hope of safety. It was done when the Titanic foundered, and it has been done still more recently. Under the heading –

"**Priests faithful unto death when ship is wrecked,**" there appeared, in the Brooklyn Tablet of February 28, 1921, the following news item from the NCWC News Service:

"Corunna, Spain, February 4th.– Among the dem-
"onstrations of magnanimous charity and fortitude
"witnessed when the S. S. "Santa Isabel" sank, off
"the Island of Salvora, in January, the most remark-
"able heroism was displayed by two priests, **Father**
"**Antonio Pascador and Monsignor Francesco Mondi-**

"**guren**, the former the Chaplain of the ship, and the other a passenger on his way to the Argentine, where he was Vicar General of the Diocese of Correintes.

"According to the testimony of one of the survivors, as soon as the ship crashed against the **Pegar Rock**, the two priests rushed to the deck, where they were immediately surrounded by a crowd of passengers and seamen, begging for absolution and blessing. **Without the slightest thought for themselves**, they devoted every moment to their travelling companions, giving absolution and blessing.

"When one of the seamen offered a life-preserver to the Chaplain, **he refused**, saying: 'I cannot abandon the ship while I still have my sacerdotal duties to perform.' A wave washed him from the deck and dashed him against the side of the ship. His body was later found on the beach at Muros, and was given the place of honor in the cemetery, among the graves of the other victims of the disaster."

MACSWINEY'S PHILOSOPHY

"Neither kingdom, republic nor commune can regenerate us. It is in a beautiful mind and a great ideal that we shall find the charter of our freedom."

"We shall rouse the world from a wicked dream of material greed, of tyrannical power, of corrupt and callous politics, to the wonder of a regenerated spirit."

"It is harder to live a consistent life than to die a brave death. To live is as daring as to die. To slip apologetically through existence is not life."

Chapter Eleven

THE VALUE OF HUMAN LIFE

GOD'S OWN EVALUATION OF IT IS MAN'S GUIDE

Each successive generation of Irishmen, from the time of O'Connell to our own, credits him with having said that the freedom of Ireland is not worth the shedding of a single drop of blood. Likely he never said it. The great Emancipator was preeminently a fighter for the people's rights, though rather a constitutional than a military fighter.

There is a subconscious sentiment, very universal, that shrinks from sacrificing human life in any cause however good. This irrational sentiment has its origin in **an exaggerated estimate of God's purpose** regarding all life, and His dominion over it. The first fruit of this exaggerated estimate is **a sense of horror** at the destruction even of brute life. Strong, resolute men have been known to impose voluntary abstinence on themselves, rather than that the spring chicken that was to supply their meat should be put to death. This is to be **more solicitous for God's creatures than God Himself is**. No one who is familiar with wild animals, or even with some of the domestic ones, can doubt God's purpose that some of them should prey upon others. Their **instincts**, their **impulses**, their **habits**, show it. Many of them **will eat nothing but flesh**, and of these, some will not eat flesh that is already dead. They insist that the flesh they eat be **of their own killing**. Others will kill **even when not in need of food at all**. In this the tiger differs from the lion. Yet others are **cannibals**, and refuse to eat any food except the bodies of their own species. The king cobra, the most deadly poisonous of all reptiles, will not feed on any other animal **except snakes**. The weasel again, will, with unerring accuracy, penetrate the jugular vein of its victim and drink its blood, leaving the body otherwise untouched. And all this happens according to an unvarying and wonderful instinct, implanted in these animals by the Creator.

WILD ANIMALS EQUIPPED FOR KILLING

It is interesting too, as well as instructive, to notice how admirably God has equipped these wild animals with organisms especially in keeping with their destructive instincts. The keen, penetrating vision of the fish-hawk, and its power of swooping down with lightning rapidity upon its prey in the water, is one conspicuous instance. So too are the wild animals of the cat kind – the lion, tiger, panther, puma, jaguar. Unlike those of the dog-kind, their claws – their invariable weapon of first attack – are capable of being protruded when it is necessary to use them, and retracted when not in use, for the evident purpose of preserving their delicate needle points. So too their teeth. In addition to the molars and cutting teeth given to the dog, they are supplied with **four terrible fangs**, one on each side above and below, and long enough to penetrate some vital part of the body of their victim.

Many lessons may be learned from all these and other innumerable varieties of instincts, habits and organic structure of the brute creation. One lesson in particular is pertinent to our present subject. Life was given by God to the brute creation **to be destroyed as well as preserved**, and man better fulfils the designs of God by a sane destruction of a brute animal than by a sentimental preservation of it.

DESTROYING HUMAN LIFE CREATES HORROR

But this sense of horror makes itself felt to a still greater extent when there is question of **sacrificing human life for any cause whatever**. Candidates for juries often suffer from it when there is question of a verdict of capital punishment, and many are disqualified on account of it. Reason tells us clearly and emphatically, that a prisoner guilty of many cruel murders, should pay the penalty with his life; that the life of an unjust aggressor may lawfully be taken if necessary, in order to defend one's own life; that the lives of soldiers and sailors, defending as well as offending, may lawfully be sacrificed to protect a nation's rights; that individuals may lawfully and gloriously **volunteer to surrender their own lives** in the interest of their **friends**, or in the **public** interest. We know all this to be right and just, but we give it, notwithstanding, our **reluctant approval**, especially if our sense of horror be heightened by close personal contact with the scaffold, the scene of a private brawl, the battle-field, the earthquake, the plague or the shipwreck. True, that world would be a better one that furnished no need for sacrificing human life for the public good or the individual good. But these manifold sacrifices of human life, to which civil society is **necessitated** in its actual existence, are not, on that account, evil. Good does not cease to be good because better is better.

NEED NOT BE ALWAYS SPARED OR PRESERVED

In wanting to spare human life **at any cost, we are wanting more than God wants Who gave the life.** The Author of life has put each one's life at his disposal, to use it for his own good and for the good of others, and when **necessary or helpful,** even to **sacrifice** it for others' sake. This has Christ's own sanction. "Greater love than this no man hath, that a man lay down his life for his friends." And even the pagan Romans were in the habit of saying that "it is sweet as well as noble to give one's life for one's country." "Dulce et decorum est pro patria mori." And the life that is thus sacrificed in the interests of others, redounds to the good and the glory of the one who hesitated not to surrender it.

It should be borne well in mind then, that God has given their lives to all men in order that they may use them to the best advantage, and, furthermore, that the best advantage to which these lives can ever be put, is the **promoting of the public welfare – a lawful, laudable, meritorious, glorious purpose.** Brutus was both ethical and noble when he said to Cassius: "If it be aught towards the general good, set honor in one eye and death in the other, and I will look on both indifferently."

MacSWINEY'S PHILOSOPHY

"Viciousness, meanness, cowardice, intolerance – every bad thing arises like a weed in the night, and blights the land where freedom is dead."

"It is the duty of the rightful power to develop the best in its subjects. It is the practice of the usurping power to develop the basest."

"Everyone should realize the duty to be high-minded and honorable in action; to regard his fellow, not as a man to be circumvented, but as a brother to be sympathized with and uplifted."

Chapter Twelve

GOD'S DOMINION OVER HUMAN LIFE

THE LORD HATH GIVEN AND MAY TAKE AWAY

If asked the question: "Could God allow a man to kill himself," the first impulse of most people would be to answer in the negative. And even after a reasoned solution had been found, the affirmative answer that the question calls for, would be given hesitatingly, grudgingly. This is principally because the deliberate destruction of one's own life is exceptionally revolting. Heaven and earth cry out against it. The instinctive promptings of Nature anticipate Reason and Law in protesting against it.

"Oh! – deaf to Nature's and to Heaven's command –
"Against thyself to lift the murdering hand!
"O damned Despair! – to shun the living light,
"And plunge thy guilty soul in endless Night!"

God's absolute dominion over man's life and the period of his earthly service, is always violated, outraged by the suicide. There may be a just cause for taking the life of another. One person may encroach so far on the rights of another, or of the Community, as to forfeit his right to his own life. This is a frequent occurrence, and when it happens, the person or Community whose rights are invaded, may lawfully take the life of the aggressor. There may even be cases in which they are obliged to do so. Public officials are not only permitted to carry out the death penalty in the case of murderers, traitors and such-like criminals, but are usually in duty bound to do it. The public good requires it, and since the public good is wider in its scope and consequently more important than any private good, it is reasonable that every subordinate good should yield to it. Even the private citizen, permitted to take another's life in defense of his own, may sometimes be in duty bound to do so, for reasons of family, conscience or the like.

GOD ABSOLUTE OWNER OF ALL HUMAN LIVES

But it is not so with suicide. One person may forfeit his right to live, and another person may acquire the right to take that life on set purpose and on his own authority. But there is no such thing as a lawful forfeiting of one's own life in one's own favor, to the extent that one may, on set purpose, take one's own life on one's own authority.

To take one's own life intentionally, and on one's own authority, is **suicide, and suicide can never be lawful**. To determine the duration of human life and human service belongs to God and Him alone. And to deliberately destroy the one, and thereby shorten the other, is therefore **an unwarranted encroachment on God's absolute right to the full term of man's natural life and the full measure of his service.**

DOCTRINE AVOIDS UNREASONABLE EXTREMES

This doctrine about God's dominion over human life is entirely reasonable. Like all distinctively Catholic teaching, **it avoids extremes** both of which are equally unreasonable. It teaches, on the one hand, that man may not unthinkingly, arbitrarily, fitfully **destroy his own life**, and, on the other, **that he is not obliged to save his life in all possible circumstances** — that there are circumstances in which it is **nobler and more perfect** to sacrifice one's life than to save it, and even circumstances in which there is **a strict obligation to do so.** The reasonableness of this becomes more evident when God's ultimate purpose in bestowing human life is considered. God gave Reason and Free Will to man that he might glorify his Maker by such voluntary, rational service as would use God's creatures — one's own life included — **for the purpose that God intended them to serve.** Now a **needless, useless destruction** of oneself, and a **selfish preservation** of oneself, are **equally opposed to the divine purpose.** No one **aimlessly** destroys possessions that he does not absolutely own, but only holds in trust for another. To do so would be neither reasonable nor just. And reason and justice demand, too, that the said trustee should not, on the other hand, **retain as his own**, things, the absolute dominion of which belongs to someone else. Whatever so belongs to another must be promptly and cheerfully surrendered whenever his reasonable wishes demand it. Now, human life, like all other created things, **belongs absolutely to God.** Man is but God's trustee — the custodian of his own life, to save it from reckless destruction, to preserve it, in the ordinary circumstances of life, by moderate means, but, when extraordinary circumstances demand its sacrifice, to make that sacrifice promptly and cheerfully.

GIVE YOUR LIFE! DON'T TAKE IT!

Sacrifice is the very soul of submission and service. Indeed the submission and service that comes not perfumed with the incense of sacrifice is a soulless, heartless thing, little acceptable to God or man. Men's devotion to any cause is correctly measured by the sacrifice they are ready to make for it. The hero of charity on the battlefield, in the pestilence, the famine, the shipwreck, the earthquake, the leper-colony, **must always pay the full price for his devotedness. If he could buy it cheaper, it would cease to be the grand thing it is.** "That from those honored dead," said President Lincoln at Gettysburg, "we take increased devotion to that cause for which they gave the last full measure of devotion."

Devotion, then, means sacrifice, and **sacrifice means a victim**. God does not forbid, at all times, the sacrifice of one's own life. He sometimes **permits** it, sometimes **recommends** it, sometimes **commands** it. "He spared not even His own Son, but delivered Him up for us all." (Romans, VIII, 32). Sooner or later every nation **needs a man to die for the people. And when the man is found to offer himself a willing victim, let us whose smaller souls are incapable of comprehending his great soul, be slow to call him "a suicide."**

MACSWINEY'S PHILOSOPHY

"No physical victory can compensate for spiritual surrender. Whatever side denies this, is not my side."

"A spiritual necessity makes the true significance of our claim for freedom. We stifle for self-development, individually and as a nation."

"It is love of country, not hate of the enemy, that inspires us. Our enemies are brothers from whom we are estranged."

Chapter Thirteen

**WHETHER HUNGER-STRIKE UNTIL DEATH IS
OR IS NOT SUICIDE**

Having defined hunger-strike and set forth its scope, as also the principles of Morals involved in its solution, two major questions regarding its morality now call for an answer. The first question is whether hunger-strike until death is or is not suicide. This question we answer in the negative, and that negative answer we propose to establish in the present chapter. The further fundamental question – whether, supposing that hunger-strike until death is not suicide, it may or may not be ever lawful – we shall answer in the next succeeding chapter.

OPPONENTS DENY ALL, BUT PROVE NOTHING

It may be well to state at the outset the respective positions of defendants and opponents of hunger-strike until death. The opponents of every true doctrine take their stand in a position much more advantageous than that of its defenders. They simply deny everything and prove nothing. And what is still more unintelligble, they are not even challenged to prove their negative position. When atheists deny God's existence, they do not attempt to prove it, nor are they even asked to do so. When materialists deny that the human soul is an immortal spirit, again they make no pretense of proving that denial, nor are they challenged to do so. The defenders of these fundamental doctrines, and of many similar doctrines, are content to do all the proving, and allow the opponents to do all the denying and nothing besides.

Now something very similar happens wherever hunger-strike until death is discussed. Every time that a case of hunger-strike until death occurs, the opposition insists that the hunger-striker intended his own death, and is therefore a suicide. How do they know? Is that intention of his own death an inseparable adjunct of every hunger-strike unto death? Or did that particular hunger-striker assure them, either before or during his hunger-strike, that it was his fixed and irrevocable intention to bring about his own death? Again we ask them how do they know just what any hunger-striker's intentions are.

SECOND PROPOSITION
A PERSON WHO DIES OF HUNGER-STRIKE UNTIL DEATH IS NOT GUILTY OF SUICIDE

Proof.
>Maj. Prop. No one is guilty of suicide unless he intends his own death either as end or as means.
>
>Min. Prop. But no hunger-striker until death intends his own death either as end or as means.
>
>Conclusion Therefore no hunger-striker until death is guilty of suicide.

The major proposition of this syllogism merely mentions one principal component of the morality of suicide.

The minor proposition we shall prove by parts as follows.

THIRD PROPOSITION
NO HUNGER-STRIKER UNTIL DEATH INTENDS HIS DEATH AS AN END

Proof I. He who protests against injustice, by hunger-strike until death, and, at the same time, intends that death as an end (for its own sake), is a veritable paradox. He is, at the same time, **a consummate hero and a consummate coward** – something impossible to realize.

Hunger-strike until death does not consist merely of the sum total of all the actual refusals of food. A hundred such refusals were an easy task, even for a man dying of hunger. That is but the surface of hunger-strike until death. The heroism belongs to a lower strata. It spells, in addition, a long, uninterrupted torture of body, with corresponding anguish of soul – a very death-agony, most keenly felt yet most courageously endured at every moment of long hours mounting up into longer days and into still longer weeks, nay even into **months interminably long**, until the kindly Angel of Death at last appears upon the scene to bid the ordeal cease and to bestow the martyr's crown.

But now the opponents of all hunger-strike until death appear in court and testify that, **throughout all the agonizing days and weeks and months** that his hunger-strike lasted, this bravest of brave men, this noblest of noble men, was a suicide, because he nursed in his innermost heart **the intention of securing his own death as an end – for its own sake.** Again we ask them how did they know. Ten years after the Lord Mayor of Cork had died of hunger-strike, in Brixton Prison, an American Catholic prelate wrote in a Catholic Review: "Yes, MacSwiney was a suicide." How did that Catholic prelate know?

SUICIDES CARE NAUGHT ABOUT JUSTICE

But we say that he who, even in the intermittent delirium of his last hours, continues his protest against injustice, does not intend his own death as an end, and, on the contrary, he who intends his own death as an end, is not concerned to protest against any injustice. The two things are impossible to combine. They are incompatible.

Proof II. There is not a single instance on record of anyone seeking his own death for its own sake (as an end) and attaining it by self-imposed starvation. A readier and easier way, known to all, is always sought and found by everyone who seeks his own death for its own sake.

FOURTH PROPOSITION
NO HUNGER-STRIKER UNTIL DEATH INTENDS HIS OWN DEATH AS A MEANS

Note. In addition to protest against injustice, which is the primary and essential good effect of hunger-strike until death, there are several secondary and accidental good effects – world **publicity** of the injustice, world **sympathy** with its victims, world **protest** against the injustice, world **inspiration** to others to resist similar injustice by every lawful means.

Now the **death** itself of the hunger-striker **is of itself a means, a powerful means**, towards obtaining these secondary and accidental good effects of hunger-strike – publicity, sympathy, protest, inspiration, etc., all of which are precious aids to the cause he has at heart.

INTENTION OF HIS OWN DEATH NOT A MEANS

Proof But we must here carefully distinguish between the hunger-striker's **death itself** as a means, and his **intention** of his own death as a means. The hunger-striker until death does not intend his own death as a means, because such intention is not a means to attain, or help to attain, any of the good effects of his hunger-strike. It is his death itself, over which he had no control, not his intention of his own death as a means, that would produce, or help to produce those secondary good effects. His intention of his own death as a means, if he were to have any such intention, **would neither hasten nor delay his death and its benefits by a single hour.** He dies at exactly the same time whether he intends his own death as a means or whether he does not. And the publicity, the sympathy, the protest and the inspiration follow, with the same assured promptness, when he does not intend his own death as if he did intend it.

UNINTENDED DEATH HELPS. INTENDED HINDERS

Furthermore, the hunger-striker's intention of his own death as a means would hinder instead of helping the cause he champions. Were he to intend his own death, even as a means, he would, to no purpose, rob himself of the glory of his marytrdom, and rob his fellows, present and future, of all inspiration to imitate and emulate his heroic endurance. The sublime grandeur of his courage and constancy under voluntary suffering even unto death, would be lost in his deliberate usurpation of his Maker's exclusive dominion over the term of every human life. In a word, the death of the hunger-striker, when unintended, is a powerful means to promote the cause he advocated. If intended, it must prove a hindrance instead of a help. Why then the intention of his own death, which achieves nothing but the transformation of a fascinating hero into a detestible suicide!

MacSwiney's Philosophy

"Every act of personal discipline is contributing to a subconscious reservoir whence our nobler energies are supplied forever."

"I came here more as a soldier stepping into the breach, than as an administrator to fill my post in the municipality."

"This is our simple resolution. We ask no mercy and we will accept no compromise."

"Our minds should be restless for noble and beautiful things. The man who cries out for the sacred thing but voices a universal need."

"Those who are strong in faith will endure to the end in triumph."

Chapter Fourteen

WHETHER HUNGER-STRIKE UNTIL DEATH IS EVER LAWFUL

THE CIRCUMSTANCE OF PROPORTION

It has been shown in our second chapter that hunger-strike is essentially a protest against injustice. In the last chapter it was shown, moreover, that hunger-strike until death is not suicide, since no hunger-striker until death intends his own death, either as an end or as a means. Now the injustice done may be very great or it may be very small. It would be altogether contrary to reason, and therefore unlawful, to attempt hunger-strike until death in order to vindicate a claim of only a few dollars or its equivalent. There is no proportion between a few dollars worth and a human life sacrificed to recover it. In order that hunger-strike until death may be lawful, the claim on account of which the protest is made, must be, **in some measure, an** equivalent of the life that is sacrificed for its vindication. Every action, in order to be lawful, must be (1) for a lawful end; (2) attained by lawful means; (3) in lawful circumstances.

FIFTH PROPOSITION

HUNGER-STRIKE UNTIL DEATH, FOR A CLAIM PROPORTIONATE TO THE LIFE SACRIFICED, IS ALWAYS LAWFUL

Proof.

Maj. Prop. Every act placed (1) for a lawful end (2) attained by lawful means (3) in lawful circumstances, is lawful.

Min. Prop. But hunger-strike until death, for a claim proportionate to the life sacrificed, is (1) for a lawful end, (2) attained by lawful means, (3) in lawful circumstances.

Conclusion Therefore hunger-strike until death for a claim proportionate to the life sacrificed is always lawful.

SIXTH PROPOSITION

EVERY ACT PLACED (1) FOR A LAWFUL END, (2) ATTAINED BY LAWFUL MEANS, (3) IN LAWFUL CIRCUMSTANCES, IS LAWFUL

Proof of Major. End, means and circumstances – sometimes called "object," "intention" and "circumstances" – are the only sources of morality, the only fountains from which human actions derive their moral goodness or moral badness.

SEVENTH PROPOSITION
HUNGER-STRIKE UNTIL DEATH, FOR A PROTEST PROPORTIONATE TO THE LIFE SACRIFICED, IS (1) FOR A LAWFUL END, (2) ATTAINED BY LAWFUL MEANS, (3) IN LAWFUL CIRCUMSTANCES

Proof of minor by parts.
1. It is for a lawful end. It is in protest against injustice, and since injustice is essentially evil, it is essentially lawful to protest against it.
2. That protest is attained by lawful means – namely by the act of refusing food until death. That act is the means, and is essentially good or indifferent, not essentially evil.

EIGHTH PROPOSITION
THE ACT OF REFUSING FOOD UNTIL DEATH IS ITSELF LAWFUL

KILLING ONESELF, NOT INTENDING DEATH

Note. The sincere inquirer about the morality of hunger-strike until death can readily understand that protest against injustice is, in itself, an entirely lawful act. Such inquirer can also easily understand that there are some circumstances in which the loss of life sacrificed for the protest is amply recompensed by the benefit to others, and the sacrifice therefore lawful and even laudable. It is the particular kind of means used to attain that end, however, it is the act itself of refusing all food until death, whose lawfulness they cannot understand. "Isn't it killing yourself" they say! Yes, it is to kill yourself, but without intending to do so. It is exactly the same killing that early Christian Martyrs did on themselves when they died of hunger rather than eat foods that had been offered to idols. True, the motive of the Christian Martyrs was high,– the very highest. But, first, the motive of the hunger-striker is also high, and, secondly, if the act of refusing, until death, food given to idols were evil in itself, intrinsically evil, no motive, however good, could justify it.

The proof we are now giving that the act of refusing food until death is itself lawful, involves some principles of Psychology and Ethics. All who are unable to grasp these principles must accept that proposition on the twofold authority cited – that of the Church and that of Theologians.

Negative Proof

No compelling reason, not even a plausible reason, has been or can be urged against the lawfulness of the action itself. The arguments of all who would pronounce the act of hunger-strike intrinsically evil, have been examined and found wanting.

Positive Proof

(1) From Reason:

> Maj. Prop. The adequate object of hunger-strike is
> (a) **protest against injustice, and**
> (b) **physical life unpreserved.**
>
> Min. Prop. But neither protest against injustice nor physical life unpreserved **is evil from itself – intrinsically evil.**
>
> Conclusion: Therefore hunger-strike is not evil from its adequate object—not intrinsically evil.

Proof of Minor Proposition

(a) Injustice is intrinsically evil, therefore protest against it is intrinsically good.

(b) If physical life unpreserved were intrinsically evil, sacrifice of physical life could never be lawful for any cause whatever. Even the self-immolation of the martyrs would then be forbidden.

OBLIGATIONS REGARDING ONE'S OWN LIFE

Different circumstances give rise to **three separate species of obligation** regarding the preservation of one's own life. First, there are **ordinary circumstances**. Here the strict obligation of preserving one's own life, by at least ordinary means, is **absolute**. Secondly, there are **extraordinary circumstances** (emergencies) in which the sacrifice of one's own life is **permitted and recommended**, but **not commanded**. Lastly, there are such **extraordinary circumstances** as forbid the preservation of one's own life, and so make its sacrifice obligatory. Whenever and wherever a choice is given between committing sin and being put to death, it is always obligatory to accept death. In that case it is always forbidden to preserve one's own life.

(2) Proof from Authority:

(a) **Authority of the Church**

REFUSING FOOD SAME AS REFUSING WARMTH

During the persecution of the Roman Emperor Licinius, the Forty Martyrs of Sebaste, in Cappadocia, were deprived of all covering and exposed on a frozen lake. Warm baths were erected near by, intended to induce them to deny Christ. They refused even till death, and the Church has put the seal of its approval on their refusal. Now the warmth they refused was the normal warmth, as naturally necessary to preserve life as food is. In fact it is principally to supply bodily heat that food is necessary at all. Will the opponents of hunger-strike say that to refuse the normal, bodily warmth naturally necessary to preserve life, is good or indifferent in itself, whereas to refuse the food normally and naturally necessary to preserve life, would have been, in the same circumstances, evil in itself! They cannot claim a disparity by urging that the warmth was offered only on the condition that the martyrs commit sin by denying Christ, whereas there is no such condition attached to the food given the hunger-striker. If refusal of food or warmth naturally and normally necessary to preserve life, were evil, then the martyrs, by refusing it rather than deny Christ, would but avoid doing one evil by actually doing another.

If it be urged that these martyrs, by refusing the warmth of the baths, did what is evil in itself, but did it in good faith – with erroneous consciences – and hence that the Church has approved the heroic constancy of their wills rather than the theological correctness of their understandings, the assertion is gratuituously made. If to refuse warmth (or food) until death were evil in itself, then the Martyrs of Sebaste would have been necessitated to the one evil or the other – either to refusal to save their own lives or to deny Christ. Evils are not to be multipled without necessity and proof.

(b) Authority of Theologians

MANY LAWFUL REFUSALS OF FOOD UNTO DEATH

A hundred different cases of omission to preserve one's own life have been discussed in the light of moral principles, and pronounced lawful by the greatest theologians of the Catholic Church. They even discussed the case of omitting to preserve one's own life by necessary food, and decided unanimously that it is sometimes lawful and praiseworthy, and even heroic. And in solving that case did they not bring us to the very verge of solving hunger-strike unto death?

The Carthusian Monk refusing meat to honor his rule; the beggar giving his last crust to another starving, and dying of hunger himself; the starving garrison refusing the food offered on condition of surrender; the criminal sentenced to death by starvation, refusing the food secretly brought him – each of these is a refusal of available food and until death – the same identical refusal of food as that of the hunger-striker – the same result (death), though not done with the same intention.

SOME BY POSITIVE ACTIONS, NOT OMISSIONS

Others of the cases already cited are **more conspicuous acts of destroying one's own life** than hunger-strike is. In some of them, the agent, not by any mere **omission**, but by his own **positive action**, precipitates the situation that is the **immediate and inevitable cause of his own death**. The sinking of the ship **is the crew's own doing**, the blowing up of the fortifications **is the work of the garrison**. The hunger-striker, on the contrary, places **no action that has any positive influence** towards bringing about his own death. His hunger-strike is an **entirely negative** entity – the omission to provide the requisites for continuing to live.

IN SOME DEATH IS CERTAIN, NOT PROBABLE

Again, in some of the instances given above, the **death of the agent was certain** beyond peradventure. The sunken vessel or the exploded fortification extends no hope to crew or garrison. Hunger-strikers, on the contrary, are **never certain** that their refusal of food **must** mean death to them. **There is, ordinarily, the reasonable presumption**, even to the last moment they live, that the responsible party will relent, or that someone, somewhere, will discover some adjustment of an unprecedented situation.

SUDDEN AND VIOLENT, NOT SLOW AND NATURAL

Finally, in many of the cases stated above, that "look like suicide" but are not, the death of the agent, besides being certain, is **sudden and violent. It follows without delay from his own action**. The hand that explodes the dynamite which is to destroy the fortification, will not long survive the explosion. Not so the hunger-striker. His death is no such **instant**, no such **violent** reality as that of the citizen who, to save the breast of his Ruler, bares his own. But every one of the several acts that "look like suicide," is either good or indifferent in itself. Theologians are agreed that none of these acts is evil in itself. On what title then can the act of hunger-strike be said to be evil in itself – intrinsically evil – evil from the object? If it be lawful to **procure** and **put in motion** the machinery that, **in its very initial movement**, must necessarily and **violently destroy** one's life, why, every thing else being the same, should it be unlawful to **passively tolerate** the **unintended** and **gradual** extinction of that life?

* * * * *

GREAT AUTHORITY MUST BE RECOGNIZED

Authority rightly understood is not and cannot be excluded from any science. So long as there are problems too intricate for the ordinary inquirer – and at what period or in what science have they not abounded – so long will the pronouncements of genius be appealed to and accepted. It is for this reason that we subjoin, in concluding this chapter, the testimony of several modern masters in Scholastic Theology, in addition to the ancient authorities already cited on page forty-seven.

FR. PATRICK GANNON, S.J.

Fr. Gannon is, at present, a professor of Dogmatic Theology at Milltown Park Scholasticate, Co. Dublin. In an article entitled "The Ethical Aspect of Hunger-Striking," published in "Studies," (Sept. 1920), he says among other things:

1. "The precept of preserving life, like all positive precepts, sometimes ceases to bind, and can, for sufficient reasons, be neglected."

2. "No hunger-striker aims at death. Quite the contrary, he desires to live. He aims at escaping from unjust detention, and to do this is willing to run the risk of death. And even if he carries the protest to its fatal conclusion, he is still not seeking death even as a means."

3. "If charity towards a single individual be held an adequate reason for not eating, and thus sacrificing life, it would seem that love of one's country, which is really charity towards the millions of one's countrymen, constitutes a far more valid excuse for neglecting the positive precept of preserving life."

FR. PATRICK H. CASEY, S.J.

Fr. Casey taught Theology for many years, and with exceptional distinction, at Woodstock College, Maryland. The following is his summing up of the MacSwiney case for the "Catholic News" (New York, Sept. 4, 1920):

"The reason for the Lord Mayor's refusal of food is of the gravest kind, and is in full proportion to the seriousness of his action. His purpose is the noblest. It is not to kill himself. It is to kill tyranny. Therefore his refusal to eat is justified, even though death may follow. 'Justified' did I say? That was all I wished to show. The heroism of this long-drawn-out agony of death is another subject. Theology does not deal with it. But Oratory will exalt it, and Poetry will linger over it, and the children of Erin will hold it in grateful and tender remembrance."

FR. PETER FINLAY, S.J.

Fr. Finlay ("theologus eximius") taught Theology for more than forty years, first in the Scholasticate at Woodstock, Md., and afterwards at Milltown Park, Dublin. He was, perhaps, the most widely-known theologian in the English-speaking world. Writing in the "Irish Catholic," he had this to say relative to hunger-strike:

"Carthusian monks have a rule which forbids them "to eat flesh meat. Suppose a Carthusian monk to have "fallen ill by this abstinence, to be in danger of death, "from which a meat diet alone can save him. Is he "bound in conscience to take it? It is certain that he "may. His rule binds no longer in such extremity. It is "**equally certain that he is not bound to do so**. He may "**lawfully refuse** flesh meats, though they be at hand, "and die to honor the rule, and to promote the spirit of "discipline and observance in his Order.

"He does not wish to die. He **does not choose death** "**as a means** of furthering religious fervor among his "brethren. That fervor he does intend, and the means "he chooses to further it is **not his own death** but the "**example of his life** – his living love of his Order, his "fidelity to its rules, his constancy in making sacrifices "for it. The object which he aims at is spiritual – the "**welfare of his Order**. The means which he adopts – "abstinence from the only food that can save his life."

"What the hunger-striker aims at ultimately is the "welfare of his country. Directly and immediately he "seeks to shame government into the ways of justice; "to draw the attention and sympathy of the world to "the cause he has at heart; to make clear that no vio-"lence can destroy it; to encourage and embolden his "fellow-citizens; to foster and hand on a spirit of fear-"less, self-sacrificing patriotism – all most excellent, "most valuable objects, to secure which no lawful price "would appear to be too great. And the price he offers? "The means he adopts to secure them? His sufferings, "the danger of dying, his long-drawn out martyrdom, "his constancy and heroism – all lawful in themselves, "and ennobled by the purpose to which they are di-"rected. What the dying Carthusian monk did, and did "lawfully for religion and his Order, the dying patriot "does, and may lawfully do, for his country's service.

"But it is self-murder! He kills himself! Only as the "Carthusian does. He does not will to die. He does not "act to bring death about. Death is not chosen by him "as a means to the end he has in view. If it comes, it "is only permitted by him, and is worked out by causes "which operate independent of his will. It may be that "the more precious of the objects he aims at, he is cer-"tain to secure. It may be that in no other way could "he secure them so effectively. If this be so, a hunger-"strike is as lawful in a prison as in a Carthusian cell."

("The Catholic Mind," April 8, 1921)

(3) In Lawful Circumstances

The only circumstance involved in hunger-strike until death is the circumstance of **proportion** or **disproportion** between the measure of justice vindicated and the life sacrificed for its vindication. Now our thesis that hunger-strike until death is lawful, **applies only to cases of hunger-strike until death in which that proportion exists – in which the benefits derived from the protest until death compensate for the life that is lost. Our thesis says expressly:– "For a claim proportionate to the life sacrificed."**

If hunger-strike unto death were unlawful, it could only be on account of the hunger-striker's obligation to preserve his own life. But the obligation to preserve one's own life is **never absolute, never universal.** We have Christ's own assurance that **laying down** one's life for a friend is not only lawful but even **the perfection of Charity.** "Greater love than this no man hath that a man lay down his life for his friend."

LAWFUL TO DESIRE ILL EFFECT PERMITTED

Note I. It should be carefully noted that the ill effect permitted is sometimes **a partial and very effective means** of attaining the end the hunger-striker is aiming at. It may therefore be lawfully desired, not for its own sake but for the good effects that sometimes flow in abundance from it.

Note II. Recall what was said at the beginning of Chapter V – that it is lawful for the hunger-striker to **foresee** his own death, to **wish** it, to **hope** for it, to **pray** for it, and if it comes, to **rejoice** in it, both for the sake of the cause he has at heart and for his own sake. He may lawfully rejoice that the fierce fight is over, that the martyr's crown is won, and that his death will make the injustice on account of which he began his hunger-strike, resound from pole to pole. In other words, though not intending his own death, and even shrinking from it in horror, the hunger-striker is **by no means obliged to be unwilling that his death should result, or to be unwilling that it should contribute to his desired object.** As he is not obliged to be positively unwilling that his death should unintentionally follow from his hunger-strike, so he is not obliged either, to be unwilling that his death should contribute anything to the result which he desires. All that is required, so far as relates to this condition, is that his own death be not sought **as an instrument or means** to attain his purpose. The foreseeing and wishing and hoping and praying and rejoicing is far removed from intentional seeking his own death either as an end or as a means.

Note III. It is not necessary for the lawfulness of hunger-strike that the entire purpose or any measure of it be realized during the lifetime of the hunger-striker. When it is said that the good effect must follow as immediately from the action as the ill effect, it is "as immediately" in the order of causation that is meant—not as immediately in time. The meaning of the principle is not that the good effect must be realised in the same instant of time—the same day or the same year that the ill effect—his death—is. It only means that the ill effect must not be used as a medium whereby to attain the good effect. If it were so used, it could not be said that it was not intended. Means are always intended whenever the corresponding end is intended.

Note IV. It is not necessary that the hunger-striker be antecedently certain that his object, or any part of it, will ever be actually realized. A reasonable presumption that the good effect, or some proportionate measure of it, will be realized, either before his death or after, is sufficient to justify the hunger-strike and its probable ill effect—the death of the hunger-striker.

Note V. There is no force in the objection that if the people be taught that hunger-strike until death may sometimes be lawful, they will disregard the conditions requisite for its lawfulness, and the way will thus be opened to serious practical abuses. Listen to two authorities on that matter:

Dr. Murray of Maynooth, in his "Essays Chiefly Theological," furnishes the answer:

> "It is no objection to any principle of morals to say "that unscrupulous men will abuse it, or that, if pub-"licly preached to such and such an audience, or in "such and such circumstances, it will lead to mischief."
> (Essay on "Mental Reservation.")

And Dr. Balmez answers the same objection in practically the same words:

> "In recommending prudence to the people, let us not "disguise it under false doctrines. Let us beware of "calming the exasperation of misfortune by circulating "errors. I may be permitted to observe that the prud-"ence of those who shrink from investigating such ques-"tions, is quite thrown away—that their foresight and "precaution are of no avail. Whether they investigate "these questions or not, they are investigated, agitated "and decided, in a manner that we must deplore."
> ("European Civilization," Chap. 54)

DISGUISED UNDER FALSE DOCTRINES

Alas that it should have to be said! "Disguised under false doctrines" is exactly what happened to the question of hunger-strike. During and after the hunger-strike controversy that raged in 1920, there was, in the very words of Dr. Balmez, a manifest attempt – on the part of some moral theologians and editors of Catholic reviews – "to calm the exasperation of misfortune by circulating errors." But, as Dr. Balmez again says very truly, the prudence of those who shrank from the investigation of hunger-strike was quite thrown away, and their foresight and precaution were of no avail. Hunger-strike was investigated and agitated and decided in a manner that we must deplore.

SUICIDAL DEATHS BUT NOT SUICIDES

For more than a year the remains of John McNeela and Anthony Darcy lie in suicidal graves. But that is not to say that each of these brave young men was guilty of the sin of suicide. Both were ignorant of what hunger-strike means, and so both believed they were practising hunger-strike when, in reality, they were only refusing food until death. Hunger-strike is ever and always a protest against injustice, and their imprisonment for revolt against their own legitimate government was no injustice to them. That is why their fast unto death was not hunger-strike at all. No injustice was done them by their government, and, no injustice, no protest against injustice, and no protest against injustice, no hunger-strike.

McNeela and Darcy were deluded heroes. Their ignorance of the catechism of hunger-strike was responsible for the wrecking of two young lives that otherwise might have been noble. Had they been taught that not every hunger-strike until death is lawful, that hunger-strike until death is sometimes but not always unlawful, they would, in this matter, have obeyed God's commandment as faithfully as their race has always been known to do. But they investigated and agitated and decided the question of hunger-strike until death, in a manner that made their fast until death suicidal.

And how could they have been other than ignorant about the morality of hunger-strike, when the clergy, their teachers, were themselves ignorant about it, yes, left ignorant and sometimes even led into error about it, by the professional moralists whose duty it was to direct the controversy, but failed to do so?

"How then are they to call upon him in whom they have not believed? But how are they to believe him whom they have not heard? And how are they to hear if no one preaches?" (Romans, x, 14.)

OUR CONCLUSIONS

The pivotal conclusions which we arrive at, as the result of all the argumentation set down in the foregoing pages, may be stated in the following propositions:

A. **Hunger-strike, even until actual death, is never suicide. No hunger-striker intends his own death, either as an end or as a means.**

B. **The primary end or purpose of hunger-strike even unto death is not intrinsically evil. Protest against injustice is intrinsically good.**

C. **The hunger-striker's means of protest – his refusal of all food even until death – is not an intrinsically evil act. It is good or indifferent.**

D. **The circumstance of proportion between the good effect from protest, and the ill effect of the hunger-striker's probable death, is the sole guide as to whether any hunger-strike is lawful or not.**

With the end of hunger-strike always good, and its essential means always good, unlawfulness can never come to hunger-strike from either of these sources of morality. If hunger-strike is ever unlawful, and it sometimes is unlawful, the unlawfulness does and must come from the only remaining source of morality,– the circumstances. Now the only circumstance involved in hunger-strike until death is the proportion or disproportion between the good effect of protest against injustice, and the probable, but never certain, death of the hunger-striker. If the benefit resulting from the protest – whether to the few or to the many – be worth the hunger-striker's risk of death, or even his actual death, then his hunger-strike until death is certainly lawful. But if, on the contrary, the injustice protested against be unreal, or if it be insignificant when compared with a human life, in every such case, hunger-strike until actual death, or even merely intended until death, is certainly unlawful, and therefore suicidal, though not suicide.

LAWFULNESS FROM PROPORTION OF GOOD

Thus the entire inquiry about the lawfulness and unlawfulness of hunger-strike until death, reduces itself to the question whether, in any specific instance, the protest against injustice is or is not worth the life sacrificed to make it – always bearing in mind that the life at stake is not merely a human life in the abstract, but a concrete individual life, laden with the authority and responsibilities of Husband, Father, Mayor, Governor, Legislator, Magistrate. And therefore everyone capable of a sober, balanced, conservative comparison between the good effected by such protest, and the probable loss of life involved in its making, is able to solve, with certainty, any and every case of hunger-strike until death.

Here we rest the case for the lawfulness of every hunger-strike producing a proportionate good. We set out to prove, first, that hunger-strike is essentially, not accidentally, a protest against injustice; secondly, that hunger-strike until death is not suicide; thirdly, that the end, the purpose of hunger-strike, is always good; fourthly, that the hunger-striker's essential means – refusal of all food – is good or indifferent; fifthly, that hunger-strike until death is sometimes lawful; sixthly, that its lawfulness or unlawfulness is determined solely by the measure of good resulting from the hunger-striker's protest until death.

CONCLUSIONS TRUE, EVIDENT, CERTAIN

We respectfully submit that everyone of these theses has been proved beyond reasonable challenge. Whoever weighs the evidence presented, will feel compelled to accept these conclusions with a firm, steadfast, unwavering assent. They are no mere slender probabilities, which may be accepted or rejected. They are true and evident and certain. To deny them would be to reject objctive evidence of certainty – to insist on shutting out the light of the noonday sun that we may seem to justify our living in darkness.

In the supreme interest of Moral Theology then, the truth, the whole truth, about hunger-strike must be told, though the heavens were to fall. It is, before all else, a question in Moral Theology, and therefore vastly more important than the issues involved in any national or political controversy. Nations, nationals and nationalities rise and fall, but the truths of Moral Theology remain forever. They are part of the deposit of truth, which Christ commanded the Apostles and their successors to teach all nations.

APPEAL TO THE TRIBUNAL OF ALL MANKIND

In its method of appeal for eternal justice, hunger-strike is democracy in flower and fruit. It is not the summoning of an offender before any Court of General Sessions, to receive the findings of one solitary judge and one solitary jury of twelve men. No! Hunger-strike is **an appeal to the tribunal of all mankind, a summoning before the bar of public opinion** – that natural, spontaneous, humane **supreme court**, founded on the lofty principles of **true justice, true liberty** and **true progress** instinct in all peoples and nations.

That court of world opinion, to which every hunger-striker has recourse, **is a just tribunal, and its decisions, when rendered, are final and compelling. There is no appeal from the common verdict of humanity, and there is no resisting it.**

OBJECTORS IN GOOD FAITH AND BAD FAITH

In Chapter Thirteen we proved conclusively that **no hunger-striker until death is guilty of suicide, because no hunger-striker intends his own death either as end or as means.** In Chapter Fourteen it is proved, with the same conclusiveness, that **the act of refusing food until death is not itself evil, and that consequently every hunger-strike until death in protest against proportionate injustice is lawful.** Each of these three points we have shown **to be true and evident and certain** – beyond any shadow of doubt or misgiving.

As a consequence, **any serious, bona fide objecting to that doctrine was and is and always must be impossible. In the face of certain evidence of their truth, the foregoing propositions can neither be denied nor doubted, much less disproved.** It cannot be denied or doubted that the sum of two and two is four.

All the same there were objectors and objections aplenty – impotent efforts to deny and disprove **what is palpably evident.** In the case of the many who, in urging their objections, entirely disregarded the sources of morality, (fontes moralitatis) they may indeed be given credit for having objected **in good faith,** even though their challenge did not deserve to be taken seriously. Others there were who, while manifesting exceptional familiarity with the moral principles involved in hunger-strike, **with faith superlatively bad, unblushingly distorted these principles and their application,** in order to arrive at the verdict of their choice.

Chapter Fifteen

SOME OBJECTORS AND THEIR OBJECTIONS

Fr. Tanquerey, S.S.

"It is essentially unlawful for prisoners to abstain "from all food –'hunger-strike,' as it is called – fore- "seeing that death must result from it, **in the hope that** "**the judges will be moved to pity** and will liberate the "prisoners. For life is of greater worth than physical "liberty, and therefore to be preferred to it. And, more- "over, human life depends on God alone. But if **the hope** "**of liberation were well founded, and such action would** "**be considered very useful or necessary for promoting** "**the public good, it is then a disputed question. The** "**solution depends on the measure of hope, and the** "**gravity of the reason for refusing food.**"*

TREATMENT INADEQUATE, CONFUSED, WRONG

How inadequate, how confused and confusing these remarks on hunger-strike are! Fr. Tanquerey begins by defining hunger-strike, and defining it wrongly. The popular notion of hunger-strike is that it is any refusal of all food until death, and nothing more. And Fr. Tanquerey seems to have shared this popular misconception. He begins by saying "it is essentially unlawful for prisoners to abstain from all food –'hunger-strike' as they call it – foreseeing" etc. Now abstention from all food until death is neither sufficient nor necessary for hunger-strike. There may be hunger-strike without refusal of food unto death, and there may be refusal of food unto death without hunger-strike. Mahatma Gandhi's refusal of food, in September of last year, was not until death, and yet was hunger-strike. On the other hand, a prisoner held on a murder charge, a few years ago, at Boonville, Mo., died after refusal of food for six weeks. But it was not hunger-strike. His detention was not an injustice.

And even if we suppose that Fr. Tanquerey's further words –"in the hope that the judges will be moved to pity and will set the prisoners free"– are part of his definition of

---

*"**Ex se** non licet captivis ab omni cibo abstinere (quod vocant "la greve de la faim) cum praevisione mortis exinde secuturae, "sperando judices misericordia motos, captivos e carcere libera- "turos esse. Nam vita est pretiosior physica libertate, ideoque ei "anteponenda; aliunde vita nostra a solo Deo pendet. Si tamen "**spes liberationis** fundata esset, et talis agendi ratio tanquam "valde utilis aut necessaria haberetur ad bonum publicum promo- "vendum, res controvertitur. Solutio pendet a gradu spei et a "gravitate rationis proter quam quis a cibo abstinet." "**Synopsis Theologiae Moralis et Pastoralis,**" Vol. III, n. 272D.

hunger-strike, his definition is still incorrect. **Hunger-strike is an appeal not to mercy but to justice.** It has been proved conclusively in Chapter II that hunger-strike is essentially a protest against injustice. In ancient times the person perpetrating the injustice and persistently refusing to rectify it was held responsible for the death of the hunger-striker.

FR. TANQUEREY ON HUNGER-STRIKE

As we have just seen, Fr. Tanquerey's entire treatment of hunger-strike consists of **two cases**, the first of which he proposes as an **unlawful** case of hunger-strike, the second as **doubtfully lawful**. In truth, **neither is a case of hunger-strike at all**. Neither the word "injustice" nor the word "protest," nor any of their equivalents, occurs in either case. The second case he sharply contrasts with the first by two compensating conditions — hope of liberation, and **promotion of public welfare**. Now, assuming, as we must do, that both of these compensating factors are absent from Fr. Tanquerey's first case, that case is **not a case of indirect voluntary at all**. It is a case of one and only one effect, notwithstanding that Fr. Tanquerey introduces it as an example of indirect self-killing, and treats it as such when he undertakes to prove its unlawfulness. The only effect of his prisoners' refusals of all food is **the evil effect of their own deaths** — foreseen because essentially resulting from their abstention, intended because it is the only effect of their actions. And intended self-killing is suicide, which Fr. Tanquerey had already proved unlawful when treating of direct self-killing. What need was there, then, of trying to prove his prisoners' refusal of all food unlawful, by saying (1) that "life is of greater worth than physical liberty and therefore to be preferred to it," and (2) that "human life depends on God alone?"

HIS PROOFS HAVE NO VALUE

It is precisely because Fr. Tanquerey misunderstands his first case that his proofs of its unlawfulness have no value. He compares life with physical liberty, thus giving his first case the appearance of a case of indirect voluntary. But, in every case of indirect voluntary, the one and only comparison is that between **the good effect intended and the ill effect permitted**. It is never betwen two things both of which are good, as life and physical liberty are. But, in Fr. Tanquerey's first case there is no good effect — nothing to compare with the ill effect — the death of his prisoners. The physical liberty of which he speaks does not belong to his first case at all. His abstainers have no **actual liberty**, since they are prisoners. Neither have they any **prospective** liberty, since, according to his own statement of the case, they have **no hope of liberation**. He makes nothing then for the solution of his case by saying that "life is more precious than physical liberty and therefore to be preferred to it." Doubtless his meaning is that loss of liberty is a lesser evil than loss of life. But this is not unqualifiedly true. It is contradicted by Patrick Henry's immortal saying —"Give me liberty or give me death."

Furthermore, if Fr. Tanquerey supposes (wrongly) that the case he is solving is a case of indirect voluntary, what does he do to solve it when he says that human life depends on God alone. Applied literally and without the needed qualifications, that principle would forbid even the heroic deaths of the Christian martyrs. Their lives depended on God alone no less than the lives of Fr. Tanquerey's prisoners, yet not with such dependence as to forbid them to voluntarily sacrifice those lives for the glory of Him who gave them.

FIRST CASE — NO GOOD EFFECT

Nor can it be urged in favor of Fr. Tanquerey that it is the **combined** compensation from hope of liberation, and promotion of public welfare, not either of them separately, that is excluded from his first case. First, neither compensating factor is mentioned at all in that case. **Secondly,** the sharp contrast of the second case with the first —"si tamen" etc.— **favors the exclusion of both** these conditions from the former. And, **thirdly,** if either condition were supposed to be present in his first case, Fr. Tanquerey's solution of that case would then, as we shall see, **be the wrong solution.** Introduce into the first case either a reasonable hope of liberation or a considerable promotion of public welfare, and that case would be lawful.

FIRST CASE CONTRADICTS ITSELF

Finally, in addition to its other shortcoming, this first case seems to contain a contradiction even in the very statement of it. Abundant reason has already been given for considering it a case in which the prisoners **have no hope of liberation**. But is not this contradicted by those other words of the case —"**in the hope that the judges will be moved to pity**"—"sperando judices" etc. If there be such a thing as "hoping against hope," theology takes no cognizance of it.

SECOND SOLUTION DOUBLY ERRONEOUS

Fr. Tanquerey is equally unsuccessful in solving his second case. Though he called his first case a case of hunger-strike, which it is not; though he called it a case of indirect self-killing, which it is not; though calling his argument that "life is preferable to liberty" a proof of its unlawfulness, which it is not; he says truly that his prisoners' abstention from all food is essentially unlawful. And we saw that the reason for its unlawfulness is that **there is no compensating good** to justify the sacrifice of their lives. But now, in Fr. Tanquerey's second case, which—though no more a case of hunger-strike than his first—is a case of **indirect voluntary**, the compensating reasons for the prisoners' abstention from all food are **superabundant** and evidently so. And therefore when Fr. Tanquerey says that the lawfulness of that case is doubtful, he says what is erroneous. For, in the first place, independently of all consideration of the public welfare, the prisoners' well-founded hope of regaining their liberty **amply justifies the risking their lives**. And, secondly, without any hope whatever either for their liberty or their lives, the great benefit to the public—"valde utilis"—adequately **compensates** for the loss of their lives. Listen to what some standard theological authors have to say about the risk of life which prisoners may lawfully take in the sole hope of regaining their liberty.

"It is lawful to hurl onself from a window, with great danger of death, to escape a death-sentence or prolonged imprisonment, provided there be some hope of avoiding death."(1)

"It is lawful for criminals detained in prison to throw themselves from a great height, with certain danger of death, in order to escape an assured death-sentence or even perpetual imprisonment, provided there is some hope of escaping death."(2)

"It is lawful for criminals detained in prison to throw themselves from a pinnacle to escape a certain death-sentence or even perpetual imprisonment, provided there be some hope of saving their lives."(3)

---

(1) "Licet se projicere e fenestra, cum magno periculo pereundi, ut aliquis evadat sententiam mortis vel durissimum carcerem, modo spes etiam evadendi mortem adsit."

(Lehmkuhl, S.J., Vol. I, n. 580.)

(2) "Licet reis detentis in carcere ex alto se praecipites dare, cum certo mortis periculo, ad evadendam certam sententiam mortis vel etiam carcerem perpetuum, dummodo adsit aliqua spes mortem evadendi." (Genicot, S.J., Vol. I, n. 362.)

(3) "Licet reis detentis in carcere ex alto se praecipites dare ad evadendum certam sententiam mortis vel carcerem perpetuum, dummodo adsit aliqua spes servandi vitam."

(Noldin, S.J., Vol. II, n. 327.)

EITHER MOTIVE ENOUGH. BOTH SUPERFLUOUS

Now if some hope of personal liberty justifies prisoners in risking their lives by throwing themselves from a great height, why should not Fr. Tanquerey's "well-founded hope" alone justify his prisoners in risking their lives in the same cause by abstention from all food? To do so is lawful—certainly lawful.

Again, if the prisoners may lawfully risk their lives in the hope of obtaining only their own personal liberty, why may they not lawfully do the same for the public welfare alone—all the more when the public welfare is greatly promoted—"valde utilis"—by the act which involves the risk? It is certain that the prisoners may lawfully risk their lives for an exceptional promotion of public welfare, independently of any private benefit to themselves or others. Nay, even in the case in which th abstention spells certain death to the prisoners, they may lawfully and laudably sacrifice their lives, provided the public welfare is proportionately promoted thereby. This Fr. Tanquerey himself teaches elsewhere in his book. In his Synopsis Theologiae Moralis et Pastoralis (Vol. III, n. 270) he writes:

> "The public good is a sufficient reason for exposing "oneself to proximate and certain danger of death. "Soldiers may lawfully set fire to a ship or dynamite "a citadel in order to drown or destroy the enemy, "though certain that it must mean their own deaths."*

Here Fr. Tanquerey says that not only the risk of one's death but certain death is certainly lawful for the public benefit of destroying a considerable portion of the enemy. In other words, he says that an ordinary measure of benefit to the public—"bonum publicum"—of itself and without any further benefit, amply compensates for the loss of the soldiers' lives, and thus justifies them in placing an act which they foresee must bring about their own certain and inevitable deaths. Why then does he say that "the solution depends on the measure of hope?" And if the marines may lawfully sink their ship without any hope for their own lives, why may not the hunger-striker place an act which leaves him no hope for his own life, if a proportionate measure of good results either to an individual or to public? In a lawful hunger-strike, Fr. Tanquerey's "measure of hope" may either be (1) the sole compensating good, or (2) only part of the compensating good, or (3) it may be absent altogether. It is not essential to a lawful hunger-strike, and so Fr. Tanquerey says what is false when he

---

*"Bonum publicum sufficiens est causa ut quis seipsum exponat "periculo etiam proximo et certo mortis; ita militibus licet incen-"dere navim vel arcem explodere ad submergendos vel delendos "hostes quamvis propria mors exinde certo sequatur."

says that "the solution depends on the measure of hope." Furthermore, that "measure of hope," if present, must always be identical, either adequately or inadequately, with his "gravity of the reason."

A DOUBLE CONTRADICTION

But now, and on the same page (n. 272D), he contradicts, doubly contradicts, all this. After saying very truly that "a greater benefit is required in proportion as the danger of death is more proximate and certain"—"eo majorem requiri causam quo periculum mortis proximius ac certius est"— he says falsely that even an extraordinary measure of public benefit—"valde utilis"— plus a reasonable prospect of their own personal liberty, does not certainly justify, we will not say the prisoners' certain deaths by their abstinence from all food, but not even their probable deaths. The lives which, in the case of soldiers, he rightly judges to be certainly of small moment compared with an ordinary measure of public welfare, those same lives he wrongly judges, in the case of the prisoners, to be probably of greater moment than the combined benefits of extraordinary public welfare and well-founded prospect of liberation. "Res controvertitur" is his verdict regarding his second case, notwithstanding that that case is placed beyond all controversy by Fr. Tanquerey's own words already cited, and by similar words of other standard authors on Moral Theology.

In proof of his verdict that the lawfulness of his second case is in dispute, he refers his readers to L'Ami Du Clergé, (1920, pp. 399-400; 529-531) the date of which plainly indicates that the subject there treated is the MacSwiney hunger-strike. Now, even if it were granted, which it is not, that the lawfulness of Mayor MacSwiney's hunger-strike was and still is in dispute, it would by no means follow that the lawfulness of Fr. Tanquerey's second case is or could be disputed. The two cases differ "toto coelo," and that is enough to discredit Fr. Tanquerey's reference to L'Ami Du Clergé.

MacSWINEY CASE NOT CONTROVERTED

But the reference to L'Ami Du Clergé is counted out on other grounds also. The MacSwiney case—which Fr. Tanquerey wrongly assumes to be similar to his own—is not controverted. A theological problem is not assigned to the list of controverted questions simply because several adventurers in that domain publicly array themselves on opposite sides in the discussion of it. In theology, as in all other arts and sciences, the distinction between amateur and professional is well emphasized. It is only the opposing conclusions of cautious, conservative professors, and authors of recognized theological superiority that justify calling a question "controverted."

And who are the professors of theology, who the recognized authorities in theology that pronounced the MasSwiney hunger-strike unlawful? What exception can any of the dissenters take to the following proof for the lawfulness of Mayor MacSwiney's act?

Maj. Prop. It is lawful to place an action even though it produces an ill effect, provided (1) the action itself is not intrinsically evil, nor the ill effect intended, either (2) as an end, or (3) as a means, and the good effect is (4) proportionate to the ill effect.

Min. Prop. But each of these four conditions is verified in MacSwiney's hunger-strike unto death.

Conclusion Therefore, MacSwiney's hunger-strike unto death was lawful.

Proof of the Major:

An action in which all the requirements just mentioned are verified, cannot be evil from the end or from the means or from the circumstances – the only sources of good or evil in human actions.

PROOF OF THE MINOR – ACTION ITSELF GOOD

(1) It is certain that the action itself of refusing food until death is good – not an intrinsically evil act. It is not forbidden by negative precept, admitting no exception, as all actions intrinsically evil are. There is no precept which says: "You must never refuse food until death." Otherwise the martyrs could not lawfully refuse unto death the food given to idols. The precept to preserve one's own life is a positive precept, and so, like all positive precepts, admits occasional exceptions, allows and recommends the sacrifice of one's own life, for charity, chastity, friendship, patriotism or any other virtue. The precept is – "You must preserve your own life, except when you sacrifice it for the love of God and your neighbour." Nay more, it is positively forbidden to preserve one's own life by any sinful means great or small.

INTENTION OF THE LORD MAYOR GOOD

(2) It is certain that the Lord Mayor did not intend his own death, either as an end or as a means. Why should he? What benefit would have accrued, either to Ireland or to himself, from intending his own death? It could only have transformed a fascinating hero – the admiration and inspiration of all men, for all time – into a loathesome suicide, abhorrent to God and man. This would not have been the MacSwiney who hoped "to reach the mountain tops in aspiring to the stars."

PROPORTION OF GOOD SUPERABUNDANT!

(3) It is certain that the heroic sacrifice of his young life, with all its prospects, **was abundantly compensated by the benefits to his country and countrymen the world over.** His protest against the injustice of his own imprisonment, and against their oppression by an alien government, resounded to the ends of the earth, **assuring and securing for him and them, world attention, world sympathy and world assistance.**

Thus is the lawfulness of MacSwiney's hunger-strike until death proved to a certainty. **Nothing, absolutely nothing, has been proved to the contrary.** How then can the lawfulness of that case be denied or doubted? **How can it be called "controverted?"**

"L'AMI DU CLERGÉ" NO AUTHORITY

By referring his readers to L'Ami Du Clergé as proof, indeed his only proof, that his second case is controverted, Fr. Tanquerey asserts implicitly (1) **that the MacSwiney case is similar to his own second case,** and (2) **that the article in L'Ami Du Clergé proves that the MacSwiney case is controverted.** Now both of those indirect assertions are false. First, the two cases are not similar. **The MacSwiney case is hunger-strike, Fr. Tanquerey's second case is not.** Again, the article in L'Ami Du Clergé **hands down no decision nor even an opinion** as to whether the MacSwiney case is lawful or not, as to whether it is controverted or not. It does not name a single authority, nor cite a single argument for or against hunger-strike. True, the writer speaks of the ethical discussions to which Mayor MacSwiney's hunger-strike gave rise—"les polemiques casuistiques dont l'affaire de Cork a été l'occasion." But this is not to say that the MacSwiney case is controverted. If discussion, orderly and disorderly, could make a question controverted, there would be no end of controverted questions.

Furthermore, the author of the article on MacSwiney in L'Ami Du Clergé declared at the outset that **he would not undertake to solve the MacSwiney case,** since he was not familiar with the facts and circumstances connected with it. If he failed to arrive at any conclusion about it, **it was not because he had weighed the reasons for and against and found them equally inconclusive.** These are his words:

"We said at the beginning of this article that we "could not and would not give a conclusive answer. We "discuss **a hypothesis according to which the behaviour** "of the hunger-striker, **far from being morally blameworthy, could certainly be lawful and even worthy of** "**admiration.** In the concrete case of the Mayor of

"Cork, did the facts correspond to the conditions of that hypothesis? We leave to others better informed than we are, the burden and responsibility of passing judgment on this."*

In the light of this protest by the writer in L'Ami Du Clergé; in the light of his article, which mentions no authority and cites no argument – merely stating the moral principles bearing on hunger-strike – in view of the fact that the MacSwiney case, even if controverted, would prove nothing as to whether Fr. Tanquerey's case was controverted or not – in the light of all this, what becomes of Fr. Tanquerey's appeal to L'Ami Du Clergé as his sole proof that his second case is a controverted case. That case he wrongly calls a case of hunger-strike. He wrongly pronounces it a controverted case. He wrongly assumes that it is similar to the MacSwiney case. He wrongly assumes that the MacSwiney case is controverted. He wrongly thinks that the article in L'Ami Du Clergé shows that the MacSwiney case is controverted. This is quite a lengthy list of wrongs done to a single simple case in Moral Theology!

CONTRADICTION AND ETHICAL PARADOX

It must be noted, in conclusion, that Fr. Tanquerey pronounces his second case doubtfully lawful, even when his prisoners' absolute abstention from all food is **necessary for the public good.** "Et talis actio est valde utilis aut necessaria ad bonum publicum promovendum." There surely is an ethical paradox. His "necessaria ad bonum publicum," joined to his "controvertitur," besides contradicting what he said before –"the public good is a sufficient reason for exposing oneself to proximate and certain danger of death"– contradicts itself. An action necessary for the public welfare, and, at the same time, doubtfully lawful, would be, at the same time, obligatory and forbidden. It would be obligatory because public officials, philanthropists, and citizens in general are obligated to what is necessary for the public good. It would, at the same time, be forbidden, because it is forbidden to place an act whose lawfulness is doubtful. In such an impossible case, the supplying of public necessities would be dependent on an action which it would be unlawful to place – a condition which could arise only from the absurd supposition of either a disordered public welfare, which needs or admits promotion by actions doubtfully

---

*"Nous l'avons déclaré dès le début de cet article: Nous ne pouvons ni ne voulons rien conclure. Nous examinons une hypothèse où l'attitude du jeûneur, loin d'étre moralment répréhensible, pouvait etre certainement licite, et même digne d'admiration. Dans le cas concrete du maire de Cork, la réalité des faits correspond – elle aux donnees de cette hypothèse? Il nous faut laisser à d'autres mieux informes le soin et la responsibilité d'en juger."

lawful, or **a defective moral code** which fails to sanction actions requisite for supplying such public necessities.

ANOTHER CONTRADICTION

Finally, the evident lawfulness of Fr. Tanquerey's second case, which he claims to be "controverted," is proved beyond challenge by the universally accepted principle regulating cases of indirect voluntary, and set down by himself in these words:

> "It is lawful to place an action (1) good or indifferent in itself, producing two effects, one good, the other ill, provided (2) the good effect be not produced by an absolutely evil effect, provided (3) there is a proportionately grave reason for the action, and (4) the intention of the agent is upright."*(Vol. II, n. 220.)

Now it is beyond question that each of the four conditions here specified by Fr. Tanquerey **is verified in his second case**. (1) The action of his prisoners in abstaining from all food **is itself indifferent**, because the precept of preserving one's own life by food – or otherwise – **is not a negative precept** forbidding ever and always any contrary action, but **a positive precept** which, like **all positive precepts, admits exceptions** for sufficient reasons. (2) Again, the **intention** of the prisoners is directed exclusively to obtaining their own liberation and **promoting the public good**. (3) These objectives, as we have seen, **superabundantly compensate** for the risk, and even for the certain loss of their own lives. (4) Neither the prisoners' risk of their lives nor the certain loss of them **is used as a means** to obtain their own liberty or to promote the public welfare. In other words, all the requisites for an evidently lawful indirect voluntary are realized in the action of Fr. Tanquerey's prisoners. **On what grounds, then, does he call his second case "controverted"?** What argument may be urged against its lawfulness?

ANOTHER UNTRUTH

His treatment of hunger-strike Fr. Tanquerey concludes by saying that "the solution depends on the measure of hope and the gravity of the reason for placing the action." **This cannot be admitted.** We have it on Fr. Tanquerey's own authority that, for the lawfulness of any action producing an ill effect, (1) the act itself must be good or indifferent; (2) the intention of the agent must be good; (3)

---

*"Licet ponere actum in se bonum aut indifferentem, ex quo sequitur duplex effectus, alter bonus et alter malus, dummodo effectus bonus non producatur mediante effectu absolute malo, adsit ratio proportionate gravis, et finis agentis sit honestus."

the good effect must not be obtained by an ill effect absolutely evil; (4) the reason for placing the action must be proportionately grave. How then can he venture to say, a moment later, that the solution of every case of fast until death depends, entirely and exclusively, on "the measure of hope" and "the gravity of the reason for placing the act?" This is equivalent to saying that neither the morality of the act of fasting itself, nor the intention of the one who fasts, nor the causality of the good effect enters at all into the solution. It is to say the contradictory of what Fr. Tanquerey himself said only a little while before. Nor is it an excuse to say that he is taking for granted the fulfilment of the omitted conditions. The solution of every case of "two effects" depends on the fulfilment or non-fulfilment not of some but of all the conditions for a lawful indirect voluntary.

The present writer has no desire to pronounce an unfavorable verdict on anything said by a theologian so widely known and so deservedly esteemed as Fr. Tanquerey. But what excuse can be offered for his saying that the solution of every case of fast until death depends exclusively on "the measure of hope" and "the gravity of the reason?" It is true that the act itself – the refusal of food even until death – is not intrinsically evil. But that is no reason for omitting that condition from his list of requirements. Moreover, it is by no means evident, and, on that account, needs to be proved. At the time of the MacSwiney fast it was not accepted by the masses because it was not proved for them. And though more than a decade of years have since passed, it still remains unproved for the average layman, the average cleric, and indeed the average theologian. Today, many theologians, and not a few professors of theology, are heard insisting that the act of refusing food until death is intrinsically evil.

THE POPULAR OBJECTION

This, in fact, was the recurring bugbear of the sincere inquirer, from the very beginning of the controversy regarding the MacSwiney hunger-strike. Canon Villiers of Birmingham, England, was a typical example. By way of objection against the lawfulness of any fast until death, the Canon wrote in The Tablet (London): "Suppose he – the hunger-striker – had said: 'If I am not freed in three days I will shoot myself,' would any sane theologian say 'that is quite allowable'? Does it alter the case if you change 'shoot' into 'starve'?" Does Fr. Tanquerey's treatment of fast until death answer this objection? Its answer is not found either in his "measure of hope" or in his "gravity of reason." To change "shoot" into "starve" alters the case to the extent of substituting **an act intrinsically indifferent for an act intrinsically evil** – quite an alteration in accordance with the first and chiefest requisite for a lawful case of "two effects," and of which Fr. Tanquerey says nothing.

PHYSICAL ASPECTS, MORAL ASPECTS

In their physical aspects there is no difference between "shoot" and "starve." Each spells inevitable death. But there is a world of difference between their **moral aspects.** Shooting oneself to death is an intrinsically evil act. Starving oneself to death is not. This crucial point in the hunger-strike controversy – the point that was mostly unthought of because mostly unheard of, doubted by very many and vehemently denied by several – this pivotal point of doctrine is not self-evident, nor is it to be accepted solely on any human authority. There is no authoritative catalogue of actions good in themselves, actions evil in themselves and actions indifferent in themselves. In a specific instance it is sometimes difficult to decide whether an action is intrinsically evil or not .And thus **the misgiving attaching, in the popular mind, and not infrequently in the theological mind, to the act itself of starving oneself to death,** was the great obstacle to a wider understanding and acceptance of the doctrine that hunger-strike until death **may sometimes be lawful.**

Neither the **intention** of the hunger-striker nor the circumstance of **proportionate benefit** created any misgivings. 'Twas easy to understand that the hunger-striker, though encompassing his own death, **could be exclusively intent on some proportionate good. But the technical distinction between destroying one's own life and not preserving it, was something which the theology of the populace could not fathom.** Simply and solely because both acts inevitably terminate in a violent death, the popular mentality, and sometimes the clerical mentality, ascribed the same morality to both. Many who might be expected to know better asked Canon Villiers' question –**"does it alter the case if you change 'shoot' into 'starve'?"**

A TYPICAL SPECIMEN

The following communication to the present writer, from a distinguished professor of Catholic Philosophy and author of a work on Apologetics, is typical of the uniformly inconsiderate thinking and writing that obtains on all sides regarding hunger-strike.

"I regard self-starvation (hunger-strike) as a form "of suicide, because it is the procuring of one's death "by equivalently direct action – supposing, of course, "that the strike is deliberately persisted in until death.

"It is urged that the abstention from food is only a "negative act and so cannot be prohibited as a positive "act is prohibited. This, in my thinking, is only an "evasion. If a person were to refuse to breathe until "death results, would you absolve such a one from the "guilt of suicide simply because the action was only "negative? You would say that breathing is not an "indifferent action since it is essentially connected with "life. Holding one's breath becomes suicidal only when "one must either take in breath or die. So too, fasting "is quite lawful until the point when one must either "eat or die. Then, if the food is at hand, the abstention "is suicidal."

WRONG SUPPOSITIONS. NO PROOFS

1. Like the author of the original inquiry in "The Ecclesiastical Review," the writer supposes wrongly that all self-starvation to death is hunger-strike. "Self-starvation (hunger-strike)" are his words.

2. He supposes wrongly too, that the fast must be until death, whereas the intention of continuing until death suffices for hunger-strike.

3. He proves hunger-strike to be suicidal by merely reasserting it. He was obliged to prove that hunger-strike is directly intended self-killing, but instead he says it is "procuring one's death by equivalently direct action." "Equivalently direct" is obscure. If it does not mean "direct self-killing," it does not prove the writer's "suicide." If it does, then the proposition of which it is a part says falsely that every hunger-striker intends his own death.

PARALLELS THAT ARE NOT PARALLEL

4. The writer would prove his "suicide" verdict by the seemingly parallel act of omitting to breathe. Parallels that are not parallel are more numerous than those that are so. Refusal to breathe is not essentially a protest against injustice, as hunger-strike is and has been, by the established convention of more than a thousand years. Therefore no parallel.

Nor does the fact that breathing and eating are "essentially connected with life" make the omission of either act intrinsically evil. Otherwise, he who gives his last crust to another dying of hunger and dies of hunger himself, would be doing something intrinsically evil, whereas theologians proclaim him a martyr of charity. Neither omission to breathe nor omission to take food is intrinsically evil. Both are intrinsically indifferent acts. If the tank contains only enough of oxygen to save the life of one, would Jones, who is in possession of the oxygen, be committing suicide by surrendering it to Smith, and dying himself of suffocation?

5. The writer's parallel further fails in that **no good effect follows essentially from omission to breathe**, while protest against injustice, publicity, sympathy, organized resistance and so forth follow essentially from hunger-strike. Hence, if the absence of every good effect creates the presumption that he who refuses to breathe intends his own death – the only effect which his act produces – the same cannot be said of the refusal to take food, **since it is essentially a protest against injustice**. And precisely because that good effect alone is intended by the hunger-striker, his act, sometimes lawful, sometimes unlawful, **can never be suicide**.

IT IS MONSIGNOR BELFORD'S PARALLEL ALSO

Parallels without end were urged for and against the lawfulness of Mayor MacSwiney's hunger-strike. Monsignor Belford, of Brooklyn, New York, urged, with greater accuracy, though not with more conviction, the case of refusal to take air into the lungs.

"Suppose we substitute for food the other vital element – air. Suppose a man unjustly condemned to two years' imprisonment and cast into a small cell in which there is just one valve for supplying air. To get the air he must open the valve. He can do it easily. He is even urged to do so but he will not.

"To serve his country by proclaiming to the world the injustice he suffers, he chooses to die of suffocation. Make the case as strong as you can. Suppose his suffering excites the sympathy of the world; suppose it wins liberty for his country; suppose it prevents similar injustice to thousands, would it be right for him to refuse to let in the air on which his life depends? Sound Ethics, it seems to us, must answer, promptly and emphatically, no! Nothing can justify the employment of a means which is evil in itself."

PERFECT PARALLEL. NO PROOF

Monsignor Belford's parallel is perfect. But it is a grand effort in a poor cause – the hopeless cause of proving that hunger-strike is suicide. In the imaginary case which the Monsignor so ably and accurately constructs, it would be lawful, laudably lawful, **heroically lawful for his prisoner to refuse to open the valve that would admit the air.** Monsignor Belford says that "sound Ethics" must answer the opposite. **But this is only to reiterate instead of proving.** And when he adds that "nothing can justify the employment of means evil in itself," **he says what is true but irrelevant**. The refusal of air is not evil in itself. To say that it is would be begging the question.

Like many other contributors to the MacSwiney controversy, Monsignor Belford, instead of undertaking to prove his position from the moral principles involved, attempts to establish it by comparing hunger-strike with other cases. Like them he failed to see that such comparisons cannot prove anything of what he wants to prove. For the case introduced by him as a parallel is either a strictly parellel case or it is not. If it is not a strictly parallel case, it is introduced to no purpose. If it is a perfect parallel, then, it presents just the same difficulties as the case it was introduced to elucidate.

ACT NOT INTRINSICALLY EVIL

It is essential, for any adequate treatment of this question to give special prominence to the thesis that the act itself of refusing food until death is not intrinsically evil, and to its proof – that it is not forbidden by negative precept, which admits no exception, but the opposite only commanded by positive precept, which admits exceptions for serious reasons. Any adequate presentation of the Catholic doctrine of hunger-strike must include this central consideration, indeed must begin with it. The entire doctrine of hunger-strike hinges on it. Nevertheless, Fr. Tanquerey doesn't make even a passing reference to it. After admitting that hunger-strike until death is a case of indirect self-killing, and that every case of indirect voluntary producing an ill effect requires for its lawfulness (1) an action good in itself, (2) a good intention, (3) a reason proportionately grave, and (4) a good effect not produced by an effect absolutely evil, he merely asserts that "the solution depends on the measure of hope, and the gravity of the reason for placing the act."

SUMMARY OF HIS "ADEQUATE" TREATMENT

Discussing in general the morality of actions producing effects indirectly voluntary, Fr. Tanquerey enunciates the general principle universally accepted by moral theologians and used by them to determine whether an action producing an ill effect is lawful or unlawful. (Vol. II, n. 220)

When he afterwards comes to consider acts of indirect self-killing, and to indicate which reasons are proportionately grave to justify that effect and which are not, he writes that the public good is a sufficient reason for placing any action which must cause indirectly the certain death of the agent. (Vol. III, n. 270)

(a) But we have already seen that, when treating the case of hunger-strike – Vol. III, 272D – Fr. Tanquerey contradicts what he said in the place just referred to. There he said that **any benefit to the general public is certainly a proportionately grave reason** for placing an action which involves the certain sacrifice of the agent's own life. But now, in his treatment of hunger-strike, he says that **such public benefit is not certainly a proportionately grave reason** for the certain sacrifice of the hunger-striker's life. Indeed he says much more. He says that **a very great measure of public good ("valde utilis") is not certainly a proportionate reason.** He even goes so far as to say that **the public benefit of supplying a public necessity, together with a well-founded hope of their own liberty** – "si tamen spes liberationis fundata esset" – **is not certainly a reason proportionate to the certain death of his hunger-striking prisoners, nor even proportionate to their probable death.** He is certain, with moral theologians generally, that, for the public benefit of destroying portion of the enemy forces, **soldiers may lawfully dynamite a fortress, and sailors lawfully sink a ship,** though certain that they themselves must die of the wreckage. But **he is not certain that hunger-striking prisoners may lawfully refuse food until certain death, or even until probable death, for a combined public and personal benefit** – for the satisfying a public necessity and probably securing their own liberation. "Res controvertitur" is Fr. Tanquerey's verdict regarding his prisoners, **although that case is put outside of any controversy by Fr. Tanquerey's own words cited above,** and indeed by similar words of standard moralists in general.

The truth is that either good is a proportionately grave reason. Fr. Noldin, S.J. says that "it is lawful for criminals detained in prison to throw themselves from a pinnacle to escape certain death, or even perpetual imprisonment, provided there be some hope ("aliqua spes") of saving their lives." (Summa Theologiae Moralis, vol. ii, n. 327). And Genicot, Lehmkuhl and others say the same thing in practically the same words. Now, when it is borne in mind that **the death of the hunger-striker is never certain,** and that many are still alive and well who have had one or more hunger-strikes, why, **it may be asked, is it not as certainly lawful for hunger-striking prisoners to risk their lives by refusing food, as it is for criminals to risk their lives by throwing themselves from a pinnacle,** especially when, according to Fr. Tanquerey, the prisoners' hope of liberation is well-founded? It is lawful, **certainly lawful, for** prisoners and criminals alike.

Again, the public good, **even a modicum of public good,** is, of itself, sufficient to justify the **certain sacrifice of the prisoners' lives.**

And if even a small measure of public benefit certainly justifies soldiers and sailors in facing certain death, is not a very great public benefit, or the supplying some public necessity, of itself a still more certain justification for the prisoners' fast until probable death? Yet Fr. Tanquerey does not recognize in that case either an a fortiori or an a pari argument. Notwithstanding that either reason is certainly sufficient, he is not certain that the prisoners' refusal of food until probable death is justified by either the one reason or the other or by both combined.

(b) Furthermore, this second of Fr. Tanquerey's two cases, besides contradicting what he says elsewhere in his book, even contradicts itself. It is an ethical paradox. His prisoners' refusal of food, even when necessary for the public good, is doubtfully lawful. "Controvertitur" is his verdict about it. Now, every action necessary for the public good is obligatory, (primarily on public officials), and every action doubtfully lawful is forbidden. Thus according to Fr. Tanquerey's own data, his prisoners' refusal of food is both commanded and forbidden in the same circumstances.

(c) The first of his two cases is equally paradoxical. It is a case in which his prisoners have no hope of liberation. This is evident both from the words in which that case is stated—"foreseeing that death must result from it"—and from the sharp contrast expressed by the introductory words of his second case:—"but if the hope of liberation were well-founded." Nevertheless, Fr. Tanquerey makes those prisoners hope. "In the hope that the judges will be moved to pity and will liberate the prisoners," says Fr. Tanquerey. Poetry or rhetoric may entertain such fictions as hoping against hope. Moral theology can not.

Moreover, either the prisoners have hope of liberation or they have none. If they have hope of liberation,—"aliqua spes"—then, according to Noldin, Genicot, Lehmkuhl, and many other moralists, their refusal of food is certainly lawful, and Fr. Tanquerey's solution is the wrong solution. If they have no hope of liberation, then this first case is not a case of "two effects" at all. The prisoners' refusal of food has one and only one effect—the evil effect of their own deaths. Their refusal of food is suicide, and Fr. Tanquerey's proof that their act is unlawful, besides being obscure and insufficient, is unnecessary. He had previously proved suicide unlawful. So much for the merits and demerits, the brevity and the inadequacy of Fr. Tanquerey's treatment of hunger-strike.

Chapter Sixteen

SOME OBJECTORS AND THEIR OBJECTIONS

Fr. Wouters, C.SS.R.

Fr. Wouters, unlike Fr. Tanquerey, does not use the term "hunger-strike" at all. Neither does he discuss the specific action for which the term "hunger-strike" stands. Of the eight hundred pages which make up the first volume of his treatise, **there are only four lines** that could be interpreted as referring expressly to hunger-strike. These are the lines:

> "To omit self-preservation – say, by abstaining from "food or drink until death – seems altogether unlawful "as carried out in practice. For it is altogether unlaw-"ful **to intend death as a means to obtain something.** "Now whoever abstains from food or drink, **intends, in** "**practice, death as a means to obtain something.**"*

NOT DISCUSSION, NOT ABOUT HUNGER-STRIKE

The brevity of this citation would seem to forbid calling it "discussion," as the Editor of The Ecclesiastical Review does. But it has, in addition, the following more serious shortcomings. First: Like Fr. Tanquerey's treatment of the same question, Fr. Wouters' discussion of it **contains nothing that expressly applies to hunger-strike.** It says **nothing whatever about injustice or protest against injustice, and hunger-strike is essentially a protest against injustice.** Thus we cannot agree with the Editor of The Ecclesiastical Review that "the last edition of Wouters' 'Manuale' discusses that problem."

A FALSE PRINCIPLE

Second: **Fr. Wouters' brief reasoning is full of ambiguity and error.** In the first sentence of his argument, he asserts, **unqualifiedly and therefore falsely, that all omission to preserve one's own life "seems altogether unlawful."** His parenthetic phrase – "say, by abstaining from food or drink" – is added only incidentally by way of illustration, and therefore does not limit or restrict his predicate "unlawful" to any particular types of omission, as would be

---

*"Omissio conservationis sui – puta, abstinendo a cibo vel potu "dum moriaris – omnino illicita videtur, scilecet ut practice exerce-"tur. Etenim ommino illicitum est intendere mortem tanquam "medium aliquid obtinendi. Atqui qui abstinet a cibo vel potu, in-"tendit – prout ista ratio agendi practice obtinet – mortem tanquam "medium aliquid obtinendi." ("Manuale Theologae Moralis," Auctore Ludovico Wouters, C.SS.R., Beyaert, Bruges, Belgium, 1932.)

the case if he had said: "To omit self-preservation, by abstaining from food or drink, seems altogether unlawful." Here the predicate "unlawful" is restricted to one type of omission to preserve life – namely that by abstention from food or drink.

Besides abstention from food or drink, there are evidently many other ways by which preservation of one's own life may be omitted. The Forty Martyrs of Sebaste, for instance, when exposed by their persecutors on a frozen lake, omitted to preserve their lives, by refusing the warmth of th baths, offered them if they would deny Christ. Now Fr. Wouters' assertion –"omission to preserve one's own life (say, by abstaining from food or drink until death) seems altogether unlawful"– predicates "unlawful" of every omission to preserve one's own life, even of the omission by the Forty Martyrs. And, on the contrary, "omission to preserve one's life, by abstention from food or drink, seems altogether unlawful" predicates "unlawful" of that one kind of omission to preserve one's own life, and of no other. Nor, may anyone say with reason that there is question here only of a modus loquendi, or that Fr. Wouters' meaning was evidently the latter and not the former. A modus loquendi obtains only between different ways of saying the same thing, and it has just been shown that the things corresponding to the phrases here contrasted are not the same. As to gathering from the context what Fr. Wouters' meaning might or might not be, it must be remarked that it is the function of language to express, with all accuracy, what the speaker or writer means.

SEVERAL AMBIGUITIES

Third: Of the ambiguity arising from such inaccurate expression, Fr. Wouters' second sentence furnishes another conspicuous example. There he says: "It is altogether unlawful to intend death as a means to obtain something." Taken at its face value, this assertion is untrue. It would forbid a soldier on the firing line in time of war, to intend the death of a single one of the enemy forces. Again, why the adjunct "as a means to obtain something?" Does anyone suppose that it might not be altogether unlawful to intend one's own death as an end? If Fr. Wouters had simply said: "It is unlawful to intend one's own death"– "mortem propriam"– the argument – if there is an argument – would remain intact and the ambiguities would be avoided.

Fourth: The third and last sentence of Fr. Wouters' discussion combines the falsity of his first sentence and the ambiguities of his second. He says: "Whoever abstains from food or drink, intends, in practice, death as a means to obtaining something." Now the entire difficulty which the case of hunger-strike presents, arises, not from refusal of food, as such, but from refusal of food unto death. Why then does Fr. Wouters omit the very specifying words "until death"–"dum moriaris?" And again, when he says that such a one "intends death," why does he not say specifically that he intends his own death – mortem propriam? To omit these specifying terms is to overwork the context, and destroy the syllogistic form that should underlie all deductive reasoning.

WHAT DOES HIS "IN PRACTICE" MEAN?

And what meaning are we to assign to the phrase "as carried out in practice,"–"ut practice exercetur"– of Fr. Wouters' first sentence, and to the same phrase, "in practice,"–"prout ista ratio agendi practice obtinet"– which occurs in his last sentence? When he says that "to omit self-preservation, etc., seems altogether unlawful as carried out in practice," does he mean that there are other ways of carrying out the same abstention which would be lawful in practice? If this be his meaning, why does he not state what those "other ways" are?

Or does he mean that, although in theory such omission is or may be lawful, it can never be so in practice? Is there any action which is sometimes theoretically lawful, but must always remain unlawful in practice? If such an action must be supposed in order to interpret Fr. Wouters' "in practice," it is for him to show why it is sometimes lawful in theory, and why it is always unlawful in practice.

ANOTHER FALSE PRINCIPLE

In his last proposition – the minor of his syllogism – he asserts that "every one who abstains from food or drink until death, intends, in practice, his own death." Here again we may interpret Fr. Wouters' "in practice" to mean that the abstainer, though professing that he does not intend his own death, does actually intend it –"as a means to obtain something." Coming from a professional moralist, who is especially committed to cautious, conservative statement, this assertion is nothing short of reckless. Fr. Wouters gives no proof of it. He has none to give. It cannot be inferred from the nature of the abstainer, nor from the nature of his act. Neither does Fr. Wouters cite any list of instances in which the abstainers themselves uniformly testified that they intended their own deaths "as a means to obtain something."

That there **could be** cases in which the abstainers might perhaps intend their own deaths "as a means to obtain something," may be readily granted. But that **every abstainer until death, does, and in practice must,** intend his own death "as a means"- this assertion of Fr. Wouters is gratuitous because it is flaringly false.

CONTRADICTS HIMSELF

And indeed Fr. Wouters himself contradicts that assertion a moment later. Continuing his reasoning with regard to abstinence from food or drink until death, he says:

> "It is otherwise in the case of one who abstains – "until death – from food or drink, **in order that it may** "save the life of another. For such a one intends to "preserve another's life, and merely permits his own "death."*

But does not such a one abstain from food and drink until death, and has not Fr. Wouters said already that "whoever abstains from food or drink until death, intends, in practice, his own death?" Thus, according to Fr. Wouters, he who abstains until death to save the life of another, **intends his own death,** and, at the same time, **places a lawful act.** "It is otherwise," etc. It is the rule regarding contradictory judgments that both cannot be true. **If it is true that the act of him who abstains until death, to save the life of another, is lawful, then it is false that "whoever abstains until death from food or drink, intends, in practice, his own death."** But, by the common consent of theologians, it is true that the act of him who abstains until death to save the life of another, is lawful and most laudable. Therefore it is false that "whoever abstains from food or drink until death, intends, in practice, his own death." And this false as well as contradictory proposition is Fr. Wouters' entire contribution to the Ethics of hunger-strike. He is no less guilty than Fr. Tanquerey in the matter of contradicting himself.

FR. WOUTERS' IMMEDIATE SELF-CONTRADICTION

In doctrinal treatises it is not often that contradictory propositions are found to follow immediately one upon the other. Fr. Tanquery contradicts, in his third volume, a principle laid down by him in his second. But Fr. Wouters makes an assertion in one sentence and contradicts it in the

---

*"Secus dicendum est de eo qui abstinet a cibo vel potu ut alius "habeat under mortem effugere possit, quia conservationem vitae "alienae intendit, propriam vero mortem solummodo permittit."
(Ibidem)

very next. He first says that "everyone who abstains from food or drink, **intends, in practice, his own death as a means** to obtain something," and then immediately adds that **he who abstains from food or drink in order to save the life of another, does not intend his own death.** "It is otherwise, etc. This is like first saying that all men are liars, and then immediately adding that it is otherwise in the case of George Washington. A single instance to the contrary contradicts a universal assertion or denial.

"IT IS OTHERWISE" IN MANY OTHER CASES

And there are **many others** of whom Fr. Wouters might as truly say "it is otherwise." It is otherwise in the case of Christians deprived of all other food, and abstaining until death rather than eat food previously offered to idols. It is otherwise with the Carthusian monk refusing until death a meat diet – the only diet which for him is food at all – in order to honor his Rule. It is otherwise in the case of many a hunger-striker. It was otherwise in the case of **Mac-Swiney, Fitzgerald, Murphy, O'Sullivan and Barry. It was otherwise** with the hunger-strike of Mahatma Gandhi, in which his abstention from food and drink was **intended until death**, in protest against the English Government's unjust discrimination against the "untouchables." Fr. Wouters' **universal** proposition that "everyone who abstains from food or drink, **intends, in practice, his own death,"** is untrue. He accordingly **contradicts it only to the extent of a single exception** – that of him who dies because he gave his last meal to save the life of another. The many other equally legitimate exceptions enumerated by authors generally, he ignores. Thus the falsity of his universal assertion is made less evident. All the same, the Editor of **"The Ecclesiastical Review"** says that "the last edition of Wouters' 'Manuale' discusses that problem," nor is there room to doubt that very many pronounce every hunger-strike unto death unlawful, **on the authority of Fr. Wouters,** C.SS.R.

MACSWINEY'S PHILOSOPHY

"You may weaken and yield, or you may stand your ground, refuse the bribe, uphold the flag, and be rated a fool and a failure. But they who rate you so will not understand that you have won a battle greater than all the triumphs of empires."

Chapter Seventeen

SOME OBJECTORS AND THEIR OBJECTIONS

Fr. Merkelbach, O.P.

CONTRADICTS HIMSELF TWICE ON SAME PAGE

Fr. Merkelbach must be added to the list of authors in Moral Theology who are guilty of contradicting themselves when writing on the morality of hunger-strike. After accurately distinguishing, in his preamble, between direct and indirect self-killing, he says immediately:

(1) "No reason can be assigned on account of which it "may be lawful to kill oneself."*

This assertion is untrue. Fr. Merkelbach himself says so twice over, thus contradicting himself twice over. In the preamble already mentioned he wrote:

(2) "No one doubts that indirect self-killing is lawful "under certain conditions, and for a cause propor- "tionately grave."**

And he says the same thing again by way of a thesis.

(3) "Indirect self-killing is unlawful except for a just "and proportionate reason."***

Thus we find Fr. Merkelbach insisting that no cause can be assigned that could justify killing oneself, and twice admitting, a moment later, that indirect self-killing, for a just and proportionate reason, is lawful beyond all doubt.

After setting forth the doctrine held by theologians generally regarding the preservation of one's own life, and the avoiding its destruction, Fr. Merkelbach says:

"For greater reasons, they sin grievously who re- "frain from taking necessary sustenance, even when it 'is done for the highest motive – for example, the lib- "eration of one's country. That is direct self-killing, "since, as St. Thomas says: 'not to take sustenance is "the same as to kill oneself' (Q. 69, a. 4, ad 2). Thus a "good end is sought through evil means."****

---

*"Nulla est causa assignabilis propter quam sit licitum occi- "dere seipsum." ("**Summa Theologiae Moralis,**" Vol. II, n. 350.)

**"Occisionem sui indirectam esse licitam, datis certis condi- "cionibus et ex causa proportionate gravi, nemo est qui dubitet." (n. 348.)

***"Indirecta occisio sui est illicita, nisi accedente justa et pro- "portionata cause." (n. 351.)

****"A fortiori qui ab alimentis necessariis sumendis absti- "nent, etiam ad optiman finem, v.g. liberationem patriae. Id enim "est directa occisio, nam, ut ait S. Thomas, 'Non sumere idem est "ac seipsum occidere.' Et bonum speratur ex malo medio." (n. 352.)

NO "A FORTIORI," NO "A PARI," NO REASON AT ALL

So far from there being a greater reason against fast until death than against the unlawful acts which the author had previously enumerated, there is not even an equal reason. There is no reason at all. "It is direct self-killing," ("directa occisio") says Fr. Merkelbach. And by means of a palpable fallacy, with which he associates the name of St. Thomas, he undertakes to prove his "direct self-killing." Reduced to syllogistic form his argument runs thus:

> "Not to take sustenance is the same as to kill one-
> "self." (St. Thomas)
>
> "But to kill oneself is the same as to kill oneself
> "directly." (Fr. Merkelbach's implied minor.)
>
> "Therefore not to take sustenance is the same as to
> "kill oneself directly." (Fr. Merkelbach's conclusion.)

Now the major proposition of this piece of argumentation is all that St. Thomas is responsible for. Fr. Merkelbach would dishonor the great name of his illustrious master by making him responsible for either the minor premise or the conclusion of the above syllogism.

The false minor premise that "to kill oneself is the same as to kill oneself directly," is Fr. Merkelbach's own, and a stepping-stone to his false conclusion that "not to take sustenance is the same as to kill oneself directly." But if to kill oneself, be the same as to kill oneself directly, there is no such thing as indirect self-killing, and so Fr. Merkelbach's accurate distinction between indirect and direct self-killing is to no purpose.

But his fallacy is too apparent to need further unveiling. And that fallacy is Fr. Merkelbach's only ground for teaching that every fast until death is direct self-killing, and therefore grievously unlawful – that it is a case of seeking a good end by grievously evil means. Since therefore he calls hunger-strike until death "direct self-killing," why does he not call it "suicide"?

──────────────── MacSwiney's Philosophy ────────────────

"If the rulers of earth fail us, we still have refuge in the Ruler of Heaven."

"A man of moral force is he who, seeing a thing to be right and essential, and claiming his allegiance, stands for it, unheeding any consequence."

Chapter Eighteen

SOME OBJECTORS AND THEIR OBJECTIONS

Fr. Daman, C.SS.R.

ANOTHER RETAILER OF CONTRADICTIONS

Like Fr. Wouters, Fr. Daman – his brother among the sons of St. Alphonsus – is bent on placing under interdict every voluntary fast until death. In his endeavor to do so, however, he does not follow in Fr. Wouters' footsteps, except in the matter of contradicting himself. He does not endorse Fr. Wouters' method of indicting voluntary abstainers. Fr. Wouters, as we have just seen, does not discuss the question. He solves it with a word – "direct self-killing," "suicide."

"CONTRARY TO LAW OF SELF-PRESERVATION"

Fr. Daman is not so explicit in asserting that all voluntary abstainers until death intend their own deaths, "as a means to obtain something." It is only at the very end of his paragraph on voluntary fast that he mentions the intention at all, and then only indirectly and ambiguously. He carefully avoids all explicit reference to any of the sources of morality. By contending, however, as he does, that voluntary fast until death is contrary to the natural law of self-preservation, his challenge is directed against the act itself – the means – rather than against the end or intention. In his "Theologia Moralis," (Torino, Italy, 1932, Vol. i, n. 566) he writes:

> "Everyone is obliged to preserve his life by ordinary "means . . . From this obligation alone of sustaining "one's own life by ordinary means, follows **the unlaw-** "**fulness of deliberate and directly voluntary abstention** "from all food or drink until death. And from this "seems to follow the unlawfulness of the so-called "hunger-strike – deliberate and directly voluntary ab- "stention, complete and permanent fast, inaugurated "until death, by some, in good faith, for political or "other reasons. And this holds true even in the case "of one who professes (pretends) that he **does not in-** "**tend to commit suicide."***

---

*"Unusquisque tenetur vitam suam conservare mediis ordi- "nariis. **Ex hoc solo officio** sustentandi propriam vitam mediis or- "dinariis, jam satis sequitur illiceitas abstinendi sese deliberate et "directe voluntarie ab cibo vel potu usque dum mors inde sequatur. "Hinc illicita videtur sic dicta **hunger-strike**, seu deliberata et "directe voluntaria abstinentia, seu inedia completa et perpetua, "ab aliquibus, bona quidem fide, ob politicas vel alias rationes, ad "mortem usque instituta; idque etiamsi praetendatur in casu "directe non intendi suicidium."

FALLACIES ARE THEIR POLICIES

To urge the obligation of preserving one's own life by ordinary means, **as if it admits no exception** – this has been **the policy and fallacy** of practically all who wrote against hunger-strike. They emphasize that obligation, in that particular case, as if Christ had never said that it is the perfection of charity to lay down one's life for one's friend. "Each is in duty bound to preserve his life by ordinary means" says Fr. Daman. This universal principle is **untrue**. It admits a thousand exceptions. There are countless circumstances in which a person is **not obliged** to use ordinary means to preserve his life, and countless other circumstances in which he is **forbidden to use the ordinary means** to preserve his life. He who gives his last meal to save the life of another, is **not bound** to the ordinary means to save his own life. The marine who is ordered by his superior officer to sink his ship, **is, in duty bound to carry out the order**, though there be no hope of saving his own life. The moral law **forbids him to use ordinary means** to preserve his life.

OBLIGED TO PRESERVE ONE'S OWN LIFE EXCEPT

That there are such exceptions to Fr. Daman's universal principle, he himself acknowledges. But in doing so, he **too contradicts himself**. He says that it is lawful to kill oneself indirectly "for a just and proportionate reason." (No. 566, iii). Now this exceptive principle contradicts his previous principle that "everyone is obliged to preserve his own life by ordinary means." If everyone were obliged to preserve his life by ordinary means, there could never be such a thing as killing oneself indirectly. Whoever failed to use those ordinary means killed himself directly. The act of indirect self-killing is incompatible with the use of ordinary means to preserve one's own life. It is the rejecting of ordinary means in order to practice heroic charity or heroic chastity or heroic patriotism or heroic friendship. Thus is Fr. Daman guilty of grave inconsistency when he says, in one place, that "everyone is obliged to preserve his life by ordinary means," and says, in another, that indirect killing oneself "for a just and proportionate reason" is lawful.

HIS CONTRADICTORY ASSERTION FALSE

As must always obtain in contradictions, one of Fr. Daman's contradictory assertions is false. It is false that "everyone is obliged to preserve his life by ordinary means." And yet it is from this false antecedent that Fr. Daman concludes that every fast until death is unlawful.

> (1) "From this obligation **alone** of sustaining one's own "life by ordinary means," says Fr. Daman, "follows "the unlawfulness of deliberate and directly volun- "tary abstention from all food until death."

FALSE CONSEQUENT FROM FALSE ANTECEDENT

Here is a false universal consequent derived from a false universal antecedent. And the consequent, like the antecedent, **is false precisely because it is universal.** Neither Fr. Daman's antecedent – that "everyone is obliged to preserve his own life by ordinary means" – nor any other antecedent, can ever yield a true universal conclusion that **every** fast until death is unlawful. This or that particular fast until death **may be unlawful.** But it is not because of Fr. Daman's principle that "**everyone** is obliged to preserve his life by ordinary means." It is either because the **intention** of him who fasts until death **is not good,** or because his **reason for fasting until death** is not "just and proportionate" – because Fr. Daman's requisites for the lawful indirect killing of oneself are not realized.

Wrongly assuming that he has established the unlawfulness of **every** fast until death, he proceeds to apply his general conclusion to the case of hunger-strike.

> (2) "And from this **seems** to follow the unlawfulness of "the so-called hunger-strike – deliberate and directly "voluntary abstention, complete and permanent fast, "inaugurated until death, by some, in good faith, for "political or other reasons."

"SEEMS TO FOLLOW" – FROM FALSE ANTECEDENT

(a) And from this **it does not follow** that any hunger-strike is unlawful. So far as Fr. Daman's principle that "everyone is obliged to preserve his own life by ordinary means," and his inferences from that principle are concerned, **any and every** hunger-strike in which the intention of the agent is good, and the reason for his hunger-strike "just and proportionate," **is lawful.** He started with the false principle that "everyone is obliged to preserve his life by ordinary means." From this false principle he derives **the false inference** that every directly voluntary fast until death is unlawful. And from this latter false inference he further falsely concludes that every hunger-strike until death is unlawful. False premises can yield only a false conclusion. "Nemo dat quod non habet."

HIS "GOOD FAITH" ASSUMES OBJECTIVE EVIL

(b) By acknowledging, as Fr. Daman does, that hunger-strikers are in good faith, ("bona quidem fide") he wrongly assumes that he has conclusively established his case against them all — wrongly assumes that he has proved conclusively that every fast until death is objectively unlawful. To enter any plea for an action is to take its apparent unlawfulness for granted. No one enters a plea for conduct which he judges to be entirely lawful. An agent is said to place an act "in good faith," only when it is certain and evident that the act is objectively wrong, and therefore forbidden, but the agent has no means of knowing that it is so. But not even Fr. Daman's efforts have made it evident or certain or probable that every fast until death is objectively unlawful. His helpless effort to prove it becomes an added presumption to the contrary. And thus his plea of "good faith" is unnecessary for the hunger-strikers' exoneration.

His indictment of hunger-strike ends here. The further remark with which he concludes has no bearing on his subject.

(3) "And this is true even in the case of one who pro-"fesses (pretends?) that he does not directly intend "to commit suicide."

PROFESSIONS AND PRETENSES IRRELEVANT

(a) What any particular hunger-striker professes or pretends or denies regarding his intention, is entirely irrelevant to the question Fr. Daman is discussing. His position is that every hunger-strike until death is unlawful, and he undertakes to show why it is unlawful — what it is that makes it unlawful. But no action is made lawful or unlawful by any profession or pretense or denial of the agent with regard to his intention. It is that intention itself, not any declaration of the agent about it, that makes every action lawful or unlawful. Independently of any affirmation or denial or profession or pretense on the part of the hunger-striker concerning his intention, his act is either good or evil — good if his intention was good, evil if his intention was evil. The question whether or not the hunger-striker intends his own death is therefore more pertinent to Fr. Daman's subject than anything he may profess or pretend regarding his intention. Yet Fr. Daman does not address himself at all to that inquiry.

UGLY INSINUATION OF SUICIDE

(b) These last words of his are obscure, and might be interpreted to imply that the hunger-strikers until death intend their own deaths, **irrespective of their professions or pretenses to the contrary**. Against this interpretation it might be asked (1) why should **Fr. Daman be content to urge, merely by implication,** a consideration that is such a factor in the morality of hunger-strike as the intention of the hunger-striker is; and (2) why should he say, even by implication, something that **he cannot prove, since it is utterly false?** It would be but to say over again what Fr. Wouters says against hunger-strike, **with the inevitable leaving the assertion unproved, as he does.** Still, the oracular ambiguity of Fr. Daman's "etiamsi praetendatur in casu non directe intendi suicidium," at the very conclusion of his commentary, leaves him suspected of saying by implication that every hunger-striker **intends his own death,** however he may profess or pretend that he does not. And Fr. Daman's **"directe voluntaria abstinentia" tempts the reader to mistake it for "directe voluntaria mors"**–something vastly different.

MACSWINEY'S PHILOSOPHY

"Now and in every phase of the coming struggle, the strong mind is a greater need than the strong hand."

"In the aberrations of the weak mind decrying resistance, let us not lose our balance and defy brute strength."

"Keeping in mind not only the ideal line of action but the line practicable at the moment as well."

"It is not those who can inflict the most but those who can suffer the most who will conquer."

Chapter Nineteen

SOME OBJECTORS AND THEIR OBJECTIONS

Fr. Vermeersch, S.J.

WRONGLY CITED IN OPPOSITION

The following references, given by Fr. Daman, at the close of his article, also call for a word of comment:

> "See Vermeersch, n. 320; N.K.S. 1921, p. 54; For opinions regarding both sides consult 'The Irish Ecclesiastical Record,' 1918, 1919; 'The Irish Theological Quarterly,' 1921 (passim); 'La Civilta Catt.' 1920, IV, p. 521."

(a) The "pros" and "cons," for which Fr. Daman gives some references, induced Fr. Tanquerey to pronounce hunger-strike a **"controverted"** question. "Res controvertitur." Why does Fr. Daman unhesitatingly pronounce all hunger-strike unlawful, and, a moment later, equivalently acknowledge, by the above references, **that its lawfulness has been defended as well as denied?** "For opinions regarding both sides," he says.

(b) Why does Fr. Daman cite Fr. Vermeersch as holding with him that every voluntary fast until death is unlawful? Notice that his first reference is to Fr. Vermeersch, and that he does not place that well-known author among the inconclusive writers **"for and against."** Here is what Fr. Vermeersch says in the place cited by Fr. Daman:

> "The same reasoning applies also to **suicide through fasting.** For this is not undergone except **through a positive volition whereby every instinct to seek necessary nourishment is violently suppressed.** But the fundamental law enjoining us to strive for our own perfection obliges us to the actions necessary for attaining that perfection."*

In his first sentence Fr. Vermeersch merely says that intended self-killing by fasting is unlawful, **for the same reasons that every other form of suicide is unlawful. But that principle has no application to any hunger-striker,** since no hunger-striker intends his own death.

The second sentence of Fr. Vermeersch does not pertain to morality at all. It only states a psychological truth – that fast until death involves a violent suppression, by

---

*"Ratiocinium istud valet quoque de **suicidio per inediam.** Haec enim non toleratur sine positiva voluntate qua omnis instinctus quaerendi alimenta necessaria violenter reprimitur. Et fundamentalis lex qua jubemur propter bonum nostrum agere, actionem quae ad bonum istud necessarium est simul nobis imponit."
"Theologia Moralis," (Tomus II, n. 320).

On Morality of Hunger-Strike 107

positive volition, of every instinct to seek necessary nourishment.

In his third and last sentence, Fr. Vermeersch says that a fundamental law obliges us to tend to our own perfection, and thus obliges us to acts necessary for attaining it. This is of course true. But that fundamental law does not say that man's striving for his own perfection must **always** be by acts of **accepting** necessary food, and **never** by acts of abstaining from it until death. As a matter of fact, the requirements of that fundamental law of tending to our own perfection are sometimes better fulfilled by acts of refusing food until death than by acts of accepting it. He who dies of hunger because he gave his last meal to save the life of another; he who refuses until death food previously offered to idols; the Carthusian who refuses meat until death, when meat alone can sustain him – all these are acting in more perfect conformity with Fr. Vermeersch's fundamental law of striving for their own perfection, than they would have done by accepting necessary food. By acts of positive volition truly heroic, they violently repress every instinct to seek the necessary sustenance. And the violence, far from making their refusals of food unlawful, makes them heroic. Without the violence there can be no heroism, and the heroism is higher as the violence is greater. "The kingdom of heaven suffereth violence, and the violent bear it away." And the same must be said of some hunger-strikers. What confirmation, then, does Fr. Daman's thesis receive from the authority of Fr. Vermeersch? Fr. Vermeersch neither condemns nor attempts to condemn any hunger-strike until death, and therefore has no need to contradict himself, as Fr. Tanquerey, Fr. Wouters, Fr. Daman and Fr. Merkelbach have done – were compelled to do in the circumstances.

TANQUEREY, WOUTERS, MERKELBACH, DAMAN, ALIKE

The treatment of this tangled question by Fr. Tanquerey, Fr. Wouters, Fr. Daman and Fr. Merkelbach has many things in common. First, Each of them dismisses a complicated subject with a single paragraph of less than ten lines. Second. Each of them set out to treat the question of hunger-strike. Third. None of them defines or attempts to define hunger-strike. Fourth. None of them seems aware that hunger-strike is essentially a protest against injustice. Thus the primary good effect of hunger-strike – all important in determining its morality – is entirely overlooked by them all. Fifth. No one of them says anything that applies specifically to hunger-strike. Sixth. Each dealt instead with the question of voluntary fast until death – the generic constituent of hunger-strike. Seventh. Each mistakenly believed that he had treated the question of hunger-strike. Eighth. In discussing voluntary fast until death, each is guilty of at least one false statement of principle, and one self-contradiction.

FR. TANQUEREY'S CONTRADICTIONS

In addition to the intrinsic contradictions involved in each of Fr. Tanquerey's paradoxical cases, there is a further contradiction in his doctrine regarding indirect self-killing. He begins by stating a general proposition that is universally true, and afterwards contradicts it by denying its truth in a particular instance. In Vol. iii, n. 270, he says that it is always certainly lawful for individuals to indirectly sacrifice their lives for the public good. But he denies, a moment after, (n. 272 D) that it is certainly lawful for prisoners to sacrifice their lives for the public good by refusal of food.

WOUTERS, MERKELBACH, DAMAN, SAY WHAT IS FALSE

The contradictions of Fr. Wouters, Fr. Daman, and Fr. Merkelbach are singularly alike, as if evolved from the same formula. In attempting to prove all voluntary fast until death unlawful, each begins with a universal proposition that is false. Fr. Wouters says that "everyone who abstains from food or drink, intends, in practice, his own death." Fr. Daman says that "everyone is obliged to preserve his own life by ordinary means." Fr. Merkelbach says that "no cause can be assigned on account of which it may be lawful to kill oneself"– Fr. Daman's assertion put in negative form.

EACH THEN MAKES TRUE CONTRARY ASSERTION

Each of these propositions being false, true propositions to the contrary had afterwards to be set down by those authors as part of the correct doctrine. And so we find Fr. Wouters saying that "it is otherwise in the case of one who abstains from food or drink in order to save the life of another." Fr. Daman says that "it is not lawful to kill oneself indirectly except for a just and proportionate cause." Fr. Merkelbach says that "indirect self-killing is unlawful except for a just and proportionate reason."

NOT RETRACTATIONS BUT SELF-CONTRADICTIONS

And, mark you, these concessions by way of exception are not made as retractations of the falsehoods to which they are contrary. They are made by way of self-contradiction.

In the face of their authors' assertions to the contrary, the falsehoods are allowed to stand. Fr. Wouters, Fr. Daman and Fr. Merkelbach assent to the true propositions and the false ones, at the same time, and, so doing, contradict themselves. What can be truly predicated only of particular cases, only of some, or of the vast majority of cases, these theologians unwarrantedly predicate of all cases, apparently in order to include within the scope of that universal predication the case of hunger-strike. Fr. Wouters says that everyone who fasts until death intends his own death, though this is true only of some, if any. Fr. Daman says that everyone is obliged to preserve his life by ordinary means, though this is never true in any extraordinary circumstances. Fr. Merkelbach says that no cause can be assigned that could make self-killing lawful, though a thousand causes can be assigned, any one of which could make indirect self-killing lawful.

EACH INDICTMENT DIFFERENT FROM ALL OTHERS

So much for what these masters in casuistry have in common, in their treatment of voluntary fast until death. That in which they differ from one another is also worthy of notice. It is very significant that, though each of them finds every hunger-striker guilty, the charge preferred by each is different from that of every other. Fr. Daman testified that it is the action itself of fasting until death that is unlawful. Fr. Wouters insists that it is rather the hunger-striker's intention of his own death that is unlawful. Fr. Tanquerey says that the unlawfulness, if any, lies in the circumstance of disproportionate good effect. Fr. Merkelbach merely says "direct killing," and for no better reason than because St. Thomas says: "not to take food is the same as to kill oneself."

THUS IT IS EVIDENT THAT THEY ARE ALL WRONG

During the discussions of hunger-strike, some years ago, Fr. Nicholas Lawless, of Dundalk, Ireland, summed up the case in favor of the hunger-striker, though intending to sum it up against him. "Of those who defended hunger-strike," wrote Fr. Lawless, "no two writers in all the correspondence gave the same motives for his action. It was plain that they could not all be right. Now I know they were all wrong" ("The Tablet," London, Nov. 6, 1920).

(1) There may be many partial motives for an action-principal, secondary, etc.– but the multiplicity is not a reason why "they could not all be right," why any one of them must be wrong. "Bonum ex integra causa; Malum ex quocumque defectu."

(2) Whoever impugns the lawfulness of an act has an easier task than the one who defends an action. To prove an action lawful, all the sources of its morality, all ends, all means, an all circumstances – must be vindicated. To prove an action unlawful, it is necessary only to discount one of them. The goodness of an action is derived from all the combined sources of morality. A single evil source makes the action evil.

Thus it is seen that the attack of Fr. Lawless on the defenders of hunger-strike is rather an attack on its opponents. In the words of Fr. Lawless himself, no two of the hunger-striker's opponents gave the same reason for the unlawfulness of his action. And it was plain they couldn't all be right. Hunger-strike is not unlawful from all the sources of morality! Yet the hunger-striker's opponents urged each of the sources in turn, as ground for the unlawfulness of his act.

TRUE THEN OF AMATEURS – OF PROFESSIONALS NOW!

This was true then, when the opponents of the hunger-strikers were, without exception, amateur moralists. It is equally true twenty years after, when all the opponents of any hunger-strike until death are professional moralists. No two or them assign the same reason why hunger-strike until death is unlawful. We have seen that each of these star witnesses against every voluntary fast until death, in addition to expressly contradicting himself, implicitly contradicts every other among them. As with the Elders of Israel, testifying falsely against Susanna, their testimony against hunger-strike until death does not agree. Similar testimony in any civil dispute, would be summarily rejected by any civil court on earth. Perhaps the testimony here discussed will one day be examined and rejected by an ecclesiastical court. But, meanwhile, notwithstanding that it has been farily shown to be false, it stands today, and will long continue to stand, an authoritative verdict against all hunger-strikers, past, present and future. In theological libraries, the world over, that false testimony stands and will stand in text-books dedicated to the cause of sound moral doctrine. It stands, too, in lectures delivered to clergy, present and prospective, as well as to forthcoming professors or moral theology, at the fountain head of theological truth – the heart of Christendom. And the "Professor of Morals in an Irish Ecclesiastical College" leads the march in the parade of dissimulation, regardless of the consequences to Moral Theology and to the consciences of all hunger-strikers present and future.

Chapter Twenty

SOME OBJECTORS AND THEIR OBJECTIONS

AN IRISH "PROFESSOR OF MORALS"
"The Tablet" (London) Dec. 4, 1920

CORRECT IN STATING, NOT IN TREATING CASE

In "The London Tablet," of December 4, 1920, a writer who signed himself "A Professor of Morals in an Irish Ecclesiastical College," stated the case at issue in hunger-strike unto death, with brevity, clearness, correctness and brilliancy that are truly admirable, and equalled by no one else. While others argued blindly about "first harmless and lawful refusals," and "last deadly and criminal refusals," the "Professor" told them very correctly that "first" and "last" refusals, and all between, are morally one inseparable refusal until death, because of the one unrevoked determination to continue until death.

But, unfortunately, the correctness for which we have thus far given the "Professor" full credit, is the last of his correctness. "Quantum mutatus ab illo," the impartial jury will exclaim, after hearing the "Professor's" answers under cross-examination. In the article here reproduced in full (Appendix A, pp. 312-314) he wrote:

(1) "To abstain from food to the point of death, clearly "militates against Reason and the Moral Law. It has "only one intrinsic, natural and necessary effect, "namely death. Whatever good accrues from hunger-"strike is entirely referable to the circumstances or "to the end in view. It is a powerful protest against "injustice. But it is not a protest of itself or of its "own nature, but only in the circumstances, and be-"cause it is extrinsically directed to this end . . . "Such an effect, however desirable, is quite extrinsic "and accidental. It may be present or absent, or may "vary, while the hunger-strike, in itself and in its "own nature, remains the same.

"If, for instance, a prisoner were spirited away "without the knowledge of his friends, and confined "unjustly in some English prison, without the knowl-"edge of the public, if he there went on hunger-"strike, the substance or nature of his act would be "precisely the same, and yet it would have no effect "on public opinion. This shows conclusively that the "effect on public opinion is quite an accidental effect, "not following from hunger-strike of its own nature, "and therefore not a determinant of its intrinsic "morality at all."

HIDES, MINIMIZES ESSENTIAL GOOD EFFECT

Notice how suddenly the "Professor" switches from protest against injustice to effect on public opinion, as if they were exactly the same. Even in the case of his prisoner "spirited away" and "secretly confined," his hunger-strike would be what it is essentially – a protest against injustice. The spiriting away and the unjust confining, without knowledge of his friends or the public, cannot stifle the hunger-striker's cry of protest, nor prevent it from resounding in the ears of the ones that perpetrated the injustice. Very logically does the "Professor" conclude from his case that the effect on public opinion is "quite an accidental effect, and therefore not a determinant of the act's intrinsic morality at all." But what follows from this? Certainly not that the effect of protest against injustice is also "quite accidental, and therefore not a determinant of the act's intrinsic morality at all." Yet this is the "Professor's" only proof that the good effect of hunger-strike is not an essential, but only a merely accidental effect. He repeats that indictment several times, as if reiteration were a substitute for proof. And when he is called to prove that hunger-strike is not essentially but only accidentally a protest against injustice, he proves instead that its effect on public opinion is not essential but accidental. It is not against the public but against him who perpetrates the injustice that any protest is directed. And so we are not told that the creditor, in ancient Ireland, conducted his hunger-strike against his debtor in the public market place. But we are told that he went and sat before his debtor's door, and, in addition to refusing food, refused to leave that place until due satisfaction was made to him.

"GOOD EFFECT ACCIDENTAL"– FLAT FALSEHOOD

The "Professor's" assertion that the good effect of hunger-strike is only accidental, and not essential, we have proved in Chapter Two to be unqualifiedly false. When Father Gannon said what is unqualifiedly true – that "no hunger-striker aims at death . . . not even as a means," the "Professor" called that statement "only a half truth." But not even as much can be said in favor of his own assertion that "whatever good accrues from hunger-striking is entirely referable to the circumstances or end in view." The essential good effect of hunger-strike, as well as its essential ill effect, is produced independently of the hunger-striker's intention, or the circumstances in which he refuses food. He could not, even if he so wished, prevent his hunger-strike from being a protest against injustice. The two are inseparable. True, the protest does not follow from the hunger-strike with the **physical** necessity of a law of physical nature, as the death of the hunger-striker does. But it does follow with the **moral necessity of a law of man's moral nature.** Who, in the world's history, has ever understood hunger-strike to mean anything except protest against injustice? It is thus that it has **always been understood and recognized**, even by the very authority against which is was directed. In every instance the authority challenged either relented or vigorously resisted the protest. Sometimes the resistance took the form of forcible feeding, sometimes that of bland persuasion, while not unfrequently the hunger-strike became, for both sides, a test of endurance. Why then is hunger-strike ever and everywhere understood to be a protest, if as the "Professor" claims, it is such **only** "extrinsically and accidentally," and why does he assert so confidently that it has only one intrinsic, natural and necessary effect – namely death?" He would even make his readers believe that his objection is that of **St. Thomas.** He says: "To this and this alone – to borrow the language of St. Thomas – it has a proportion, and by this its intrinsic character is determined." No, "Professor," if this be the language of St. Thomas, **you apply it wrongly. Rather is the intrinsic character of hunger-strike determined by its intrinsic, essential, proportionately good and equally immediate effect** – protest against injustice. Whenever, in addition, that protest **receives publicity,** the hunger-strike has then the secondary and accidental good effect of bringing the injustice to the attention of others, and thus securing their sympathy and protest.

EXTRINSIC DIRECTING. WHY, HOW A PROTEST?

When the "Professor," and others who imitated him, objected that hunger-strike "is not a protest **of its own nature,** but only in the circumstances, and because **extrinsically directed to this end**," why did they not feel **obligated to prove or attempt to prove their assertion, by canvassing the list of circumstances,** pointing out the **circumstances** which, in their opinion, constitute hunger-strike a protest, and showing how it is "**extrinsically directed to that end**"? What is the "direction" of which the "Professor" speaks? Every rational directing consists in **choosing and using suitable means to the end proposed.** That was exactly what Mayor MacSwiney did when he chose and used hunger-strike as a protest against the English Government's injustice to himself and his country. But why did he choose refusal of food rather than refusal to speak, or refusal to sleep, or refusal to breathe? If it be the directing, and not the refusal itself, that produces the protest, why does it not make a protest out of any other action except hunger-strike? According to the "Professor's" false hypothesis, any action could be made to mean anything whatever for the public at large, simply because the agent extrinsically directs it to that specific end. A wake might be made a wedding instead, or a wedding a wake, simply because the parties to the performance "extrinsically direct it" to that end! Similarly, Smith or Jones might celebrate the Declaration of Independence with his flag at half-mast, and might mourn the passing of great public benefactors with flag at top-mast, provided his act of so hoisting his flag was "extrinsically directed to that end." And he might even wrench language from its conventional meaning and make the word "black" mean "white," by the "Professor's" process of extrinsic directing. Absurd consequents from an absurd antecedent.

NO CIRCUMSTANCE MAKES FASTING A PROTEST

Let us now examine the several circumstances, to see if any of them could convert refusal of food into a protest against injustice. All the circumstances which modify the morality of any human act are included in the answers to the questions "who," "what," "why," "when," "where," "how," "what means." Now the MacSwiney hunger-strike was not made a protest (1) because it happened to be Terence MacSwiney rather than his sister, Mary MacSwiney, because it was the Lord Mayor of Cork and not the Lord Bishop of Cork; nor (2) because it lasted seventy-four days rather than forty-seven; nor (3) because it was "extrinsically directed to that end" by the merely mental intention of the Lord Mayor; nor (4) because it occurred in the fall of 1920, instead of the springtime of 1890. Again it was not made a protest (5) because it was staged in Brixton Prison rather than in Cork or Kilmainham; nor (6) because it was done with full deliberation and a right conscience, rather than with imperfect deliberation and an erroneous conscience; nor (7) because the Lord Mayor's refusal of food was signified by gestures rather than by words, or by simple refusals, not by oaths.

Thus the entire list of circumstances has been canvassed without finding among them any accidental characteristic which actually did or could convert Mayor MacSwiney's refusal for food into a protest against injustice. If, when proposing their false explanation that hunger-strike is made a protest, against injustice by "the circumstances or the end in view," the "Professor," and those who copied him, had believed that it was the true explanation, they would have felt called on to point out **the specific circumstance** which converted Mayor MacSwiney's hunger-strike into a protest against injustice or how his refusal of all food signified such protest simply because he intended that it should.

ABSURD CONCLUSIONS FROM HIS FALSE DICTUM

Notice now the **absurd conclusions** that must be inferred from the "Professor's" reasoning. It would make **countless acts of the most heroic virtue intrinsically evil. The act whereby a man dying of hunger gives his last crust to save the life of another** – this act of the most perfect charity, no more fulfills the "Professor's" requirement for an intrinsically good act than the act of hunger-striking does. So too, the heroes of the "forlorn hope," the crew who sink their ship, the garrison who dynamite the fortress, the seamen who leave the life-boats to others, the martyrs yielding their lives at the stake, on the scaffold, in the amphitheatre – all, all, all of these are, according to the "Professor's" dictum, acting contrary to the Moral Law. As truly as of the act of hunger-strike must the "Professor" say of every one of their countless acts of refusing to preserve their own lives, that "of its own nature it has only the one effect of death." Notwithstanding their glory with God and men – their glory in Heaven and on earth – they are, all of them according to the "Professor" **revolting suicides and nothing better.** If the "Professor" declares the one act unlawful and suicidal, he must do the same for all the others. His rule applies to each and all in exactly the same way, and for exactly the same reasons. And he says that to enter on hunger-strike **"is to sin against the law of self preservation, and to violate God's dominion over human life."**

The lawfulness of hunger-strike **from the object – the goodness of the act itself** – is, moreover, proved beyond challenge, by the positive precept commanding that life be preserved in **all ordinary circumstances,** but not in **all possible circumstances.** Were the act of hunger-striking intrinsically evil, as the "Professor" contends, **it would, like all other actions intrinsically evil, be forbidden by a negative precept** "thou shalt not, thou shalt never, for any reason, or in any circumstances, omit to preserve thy life." A new commandment this of the "Professor."

HIS IMPUTABILITY FROM INDIRECT INTENDING

Having disposed of the object of hunger-strike, he next undertakes to prove that the intention of the hunger-strikers is also evil, since they implicitly and indirectly intend their own deaths. "It is sufficient," he says "for the voluntariety and imputability of an evil effect, that it be willed implicity and indirectly." Here once more we have from the "Professor of Morals" another verdict against every hero of Patriotism, against every hero of Religion, against every hero of Charity. Their own deaths were intended implicitly and indirectly by the millions of martyrs, who, in love for Christ, and in testimony to Him, and in imitation of Him, refused to preserve their own lives, and even gloried in their own deaths. And, according to the "Professor of Morals," that is "sufficient for the voluntariety and imputability of their evil effect"–their own deaths. What undesirable conclusions from the "Professor's" principle, and because it is "only a half truth"!

FALSIFIED STATEMENT OF MORAL PRINCIPLE

He who enunciates such a principle without the qualification that belongs to it, deserves no recognition as a moralist. To prove hunger-strike evil from the intention, the "Professor" invokes a principle of Moral Theology that is most fundamental and most far-reaching in its application. Professing to enunciate that principle in its entirety, he states only a part of it, omitting altogether the qualifying clause which distinguishes the evil effects that are imputable, from the ill effects that are not.

WHEN INDIRECTLY INTENDED IS NOT IMPUTABLE

As to how the principle in question should be enunciated, moral theologians are in entire agreement. To the entire statement of the "Professor" that "it is sufficient for the voluntariety and imputability of an evil effect that it be willed impliciy and indirectly," every writer on Moral Theology, without a single exception, has added the very restricting clause –"provided there is an obligation to prevent the ill effect." "Si obligatio praecavendi adfuit" are the words of Father Lehmkukl, whom the "Professor" has taken for his guide. That qualifying phrase shows plainly that ill effects implicitly and indirectly intended, are not always imputable, as the Professor claims they are – shows that some such ill effects are imputable, and that others are not.

Moral Theologians not only assert this, but give rules, moreover, to determine which ill effects are imputable and which are not. They are unanimous in teaching that whenever the familiar conditions already mentioned are realized, an ill effect implicitly and indirectly intended is not imputable – the "Professor of Morals in an Irish Ecclesiastical College" to the contrary notwithstanding.

WAS THE "PROFESSOR" AWARE? IF NOT! IF SO!

Was the "Professor" aware that some ill effects implicitly and indirectly intended, are not imputable? If not, then the morals taught in that "Irish Ecclesiastical College" are not very "ecclesiastical." If he was aware of it, he is guilty of deliberately distorting a great principle of morals in order to prove the intention of the hunger-striker unlawful. Such conduct is popularly called "poisoning the wells." It substitutes a foul falsehood for the truth of God. It would brand a million innocent souls with the foul stigma of sin, in order that the infamous imputation of suicide may fall on the guiltless hearts of heroic hunger-strikers, martyr champions that they are, one and all, of the cardinal virtue of eternal justice.

The "Professor" next says: "The hunger-striker wills directly not only the end in view but also the means, namely the continued abstention from food even to its fatal conclusion." It is true that the hunger-striker wills directly both the protest, which is the end in view, and the refusal of all food, which is the means of protesting. But this does not say that he wills his own death directly. He wills it only because it is inseparable from the refusal of all food. In other words, he wills his death only indirectly. "Death, therefore," adds the "Professor," "the finis operis of the means, is imputed to him, even though he may not will it directly and explicitly; he wills it at least implicitly and indirectly, precisely because of the obligation he is under to avoid it."

IMPLICITLY WILLED, THEREFORE IMPUTABLE!

Combating the assertion of Fr. Patrick Gannon, S.J., that "no hunger-striker aims at death, not even as a means," the "Professor" says:

(2) "And here it is to be observed that the conclusion "we have come to is not invalidated in the least by "the fact that 'no hunger-striker aims at death, not "even as a means.' This is true, but it is really only "a half-truth. It is sufficient for the voluntariety and "imputability of an evil effect that it be willed im-"plicity and indirectly. The hunger-striker wills di-"rectly not only the end in view, but also the means, "namely, the continued abstention from food even

"to its fatal conclusion. Death, therefore, the **finis
"operis** of the means, is imputed to him, even though
"he may not will it directly and explicitly. He wills
"it at least implicity and indirectly, precisely because
"of the obligation he is under to avoid it.

"We conclude, therefore, that hunger-striking in
"the sense explained, is morally wrong **ex objecto** or
"as a means, and therefore may not be employed as
"a political weapon."

FALSE! FALSER! FALSEST!

This paragraph is filled with false assertions and false implications. It has just been remarked that, pretending to enunciate, in its entirely, a fundamental principle of Moral Theology, he dishonestly omits an essential portion of it. All moralists, without a single exception, enunciate that fundamental principle thus:

"It is sufficient for the voluntariety and imputability
"of an evil effect that it be willed implicitly and in-
"directly, **provided there is an obligation to prevent it.**"

Note well the proviso—"**provided there is an obligation.**" Sometimes there is no such obligation. The firemen, in putting out the fire, implicitly and indirectly will to drench and destroy much valuable merchandise. Have they an obligation to prevent it? The Christian martyrs willed their own deaths implicitly and indirectly, by explicitly and directly refusing to deny Christ. Did they have an obligation to prevent their own deaths? According to the "Professor" they had such obligation. He says: "It is sufficient for the voluntariety and imputability of an evil effect that it be willed implicitly and indirectly." Why does he leave out the proviso—"provided there is an obligation to prevent it?" He omits the proviso, on which everything depends, in order to return a verdict of guilt against every hunger-striker until death. But is he not returning the same verdict of guilt against the firemen, and even against the Christian martyrs? The "Professor" manufactures a premise which he knows to be false, in order to derive a conclusion which he knows to be false, yet presents to his readers as true.

ESSENTIAL GOOD EFFECT AGAIN SIDETRACKED

Immediately before, the "Professor" had asserted the mercenary falsehood that hunger-strike has only **one essential effect**, namely death—that the good effect of protest is **only accidental**. The purpose of that assertion is, of course,

On Morality of Hunger-Strike 119

to hide the essential good effect, and thus give hunger-strike the appearance of suicide pure and simple. Very complete refutation of that calumny is found in our second chapter. In the present citation, he accordingly makes no mention whatever of any good effect, thus making it appear that hunger-strike is not a case of "two effects" at all. Let us examine his pronouncement more in detail. He writes:

(a) "The hunger-striker wills directly not only the end "in view but also the means, namely, continued ab-"stention, etc."

Why does he not specify what the end in view is, as he states what 'the means" are? Why does he not say "the end in view, namely protest against injustice," just as he says "the means, namely continued abstention?" He hides the primary end in view – the essential good effect of protest against injustice.

(b) "Death, therefore, the finis operis of the means."

Why does he say "the" finis operis of the means; and not one "finis operis" of the means? Because he wants to make it seem that the death of the hunger-striker is the one and only essential effect of hunger-strike – the only "finis operis" of the means. The essential good effect of protest – the only "end in view" that is directly willed – the "Professor" is careful to say nothing about. Why does he not say "death, one finis operis of the means," instead of "death, 'the' finish operis of the means?" He treats hunger-strike as if it were not a case of "two effects" atall.

(c) "Even though he may not will it directly and ex-"plicitly."

Why "may not" and not "does not?" He wants to imply that the hunger-striker probably intends his own death directly. Casting around for a verdict of imputability, he repeats the same implication a moment later –"he wills it at least implicitly and indirectly" and again insists that this is "sufficient for its voluntariety and imputability."

INDICTMENT FROM INTENTION NOW DROPPED

The closing words of his article are: "We conclude, therefore, that hunger-striking, in the sense explained, is morally wrong ex objecto, or as a means, and therefore may not be employed as a political weapon." In the course of his article, the "Professor" challenged not only the act of refusing food – the object – but also the intention of the hunger-striker, who "wills his own death at least implicitly and indirectly." Why does the "Professor" now change the indictment, and no longer accuse the hunger-striker of intending his own death to the extent and in the manner that would make him responsible for it?

HE USES NO "IF," NO "PROVISO"

Note that the "Professor" has already found the hunger-striker guilty of his own death. His antecedent and conclusion contain his entire evidence and verdict. Notice, too, that he has arrived at his verdict without any use of the proviso – "provided there is an obligation to prevent it" – the evil effect. "If," "if," "if," "provided," "provided," "provided there is an obligation to prevent the evil effect," are the words of Fr. Lehmkuhl, to whom the "Professor" refers his readers. But the "Professor's" own enunciation of the principle of two effects (indirect voluntary) contains no "ifs," no "provisos."

HIS SPURIOUS SUBSTITUTE FOR "PROVISO"

And isn't the "Professor's" complete elimination of the "proviso" all the more ludicrous when we reflect that the entire question which he undertakes to answer in his article is involved in that "proviso"! Is not the question whether the hunger-striker until death is or is not obliged in conscience to prevent his own death – is not this the whole and sole issue involved in all the hunger-strike controversies!

But his sidetracking of the proviso ("provided," etc.), was so palpable an outrage against Moral Theology that he felt compelled to some form of restitution. He therefore invented and inserted **a spurious substitute**, but only after he had already anchored in the conclusion that the hunger-striker's death is imputed to him. "Death, therefore, is imputed to him." Here is his new version of the proviso. It will be better understood when placed in juxtaposition with the standard enunciation of that principle.

The "Professor's" Principle	Principle of all Moralists
"It is sufficient for the "voluntariety and impu-"tability of an evil effect "that it be willed impli-"citly and indirectly, pre-"cisely because of the ob-"ligation he is under to "avoid it."	"It is sufficient for the vol-"untariety and imputabil-"ity of an evil effect that "it be willed implicitly and "indirectly, **provided there** "is an obligation to prevent "it."

BECAUSE OBLIGED – PROVIDED HE IS OBLIGED

"Precisely because he is obliged" is surely something vastly different from "provided he is obliged." (a) It begs the entire question. It reiterates and rereiterates instead of proving. (b) It is a categorical condemnation of any and every act which produces a foreseen ill effect inseparable from a good effect. The firemen destroying the merchandise, the surgeon inflicting necessary pain, and even the martyrs dying for Christ are interdicted by the "Professor's" bogus moral principle –"it is sufficient," etc.

In the present context it is impossible not to recall the story of Professor Haeckel. Aiming to show that the human embryo and that of the monkey are entirely similar, he removed fifteen vertebrae from the diagram of the monkey, and added eleven to the diagram of the human. On that behavior of Dr. Haeckel, the Kepler-Bund – a society for the advancement of Science – made the following comment:

> "What should we say of a historian who altered the "letters of an inscription in order to push through a "preconceived personal opinion"!

WHAT SHOULD WE SAY OF THE "PROFESSOR"!

And what shall we say of the "Professor of Morals in an Irish Eccleciastical College," who deliberately alters the sacred words of a principle fundamental in Moral Theology, in order to deceive the Catholic millions, by making them believe that martyrs in this sacred cause of justice are, everyone of them, base and revolting suicides? The bulk of his indictment against hunger-strike unto death is contained in the two citations we have already examined – Nos. (1) and (2). TOGETHER THEY ARE MADE UP OF SIXTEEN ASSERTIONS, THIRTEEN OF WHICH ARE UNQUALIFIEDLY FALSE – HAVE NOT A SHRED OF TRUTH IN THEM, NO MATTER IN WHAT SENSE THE WORDS MAY BE TAKEN.

ALL FALSE FUNDAMENTAL PRINCIPLES

FURTHERMORE, NOT A SINGLE ONE OF THE "PROFESSOR'S" THIRTEEN FALSE ASSERTIONS IS A FALSE ASSERTION OF FACT – FREQUENTLY FRAUGHT WITH NO SERIOUS CONSEQUENCES. EVERYONE OF THE THIRTEEN IS THE ASSERTION OF A FALSE PRINCIPLE IN MORALS – A DELIBERATE PERVERSION OF TRUTHS THAT ARE THE FOUNDATIONS OF MORAL THEOLOGY. PULLING

STONES OUT OF THE FOUNDATIONS OF THE ETHICAL STRUCTURE IS THE HIGH-POWER MORALIZING OF THE "PROFESSOR OF MORALS IN AN IRISH ECCLESIASTICAL COLLEGE."

He was careful to conceal his **personal identity.** Though he cannot be credited with any devotion to the cause of theological truth, he must be given credit for ability to manufacture skillful sophistry. That many, very many, were led astray by him and others of his type, regarding the morality of hunger-strike, is very certain and **very regrettable. Their published sophisms on that subject must be counted, not in ones or twos, but in twenties and thirties and forties.** But the teaching Church never accepted their findings, and the overwhelming majority of the people **revolted and continue to revolt against them.** Untaught by the Clergy, whose duty it is to teach, **but who unfortunately are themselves untaught regarding the Ethics of hunger-strike,** many of the laity **become their own moralists,** and justify their own hunger-strikes until death, **even in instances that admit no justification.** The so called **"prudence" of silence,** linked with the base **equivocations** of partisan politicians, continues to fill **suicidal graves.** Only two months ago, **John McNeela** and **Anthony Darcy** – both young, brave and noble Irishmen – died deaths **loathesomely suicidal,** only because they were never taught, as they should have been, that refusal of food until death **is sometimes unlawful.**

MACSWINEY'S PHILOSOPHY

"The true antithesis is not between moral force and physical force, but between moral force and moral weakness."

"A man must be prepared to labor for an end that may be realized only in another generation."

"Every act of personal discipline is contributing to a subconscious reservoir whence our nobler energies are supplied forever."

Chapter Twenty One

SOME OBJECTORS AND THEIR OBJECTIONS

LA "CIVILTA CATTOLICA," ROME, ITALY
(Dec. 18, 1920)

AUTHOR'S TASK OF MAKING FALSE APPEAR TRUE

The Civilta article on Mayor MacSwiney's hunger-strike is lame, limping theology. The student who would present it as a qualifying test would be disqualified by any board of examiners in the world. The writer of that article – like all others who wrote against the Irish hunger-strike – had the embarrassing task of making a doctrinal falsehood appear true. How this could best be done, how each of the said writers could most effectively pretend to have proved his case conclusively – there was the rub.

Whoever impugns the lawfulness of any act has an easier task than the one who defends it. To prove an action lawful, all the sources of its morality – end, means and circumstances – must be vindicated. To prove it unlawful, it is only necessary to discount any one of them. "Bonum ex integra causa; malum ex quocumque defectu." Good if all the sources of its morality are good; evil if any one of them is evil.

CONFLICTING TESTIMONY DISCREDITS ALL

Why then were not all the opponents of Irish hunger-strike agreed about the source of its unlawfulness? Some of them insisted that every hunger-strike until death is unlawful from the action itself. Others of them denied this. And there was a similar conflict among them regarding the hunger-striker's intention, and the circumstances of the Irish hunger-strike. "Their witnesses did not agree," and that fact creates a strong presumption against them all. How could such conflicting testimony do less than discredit all the witnesses! It was but a reenacting of the case of Susanna and the elders of Israel. And so when Fr. Nicholas Lawless hurled at the defenders of Mayor MacSwiney the challenge that no two of them gave the same reason for the lawfulness of his act, he unconsciously wielded a two-edged sword. No two of those who condemned the Irish hunger-strike gave the same reason for condemning it.

ALL OBJECTIONS THEOLOGICALLY EMPTY

And indeed the theological emptiness of all the articles against the Irish hunger-strike showed very plainly that their authors entered the controversy, **not because they had something to write, but because they had to write something – had to condemn Mayor MacSwiney whether he deserved condemnation or not.** That, in deriving their verdict, they had accorded but scant recognition to the principles of Theology and Logic, **was not their concern.** Cardinal Newman, speaking of the extent to which an Established Church can afford to be orthodox, aptly remarks that **it must first be national, and, after that, be as othodox as it can.** Similarly the writers in question had first to condemn Mayor MacSwiney's hunger-strike, and after that be as orthodox as they could.

LURKING FALLACIES THEIR PRINCIPAL MEANS

And the means they use are in keeping with the end. They begin with protestations of **impartiality in motive, and of order and accuracy in exposition** – all of which they accuse their adversaries of lacking. When they come, a moment later, to state the fundamental principles of Theology involved in the MacSwiney case, they fail to state those principles **adequately and accurately.** The inferences which they draw, while **affecting logical rigor, abound in lurking fallacies.** And, as a consequence, **their ultimate findings are not logical conclusions from any true premises.**

If this seems a damning indictment, the reader is aware that it has been well substantiated in the pages that have gone before. And it shall receive further confirmation from the pages that follow. The writer in the Civilta begins thus:

(1) "The case of MacSwiney, Mayor of Cork, who, to "vindicate the independence of Ireland against Eng-"land, had recourse to hunger-strike or voluntary "fast, etc."

TWO FALSEHOODS

(a) This opening sentence of the Civilta article **contains two falsehoods.** It is false and foolish to say that the aim of Mayor MacSwiney's hunger-strike was **to vindicate the independence of Ireland against England.** No one aims to quarry a granite rock with a razor. The aim of the Lord Mayor's hunger-strike was to **protest against the injustice of his own personal arrest and imprisonment, and of his country's oppression, by an alien government.** Let the reader remember this when we find the Civilta writer afterwards condemning the MacSwiney hunger-strike because it was incapable of producing the good effect **desired.** Notice he does not say "the good effect **intended.**"

(b) It is **false** to say that hunger-strike and voluntary fast are the same thing. Voluntary fast even until death, as a scientific experiment, is not hunger-strike. **It is only in protest against injustice that voluntary fast is hunger-strike.**

(2) "We think it useful to briefly examine this question "in its theological aspect, because some newspapers "and reviews have, in our opinion, **treated it very "superficially, and without that impartiality and "composure of judgment** which is indispensable in "all theological discussions."

TRANSPARENT PROFESSIONS OF IMPARTIALITY

This complaint is well founded. When the writer of the Civilta article took up his pen, in December 1920, **much that was both superficial and partisan** had been spoken and written about the theology of hunger-strike in general, and in particular about the MacSwiney hunger-strike. Our present chapters of "comments" present to the reader many rare specimens of **dullest superficiality and most obdurate partisanship**. It may, however, be said, **to the credit of some of the writers, that they were superficial without being partisan**, while, **to the discredit of others, it must be said that their partisanship was criminal precisely because it was not superficial**. They sent forth from their pens false ethical principles, in order to prove Mayor MacSwiney's hunger-strike suicidal, with no plea of ignorance, invincible or vincible, to palliate their deed. They used professions of impartiality in order to be partial, and, while actually using them, accused even their impartial adversaries of being partial.

Where does the author himself of the Civilta article stand with regard to the superficiality and partiality which he condemns in other writers on the MacSwiney hunger-strike? The measure of his own impartiality will appear at intervals in the course of this review. His own superficiality is in evidence on his opening page, and even in his opening sentence. He there writes:

(3) "We shall do no more than state, **in clear and precise "terms, the Catholic doctrine of direct and indirect "suicide . . ."**

"DO NO MORE THAN STATE," IS TO DO NOTHING!

(a) Does the writer intend to solve the MacSwiney case? To merely "state" the Catholic doctrine on suicide and "do no more" – this is to leave the MacSwiney case just where he found it – to leave unsolved the case he apparently set out to solve. Cases are solved not by stating but by applying the principles which they involve. It is not merely the stating of the Catholic doctrine on suicide that was needed when the Civilta writer took up his pen, but **the application of that doctrine to the unprecedented case of Mayor MacSwiney.** Nobody needs to be told what suicide is. Everyone knows what it is. Nor does anyone need to have its unlawfulness demonstrated to them. Everyone admits that it is unlawful. But for many, very many, the vexed question was (and is today) whether Mayor MacSwiney's fast until death was suicide or not. Therefore to "state" the Catholic doctrine on suicide, as the author proposes, **and to "do no more,"** as he also proposes, **is to do nothing to solve the MacSwiney case,** to do nothing to answer the burning question whether MacSwiney was a suicide or not. **Yet that is precisely what the author does.** As we shall afterwards see, he was true to his proposal to "do no more than state the Catholic doctrine on suicide." He proves at great length that suicide is unlawful, and then dismisses his "Catholic doctrine on suicide," without even raising the question whether that doctrine applies or does not apply to Mayor MacSwiney's hunger-strike.

AUTHOR NOT CLEAR, NOT CONCISE, NOT CORRECT

(b) As to the author's clearness and precision, it will be here shown that the Catholic doctrine on suicide **is stated more clearly,** more precisely, and indeed more **correctly,** in any one of the countless text-books on Ethics or Moral Theology than the Civilta writer states it. He begins with an explanation of the terms "direct" and "indirect." These terms have **at least ten different meanings** in Catholic Philosophy and Theology, and, for that reason, **lend themselves readily to equivocation and fallacy.** More than once have they been made to serve that sinister purpose, by some who pronounced **all hunger-strike until death unlawful and suicidal,** in order the more surely to return a verdict against Mayor MacSwiney. The very sentence in the writer's article which contains his promise of "clear and precise terms" contains both a tautology and a contradiction in terms. Suicide is direct self-killing on private authority, and therefore the **"direct suicide"** of the author means direct, direct self-killing – a palpable tautology. Again, according to the definition of suicide just given – and it is the standard definition – the Civilta writer's **"indirect suicide"** is indirect, direct self-killing – a palpable contradiction in the very terms whose **clearness** and **conciseness** he guarantees, and even in the very sentence in which he guarantees them.

TAUTOLOGY AND CONTRADICTION

It is no defense for the Civilta writer to say that he uses the word "suicide" in the generic sense of any self-killing, prescinding from whether it is intended or unintended. It is not the mere etymology of the word "suicide" that gives its specific meaning. As in the case of many other words, the specific meaning of the term "suicide" is fixed by **conventional usage**. And, according to conventional usage, no one is called a "suicide" simply because he swallows poison by mistake, or accidentally sends a bullet through his own body, or drowns while striving to save another from drowning. "Deliberate, premeditated, direct (i. e. intended) **self-killing on private authority**"— that is the fixed, irreducible minimum signified by the term "suicide," for the moralist, the coroner's jury, and the man in the street. In criminal legislation, the distinction between **murder** and **manslaughter** is made very clear. "Indirect murder" is never heard of in criminal jurisprudence, for the same reason that "indirect suicide" is never heard of. Indirect murder is not murder at all, for the same reason that **indirect suicide is not suicide at all**, that indirect perjury is not perjury at all, that indirect blasphemy is not blasphemy at all. And the same must be said of "direct murder" and "direct suicide." There is no such terminology. **Every murder is direct** (i. e. intended) and **every suicide is direct**. "Suicide is indirect — and not usually called by that name — when a man does not desire his own death, either as an end or as a means, but when he nevertheless commits an act which in effect involves his own death." (Catholic Encyclopedia, page 326) "**And not usually called by that name**" says the Encyclopedia.

SO, TOO, THE TECHNICAL USAGE OF THE SCHOOLS

Nor is it solely in the language of the populace and the language of civil law that the term **"suicide"** is reserved exclusively to **direct** or **intended** self-killing. The same usage obtains in the technical language of the Schools, as we shall see by the following instances.

Rickaby, S.J.—"Moral Philosophy," (p. 213)
"By suicide we shall here understand the **direct**
"compassing of one's own death."

Brosnahan, S.J.—"Adversaria in Ethicam," (p. 171)
"Suicide is defined as **direct killing of oneself on**
"one's own authority."

Cathrein, S.J.—"Philosophia Moralis," (n. 282)
"Suicide is **direct killing** of oneself on private
"authority."

Russo, S.J.—"De Philosophia Morali," (p. 127)
"Whoever does something from which his own death
"follows, and in order that it may follow, **directly kills**
"himself — is a suicide."

None of the authors just cited – and they are all standard authors – knows anything about **indirect** suicide or about **direct** suicide either. It is therefore difficult to believe that the Civilita writer wants "clear and precise terms." Here, at the very beginning of his article, and again in several other parts of it, **he tampers with the clearest and most precise terms that language ever knew.**

"INDIRECT SUICIDE" NOT SINFUL. OFTEN HEROIC

But if, contrary to usage that is practically universal, he will insist on giving the opprobrious name of "suicide" even to the self-killing that is **nowise intended, let the reader understand and bear well in mind,** first, that such self-killing is **never suicide proper,** so abhorrent to God and man; and secondly, that it is **almost invariably lawful and even most laudable,** since it is **not taking one's own life but giving it** – laying it down – for God or country or friend. According to the terminology of the Civilita writer, St. Peter and St. Paul were suicides. So was St. Sebastian, St. Lawrence, St. Catherine of Alexandria. So was every one of the millions of heroes and heroines who, at every period of the world's history, sacrificed their lives for any worthy cause. To be called "a suicide" with them would redound to Mayor MacSwiney's immortal glory. True, the Civilita writer does not call the Lord Mayor either a **direct** or an **indirect** suicide. But he does conclude his article by calling MacSwiney's act of hunger-strike until death "unlawful," and every unlawful act producing one's own unintended death is suicidal, though not suicide. That is precisely what every **unlawful** act of hunger-strike until death is.

(4) "An **action** (un 'azione), as all know, may be directly "or indirectly voluntary, that is, voluntary "**in itself,**" "or only "**in its cause.**"

ACTS NOT WILLED DIRECTLY OR INDIRECTLY

(a) It is false to say that an action, **as an action,** is ever voluntary "in itself" or "in its cause." This is **more of the Civilita writer's terms, and they are neither clear nor precise nor correct.** Let us hope that all do not know that "an action may be directly or indirectly voluntary, that is, voluntary in itself or voluntary in its cause." It is **sheer distortion** to call an **action,** as such, "directly or indirectly voluntary, voluntary "**in itself,**" or voluntary "**in its cause.**" Actions, as such, are either **simply voluntary or simply involuntary.** The expressions "in itself" and "in its cause" have no meaning when applied to **actions** as actions. It is only **the effects of actions** that can rightly be denominated "directly" or "indirectly" voluntary – voluntary "in themselves" or voluntary only "in their causes." **The action, as such, is the cause.** If an action were ever called "voluntary in itself" or "voluntary in its cause," it is only as an effect, not as an action, that it would be so designated. External actions are effects of internal acts of willing. An external act of murder is an effect of the internal act of willing that murder. And so, aside from cases in which they are regarded as effects of internal actions, external actions are either simply voluntary or simply involuntary, but never "voluntary "in themselves" or voluntary "in their causes."

Principle I regarding indirect voluntary is expressed by all moralists in the same identical words – "an ill effect is imputable to the agent, that is, to him who places its cause, only when three requisite conditions are present.* And Principle II on the same subject says: "It is lawful to place a cause, good or indifferent, from which immediately follow two effects – one good, the other ill, etc."** Note well that both Prin. I and Prin. II deal with effects indirectly voluntary. Neither principle knows anything about actions indirectly voluntary.

EFFECTS WILLED DIRECTLY OR INDIRECTLY

No. It is not on actions themselves but on their effects that the distinction between direct and indirect voluntary, between voluntary "in itself" and voluntary "in its cause," falls. Effects, and effects alone, can be said to be "voluntary in themselves" or "voluntary in their causes." True, it is only acts of the will that are strictly and properly voluntary. But their effects are denominated voluntary from the voluntary actions that produce them, just as food, for instance, is called "healthy" merely because it produces health, and color is called "healthy" only because it is a sign of health.

Note that whenever an agent wills an action, he thereby wills every foreseen effect of that action. Whoever wills a cause, thereby wills (directly or indirectly) its every foreseen effect. Now the same action often produces two inseparable effects, one good, the other ill. The good effect cannot be produced without the accompanying ill effect. The act of pouring a flood of water on a burning building, extinguishes the fire, but destroys plastered ceilings, merchandise, etc. The effect of extinguishing the blaze is directly willed by the firemen. Only indirectly do they will the destruction of ceilings and merchandise. That destruction is inseparable

---

*"**Effectus** malus tunc tantum ad culpam agentis seu ponentis "causam imputatur, cum tres sequentes conditiones verificantur."

"Licet ponere **causam bonam aut indifferentem, ex qua immediate sequitur duplex **effectus**, unus bonus alter vero malus, "etc."

from the extinguishing of the fire. Both effects are foreseen by the firemen, and hence **both are willed, though not in the same way. The destruction of the merchandise is merely permitted – tolerated.**

EFFECT WILLED FOR ITSELF OR FOR ANOTHER

And, in general, an effect is **directly voluntary** when it is willed **for itself**. The extinguishing of the fire is willed **for itself. An** effect is **only indirectly voluntary** when it is **not willed for itself, but only for the sake of some other effect** which cannot be produced without it. The destruction of the ceilings, merchandise and the like, is willed **only indirectly** – only because the fire cannot be extinguished without it. Similarly, the captain who sinks his ship lest the enemy capture it, **directly wills** the destruction of the ship. The death of himself and his crew **he wills only indirectly.** Each of these cases furnishes an example of both direct and indirect voluntary. But it is the **effects of the actions** involved, **not the actions themselves,** that are either directly or indirectly voluntary. "Direct" and "indirect" regard the **object** which is attained by the action, **and the manner of its attaining, not the action** whereby it is attained. This the writer in the Civilta either does not understand, or **affects not to understand.** But his lack of understanding, real or affected, does not stay him from denouncing as "superficial" some other writers on the question he is discussing, and boasting **his own exposition of it as a model of clearness and precision.** There is not a Catholic author in existence who speaks of **actions themselves** as directly or indirectly voluntary – a very pertinent fact, well known to the Civilta writer. He says he knows that **"an action"** may be directly or indirectly voluntary, and he nonchalantly says that **everyone knows it.**

(b) Nor must it be supposed that what is voluntary only in its cause **is not really voluntary, really willed.** An otherwise good action is sometimes forbidden precisely because it produces such effect. And no effect is imputed for good or ill unless it is **in some sense voluntary.** Effects indirectly voluntary **are as truly willed by the agent as those that are** directly voluntary. They are willed, not in themselves or for themselves, but only in their causes, and for the directly voluntary effects inseparable from them.

(5) "Killing is indirect when death is neither intended "nor willed, but only permitted, inasmuch **as it oc-** "curs **praeter intentionem,** as a consequence of a "human action which is not directed to cause death, "but only to obtain some good end."

ACTS NOT INTENDED NOR WILLED NOT HUMAN

(a) Here again the writer's psychology is both **new and bad.** For the third time within the same first paragraph of his article, he gives a wrong explanation of the theological terms involved in the question he is discussing. In the previous citation he wrongly explained what is meant by direct and indirect voluntary. In the present citation he does the same with regard to direct and indirect **killing.** It is **false** that "killing is indirect where death is neither intended nor willed." The death that is neither intended **nor willed is in no way voluntary,** and hence such killing is **neither direct nor indirect,** both of which are **voluntary.**

(b) "Neither intended nor willed, but only permitted," says the Civilita. Here again the writer **either does not know or affects not to know** the meaning of the term "permitted." He says, equivalently and falsely, that permitted effects of an agent's actions are not willed by him. But is not every permitted effect of his actions **foreseen by the agent?** No one can be said to "permit" an effect which he **does not foresee.** And since every permitted effect of his actions is a foreseen effect, **it is also willed by him, in willing the action that produces it.** Whoever wills a cause, wills, at the same time, **every effect that he knows to be inseparable from it.** "Causa causae est causa causati." Hence the killing which the agent foresees to result **unintentionally from his action, he wills no less than the killing** which he both foresees and intends. The latter effect he wills **directly,** the former **only indirectly,** that is to say, he **permits** it, **tolerates** it. In this connection, "permitted" or "tolerated" means "willed indirectly."

(6) "In order to have direct killing, in the strict sense of "the word, it is necessary that, of its nature, immedi-"ately and exclusively, or at least by the intention "of the agent, the action aim at the destruction of "life."

THREE FLARING FALSEHOODS

(a) It is **false** that for **direct killing,** the action must, **of its nature,** aim at the destruction of life. It is **false** that the action must aim "immediately" at the destruction of life. It is **false** that the action must aim "exclusively" at the destruction of life. Smith, wishing to take revenge on Jones, steals into his house when himself and his family are sound asleep, turns on the gas, and suffocates the entire family. Here is **a manifest act of direct killing.** Yet Smith's action is the opening of a valve and nothing more. But the opening of a valve does not, **of its nature,** aim at the destruction of life. If it did, then **every act of opening every valve**,— gas valve, steam valve, water valve, air valve — would aim at the destruction of life — an inference contradicted by daily experience. For direct killing it is not necessary that the action be, **of its nature, deadly. If death be intended**, it is sufficient **that it be brought about "per accidens"**— by an action that is, de facto, deadly, not by its **nature, as prolonged fasting, but by the attendant circumstances**. In the example given, the opening of the **valve** causes death, only from **the circumstance** that the Jones family are **asleep** within the **confined area** in which the gas is released.

(b) Again, Smith's act of opening the gas valve **has not for "immediate" effect** the death of the family. Its immediate effect is **an open valve instead of a closed one**. One of its mediate effects is **the expansion and diffusion of the gas** until the entire house and the lungs of the sleepers are filled with it. The death of the family is **another of the effects — not an immediate effect, but a decidedly remote one.**

(c) And it is proved conclusively by the same example that, for direct killing, **it is not necessary** that the action aim **"exclusively"** at the destruction of life. **Several effects** of a single act of direct killing have just been cited.

DIRECT KILLING EXPLAINED AWAY

(d) When the writer undertook **to explain direct killing**, he was expected to state the **unvarying essentials** of it. Instead he begins by saying wrongly that the action must be deadly by its nature, and he immediately **contradicts** that assertion by adding that it is sufficient that the action aim at death **"by the intention of the agent."** He presents two contradictory statements of his essentials for direct killing, and invites the reader to choose between them. "It is necessary that, **of its nature . . . or at least by the intention of the agent, the action aim at the destruction of life."** Essentials are fixed beyond the possibility of any "at least" or "at most." Moreover, the writer's "at least by the intention of the agent" makes it difficult to understand what part the **intention** of the agent has in his explanation of direct killing. He speaks of it as an alternative. But an action may, of its nature, aim at the destruction of life, may actually kill, without being direct killing, **may actually kill the agent without being direct selfkilling**. It is the case of the captain who sinks his ship in war. Direct self-killing is **intended** self-killing.

(e) It is foolish to speak of an **action** as "aiming at the destruction of life **by the intention of the agent."** The intention of the agent is **not a constituent part of the action,**

but only **a prerequisite for its placing, and an essential of
its morality.** How then can it make the action **"aim at the
destruction of life?"** The unintentional turning on the gas,
works the same destruction of life to the sleepers that it
does when intended. Therefore the action does not aim at
the destruction of life **by the intention of the agent.** What
the intention does is to bring the agent to **choose** (and use)
**the kind of action that produces death either per se - of its
nature - or per accidens -** in the circumstances of gas, sleeping, confined area, etc.

(f) And why the introductory adjunct - "in the strict
sense of the word?" Is there such a thing as direct killing
in the broad sense of the word? If the killing be **intended,**
it is direct killing **in the strict** sense of the word. If not
intended, it is not direct killing **in any sense at all.** What
then does direct killing "in the strict sense of the word--
add to direct killing? "Vox et praeterea nihil!" "Words!
words! words!" says Hamlet.

> (7) "If, on the contrary, the action, even though neces-
> "sarily causing death, aims, **by its very nature –** and
> "not merely by the intention or declaration of the
> "agent, nor by accidental or purely extrinsic cir-
> "cumstances – to produce some other effect, **the
> "formal intention of death is excluded and we have
> "indirect killing."**

MORE OF THE EXPLAINING AWAY

**This is another piece of bad philosophy, an astonishing
pronouncement, as false as it is fitful.** The formal intention of death is not **excluded** simply because the action
which necessarily causes death, aims, by its very nature,
to produce some other effect. The formal intention of death
is not excluded from the captain's will, simply because his
act of sinking his ship, while necessarily causing the death
of himself and his crew, aims, by its very nature, to produce another effect – **to prevent its being taken by the
enemy.** Why and how and by what is the formal intention
of death excluded from the captain's mind and heart?
Only the intention of **living** can preclude or exclude from
the captain the formal intention of death, and such intention of living is not begotten in the captain by the fact
that his action aims, by is very nature, to produce some
other effect in addition to producing death. **May it not be
that the captain is weary of life, and so, in sinking his
ship, intends, at the same time, an act of patriotism for his
country and an act of self-destruction for himself? Or**
perhaps he has long cherished a deadly enmity towards

some subordinate officer and welcomes the present opportunity to kill him intentionally. "Impossible" exclaims the Civilta writer. "The formal intention of death is excluded, whenever the action though necessarily causing death, aims, by its very nature, to produce some other effect." And one error leads our writer into another. On his absurd supposition that, in the case proposed by him, "the formal intention of death is excluded" simply because the action by its very nature aims to produce some other effect – on that false supposition, he falsely calls that case **a case of indirect killing**. He furthermore falsely calls it "the contrary" of his previous case –(No. 6). "If, on the contrary," etc. The term "direct" occurs in the former case, and the term "indirect" in the latter. Let the reader find, if he can, a further reason for calling those two cases "contraries."

Further elucidating direct and indirect killing, the author says:

(8) "In the former case, life is destroyed; in the latter, it is not preserved. In the former, death is inflicted; in the latter it is only permitted."

TWO FURTHER FALSE EXPLANATIONS

The writer says that the difference between **direct and indirect** killing is the difference between the **positive act of destroying** life and the **negative act of not preserving** it. That assertion is false. It is also false to say that the difference between direct and indirect killing is the difference between inflicting death and merely permitting it. The difference between direct and indirect killing does not hinge on the distinction between destroying and not preserving, or on that between inflicting and only permitting. A little further on, the writer rightly says: "It is lawful for the soldier, in war-time, to explode a munition depot in order that it should not fall into the hands of the enemy, although he foresees that he shall die in the wreck of the explosion." Here the soldier does not merely **omit to preserve** his life. He positively destroys his own life by his own positive act of exploding the powder. It is not that he merely permits his own death. He inflicts it with his own hand. Of what use then is the writer's seemingly decisive distinction between destroying life and not preserving it, between inflicting death and only permitting it? The soldier, whose self-killing is only indirect, destroys his own life, inflicts his own death. The writer's distinctions serve only to mislead his readers.

DIRECT KILLING DEFINED WITHOUT INTENTION

No! It is the intention, and the intention alone, that constitutes the essential difference between direct and indirect killing. Direct killing is intended killing, and indirect killing is unintended killing. And, nevertheless, the writer of the Civilta article, explaining the difference between direct and indirect killing, omits all mention of the intention of him who kills. Citation No. 8 had been all that could be desired if the writer had said: "In the former case, (direct killing) life is intentionally destroyed; in the latter, its destruction is unintentional – only permitted." The writer's "soldier" destroys his own life, inflicts death on himself. But he does not intend his own death. Does our writer need to be reminded that the intention of the agent holds the chief place in all morality?

(9) "Note well that while the intention of the agent can "change into direct voluntary that which otherwise "had been only indirect, it cannot, on the contrary, "change into indirect that which is, by its own na- "ture, direct."

HE TAMPERS WITH STRICTLY TECHNICAL TERMS

(a) Tampering with standard terminology is a favorite refuge of those who have the task of befogging a clear issue and appearing to save a lost cause. What is meant by "voluntary by its own nature direct?" Has it any meaning? If voluntary is direct, can it ever be such except by its own nature? And if it is indirect, can it be so other than "by its own nature?" According to the Civilta writer there is a voluntary that is direct by its own nature, and a voluntary that is direct, but not by its own nature. Is not everything what it is by its own nature and not by anything besides?

What he wants to say, and says by implication, is that hunger-strike unto death is, by its nature, suicide, and therefore cannot be changed by any protestations of the hunger-striker that he does not intend his own death.

CHANGING INDIRECT VOLUNTARY TO DIRECT?

Again, what does the author mean by "changing" indirect voluntary into direct, or direct voluntary into indirect? Has it any meaning? The same object may, at one time, be willed indirectly, and, at another, be willed directly. But can this be called a "change" of an indirect volition into a direct volition? It is no more than a mere succession of the one volition upon the other. It is not a transmutation of indirect voluntary into direct. It is not a change.

(b) Nevertheless, the author asserts, without hesitation, without proof, and without meaning, that "the intention can change into direct voluntary that which otherwise had been only indirect." He does, however, undertake to show why "the intention cannot change into indirect, that which is, by its own nature, direct."

(10) "The reason is manifest. When an action is, by its "own nature, ordained to immediately and exclu-"sively produce an effect, he who places such action "wills also the effect, and wills it directly, even "though he protests by words that he does not will "it. Since there is not another immediate and direct "effect of the action, the will directly and immedi-"ately wills the action, and, by it and in it, wills also "the contained effect."

Since to "change into indirect that which is by its own nature direct," is meaningless, it is useless to inquire whether it can or cannot be done by means of the intention, or whether the author's "manifest reason" proves that it cannot. The following might, however, be remarked about that "manifest reason."

I. It makes no mention of the intention, though proposing to prove that the intention of the agent cannot change direct voluntary into indirect.

II. Summarized and syllogised, the writer's "manifest reason" runs as follows: Whoever places an action essentially, immediately and exclusively productive of one effect, wills that effect directly – expressed major proposition. But MacSwiney's act of hunger-strike was essentially, immediately and exclusively productive of his own death – implied minor proposition. Therefore, MacSwiney willed his own death directly. (Conclusion)

PROTEST AN IMMEDIATE GOOD EFFECT OF ACT

The conclusion of this "manifest reason" is false because the implied minor proposition is false. Every hunger-strike essentially produces protest against injustice. And what is this "manifest reason" of the Civilta writer but the objection of the "Professor of Morals," copied, word for word, from his article in The Tablet (London) of Dec. 4th, 1920 – fourteen days before the Civilta writer took up his pen. The "Professor" wrote: "It" – the act of hunger-strike – "has only one intrinsic, natural and necessary effect – namely death."

Thus it is evident that the sole purpose of the Civilta writer's "manifest reason" is to say indirectly that Mayor MacSwiney, by placing an action "essentially, immediately and exclusively productive of his own death," willed his own death directly, notwithstanding the protests of his defenders that no hunger-striker directly wills his own death.

And fearing lest the general principle he is considering might not of itself suggest to his readers the case of the Lord Mayor, the Civilta writer supplements it with two examples essentially different from the MacSwiney case, yet carrying the implication of being exact parallels for it. Here are the examples.

(11) "Let us explain this by an example. Titius is affected "with a grave and incurable disease. Giving himself "up to despair, he conceives the insane determination "of poisoning himself. Yet he formally protests that "he does not will death, but only the cessation of his "sufferings. Despite his declarations and protests, "his death is voluntary in itself, that is directly "voluntary. The same must be said of an unmar- "ried woman arrived at motherhood, who, to avoid "infamy, procures abortion, protesting that she does "not will the death of her innocent babe, but solely "the guarding of her own reputation."

EXAMPLES NO PARALLELS FOR HUNGER-STRIKE

These examples, while introduced to show that "the intention cannot change into indirect that which is, by its own nature, direct," are also designed to appear exact parallels for the case of Mayor MacSwiney. And since, in each of these two examples, death is proposed as a means to obtain the end desired, and since means are always intended, it is absurd for "Titius" and the "unmarried woman" to contend that they do not intend death, but, in the one case, the "cessation of suffering," and in the other, the "guarding of reputation." "Similarly," insinuates the Civilta writer, "it is absurd to contend that Mayor MacSwiney does not directly will his own death, when he places an act which is, by its nature, exclusively ordained to cause his death. Whoever places such an action wills also its effect, and wills it directly, even though he protests in words that he does not so will it." This theological bubble bursts immediately when the defenders of Mayor MacSwiney deny that his death is the exclusive effect which his hunger-strike, of its nature, produces. They insist that, of its nature, hunger-strike also produces a protest against injustice.

This point will be discussed more fully in a later citation (No. 14). It is not an original objection of the Civilta writer. A fortnight before his article appeared, it was urged in "The Tablet" (London) by the Irish "Professor of Morals", when he said, explicitly but falsely, that hunger-strike "has only one intrinsic, natural and necessary effect, namely death." "Only the one effect of death," reiterates the "Professor." "Ordained **exclusively** to produce an effect," says the Civilta writer. "There is nothing new under the sun!"

FALSE IMPLICATIONS BY FALSE PARALLELS

Notice too the artful simplicity with which the Civilta writer presents the case of "Titius" and that of the "unmarried woman." This method of false implication by false parallels was soon after developed to its highest perfection by the editorial writer of "The Examiner," (Bombay). He wrote: "It is mere sophistry to say: 'Although I am acting in such a way as to encompass my own death, I do not intend my own death, but only to promote the cause of my country!' One might as well argue: 'In taking prussic acid, I do not intend my own death but only to demonstrate scientifically the effects of poison.' I might just as well argue: 'In putting a bullet through my brain I do not intend to kill myself. I merely want to prove the efficacy of my revolver.' The sati woman of India might as well argue when she throws herself on the pyre: 'I do not intend to kill myself. I merely wish to add glory to my husband's funeral.' The bankrupt suicide might just as well argue: 'I do not mean to kill myself. I merely mean to shun disgrace.' A sufferer might argue: 'I do not mean to kill myself, but merely to relieve myself of intolerable pain and spare my relations the burden of nursing me'."

At the time that "The Examiner" was evolving all this miserable sophistry, and much more, its writer had before him, as model, the Civilta writer's case of "Titius," and his other case of the "unmarried woman"–published more than a month before The Examiner's article. Again, "nihil novi sub sole!"

It might also be remarked that the Civilta writer's "examples" are neither parallels for the MacSwiney case nor instances of the principle they are cited to illustrate. In both "examples," death – the evil effect – is used as a means to attain the good effect, and must, therefore, have been intended. But no hunger-striker intends his own death, either as an end or as a means. Therefore no parallel.

Again, each of the actions mentioned in the Civilta writer's "examples," produces two effects – one evil, the other good – whereas his "manifest reason,"– according to his own account of it in No. 10 – refers to "an action, by its own nature, ordained to **exclusively** produce **one** effect." Therefore no illustration of what the writer wished to illustrate.

WRONG TRANSLATION OF LATIN DEFINITION

The Civilta writer next proceeds to define "suicide," and, in so doing, he again slights the terms "intention" and "intended." Is it because they do not readily lend themselves to equivocations, as the terms "direct" and "indirect" do?

> (12) "Suicide properly so-called, (autochiria) is defined "by moralists: 'Directa et proprio voluntatis motu "suscepta, sui ipsius occisio,' that is, the direct kill-"ing of oneself by one's own will and authority."

The Latin definition of "suicide," quoted by the author, is the traditional definition of Catholic Philosophy and Theology. His own translation of that definition is **not accurate**. It is **tautological**. That suicide is self-killing "by one's own will," is already expressed by the word "direct." Here 'direct" means "intended," and intended includes and presupposes "willed." **No one uses means to attain an object without having previously willed it.** Why then "by one's own will?" "Intended self-killing on one's own authority" is an accurate definition of suicide, and an accurate translation of the Latin original.

We are now come to what the writer calls "**suicide improperly so-called.**"

> (13) "**Suicide improperly so-called,** that is, indirect self-"killing, is also unlawful. (e "illecita). It is per-"mitted only in some cases, that is, in the case in "which the conditions of indirect voluntary are "verified."

"SUICIDE IMPROPERLY CALLED," AN UGLY PHRASE

(a) As has been already remarked, the specific meaning of the term "suicide" is irrevocably fixed, **not by the mere etymology of the word, but by conventional usage.** This being so, suicide improperly so-called **is not suicide at all, just as evil improperly so-called is not evil at all.**

(b) "Suicide improperly so-called" is an **ugly phrase** in addition to being a **foolish phrase.** Suicide is an **abhorrent act** – abhorrent alike to Nature and to God. And the abhorrence passes even from the act to its name. Unhappily the cases to which the name fitly applies are numerous – all too numerous in recent times. This is but one of many reasons **for not branding with the foul stigma of suicide, actions that nowise deserve it.**

(c) But worse must be said of "suicide improperly so-called." It is, as already remarked, a **paradox, a contradiction.** Suicide improperly so-called is intended self-killing that is not intended. For both of these reasons – which are ultimately reducible to one and the same reason – the generality of moralists do not speak of "suicide **improperly so called.**" "Suicidium improprie dictum" is an expression not generally found in books on Moral Theology. "**Not usually called by that name,**" says the **Catholic Encyclopedia,** (See No. 3).

"UNLAWFUL BUT PERMITTED SOMETIMES"!

(d) It is surely an unheard of way of stating the morality of unintended self-killing to say that "it is **unlawful, but permitted only in some cases.**" The true doctrine would have been more nearly stated if the author had said that unintended self-killing is lawful, but forbidden in some cases. His "**unlawful but permitted only in some cases**" is very like saying that it is **always unlawful, but occasionally permitted,** for the same reason that divorce was permitted in the Old Law – "by reason of the hardness of your hearts."

And is merely "permitted" ("tolerated") the best thing that can be said in favor of any indirect self-killing? Remember it may be done either by a **positive act** of commission – as when the captain sinks his ship, or the commander dynamites the fortress, and perishes in the wreckage – or by a **merely negative act** of omission to save one's own life, as when men, in a shipwreck, surrender life-boats, life-buoys, and every other means of safety, to women, children, the aged and infirm, and die themselves of drowning. Are these and a million such-like actions merely "**permitted,**" merely tolerated? They are approved and lauded both by God and man. Many of them are acts of the noblest heroism; many others are acts of the sublimest charity – prompted by such love of God and man as impels **them to give their very lives for the objects of their love.**

ONLY "PERMITTED"! ONLY TOLERATED!

The number of Christian martyrs mounts up to many millions – every one of them a case of unintended self-killing, either by their own positive acts, like that of the sea captain and the commander of the fortress, **or by their own omission** (like the heroes of the shipwreck) **to preserve their lives when it was in their power to do so.** And all those **acts of the most exalted virtue that mortal man is capable of** – all these acts of unintended self-killing are, according to the Civilta writer, only "permitted." He does not pronounce them – any of them – laudable or even "lawful." He would lead the reader to think that they **can never be either the one or the other.** "Suicide improperly so-called, that is, **indirect self-killing, is also unlawful. It is permitted** only in some cases."

LEADS HIS READERS INTO MANY ERRORS

Thus far the author's "**clearness**" and "**precision**" have stood out in bold relief. His impartiality shall hereafter be equally conspicuous, to the very end of his article. He imposed on his readers the laborious yet unprofitable task of seeing him **define the theological terms involved in hunger-strike**, and, almost without exception, define them wrongly. We have just heard him say "the reason is manifest," and again, "let us explain this by an example," when both the "reason" and the "example" entirely ignored the point which he proposed to prove or explain. We have seen him **explain at great length, and wrongly, the meaning of direct and indirect voluntary, direct and indirect killing.** His crime is not merely the negative one of not having put his readers on the right road and kept them there as he professed to do. **He began by leading his readers astray. He has put them on the wrong road and kept them there.**

With theologians generally he now states the four conditions required in order that an ill effect be permitted.

(14) "It is lawful to place a cause, good or indifferent in "itself, from which follows immediately a double "effect — one good, the other ill — provided the ill "effect, although foreseen, be not intended, and there "is a just and proportionately grave reason for per-"mitting such ill effect.

"To eliminate every doubt, and throw further light "on the above-mentioned conditions, we call the at-"tention of our readers to the following **indisputable considerations which determine whether an affirma-"tive or negative answer** must be given to the pres-"ent question.

"1st. The good effect **must be certain**. It might be "doubtful only when the ill effect would also be "doubtful.

"2nd. **The cause (the action) must be capable of pro-"ducing the good effect.** St. Thomas, speaking specifi-"cally of unintended killing, says: 'An action placed "with a good intention **may become unlawful from "its incapacity to produce the good effect intended.**'

"3rd. **The cause must, by its own nature, produce "the good effect, and not merely by the intention or "protest of the agent, or by purely extrinsic cir-"cumstances.**

"4th. It is necessary that the good effect be not "obtainable without the ill effect."

DOES NOT ATTEMPT TO APPLY ABOVE CONDITIONS

(a) This is the only portion of his entire article to which the writer especially directs the attention of his readers. The issues here involved must, therefore, be **especially** momentous. What "doubt" is he anxious to "eliminate"? Which of "the above-mentioned conditions" does he undertake to "throw further light on?" Why is he anxious to "throw further light on the above-mentioned conditions," when he neither applies nor attempts to apply, nor intends to apply them at any succeeding stage of his article? To what purpose has he expounded, at great length, though wrongly, the doctrine of indirect voluntary, if he is now bent on solving the MacSwiney case independently of that "doctrine"—if, to use his own words, some other "indisputable considerations determine whether an affirmative or negative answer must be given to the present question?"

FALSEHOODS AND CONTRADICTIONS

(b) The foregoing "indisputable considerations" of the author have much noise but little truth in them. The first of these "indisputable considerations" contradicts itself. It first says, without qualification, that the good effect must be certain, and then says, immediately after, that it need not be certain—that "it might be doubtful when the ill effect would also be doubtful."

(c) The author, moreover, says what is false when he says unqualifiedly that "the good effect must be certain." He himself admits that it may sometimes be doubtful. He also says what is false when he says that "it might be doubtful only when the ill effect is doubtful." What about the case in which the certain ill effect is very small and the probable good effect very great? Would the Civilta writer insist that this case is unlawful because of disproportion? And what about the other case in which the good effect is doubtful and the ill effect is certain, but the influx of the action towards producing the ill effect is very remote? In this case, as in that immediately preceding, the action is lawful, notwithstanding that the ill effect is certain and the good effect only probable.

Thus is the first of the author's "indisputable considerations" disposed of. It consists of two assertions, each of them false, and each, in substance, if not in form, contradicting the other. What doubt does it remove? What light does it throw on the requisites that an action may be lawful even though it produces an ill effect?

SECOND OF HIS "INDISPUTABLES" SUPERFLUOUS

(d) The second of the writer's "indisputable considerations" is that "the cause (the action) must be capable of producing the good effect." This consideration is superfluous. In every case of "two effects," the good effect is either certain or probable. Otherwise it is not a case of two effects at all. But all certainty and all probability of the good effect is based on the anterior certainty or probability that its cause is able to produce it. Whence could it be derived otherwise? What "doubt" does this second of the author's "indisputable considerations" remove? What light does it "throw" on the conditions for lawful indirect voluntary?

WHY HOLD "THE GOOD EFFECT MUST BE CERTAIN"

The writer began this article with the false statement that the purpose or intention of MacSwiney's hunger-strike was "to vindicate the independence of Ireland against England." "Per difendere l'autonomia dell'Irlanda contro l'Inghilterra." MacSwiney's purpose was no such impossible thing. That was the purpose of the entire revolutionary movement, of which MacSwiney's hunger-strike in protest was only one small part. When he now insists that the good effect must be certain, he is getting ready to condemn MacSwiney's act of protest because it is incapable of producing an effect to which it was never directed — "to vindicate the independence of Ireland against England." And he quotes St. Thomas to the effect that "an action placed with a good intention may become unlawful from its incapacity to produce the good effect intended."

HIS THIRD "INDISPUTABLE" FALSE

(e) The third "indisputable consideration" of the writer is that "the cause must, by its own nature, produce the good effect." This, besides being false, is contradicted by the author's first "consideration." There he said that the good effect "might be doubtful, when the ill effect would also be doubtful." But to say that the good effect "might be doubtful" is to say that the action does not, by its own nature — that is to say, need not — produce the good effect. An effect which an action produces by its own nature, is never doubtful. It is always certain. Whenever that action is placed, that effect must follow. Thus "consideration" three, besides being false, contradicts "consideration" one, which itself consists of two pronouncements, one of them false and contradictory of the other. Does this third of the writer's "indisputable considerations" remove any doubt from the question of hunger-strike, or throw any light on it?

URGED BY "PROFESSOR" FORTNIGHT BEFORE

This third of the Civilta writer's "indisputable considerations" was urged against hunger-strike, in an article which appeared in "The Tablet," (London) of Dec. 4, 1920, over the signature of "A Professor of Morals in an Irish Ecclesiastical College." Here is the "Professor's" reasoning in his own words:

Major Prop. "For one freely to adopt a course which, "of its own nature, has only the one effect "of death, is to sin against the law of self-"preservation?"

Minor Prop. "But hunger strike has only one intrinsic, "natural and necessary effect, the finis "operis – death."

Conclusion. "Therefore to freely adopt hunger-strike is "to sin against the law of self-preserva-"tion."

As is evident from what has been already said in our second chapter, the minor premise of this syllogism is not even half true. The conclusion is unqualifiedly false because the minor premise is unqualifiedly false. But the "Professor" would prove that minor premise true by the three following false reiterations.

A CLEAR CASE OF "IDEM PER IDEM"

(1) "To this and this only – to use the language of St. "Thomas – it has a proportion."

(2) "Whatever good accrues from hunger-striking is "entirely referable to the circumstances or the end "in view."

(3) "It is not a protest of itself or of its nature, but only "in the circumstances, and because it is extrinsically "directed to that end."

In other words, the "Professor" proves that hunger-strike has only the one essential effect of death, by saying that (a) to this alone is the action proportionate; that (b) its good effect is entirely due to circumstances and intention; that (c) it is not a protest by its own nature. This is like proving that a man is young, first, because he is not old; secondly, because he is juvenile; thirdly, because he is not senile.

"IDEM PER IDEM" FOR MAJOR AND MINOR

This objection of the "Professor," the Civilta writer copies almost word for word. One of his guides as to "whether an affirmative or negative answer must be given to the present question" is the "indisputable consideration" we have been considering – "the cause must, by its own nature, produce the good effect, and not merely by the intention of the agent or by purely extrinsic circumstances." That is his major premise. As it stands it is false. His "proof" of his minor premise he defers until the closing paragraph of his article, and so we shall defer our examination of his argument. Suffice it now to say that when he comes to the impossible task of proving that minor proposition true, he will, like the "Professor," reiterate and rereiterate instead, though aware that reiteration is not a substitute for proof.

HOW MADE BY INTENTION OR CIRCUMSTANCES

Both the "Professor" and the Civilta writer speak of the good effect (protest) being produced, not by the act of hunger-strike itself but by the intention and the circumstances. But here, as elsewhere, they take no pains to prove their assertions. The reader must accept them on their authority. Why do thy not show that hunger-strike is constituted a protest by being "extrinsically directed to that end?" Why do they not select from the classified list of circumstances the ones which convert hunger-strike into a protest? Surely these questions are both pertinent and reasonable. But again the answer is the same. No one can prove that two and two make five, and hence no one is obligated to it. "Ad impossibilia nemo tenetur."

HIS FOURTH "INDISPUTABLE" ALSO SUPERFLUOUS

(f) The fourth and last of the writer's "indisputable considerations"—"that the good effect be not obtainable without the ill-effect."—is also superfluous. Without it there would be no indirect voluntary atall. But the impossibility of obtaining the good effect without the accompanying ill effect, need not be absolute. Moral impossibility is sufficient to justify the action. A dentist, treating a charity patient, is not morally obliged to administer a costly anesthetic, in order to save his patient the pain otherwise inseparable from cutting, drilling, extracting and the like. In general, it may be absolutely possible to obtain the good effect without the ill effect, yet practically impossible to do so. And it is the practical, not the absolute, possibility or impossibility that is a determining factor of the morality of the act. The Lord Mayor was not bound in conscience to go to the ends of the earth in search for means to produce the good effect of his hunger-strike without sacrificing his own life.

TWO FALSE "INDISPUTABLES" AND TWO TRUISMS

We have now considered each of the Civilta writer's "indisputable considerations." They are four in number. The first contains two assertions, one false and contradictory of the other. The second is a truism. The third, besides being false, contradicts the first. The fourth is only half true and entirely irrelevant. Is there much hope that these "considerations" will remove doubt, or throw light on the question of hunger-strike? Is there much ground for considering or calling them "indisputable," and taking them for guides in solving the case of hunger-strike until death? Yet the Civilta writer says that he will solve the MacSwiney hunger-strike by means of his "indisputable considerations, which determine whether an affirmative or a negative answer must be given to the present question."

The writer now pretends to state and refute the arguments of those who defended the MacSwiney hunger-strike.

(15) "The doctrine of direct and indirect killing being "stated, let us examine the question of hunger-strike. "And first let us see what value the arguments pro- "posed by the defenders of hunger-strike have. The "only argument which has any value as proof is the "accurate exposition and application of the Catholic "doctrine of indirect voluntary. The other arguments "of the said defenders either do not prove anything "or prove very little. They are: (1) The examples "of Jesus Christ and of Elias, who fasted forty days. "(2) The case of Sampson, who pulled down the "columns which supported the building, and perished "with the others under the ruins. (3) The case of "Eusebius, told by Baronius in his annals. (4) The "doctrine of Suarez,—"De Legibus," Book iii. Chap. "30, n.n. i-ii, and Book vi, Chap. 7, n. 9. (5) The "doctrine of Lessius,—"De Justitia et Jure." Book ii, "Chap. 9, Dubit. 6. n. 29. (6) The example of the "soldier who explodes the powder magazine; the case "of the shipwrecked person who gives to another the "plank of safety; the case of the Religious who, in "order to be faithful to his Rules, abstains from those "foods which are necessary for his health."

DOCTRINE STATED WRONGLY AT EVERY STEP

(a) The "doctrine of direct and indirect voluntary" is not stated in the Civilta article. The stating of any doctrine presupposes, before all else, correct defining and explaining of all the technical terms involved. Now the Civilta writer does not merely fail to define and explain the technical terms involved in "the doctrine of direct and indirect voluntary." He does worse. He defines and explains them wrongly, even when proposing to do so "in clear and precise terms." (See Nos. 2, 3, 4, 5, 6, 7, 8, 9, 10, 11.)

Thus instead of helping his readers to understand the doctrine of direct and indirect voluntary, he prevents them from understanding it, and even leads them to misunderstand it.

(b) When the writer says that "the only argument which has any value as proof is the accurate exposition and application of the Catholic doctrine of indirect voluntary," he enunciates a **veritable platitude**. When he asserts that the **"other arguments"** either prove nothing or prove very little, he says what is **false**.

NOT "OTHER" ARGUMENTS

(c) The proofs enumerated by him under (1), (2), (3), (4), (5) and (6), he calls **"other arguments,"** although, in truth, they are **not "other."** The cases under Nos. (1), (2), (3), and (6) are all examples of **lawful indirect voluntary**, while, in Nos. (4) and (5), **Suarez and Lessius** explain why indirect destroying one's own life can be lawful. Why then call either the examples or the explanations **"other arguments?"** Let us hear him, in addition, review and reject them. He writes:

(16) "The first argument **has no value**, and it is the very "height of irreverence to compare the fast of the "Mayor of Cork with that of Elias or of the Divine "Master."

VALUE AS PROOF; NO "HEIGHT OF IRREVERENCE"

(a) The forty days fast of Christ – and the similar fast of Elias – **proves with certainty that refusal of all food for a prolonged period is not an intrinsically evil act**. Is this proving nothing or very little? It is false to say that the fast of Christ has no value in **determining the morality of hunger-strike**.

(b) The writer's charge of irreverence –"the height of irreverence"– is both **a falsehood and a grave calumny**. Notice, first, that the writer says **nothing to substantiate so serious a charge**. Secondly, his charge is **false and evidently so**, and therefore cannot be substantiated. If a man be accused of lacking Christian fortitude because he sheds a tear at the grave of a cherished friend, **is he guilty of the "height of irreverence" when he answers that Christ wept at the grave of Lazarus?** If Fr. Charles Coughlin be challenged because, in his radio talks, he denounces the greedy rich, **is there no defense in his rejoinder that Christ did the same? Is it the height of irreverence?**

(17) "As to Sampson, we may answer with the Angelic "Doctor, in the words of St. Augustine: 'Samson is "excused for killing himself and his enemies, by pre- "suming that he did so **under the inspiration of the** "**Holy Spirit**, who wrought many miracles through "him'."

"TWO EFFECTS" IN FORESEEN SELF-KILLING

Assuming, as we may, that Samson acted under the inspiration of the Holy Spirit in placing the act which brought about his own death, **his case proves that an action may be lawful even though the agent foresees with certainty that his own death must inevitably result from it.** The Holy Spirit does not inspire any one to acts intrinsically evil. Is this principle or argument other than the Catholic doctrine of indirect voluntary? Is it not rather the doctrine of indirect voluntary applied to an act of foreseen self-killing? It is false that it proves "nothing or very little" regarding hunger-strike?

> (18) "The words which St. Eusebius of Vercelli, while imprisoned for the Faith, addressed to the heretic Patrofilus, **do not apply.** They are an open profession of faith, a generous protest of preferring rather to die than receive food from the hands of heretics, lest it should seem that he made common cause with them."

NOT MERELY "TO DIE," BUT "TO DIE OF HUNGER"

(a) It is false that the words of St. Eusebius do not apply to hunger-strike. He told Patrofilus that he **preferred to die of hunger** rather than accept food which might appear to signify **communing with heretics.** The saint's words apply specifically to hunger-strike, not because he said he **preferred to die,** but because he said he chose rather to die of hunger*. This canonized saint, and even one of the Fathers of the Church, judged the refusal of all food, even until death, to be lawful and praiseworthy, whenever a proportionate benefit resulted from it. Is the argument contained in the words of St. Eusebius something "other" than the Catholic doctrine of indirect voluntary? Does that argument "prove nothing at all or very little" for the lawfulness of the MacSwiney hunger-strike?

(b) Why does the Civilta writer represent St. Eusebius as only saying that he preferred **to die,** when, in reality, what the saint had said was that he had decided to die **of hunger** –"non panem manducaturum neque aquam bibiturum," are the saint's own words – rather than commune in food with the Arian heretics, when, in reality, what he told Patrofilus was that he had decided to die **of hunger,** rather than partake of the food which they brought him?

---

*These are the Saint's own words: "Interim me hoc decrevisse "sciatis, **non panem manducaturum neque aquam bibiturum** nisi "ante singuli professi fueritis vos non prohibituros fratres meos "necessarias escas offere. Nisi professi et verbo et conscriptione "fueritis, eritis homicidae prohibendo."
(Patrologia Latina, vol. xii, p. 950)

The words of St. Eusebius which make his position exactly the position of the hunger-striker, these words the Civilta writer **advisedly suppresses,** that he may seem to say with truth: "The words of St. Eusebius do not apply." And more of this purposeful suppression of the truth is yet to come!

(19) "Suarez (De Legibus, Book iii, Chap. 30, n.n. 1-11) "does no more than expound the doctrine of the ob- "ligation to sometimes observe the law even at the "risk of one's own life. Here is the title of the chap- "ter: 'Can the civil law oblige its subjects to its "observance at the risk of every temporal evil and "even of death?' And he answers affirmatively, add- "ing that this opinion is 'common and to my mind "certain' (loc. cit. n. 4). And undoubtedly it is cer- "tain. But in our case there is no human law which "imposes the hunger-strike."

HE IGNORED ARGUMENT, ARTICLE AND AUTHOR

Professional blind beggars are sometimes suspected of affecting blindness. Is the Civilta writer here affecting a kindred lack of vision? His remarks on this portion of his subject are so shortsighted as to leave the reader wondering whether his shortsightedness is genuine. He asserts correctly that "the only argument that has any value as proof is the accurate exposition and application of the doctrine of indirect voluntary." Now of this "accurate exposition and explanation" he had an admirable specimen furnished him by Fr. Patrick Gannon, S.J., in an article entitled "The Ethical Aspect of Hunger-Strike," which appeared in "Studies" for September, 1920. That article – by far the most lengthy and complete exposition of the doctrine of hunger-strike that the entire controversy produced – was published in a widely circulated quarterly review, two months before the Civilta writer took up his pen. Moreover, his references to the doctrine of Suarez and Lessius seem to have been copied, word for word, from Fr. Gannon's article. No other writer on hunger-strike cited either of these authors. Thus is the evidence fairly conclusive that the Civilta writer, previous to composing his own article, had before his eyes Fr. Gannon's accurate exposition, and application of the doctrine of indirect voluntary to the MacSwiney hunger-strike. In that article he read the five following propositions:

Prop. I "The precept of preserving one's own life, like "all positive precepts, sometimes ceases to "bind, and can, for sufficient reasons be "neglected."

" II "No hunger-striker aims at death. Quite the "contrary. He aims at escaping from unjust "detention."

Prop. III "And even if he carries the protest to its fatal "conclusion, he is still not seeking death, not "even as a means."

" IV "His object is to bring the pressure of public "opinion to bear upon an unjust aggressor, "and advance a cause for which he might face "certain death in the field."

" V "If charity towards a single individual be held "an adequate reason for not eating, and thus "sacrificing life, it would seem that love of "one's country, which is really charity towards "the millions of one's countrymen, constitutes "a far more valid excuse for neglecting the "positive precept of preserving life."

SLYLY OMITS PARAGRAPH ON HUNGER-STRIKE

The foregoing propositions accurately represent the doctrine of indirect voluntary in its application to the MacSwiney hunger-strike. And the Civilta writer read and ignored the argument, the article and the author – did so while professedly examining the arguments in the Lord Mayor's defense, and finding that "they either do not prove anything or prove very little." Nor is that the end of his ignoring. In his citation from Suarez which we are now considering, he quotes only the portion which does not apply to hunger-strike. The paragraph immediately succeeding, which applies to hunger-strike, he studiously omits. He mentions the words of Suarez which say that the State may oblige its subjects to sacrifice their lives for the public good. He omits the words immediately following, in which the same author states the reason why individuals, even when not obligated to sacrifice their lives, may nevertheless do so for friendship, or any worthy reason.

In the place referred to and partially cited by the Civilta writer – "De Legibus," Book iii, Chap. 30, n.n. 1-11 – Suarez says, much to our purpose:

"A confirmation of this – i.e. that the State 'can de-"mand works of supererogation involving danger of "death, when the common good requires them'– is found "in the reply that the precept of self-preservation "really involves two precepts, one negative, which "binds ever and always, namely, not to take one's own "life, and against this, human legislation can give no "command; the other positive, namely, to take steps "to preserve life and avoid death, which does not al-"ways bind, but often can be neglected not only to "observe a law but also in the interest of friendship."

CITES QUESTION AND ANSWER. OMITS THE WHY

Here Suarez asks whether the State can oblige its subjects to works involving danger of death. And he answers that it can, adding that this opinion is, "common, and to my mind, certain." Then he asks why can the State do this – why can the State oblige its subjects to destroy their lives by omission to preserve them, but not by positive violence. And Suarez answers: "Because violent destruction of one's own life is forbidden by negative precept, which never admits an exception, whereas preservation of it is only commanded by positive precept, which, like all positive precepts, admits exceptions."

Thus in the single paragraph from Suarez, cited by Fr. Gannon, the Civilta writer found (1) the question which Suarez asked; (2) the affirmative answer of Suarez to his own question; and (3) the reason which Suarez gives for his affirmative answer. And it was on account of this reason that Fr. Gannon introduced the citation at all. He was not concerned about the question of Suarez, or its affirmative answer. As the Civilta writer keeps contending, "there is no law obliging the fast of the hunger-striker." The proof Fr. Gannon was in quest of, lay not in either the question of Suarez, or in the answer, or in both. But the basic reason why the State can oblige its subjects to works involving danger of death, is the same reason why the hunger-striker may lawfully omit to preserve his own life – because preservation of life is only commanded by positive precept, which admits exceptions. Thus does Suarez interpret the Fifth Commandment, and prove by his interpretation that the act of hunger-strike until death, for any proportionate benefit, public or private, is not forbidden by that or by any other of the Commandments.

BY MERE ACCIDENT OR WELL-PLANNED PURPOSE?

Here it is that the "impartiality" of the Civilta writer, avowed at the beginning, his love for the truth that should be passionate, and his sense of honesty that should be uncompromising, appear in him to sorry disadvantage. Will anyone say that it is by mere accident, and not by a carefully planned purpose that he mentions the question which Suarez asked, and the answer which he gives to it, but omits altogether the reason which Suarez gives – the proof of Fr. Gannon's thesis? He suppresses the proof of Suarez, in order to accuse him of proving "nothing at all or very little" for the lawfulness of hunger-strike, just as he suppressed some of the words of St. Eusebius in order to say "they do not apply."

By the same shuffling evasion, expressed in another form, the Civilta writer would again strive to draw the attention of his readers away from the arguments of Suarez. He writes:

(20) "In Book vi, Chap. 7, n. 9, Suarez says: 'So too a person justly sentenced to death by starvation is not obliged in conscience to abstain from food if he can get it. He may, however, abstain from the food if he chooses to do so.' His case, as we may see, is altogether different from ours. It is the case of one who has been justly condemned to the penalty of death, and that by starvation."

PARTIALLY DIFFERENT. NOT "ALTOGETHER" SO

Does the circumstance that the criminal justly sentenced to death by starvation, lawfully starves himself to death in order to obey a civil law, make his case "altogether different" from the case of the hunger-striker, who starves himself to death in protest against injustice? Are not both cases justified by the same principle of Suarez – that the positive precept of preserving one's own life admits exception whenever some proportionate goal is realized by the sacrifice of that life? Does not Suarez say expressly, in the place cited by the Civilta writer, that the precept of preserving life does not always bind, but can often be neglected, in order to observe a law. The criminal sentenced to death by starvation may lawfully refuse food secretly brought to him. If his act were intrinsically evil, he could not in conscience place it even in order to carry out the sentence of death by starvation imposed on him. And so, in the act of refusing food until death for a proportionately grave reason, the criminal and the hunger-striker are exactly alike. That the criminal does so in order to carry out a just sentence, and the hunger-striker in order to protest against injustice – that does not make the two cases "altogether different."

All the same, the Civilta writer cries "altogether different," though the difference between the case of the criminal and that of the hunger-striker is only partial, and, moreover, irrelevant to the question which is the issue.

And, in order to more surely conceal the point of Suarez' proof, he adds: "But in our case there is no human law which imposes the hunger-strike." This is but saying over again that when Suarez asks whether the civil law can oblige its subjects at the risk of death, his question is irrelevant to the subject of hunger-strike, since the Irish hunger-strike was not imposed by any civil law. As has been already remarked, the question of Suarez and its answer are irrelevant to hunger-strike. But his reason for the answer – the reason that preservation of one's own life is only commanded by positive precept, and therefore admits exceptions – is not irrelevant. The reason for the answer – which reason the Civilta writer suppressed – is very relevant. The same ethical principle underlies both cases.

"ALTOGETHER DIFFERENT," AN EFFORT TO EVADE

Thus, for a second time, does he pretend to evade the argument of Suarez by an "altogether different" retort, another petty effort to throw proverbial dust in unwary eyes. "Altogether different" is too sweepingly general to be the language of Moral Theology. Actions are "altogether different" only when all the sources of their morality – objects, intentions and circumstances – are "altogether different." True, the intention of the hunger-striker is different from that of the criminal. The circumstances too are different. But what about the respective objects? They are absolutely identical. In both cases, the action itself is the repeated refusal of food as long as life lasts, and its essential physical object – its inevitable effect – is, in both cases, life unpreserved – permitted death. And if the actions themselves, their formal objects, and consequently the morality derived from those objects as the primary determinants of morality – if all these are exactly alike, what becomes of the "altogether different" of the Civilta writer? The actions themselves of hunger-striker and criminal are exactly alike, however much their morality may differ by reason of different intentions and circumstances. And the same must be said of the other cases mentioned by Suarez – the case of famine, and that of the Carthusian monk. One and all they refuse food until death.

MORALITY FROM ACT (OBJECT) SOLE ISSUE HERE

And it is precisely because, in all of them, the actions themselves are similar, that the argument of Suarez applies equally to them all. It is not with the intention or circumstances that the reasoning of Suarez is concerned, but with the actions themselves – the objects. He is careful to distinguish the taking one's own life from the omission to preserve it. He insists that the former is always forbidden, whereas the latter is sometimes permitted. And if the acts themselves of hunger-striker and criminal are exactly similar – both being the refusal of food until death – and if, furthermore, the argument of Suarez proves the criminal's refusal of food until death to be lawful, why should it not prove too that the hunger-striker's act of refusing food until death is also lawful. Was it out of the abundance of his simplicity, or was it out of the depth of his guile, that the Civilta writer insisted that the case of the hunger-striker is "altogether different" from that of the criminal of Suarez?

Suarez cites several cases also, in which, according to the principle just laid down by him, the omission to preserve one's own life is justified.

(1) "In a case of extreme need from famine or shipwreck, a person could lawfully subordinate his own interest, and surrender bread or a spar to a friend in like emergency." (l.c.n. 10)

(2) "A person justly condemned to death by starvation is not bound to abstain from food if he can obtain it, though he may do so without sin if he wishes."

(3) "In the Carthusian Institute, the precept of abstaining from flesh meats, even if it were a strict law binding of itself in conscience, could be neglected without sin, on account of the danger of death. Yet it is most probable that it could be observed even then if one wishes to use such rigor with oneself."

DOES SUAREZ "PROVE NOTHING OR VERY LITTLE"?

Suarez here applies to several concrete examples his general principle that the precept of preserving one's life admits exceptions. We have it on his authority that, because the precept of preserving one's own life is positive, and therefore admits exceptions, a person in extreme hunger may, for charity, friendship or any worthy motive, lawfully give his last crust to another in like extremity, and die himself of hunger; that a criminal justly sentenced to death by starvation, may, in order to carry out his sentence, lawfully refuse food secretly brought to him; that a Carthusian monk, in order to honor his Rule, may lawfully refuse a meat diet when it is the only food capable of saving his life. In other words, Suarez proves, both by a general reasoning and by several concrete instances of its application, that, for a proportionately worthy motive, it is always lawful to refuse food until death. Dear writer in the Civilta! It is false that Suarez, in the places cited by Fr. Gannon, "either proves nothing or proves very little." It is false that his reasoning on this subject is an argument "other than the Catholic doctrine of indirect voluntary."

After affecting to analyse the reasoning of Suarez and show that it does not apply to hunger-strike, the author adopts exactly the same tactics towards the reasoning of Lessius.

(21) "The doctrine of Lessius in the place cited (De Justitia et Jure, Book 11, Chap. 9, Dubit. 6,n.29) is the

"same as that of Suarez. Here are his precise words: "'A person condemned to death by starvation may lawfully abstain from food surreptitiously brought to him. . . . For this he has a just reason, namely that he may conform to a just sentence.'"

"ALTOGETHER DIFFERENT" OVER AGAIN

At this point the reasoning of the Civilta writer is very simple. He states that "the doctrine of Lessius in the place cited"—he is careful not to say by whom—"is the same as that of Suarez." This is his major proposition, suggesting to the reader the minor proposition that the doctrine of Suarez has been already shown to have no application to hunger-strike, and the conclusion that the same is true of the doctrine of Lessius. And that the Civilta writer may not seem to repudiate the doctrine of Lessius without having examined it, he cites the case, already mentioned by Suarez, of the criminal justly sentenced to death by starvation,—**the case which he previously declared to be "altogether different" from that of the hunger-striker.** If the case of the hunger-striker is altogether different from the case of Suarez, as the Civilta writer claims, why is it not also different from the case of Lessius—**the same identical case as that of Suarez?** Yet, the Civilta writer does not say so.

The writer in the Civilta wrote one truth when he said that the doctrine of Lessius is the same as that of Suarez. Both these great theologians hold exactly the same doctrine on this point, and enunciate it in practically the same words. Here is the entire citation from Lessius, which Fr. Gannon introduced into his article.

> "Though one may never slay oneself directly, it is lawful, when there is a just reason, to do or omit something from which it is certainly foreseen that death will ensue indirectly. So hold, in general, the doctors cited below. The reason is that it is not forbidden to a man ever to expose his life to danger, or commanded that he should always endeavor to conserve it, **but only forbidden to destroy it deliberately,** as distasteful to him, or to expose it to danger, or cease to conserve it without reason, for then he would be held to end it intentionally." ("De Justitia et Jure," Book 11, Chap. 9, Dubit 6, n. 27).

(1) "A man condemned to death by starvation **can abstain from food secretly offered to him,** as is rightly taught by Henriquez, Sotus and Lopez" . . .

(2) "If a person in extreme necessity had only food offered to idols at hand, **he might abstain from eating it and prefer to die.**"

(3) "If two are placed in extreme necessity, **one can yield the other the bread by which he could preserve his**

"life, and allow himself to die, for he has a just rea-
"son for not eating, namely, the duty of charity to-
"wards his neighbor." (l.c.n.29).

LESSIUS "PROVES NOTHING OR VERY LITTLE"?

Though Lessius does not mention here, as Suarez does above, the negative precept which always forbids death by one's own violence, or the positive precept which sometimes permits death by one's own omission to preserve it, he does assert that, for a just reason, it is lawful to do or omit something from which it is certainly seen that death will ensue indirectly. He does assert that it is not commanded that a person should always endeavor to preserve his life. And, like Suarez, Lessius cites, as examples, a man sentenced to death by starvation, who may lawfully refuse food secretly brought to him; a person in extreme hunger who may lawfully refuse food offered to idols, and thus die of starvation; a person in extremity of hunger who may lawfully give his food to another in like extremity and die himself. Once again, dear Civilta writer, you are called to answer the question—Does this doctrine of Lessius "prove nothing at all or prove very little" about the lawfulness of hunger-strike?

OMITS PERTINENT PART OF LESSIUS CITATION

And is it not worthy of special notice, and indeed of special comment, that the Civilta writer should have disregarded all besides that Lessius said, and singled out for citation, a second time, the case of the criminal sentenced to death by starvation, and already cited by him from Suarez? Now, however, he merely states that case, in proof of his assertion that the doctrine of Lessius is the same as that of Suarez? He omits the comment which he himself had previously made on that case, implying thereby that that case was already disposed of when he pronounced it "altogether different" from the case of the hunger-striker. But, as before, he may again be asked: Is the case of the person who dies because he refused food offered to idols, another "altogether different" case? And is the case of the person in extremity of hunger, and dying because he gave his last morsel of food to another in like necessity—is this case also "altogether different" from that of the hunger-striker?

His sham examination and refutation of partial proofs for the lawfulness of some hunger-strikes until death, the Civilta writer concludes with the following remark, which would deserve to be considered imbecile if it did not seem disingenuous.

(22) "The case of the soldier who explodes the powder-
"magazine, even though he foresees that he will be

"the victim of the explosion; of the shipwrecked per-
"son who gave the life-preserver to another; of the
"Religious, who, to be faithful to his Rule, does the
"heroic act of refusing those foods which are neces-
"sary for his health—these and similar examples
"aptly illustrate the doctrine of indirect voluntary in
"its practical applications."

SUPPRESSION AND EVASION WRITER'S METHOD

(a) In the case of the Religious, the question is not of foods "necessary for his health" but of foods necessary to save his life. The question throughout is not whether the Religious may, in the circumstances, sacrifice his health, but whether he may lawfully sacrifice his life.

(b) In addition to the doctrine of Suarez and that of Lessius, the Civilta writer includes the three cases he has just mentioned, in his list of the proofs that "either do not prove anything of prove very little." A responsible writer, making so grave a charge, would feel an obligation in fairness to prove his own sweeping indictment. He would first state clearly the thesis which his opponents proposed to prove. Next he would make a fair analysis of their alleged proofs. Finally he would show that they do not prove the thesis. This would save him the necessity of having recourse to the "nothing at all or very little" expedient—to labyrinths of suppression, evasion and what not.

But such is not the type of discussion that the Civilta writer is in quest of. His case is one that does not permit the methods of candid controversy. 'Tis easier, and indeed less embarrassing for him, to dismiss the whole question with an "altogether different from ours" gesture. " 'Tis so like truth 'twill serve the turn as well."

SUAREZ, LESSIUS, EXAMPLES PROVE ACT LAWFUL

(c) It has been shown that the doctrine of Suarez does prove, and that the doctrine of Lessius does prove all that each was cited to prove. Each proves that it is sometimes lawful to refuse food until death. And the same is proved by each of the concrete examples cited by Suarez and Lessius. For if a single instance can be named in which it is lawful to refuse food unto death, it follows inevitably that the act itself of refusing food until death is not intrinsically evil, but, on the contrary, good or indifferent, and, consequently, may be lawfully placed as often as the intention is good and the good effect proportionate.

Do the case of the soldier, of the victim of shipwreck, of the Religious, "either prove nothing or prove very little" regarding the lawfulness of hunger-strike? Like the act of hunger-strike, everyone of these cases is **an action which tends to cause the death of the agent, at the same time that it is directed exclusively to produce some proportionate good effect.** Thus their formal objects are similar, and since actions are specified by their formal objects, **the actions themselves are of similar morality.** Now every case that is known to be lawful proves that every **parallel case is also** lawful, and hunger-strike, instead of being "altogether different" from the cases of Suarez and Lessius, offers a deadly parallel to them as regards their object. The alibi of "altogether different," bolstering up an "either do not prove anything or prove very little" is exploded.

"APTLY ILLUSTRATE DOCTRINE" NOT THE ISSUE

(d) The **direct issue** is not whether the cases cited above **illustrate** or **do not illustrate the doctrine** of indirect voluntary. The question is, **do they or do they not prove that hunger-strike until death is sometimes lawful.** These cases are included **in the author's list of counterfeit proofs.** He mentions them in his sixth series of arguments that "prove little or nothing." But, where he might reasonably be expected to give proof of the faith that is in him, by proving that they "prove little or nothing," he says instead, with grand theological flourish, that the cases in question "aptly illustrate the doctrine of indirect voluntary in its practical applications." Is it possible for any lawful case to aptly illustrate any doctrine, and, at the same time, either not prove anything or prove very little? If masters in Theology state general moral principles and apply them to solve particular cases, do they not thereby solve all parallel cases? Yet the Civilta writer **conceals the light which Suarez and** Lessius throw on the question of hunger-strike, **and then accuses them of leaving it in darkness.** And suppression of the truth, wholly or in part, **is one species of falsification.** It is **false** that the soldier who lawfully explodes the powder-magazine and loses his life in the explosion, **proves little or nothing about hunger-strike.** It is false that the case of the shipwrecked person who gives to another the plank of safety, proves little or nothing about the morality of hunger-strike. It is false that the case of the Carthusian monk – who, to honor his rule of perpetual abstinence, **freely refuses a meat diet, when a meat diet is necessary to save his life** – proves nothing or very little for the lawfulness of hunger-strike.

And now having introduced a lengthy list of **wrong definitions, wrong explanations and wrong refutations,** he pretends to test the MacSwiney hunger-strike by the requirements for every lawful case of indirect voluntary.

(23) "Voluntary fast is not an act intrinsically bad. That "is certain. Hence, if voluntary fast is not an act "intrinsically bad, and therefore may even be good, "or at least indifferent – e guindi puo essere anche "buono o almeno indifferente – it evidently follows "that the doctrine of indirect voluntary is applicable "to it."

NOT INTRINSICALLY BAD, HENCE TWO EFFECTS?

(a) "Not intrinsically bad and therefore may even be good, or at least indifferent." That is a new and false method of inference regarding disjunctives. Actions are either good, bad or indifferent. If they are not one of these classes, they must (not may) be either of the remaining alternatives.

(b) In addition to being false, it is absurd to say that the principle of "two effects" is applicable to voluntary fast, or to any other action, simply because it is not intrinsically bad. An act of prayer is not intrinsically bad, yet the principle of indirect voluntary is not applicable to it. And the falsity and the absurdity are multiplied when the writer insists that it is evidently applicable, for the reason that he assigns. If the Civilta writer's reason why the principle of indirect voluntary is applicable to voluntary fast, were true, then every action not intrinsically bad would be, ipso facto, a case of "two effects" – an evident absurdity.

(c) Here the Civilta writer says expressly that every voluntary fast until death is a case of "indirect voluntary," or "two effects." He therefore says equivalently: (1) that the act itself is good; (2) that it produces a good effect; and (3) an inseparable ill effect, (4) not intended. That is the minimum requirement for any and every case of "two effects." There is no case of "two effects" (a) if the action is intrinsically evil, or (b) if the ill effect is intended, or (c) if the good effect is obtainable without the ill effect. Of course a lawful case of "two effects" further requires due proportion of good effect.

ADMITS FAST IS "TWO EFFECTS." EVADES USING

And now it might be expected that the writer would proceed to solve the MacSwiney case, by applying to it the requisites for the lawfulness of every indirect voluntary – stated by himself in No. 14. But he turns instead to his "indisputable considerations," as we shall afterwards see, and denies that MacSwiney's act was able to produce the good effect intended. In other words, he denies that the Mac-

Swiney hunger-strike was a case of "indirect voluntary," or "two effects" at all, thus contradicting what he said a moment before in No. 23.

(24) "Neither can it be said that voluntary fast is, within "certain limits, good, or at least indifferent, but be-"comes unlawful if prolonged until it causes death. "Undoubtedly a time comes when it necessarily pro-"duces death. But not for this and this alone does it "become bad. It cannot become bad so long as the "agent has a right intention and a just reason."

ACT OF FASTING ADMITTED LAWFUL. NOT PROVED

This the Civilta writer should have proved but did not. Of his article, comprising eleven pages, he devotes three entire pages to defining suicide, proving it intrinsically unlawful, and corroborating his proof by citations from St. Thomas, as if any of his readers was unaware what suicide is, or disputed its unlawfulness. And the point that was doubted by very many – one may safely say, by the vast majority – and vehemently denied by several, this crucial point in the doctrine of hunger-strike, he accepts without challenge. He does not prove nor attempt to prove it. He admits it, assents to it, but does not tell his readers why he does so. It is not self-evident, nor does he receive it solely on any authority. That hunger-strike unto death is not intrinsically evil needed proof, and whence did he derive that proof? The argument of Suarez – that interpretation of the Fifth Commandment which forbids the taking one's own life, but allows the giving it, the laying it down as an act of supreme love – that argument proved conclusively to the Civilta writer that hunger-strike until death is not an intrinsically evil act. And that argument, at the same time that it is conclusive, is also exclusive. Theology has no other proof of the thesis in question, nor does it need any other. It rests on Christ's own assurance that it is most laudable to sacrifice one's life for a friend, or for any proportionate good. The Civilta writer, while using the conclusion of that argument himself, concealed the argument from his readers!

PROOF NEEDED. WRITER HIDES PROOF INSTEAD

It was incumbent on him to give special prominence to his thesis that hunger-strike until death is not intrinsically evil, and most of all, to its proof – because its opposite is only commanded by positive precept. In the interest of theological truth and Catholic teaching, he was called to make a prominent display of that pivotal proof. But he hides it instead. Professing an impartial, clear and precise presentation of Catholic doctrine on self-killing, **he excludes from his exposition the central consideration on which that entire doctrine hinges.** Professing to lead his readers to an understanding of the theology of hunger-strike, he **misleads them** – leads them to misunderstand it. To prove that hunger-strike is not intrinsically evil, **he would be compelled to invoke the argument of Suarez, just as Fr. Gannon did.** But then he would be prevented from accusing Suarez of "either proving nothing at all or proving very little."

(25) "This only must be added that the ill effects of the "fast increasing, and the fast becoming the proxi- "mate cause of inevitable death, the motive (the "good effect), which at the beginning could make it "lawful, does not any longer do so. For, according 'to the principles before mentioned, the reason for "placing the action must be proportionate to the "gravity of the ill effect, and to the greater or lesser "influx which the cause exerts in producing it."

(a) This is purblind reasoning, based on an entire misconception of the nature of hunger-strike. That entire misconception, misunderstanding, ignorance, or whatever the reader wishes to call it, will be apparent from the analysis of the act itself.

EXCOGITATES PUZZLE WHERE NONE EXISTS

The fundamental error of the Civilta writer is that of considering hunger-strike at different stages of its progress, and dividing what is really **one act, with one morality,** into several separate acts with several separate moralities. In other words, he makes several hunger-strikes out of what is, in reality, only one. In a series of taps of an electric hammer, **no single tap is "riveting;"** in a series of strokes of arm or oar, **no single stroke is "swimming"** or **"rowing;"** in a series of stitches with a needle, **no single stitch is "sewing."** It is the entire series, the aggregation of taps, strokes, stitches, and so forth, that is, and is called "riveting," "swimming," "rowing," "sewing." And, similarly, **in a series of refusals of food, it is the sum total of them all, that is hunger-strike.** No single member of any such series is hunger-strike, and, therefore, no single refusal has a separate morality of its own. Otherwise Mayor MacSwiney would have had to his credit two hundred and twenty-two hunger-strikes, each of which, according to the calculating of the Civilta writer, had a separate morality of its own, different from the morality of every other refusal. Hence, to inquire whether the motive for this or that particular refusal is sufficient, would be like investigating a single stitch in its own series, and determining how much is due the tailor for setting it.

HIS PROPORTION IMPOSSIBLE TO CALCULATE

And since it is not any single one in a series of refusals, but the entire series, that is hunger-strike; since its formal objects – protest and probable death – are unvarying throughout; since the original intention of continuing until death, perseveres in them all; since each refusal of food is an exact reproduction, and practically a continuation of the previous one – it follows that all the refusals are virtually and morally one, having, at the very beginning, and retaining to the very end, the same unvarying proportion of good effect, to compensate for the equally unvarying ill effect – probable death. What place is there then for the author's ruling that "the motive (the good effect) which, at the beginning, could make it lawful, now perhaps does not any longer do so?"

REMOTE, PROXIMATE CAUSE OF DEATH FOREIGN

(b) The writer's reason for saying that, as the hunger-strike progresses, the original motive may no longer be sufficient, is as false as the saying itself. He says it is because, with the advance of the hunger-strike, the refusal of food, which previously had been only the remote cause of death, now becomes its proximate cause – "the ill effects of the fast increasing and the fast becoming the proximate cause of inevitable death." Whoever enters on a hunger-strike, intending to continue it, if necessary, until actual death, must from the very beginning, have a motive (good effect) proportionate to the loss of his own life, even when he does not actually continue until death. Thus there is no need of new calculating of proportionate motive at any stage as the hunger-strike progresses.

But the Civilta writer would, at every separate instant during the entire period of the hunger-strike, exercise a new microscopic scrutiny over the act of refusing food and its varying physical effect on the hunger-striker, without however being able to point out – even if there were need to point out – the exact refusal which first ceases to be the remote cause, and now becomes the proximate cause of the hunger-striker's death. And since, that is so, the Civilta writer is equally helpless to decide at which stage the motive for the hunger-strike must become greater in order that the hunger-strike may be lawful. For his solution of hunger-strike, or of any other case in Moral Theology for that matter, the decimal system of Mathematics is not sufficient. The infinitesimal system is needed.

PUZZLE COPIED LATER BY WRITER IN "TABLET"

This fallacious reasoning of the Civilta writer was copied, word for word, a fortnight later, by a writer in The Tablet (London), who signed himself "An Irish Student of Morals." There can hardly be any doubt that in both cases **the sophistry was intended to make readers despair of ever understanding the case of hunger-strike.**

We have heard the author **falsely assert** that the motive must be greater as the hunger-strike continues. We have seen that it **need not, does not, cannot.** If hunger-strike **until death** was intended from the very beginning, a proportionate good effect was necessary from the very beginning, in order that the hunger-strike may be lawful. Why then a need of an ever **increasing** motive, or good effect?

He wrongly reasons that the motive must then be greater, because the hunger-strike then **passes from remote to proximate cause of death.** We have seen that his "reason," like every reason for something that is not so, is not only unconvincing but even false.

(26) "Therefore the whole question, objectively con-
"sidered, resolves itself into inquiring whether he
"who has recourse to a voluntary fast producing
"death, has a reason just in itself, and if that rea-
"son is sufficient."

WHOLE QUESTION IS ABOUT FOUR CONDITIONS

This pronouncement is false, and, moreover **contradicts** what the writer has already laid down. He said previously that "four conditions are required in order that an ill effect be permitted," one of which is that "the ill effect must not be willed (he should have said 'intended') either as an end or as a means." The whole question, therefore, resolves itself into inquiring whether the **four** requisite conditions are verified or not. If they are all realized, the action is lawful. If anyone of them is wanting the action is unlawful. But the writer whittles down the four conditions to two—"a reason just and sufficient." He continues the juggling process even to the very end of his article. True he has already pronounced the act itself to be certainly lawful. But what about the intention **with regard to both end and means?** And what does he mean by "a reason just in itself and sufficient?" In every indirect voluntary **is not the sufficiency (proportion) of the "reason" its entire justification?**

(27) "Even the defenders of the lawfulness of the Cork
"case admit that the desire of shortening imprison-
"ment in order to regain liberty; the wish to place
"an act of protest against the sentence pronounced

"by the judges, the wish to excite public opinion in "one's own favor, would not be just and sufficient "reasons."

DEFENDERS ADMIT NOTHING ABOUT "REASONS"

The number of "reasons that would not be just and sufficient" is legion, and the defenders of Mayor MacSwiney have not undertaken to enumerate and estimate them. But when and where and by which of the Lord Mayor's defenders was it acknowledged that the reasons involved in his hunger-strike were "not just and sufficient?" It is false, notoriously false, that the defenders of Mayor MacSwiney admitted their insufficiency.

Much of what was spoken or written in defense as well as condemnation of Mayor MacSwiney, is reproduced in these pages, and nowhere in that collection is there any trace of such acknowledgment as the author asserts, or indeed of anything that approximates to it. Why does he ask his readers to accept that statement on his "say so?" Why does he dispense himself from the rules of fair discussion? Common convention obliged him to mention the names of at least some of those who made the acknowledgment he claims; to cite, in substance if not verbatim, at least one or other of the acknowledgments themselves; or, as a last resort, to refer his readers to the places where they could be found. But he does none of these. Besides being unauthentic, it is false that the defenders of Mayor MacSwiney made any such acknowledgment as the author speaks of. So much for the acknowledgment which the defenders of Mayor MacSwiney did not make.

FICTITIOUS REASONS INSTEAD OF MacSWINEY'S

(b) The question which the Civilta writer proposed to answer is not whether such and such imaginary reasons would or would not be "just and sufficient." He rather undertook to state the real reasons involved in the MacSwiney hunger-strike, and to decide whether or not they were "just and sufficient." But this he does not do. It would be too intelligible for his readers! Instead, he proposes reasons bearing a superficial similarity to the MacSwiney reasons, and then falsely accuses the Lord Mayor's defenders of acknowledging their insufficiency, though, in truth, they had neither rejected, accepted or considered them. And thus, unwary readers, unskilled in subtle distinction, are artfully led into the settled conviction that the MacSwiney reasons are also insufficient – so identical do they seem with the reasons already said to be rejected even by the defenders of MacSwiney. The art employed by the Civilta writer will be more evident when his forged "reasons" and the real reasons of Mayor MacSwiney are set forth in parallel columns.

(a) Civilta's False Reasons	(b) MacSwiney's Own Reasons
(1) "The desire of shortening imprisonment in order to regain liberty."	(1) The desire of ending unjust imprisonment in order to regain liberty.
(2) "The wish to place an act of protest against the sentence pronounced by the judges."	(2) The wish to place an act of protest against (a) the unjust sentence of his judges and (b) his country's oppression.
(3) "The wish to excite public opinion in one's own favor."	(3) The wish to excite public opinion in favor of his country.

(c) Civilta's "Sufficient" Reasons
"The autonomy, the liberty of Ireland – the public welfare of the Nation."

Now, there is a world of difference, for the moralist, between desire to shorten imprisonment and desire to end unjust imprisonment; between protesting against the sentence of the judges and protesting against an unjust sentence; between wishing to excite public opinion in one's own favor, and in favor of one's country. We are not concerned to decide whether the "Civilta's reasons" are sufficient or not. We merely point out that they are very different from the real reasons of Mayor MacSwiney, though ingeniously made to appear like them. The Civilta writer's own grounds for their insufficiency, he state as follows:

(28) "These reasons are grave, it is true, but pertain to private, individual welfare, and, as such, are not sufficient to render lawful an act which brings about the loss of a good supreme in the natural order – the loss of life."

AUTHOR'S SCALES EXCLUDE PRIVATE WELFARE

(a) "Grave, yet not grave enough," says the Civilta writer. It is difficult to surmise on what basis he makes his calculations. His "grave but not sufficient" suggests the impossible task of measuring with fractional accuracy the value of a human life. It is remarkable how much more profoundly the supreme value of human life impressed itself, at the time of the hunger-strike controversy, on the writers who opposed it, than it had done at any other time. "Grave and irreparable evil" is one writer's estimating of it. Those writers are greatly distressed about a single life sacrificed for Ireland's freedom, but the **millions of lives immolated, on the battle-fields of the world, to national greed** and **international intrigue** – all this **commerce in human lives** does not cause those same writers a single pang!

(b) **And why "not sufficient?"** Because it "**pertains to private, individual welfare**," answers the Civilta writer. This is to say equivalently that no "private, individual welfare" **justifies the sacrifice of a human life** – a saying **too false** and **too absurd** to call for refutation. Theologians are agreed about cases without number in which one's own life may be lawfully and even laudably sacrificed **to save the life of another,** be that other **young or old, rich or poor, sickly or healthy, superior or subject, obscure or illustrious.** It must be again remarked that we are not concerned about defending the sufficiency of the Civilta "reasons." **Perhaps they are insufficient.** But the writer's rejection of them because they pertain to "**private, individual welfare**," is, like much else that he has written – foolish. Suárez says that the obligation to preserve one's own life "can be neglected, **not only to observe a law but also in the interest of friendship**"– in the interest of a friend. (See No. 19.)

(29) "In our case, the good effect which is desired through "the voluntary fast is the autonomy, the liberty of "Ireland – the public welfare of the Nation."

WRITER MAKES ABSURD ASSERTION UNABASHED

(a) Why does he say "the good effect **desired?**" It is not the sufficiency or insufficiency of the good effect **desired,** but rather of the good effect **actually produced** that constitutes proportion or disproportion to the ill effect. Why then does he say "the good effect **desired?**"

(b) We have already met a goodly number of the writer's **misstatements.** Here he adds another to them. The good effect, or rather the good **effects,** desired through the MacSwiney fast have been enumerated several times already, but nowhere among them is "**the autonomy, the liberty of Ireland** – the public welfare of the Nation." It was the same misrepresentation of the objectives of MacSwiney that called forth from Fr. Nicholas Lawless the stupid as well as cynical remark that "glowing reasons were given (by the defenders of the Lord Mayor) about Ireland's freedom to be won in right chivalrous fashion by a solitary hunger-striker." "Autonomy of Ireland" was no more necessary to justify the MacSwiney hunger-strike than the independence of the United States was necessary to justify Nathan Hale's sacrifice of his own life. In neither case was the "just and sufficient reason" **the absurd one of** their nation's independence – to whose achievement ten thousand other agencies were cooperating – but something which, **as their proximate aim**, would, **to some small extent**, contribute to their country's independence. Nathan Hale's actual contribution to American Independence was an unsuccessful effort to discover for General Washington, the numbers and plans of the Continental forces assembled at Harlem Heights, New York. Nor has any one been heard to say that this reason was not proportionate to the life which he sacrificed in attempting it. And, similarly, Mayor MacSwiney's motive was **protest** against personal imprisonment by an alien government, protest against his country's oppression by that alien government, **inspiration** to others to likewise protest, and **appeal** to the sympathy of other nations. We shall see, a moment later, the **"impartial" maneuvering** which brought the Civilta writer to state falsely that the good effect which Mayor MacSwiney aimed at was "the autonomy, the liberty of Ireland – the public welfare of the Nation."

(30) "This reason is **certainly just in itself**. Nobody can "doubt it. But is it just and sufficient also **when all** "**the circumstances of this case are considered?** In "other words, **are there verified in this case all the** "**before-mentioned conditions of an indirect volun-** "**tary?** 1st. Is the good effect **certain?** 2nd. Is the "**cause adapted to producing that effect?** 3rd. Is it "**impossible to obtain the good effect without the ill** "**effect?** This we do not see." (Non lo vidiamo.")

"GRAVE, NOT ENOUGH." "JUST, NOT IN CONTEXT"!!

(a) A while ago (No. 28) it was "grave but not sufficient." Now, it is "just in itself but **not just in the circumstances.**" There, the writer emasculated MacSwiney's real reasons **in order to call them insufficient.** Here, he magnifies the MacSwiney reasons **a thousand fold, in order to call the Lord Mayor's hunger-strike inadequate to realize them.** Then, he pretended to show that **the good effect** is not proportionate to the **ill effect.** Now, he pretends to show that the **act** is not proportioned to **producing** the good effect. But we have shown that in neither case are the author's good effects the good effects **intended and achieved by Mayor MacSwiney**. The truth is, the Civilta writer **never stated the true aims** of the Irish hunger-strike atall. He misstates them, falsifies them. Let the reader decide for himself whether the evident and oft-repeated misstatement and falsification could, by any possibility, be unpremeditated. Is there no premeditation in assigning to a sword or rapier the weight and dimensions of a crowbar, in order to charge the military officer with being unable to wield it?

(b) See now the position of this adventurer in the domain of Moral Theology. He wrote the following:

1. "The only argument which has any value as proof "is the accurate exposition and application of the "Catholic doctrine of **indirect voluntary**." (p. 528)

2. "Voluntary fast is not an act intrinsically bad, and "therefore, the doctrine of indirect voluntary is evi- "dently applicable to it." (p. 530)

3. "It is lawful to place a cause (action) good or in- "different in itself, from which follows immediately "a double effect – one good, the other ill – provided "the ill effect, although foreseen, be not intended, "and there is a just and proportionate reason for "permitting the ill effect." (p. 526)

"CATHOLIC DOCTRINE OF INDIRECT VOLUNTARY"!

(c) Now the writer asks are there verified in this case **all the above-mentioned conditions of an indirect voluntary.** Remember, his above-mentioned conditions are of two kinds – first, his four "indisputable considerations," (p. 527), which he introduced with so much solemnity, and secondly, the four conditions, (p. 526) requisites – from **end, means,** and **circumstances** – for every **lawful** case of "two effects." Is he asking about the first alone, or about the second alone, or about both? Are all the foregoing considerations included in his "before-mentioned conditions?" Apparently not.

Becoming more specific, he asks if his "indisputable considerations" are realized, but **makes no inquiry about the "four conditions." He does not ask if the action of the Lord** Mayor is good (or indifferent); if his end or intention is good; if the good effect of his hunger-strike is proportionate: if it is or is not obtained by **means of the ill effect.** But he does ask if the good effect is certain, though the good effect of hunger-strike **need never be certain,** since the ill effect – the hunger-striker's death – is never certain. Did not the writer say already that the good effect may be doubtful whenever the ill effect is doubtful? (See No. 14.)

Again, he asks if the act of hunger-strike is capable of producing the good effect. We answer that every hunger-strike essentially produces the good effect of protest against injustice – in the case of MacSwiney, protest against his own imprisonment and his country's oppression. His hunger-strike was not capable of producing "the autonomy, the liberty of Ireland," nor was there any need that it should in order to be lawful.

The third of his indisputable considerations, namely that the action must, of its nature, produce the good effect – he now makes no mention of. Was it because he saw plainly that hunger-strike, of its nature produces the essential effect of protest against injustice?

Finally, the writer asks, rhetorically rather than interrogatively whether it is impossible to obtain the good effect without the ill effect. A moment later he denies that it is impossible, insists that there are several means whereby "the autonomy, the liberty of Ireland" may be achieved, without the loss of a single life. But he is very careful not to attempt to specify a single one of his "many and more efficacious means."

BEHOLD HIS "ACCURATE APPLICATION"!

After admitting (1) that the doctrine of indirect voluntary is applicable to voluntary fast until death, and (2) that it is the only argument which has any value as proof; after promising an accurate exposition and application of that doctrine to that action, the writer furnishes the exposition without the accuracy and without the application. He turns his back on the conditions requisite for lawful indirect voluntary, and turns his face to some but not all of his indisputable considerations, every one of which we have shown to be either false or superfluous, while some of them contradict others and even themselves.

And to his own questions – is the good effect certain; is the action adapted to producing it; is it impossible to obtain the good effect without the ill effect – to all these questions he gives the single, summary answer: "This we do not see" ("Non lo vediamo"). Here his grammar is as ungrammatical as his theology is untheological. It is not what the author does not see, but what he does see that concerns his readers. It is one thing not to see that a thing is so, and quite another to see that it is not so. Both may mean the same for the man of the street, but not for the logician. Does the Civilta writer see that MacSwiney's own good effect of protest, etc., is not certain? He does not, cannot. Every hunger-strike is essentially a protest against injustice, and therefore always certain to produce it. Does he see that the act is not adapted to producing it? Does he see that it is not impossible to obtain MacSwiney's own good effect without the ill effect? When he says with oracular ambiguity: "This we do not see," does he mean "we do not know," "we are in doubt," "we cannot say?" Or does he mean: "We see, we know that not one of our 'indisputable considerations' is verified in the MacSwiney case?" The concluding words of his article remove all doubt as to where he stands with regard to this case. There he says with all the declamatory verbosity of the stump orator:

(31) "Therefore we cannot admit that the so-called hun-"ger-strike is a means, sure, of its nature efficacious, "necessary, proportionate to obtaining national lib-"erty and independence, and that there are no other "and more efficacious means to assert and vindicate "the one and the other. How many are the means to "secure public opinion, to safeguard one's own rights, "to uphold the cause of one's own Nation? Is it really "necessary to have recourse to a voluntary fast and "die of hunger?"

MORE OF WRITER'S "ACCURATE APPLICATION"!

This is manifestly a deliberate attempt to substitute bombast for theological reasoning. He was obligated by the rules of respectable controversy, and still more by the supreme interest of theological truth, to separately consider and discuss each of the four requisites for a lawful indirect voluntary, and point out to his readers his reasons for denying that all of them were realized in the MacSwiney case. Instead, he turns to his "indisputable considerations" and denies them all in bulk, with an unreasoned "this we do not see," omitting all reference to the how and why and wherefore. This cannot be called bad theology. It is not theology at all – good, bad or indifferent. Theology proves its conclusions. The Civilta writer asks his readers to accept his conclusions on his authority. If they accept them, they do so at their own risk.

Who among the defenders of Mayor MacSwiney ever claimed that his hunger-strike was "proportionate to obtaining national liberty and independence" for Ireland? What need was there that the Civilta writer, or anyone else, should "admit" such a claim, as a condition of the lawfulness of the Lord Mayor's hunger-strike? It has been already pointed out that he magnifiees the needed proportion of good effort to a fabulous degree, in order to charge Mayor MacSwiney's act with incapacity to produce it.

It is significant that, in presenting their arguments, all the opponents of the MacSwiney hunger-strike shunned the syllogism. The strength of an argument, if it be strong, and its weakness, if it be weak, is clearly shown and easily seen when the argument is set forth in syllogistic form. Thus expressed the Civilta writer's summing up of the MacSwiney case – contained in Nos. 30 and 31 – is as follows:

Major Prop. In order that hunger-strike may be lawful, (1) the good effect must be certain; (2)

	the act of hunger-strike must be **capable of producing it;** (3) it must be **otherwise impossible** to obtain.
Minor Prop.	But in the MacSwiney hunger-strike (1) the good effect **was not certain;** (2) his act was not capable of producing it; (3) it was otherwise obtainable.
Conclusion	Therefore Mayor MacSwiney's hunger-strike was unlawful.

DENIES MAYOR'S CASE IS "INDIRECT VOLUNTARY"

Notice that one of the writer's "indisputable considerations"—that the act must, of its nature, produce the good effect—is here entirely lost sight of. Another of them—that the good effect must be certain—he could also afford to overlook. By denying, as he does—in the minor proposition—that the act is capable of producing the good effect, he equivalently denies (1) that the act by its nature produces the good effect, and consequently denies (2) that the good effect is certain. Thus is his whole indictment of Mayor MacSwiney reduced to the two following denials. First, he denies that the Lord Mayor's hunger-strike was **capable of producing the good effect,** and, secondly, he denies that the good effect was otherwise unobtainable. But isn't each of those two denials a denial that hunger-strike is a case of indirect voluntary atall? Every indirect voluntary is a case of (1) two effects (2) the ill effect inseparable from the good effect. Thus the writer gives us two farther contradictions!

DENIES WHAT IS NOT NEEDED FOR LAWFULNESS

But both these denials are sound without sense. He denies what is not necessary for the lawfulness of MacSwiney's hunger-strike. What is sufficient, if not necessary, for its lawfulness, he does not deny. He does not deny that the Lord Mayor's act produced a **protest** against injustice, and an **inspiration** to other protests, and an **appeal** to humanity. What he does deny is (1) that the MacSwiney hunger-strike was capable of bringing about "the autonomy, the liberty of Ireland," and (2) that this autonomy, this liberty, was otherwise impossible. But neither of these was necessary in order to justify Mayor MacSwiney's sacrifice of his own life. It is churlish to say that the aforesaid protest and inspiration and appeal are not sufficient proportion of good effect to compensate for the sacrifice of a single life, or that "national liberty and independence" is needed for that proportion. Again, to justify the Lord Mayor's death, it was not necessary that the "national liberty and independence" of his counry be otherwise impossible. It was only necessary that **his protest, his inspiration and his appeal be otherwise morally unobtainable.** "I do not see" ("Non lo vidiamo"), says the Civilta writer, "that MacSwiney's act was capable of producing the autonomy, the liberty of Ireland. Therefore that act was unlawful." Here is surely a non sequitur if there ever was one. Again he says: "I do not see that the autonomy, the liberty of Ireland is not obtainable by other means besides the MacSwiney hunger-strike. Therefore the MacSwiney hunger-strike was unlawful." Here is a second grossly unwarranted inference following fast upon the former. That was only **one of many truths of fact which the Civilta writer did not see.** Having eyes he saw not!

And since the writer's denials are thus wide of the mark, and do not touch the MacSwiney case atall, if we go on to consider how he substantiates those denials, it is not in order to further disprove and discredit his conclusions, but **to further illustrate his unseemly method of discussing a grave question in Moral Theology.**

DOES NOT SEE BECAUSE HE DOES NOT LOOK!

"We do not see," he says "**and therefore we cannot admit.**" That is correct psychology. It would be **irrational to admit anything without sufficient grounds for doing so. Every rational assent** is given either on intrinsic evidence or on some reliable authority. In order to "admit," it is necessary to see.

But in order to see, it is necessary to look, and the Civilta writer has not looked – has refused to look. We have just seen (No. 27) that he has not considered and weighed Mayor MacSwiney's reasons at all, that he **misrepresents, falsifies them.** He shuts his eyes to the evidence and then exclaims: "I do not see, and therefore I cannot admit, that hunger-strike is a means, sure, of its nature efficacious, necessary, proportionate, to obtaining national liberty and independence."

Moreover, if the Civilta writer's "I do not see and therefore I cannot admit," is good psychology, it would be equally good psychology if he were to say: "**I do not see and therefore I cannot deny.**" The same lack of evidence which forbids him to "admit," **equally forbids him to** "deny." If he would be consistent his position **must be that of an agnostic, who neither admits nor denies.**

DENIES LIBERTY OTHERWISE UNOBTAINABLE

Let no one suppose, however, that this is the stand taken by the Civilta writer. After **falsely** stating that "national liberty and independence" were the objectives of Mayor MacSwiney's hunger-strike, he, still more falsely, and with his accustomed declamation, denies that the said "national liberty and independence" was otherwise unobtainable. "Therefore we cannot admit that there are no other and more efficacious means to assert and vindicate the one and the other."

The impossibility which the writer here denies is not intrinsic but extrinsic impossibility. The question is not whether accomplishing "the national liberty and independence" of Ireland, without the death of a single hunger-striker, involves a contradiction. It manifestly does not. The question is whether there is a cause capable of producing that "national liberty and independence," without the ill effect of death. Furthermore, the question is not merely whether such a cause exists, but whether, in the circumstances of Mayor MacSwiney's hunger-strike, such a cause was practically available. As has been already remarked, the Lord Mayor was not obliged to canvass all creation in order to find that cause and substitute it for his hunger-strike.

IRISH HISTORY DENIES HIS DENIAL

As to the merits of the Civilta writer's denial that "other and more efficacious means" were not practically available for the Lord Mayor, it must be urged that the oft-repeated but always inefficacious efforts of the Irish people, during seven hundred and fifty years, to achieve their "national liberty and independence," creates the strongest presumption against that denial. If, when the writer penned his "other and more efficacious means," he had one or more or several of those "efficacious means" in mind, how was he able to resist every impulse to enumerate and specify them? Such enumerating and specifying of the "efficacious means" he was contending for, would have greatly strengthened his denial that they were practically unavailable. But, while insisting that such "efficacious means" existed at the time of Mayor MacSwiney's hunger-strike, and were ready to hand, he cautiously avoids all specific enumeration of them, substituting in their stead another piece of noisy, vapid declamation—"how many are the means to secure public opinion, to safeguard one's own rights, to uphold the cause of one's own Nation! Is it really necessary to have recourse to a voluntary fast and die of hunger?"

And even as the curtain is about to fall for the last time upon the scene, he is found still declaiming instead of reasoning.

(32) "Then only could the lawfulness of this fast result-in death be admitted, **when it would be demonstrated that it is the means, certain, efficacious, necessary, proportionate to achieving national freedom and independence** – in other words, when there **are verified each and all the conditions of indirect voluntary.**"

HIS DEMONSTRATION NOT NEEDED, NOT ENOUGH

(a) What a moralist this Civilta writer is! The demonstration which he now demands, as a condition of admitting that the Lord Mayor's hunger-strike was lawful, is **neither sufficient to demonstrate its lawfulness, nor necessary for admission that it is lawful.** First, it is not sufficient. The lawfulness of Mayor MacSwiney's hunger-strike, or of any hunger-strike, could not be admitted even when "each and all" the requirements just enumerated were realizd in it. It could b a means, certain, efficacious, necessary, and proportionate, at the same time that the hunger-striker **intended his own death** either as an end or as a means or as both together. Is it not significant that **nowhere in his article does he even make mention of Mayor MacSwiney's intention**, though he rightly requires, as one of the four conditions for lawful indirect voluntary, that the **intention must be good both as regards end and means.** And he also mentions the intention as one of the three **sources of morality**?

(b) And who, besides the Civilta writer, ever considered, "certain," "efficacious," "necessary" and "proportionate" to be "all the conditions of indirect voluntary?" Did he not say (in section iii) that "the cause or action must be good or at least indifferent?" Yet he does not examine the act of hunger-strike, or seek to determine by any test whether it is **good, indifferent** or **bad** in itself. Acknowledging that Mayor MacSwiney's hunger-strike is a case of indirect voluntary, he solves it without even inquiring whether the essentials from end or means are verified or not. "Means **certain, efficacious, necessary, proportionate** – in other words, each and all the conditions of indirect voluntary." What theology!

(c) Again, the impossible demonstration which the Civilta writer demands, is **not necessary** in order to admit that Mayor MacSwiney's hunger-strike was lawful. The writer himself admits that **the act** of hunger-strike until death is **not intrinsically bad.** Second, he does not challenge the Lord Mayor's **intention** with regard to either **end or means**, and this is an implicit acknowledgment that the Lord Mayor's **intention was good.** It is only at the **production** of the good effect, and its **proportion** to the ill effect, that his batteries are levelled. On these considerations he hangs all his quibbles. What was that good effect which (1) must be **certainly produced**, and (2) must be **proportionate** to the Lord Mayor's death? "The Civilta writer's answer is: In our case, the good effect desired, through the voluntary fast, is the autonomy, the liberty of Ireland."

PROPORTION FROM GOOD GAINED, NOT "DESIRED"

Notice that he says **the good effect "desired"** through the voluntary fast—"l'effetto buono che si viole ottenere." Why does he not say, "the good effect intended," instead of the good effect "desired." The proportion of good effect necessary for the lawfulness of an action producing an ill effect, is not measured by the agents desire but by his intention. His desires may reach to the stars. His intention is restricted to the limited means of his disposal. And it is the intention, not the desire, that is a source of the morality of all human actions. Why then does the Civilta writer speak of the good effect "desired," when the issue is the good effect "intended"?

THEN DESIRED. NOW "DESIRED AND NECESSARY"

And a moment later, the writer passes, suddenly and surreptitiously, from merely "desired," to "desired and necessary." He says that the act of hunger-strike, in order to be lawful, must be proportionate to attaining "national liberty and independence." Is not this to say that "national liberty and independence" is necessary for due proportion of good effect? The author's position is that Mayor MaSwiney's hunger-strike would have to be capable of attaining national liberty and independence, and would, in addition, have to be proven such, before its lawfulness could be admitted. This is his major premise. His suppressed minor premise and conclusion are that all this cannot be demonstrated, and therefore the lawfulness of the Lord Mayor's act cannot be admitted.

DEMONSTRATION ALREADY IN WRITER'S HANDS

But isn't it ludicrous to find the writer insisting, in the very last paragraph of his article, that the lawfulness of Mayor MacSwiney's hunger-strike has not been, and cannot be demonstrated. It has been already pointed out that "Studies" contained, in its number of Sept. 1920, the very demonstration which the Civilta writer declares impossible. It was there demonstrated that all the requisites for a lawful hunger-strike were verified in the MacSwiney fast unto death. That article—by Fr. Patrick Gannon, S.J., Professor of Theology in the Jesuit Scholasticate at Miltown Park, Dublin—was in the Civilta writer's hands when he wrote his own article. While examining the arguments of MacSwiney's defenders, he cites the reasoning of Suarez and Lessius, introduced by Fr. Gannon, and by no one else.

Though daring much, he does not dare to say that these arguments prove nothing. It is a little less untrue and less impolitic to say that they "prove very little," and so he says it. But do not the arguments of Suarez and Lessius rightly assert that the obligation to preserve one's own life is not a negative precept, always binding, but a positive precept, admitting exceptions? And does not this argument prove that it is sometimes lawful to omit preserving one's own life (by food), in other words, that hunger-strike until death is not unlawful from its object – the first of the three sources of morality. Is this to "prove very little"?

"ALTOGETHER DIFFERENT" SUBTERFUGE!

It is in a vain effort to escape the cogency of this proof that the Civilta writer sets up his cry of "altogether different from ours." The correctness of that argument, and the truth of its conclusion, being beyond challenge, nothing remains for him except to challenge its application. And so he exclaims:

> "This case is altogether different from ours. It is "the case of one who has been justly condemned to "the penalty of death and that by starvation. But, in "our case there is no human law which imposes the "hunger-strike."

To which we answer:

> "Not altogether different. Different as to intention "and circumstances – with which Fr. Gannon was not "then concerned – but not different as to object, whose "intrinsic goodness (or indifference) he was then con-"cerned to prove, and did effectively prove, by the "argument of Suarez and Lessius."

STILL CLAMORS FOR DEMONSTRATION

It should be further noticed that it is on the strength of that argument that the writer himself acknowledges that "voluntary fast is not an act intrinsically bad." Why does he recognize the conclusion, while refusing to recognize its connection with the only premises from which it can be derived? He does so in order to be able to tell his readers, with at least a semblance of truth, that the arguments of Suarez and Lessius "prove very little." And while actually perpetrating that crime against Theology, against the readers of the Civilta, against Mayor MacSwiney and Ireland, the writer clamors for demonstration. "Then only could the lawfulness of this fast resulting in death be admitted, when it could be demonstrated that it is a means, certain, efficacious, necessary, proportionate to attaining national liberty and independence!"

As already pointed out (No. 32) this proposition is fantastic and false. The author's contention is that unless Mayor MacSwiney's hunger-strike could certainly achieve the autonomy of Ireland, it would be unlawful. In his effort to discover a good effect which, while superabundantly proportionate, would be impossible of realization, he passed over none except the bridging of chaos. Would every good effect short of the "autonomy, the liberty of Ireland," lack due proportion to the loss of the Lord Mayor's life? Antecedently to every good effect for his country, there resulted to Mayor MacSwiney himself the benefit of protest against the injustice of his arrest and trial and imprisonment. Would the Civilta writer call this good effect "insufficient"? And when, to this personal benefit to the Lord Mayor himself, there was added a measure of new impetus to the national movement for Irish independence, and a new sympathy from all the nations, would the Civilta writer insist that this aggregate of good effects was still insufficient to compensate for the loss of a single life? Was there no good effect short of "the autonomy, the liberty of Ireland" that could justify Mayor MacSwiney's death?

USES FALSE STATEMENT OF MAYOR'S PURPOSE

The writer begins with a false statement of fact, and then uses that false statement as a stepping-stone to a false conclusion. He first says falsely that "the autonomy, the liberty of Ireland" was the good effect "desired" through the voluntary fast of the Lord Mayor. That statement, like every false statement, was made gratuitously. The writer hadn't a shred of evidence that the liberty of Ireland was, as a matter of fact, the objective of Mayor MacSwiney. And isn't it irresponsible and even unprincipled discussion to make such an assertion about so grave an issue, without any grounds whatever! Where in the public press did he read, where on any public platform did he hear that "the autonomy, the liberty of Ireland" was the good effect "desired" through the hunger-strike of Terence MacSwiney? Such an assertion does small credit to the Lord Mayor's sense of proportion. He was a victim of no illusions about the liberty of Ireland as the goal of his hunger-strike. He aimed primarily to protest against his own unjust arrest and trial and sentence. His secondary aim was to cooperate with thousands of others, striving, in various ways, to achieve "the liberty of Ireland."

What purpose did the author have in thus flagrantly misstating the aims of the Lord Mayor? By **falsifying the good effect which MacSwiney intended – and did actually attain – he substitutes a good effect antecedently impossible, and thus invents a reason for pronouncing the Lord Mayor's action unlawful.** It is easier now to see the trend of his "indisputable consideration" (No. 14) that **"the cause – the action – must be capable of producing the good effect."**

AND NOW HIS "INDISPUTABLE CONSIDERATIONS"

Having **falsely** stated the objectives of Mayor MacSwiney's hunger-strike, the stage is now ready for the reappearance of the writer's "indisputable considerations"– (1) the **capability** of the action to **produce**, (2) **with certainty**, the good effect, (3) otherwise unobtainable. Now, the author says in No. 14 that these "indisputable considerations" were intended **to throw further light on the above mentioned conditions**, i.e. the familiar requisites from **end, means** and **proportion of good**, that an action may be lawful though producing an ill effect. In the present citation he nonchalantly calls his "indisputable considerations" **"all the before-mentioned conditions of indirect voluntary."**

PURPOSE PURPOSELY IMPOSSIBLE TO ATTAIN

The author says he does not see that his "indisputable considerations" are realized in the MacSwiney case, and by this he means that **he sees they are not** realized. **Small wonder** he should see that they are not realized! **Did he not purposely make them impossible to realize –"the autonomy, the liberty of Ireland"!!** Nor is it surprising that the author **does not attempt to evaluate the evidence and state the reasons why he does not see.** When he had fixed the object of Mayor MacSwiney's hunger-strike to be "the autonomy, the liberty of Ireland," all weighing of evidence and assigning of reasons was at an end.

HE SUMS UP AND SOLVES THE MacSWINEY CASE

Here the writer sums up and solves the MacSwiney case thus: **"MacSwiney's hunger-strike until death was unlawful for the two following reasons: first, because his hunger-strike was incapable of attaining the 'national liberty and independence' of Ireland, and, secondly, because 'the autonomy, the liberty of Ireland' could have been attained without the loss of a single life."** The author's **absurdly false** assertion that the "national liberty and independence" of Ireland was the Lord Mayor's aim and object, does but make **more false** and **absurd** his further assertion that Ireland's independence **could then or now be realized without any sacrifice of life.**

Moreover, it does not seem to have occurred to the writer that if his second "reason"–"How many are the means," etc.– were true, his first "reason" would be superfluous. It is fundamental that an action producing an ill effect is forbidden if the good effect be otherwise obtainable. Thus would the writer be spared the ludicrous machination of making Ireland's independence the actual object of Mayor MacSwiney's hunger-strike, and necessary to justify his death.

The tribunal of the Civilta writer has completed its findings. Nothing now remains for him to do except to pronounce the fatal verdict. That he now does.

(33) "Until this be demonstrated, we shall, in conclusion, "say with St. Thomas (l.c.): 'An action placed with "a good intention, may nevertheless be unlawful, by "being incapable of producing the good effect in-"tended'."

"WITH ST. THOMAS" HE STATES FATAL VERDICT

(a) Thus ends the article of the Civilta writer. He has been, in turn, prosecutor, judge and jury, during the public trial of Mayor MacSwiney. In the course of his article he repeatedly invoked the authority of St. Thomas. Now, at the conclusion, he would make his readers believe that the Angelic Doctor endorses the sentence and applauds the execution. "Until this be demonstrated, we say, with St. Thomas," etc. Was St. Thomas aware that he was represented as sanctioning the low travesty on Moral Theology which the Civilta writer perpetrates at every stage of the article we are reviewing? If so, his beatitude must have suffered at least a momentary interruption.

OPPONENTS' PRETENSE OF ORTHODOXY

Throughout this hunger-strike controversy, it has been the favorite practice of those who condemned Mayor MacSwiney, to array on their side the great Masters and Schools of Theology. When the article on hunger-strike, in "The Examiner" (Bombay), was wreaking with falsehoods and fallacies, the writer kept piously telling his readers what he found, and what he did not find, in "the standard theological schools." "I cannot remember a single case in Moral Theology," etc. "I have never found theologians justifying any case analogous," etc. "Which, as far as I can see, has never been done by the standard theological schools." And, similarly, the Civilta writer! Whatever he says, he makes it a point to say "with St. Thomas"–"con S. Tomasso." And he is particularly careful to say, in conclusion, with St. Thomas: "An action placed with a good intention may, nevertheless, be unlawful by being incapable of producing the good effect intended." Notice that St. Thomas does not say with the writer, "the good effect DESIRED." He says "the good effect INTENDED."

CASE SOLVED BY REASON, NOT BY AUTHORITY

(b) But if the diplomacy employed by the Civilta writer is questionable, his statement itself is imbecile – a worthy sequel to all that went before. With as much meaning, that is to say, with as little meaning, might he have said: "Until the MacSwiney hunger-strike is demonstrated to be lawful, we shall say with St. Thomas that good is to be done and evil is to be avoided." Independently of what has or has not been proved, can or cannot be proved, regarding any hunger-strike, we all say with St. Thomas: "An action placed with a good intention may nevertheless be unlawful by being incapable of producing the good effect intended." The evident truth of that general principle is not conditioned or restricted by the demonstration which the writer speaks of, nor indeed by any other antecedent requirement. The principle which St. Thomas states is universal and universally true, and therefore excludes the "until" of the Civilta writer and every other "until."

STATING TRUE MAJOR IMPLYING FALSE MINOR

(c) The citation we are considering also exemplifies another favorite practice of others who wrote against Mayor MacSwiney's hunger-strike – the practice of stating a true major proposition in such a way as to imply a false minor premise regarding the Lord Mayor's act. Thus do they establish their readers in a false conclusion, while escaping responsibility for having openly asserted it. "Willing to wound and yet afraid to strike." They are, one and all, very willing, indeed very anxious, to attach a foul imputation on the name and memory of Mayor MacSwiney, yet afraid to be caught in the act of doing it openly. And so they insinuate it instead, as the Civilta writer now does when he states, as his major premise, the true principle of St. Thomas – that "an action placed with a good intention may nevertheless be unlawful because incapable of producing the effect intended,"– and thus leads his readers into the false minor premise that the Lord Mayor's action was incapable of producing the effect intended, and the false conclusion that his hunger-strike was therefore unlawful.

> "Damn with faint praise, assent with civil leer,
> "And, without sneering, teach the rest to sneer,"

Here ends our review of the Civilta article. That article occupies eleven pages of standard magazine size – eleven shuffling, wriggling, juggling pages!

SEE HOW HE ARRIVED AT HIS FATAL CONCLUSION

It is not the few things which, here or elsewhere in his article, the writer says truly, with St. Thomas, that are in any opposition to the MacSwiney hunger-strike, but rather the many things which he says falsely, without St. Thomas. Reviewing our review of his article, we find, by a sum in simple addition, that he has perpetrated on his readers TWENTY-SIX WRONG EXPLANATIONS,(a) FIVE CONTRADICTORY EXPLANATIONS,(b) FOUR ABSURDITIES,(c) TWO FALSE-PARALLELS,(d) THREE TAUTOLOGIES,(e) TWELVE EVASIONS,(f) EIGHTEEN FALSE STATEMENTS OF FACT,(g) NINE FALSE DENIALS,(h) SEVEN FALSE ASSUMPTIONS,(i) TWO FALSE PROTESTATIONS,(j) FIVE WRONG CONCLUSIONS,(k) AND ELEVEN WRONG DEFINITIONS.(l)

HIS LONG LIST OF CRIMES AGAINST THEOLOGY

Surely this is a long list of crimes against theological truth. Two from among them might, in particular, be singled out as exceptionally revolting to the impartial reader, in that they are more designedly directed to deceive on points of greater moment. The first is the author's refusal to recognize, nay even his futile effort to conceal from his readers, the principle – invoked by Suarez and Lessius – that it is sometimes lawful to omit preservation (by food or otherwise) of one's own life – the principle which has been, from the beginning, and must continue to be until the end, the justification of every noblest, every holiest sacrifice of one's own life, whether for faith or charity or patriotism or friendship or any other worthy motive.

The author's second flagrant crime against theology is the preposterous statement that the aim and object, necessary for the justification of Mayor MacSwiney's hunger-strike, was "the autonomy, the liberty of Ireland," and

---

(a) See Nos. 6. 7. 8. 9. 10 13. 14. 23. 24. 25 . 26. 28. 30. 32

(b) " " 6. 14. 15. 25. 26
(c) " " . . 4. 5. 6
(d) " " 11
(e) " " . . . 3. 12
(f) " " . 15. 16. 17. 18 . 19. 20. 21. 22 . 28. 30. 31. 33

(g) See Nos. 1. 4. 16. 17. 18 20. 21. 23. 24. 25 26. 27. 28 .

(h) " " 15. 16. 17. 18. 23
(i) " " 1. 27. 28. 29 .
(j) " " 2. 3 . . . .
(k) " " 23. 26. 31. 32 .
(l) " " 1. 4. 5. 6 . . 7. 8. 12 . .

that, moreover, this autonomy and liberty could, in the then existing circumstances, have been attained by any one of several other means, without the loss of a single life. What recognition, what confidence does a writer deserve who behaves thus in solving a case in Moral Theology wherein the immortal glory or the immortal shame, not only of MacSwiney himself but of his race and nation, was at stake? In the light of such behaviour, it is charity to refrain from calling the writer's opening protest against partiality, by the name it deserves.

OUTRAGE ON THEOLOGY AND ON PAGAN JUSTICE

At the beginning of this review we said that the author, like all the opponents of the MacSwiney hunger-strike, entered upon his task not because he had something to write but because he had to write something. Is not this charge amply substantiated by the false protestations, and false statements of fact, and false principles, and false definitions, and false parallels, and ambiguities, and absurdities, and contradictions in which his article abounds! We also called that article "lame, limping theology." Is this too much? It is not half enough! The composition of the Civilta writer is an outrage on theology, and an outrage even on pagan justice. As has been already remarked, such unprincipled discussion of a grave question involving the cherished interests of millions of loyal Catholics, and the still more precious interests of theological truth, utterly disredits the author and deprives his article of every claim to recognition. That article is not published over any signature, and thus the author's identity is known only to the editors of the Civilta Cattolica. But while the fact that the publication was anonymous does not in the least dispense the writer from the obligations of honest and honorable controversy, it does transfer to the shoulders of the said editors a large measure of responsibility for the article's contents.

REACHED THE REPUTABLE CIVILTA. HOW?

Indeed the article would have received but scant recognition from its present reviewer were it not that it found its way, in some inexplicable manner, into the pages of the reputable "Civilta Cattolica." The propagandist methods of those most interested in condemning Mayor MacSwiney are notorious. But it is beyond conception that they should succeed in enlisting, as part of their nefarious system, this ancient and irreproachable periodical, dedicated to the cause of truth, and most of all to the cause of theological truth, at the fountain-head of theological truth – the City Eternal.

Chapter Twenty Two

SOME OBJECTORS AND THEIR OBJECTIONS

"THE EXAMINER," BOMBAY, INDIA
(Editorials, Jan. 8 and 15, 1921)

SYNTHESIS OF ALL PREVIOUS FALLACIES

Pope Pius X called Modernism "a synthesis of all the heresies." The Examiner's article on Mayor MacSwiney's hunger-strike is a synthesis of all the fallacies previously conjured up to prove it suicide, and supplemented by a goodly number of fallacies of its own inventing. Like the Civilta article, it professes, at the very outset, to want impartial thinking, and begins its article with this protestation to that effect:

(1) "The Examiner has a rather irritating way of keep-"ing silence on a current controversy while excite-"ment is on, and tackling it only after feeling has "died away, and people are in a position to think "impartially."

This is admirable. Whoever reads even a few of the numerous articles on Mayor MacSwiney's hunger-strike – published principally in Catholic periodicals – will readily recognize that, in many instances, Catholic truths were violently distorted to suit the partisanship of the contending writers.

But impartiality is easier to profess than to practice. After an explicit protestation of impartiality in the first paragraph, The Examiner says in the second:

(2) "MacSwiney had pitted his determination against "the Government, and the Government bucked up and "stood firm and held its own. The defeat of Mac-"Swiney is then converted into a victory, by calling "him a martyr."

HOW "IMPARTIAL" THIS BEGINNING!

This is an inauspicious beginning. It does not sound very impartial. The wolf in the fable said to the lamb: "How dare you disturb the water which I am drinking." "Impossible," replied the lamb, "since the stream flows from you to me." "Two years ago you slandered me," subsumed the wolf. "Impossible," reiterated the lamb, "for I was not born then." "Well," concluded the wolf, "it was your father then or some other of your relations." And he then and there seized the innocent lamb and tore him to pieces! The wolf "bucked up and stood firm and held its own."

The victory of brute violence was his. But the moral victory was the lamb's. And it was also MacSwiney's. "He has won his battle," was the verdict of the Westminster Gazette. And the secular press of the entire world recorded scores of similar verdicts. The consensus of humanity is that what The Examiner calls the Lord Mayor's "defeat," was in reality, his victory.

And now The Examiner makes a gesture of seeming defense of Mayor MacSwiney.

> (3) "We had admitted two pleas which might possibly "exonerate the Mayor from the guilt of suicide."

"PLEAS WHICH MIGHT POSSIBLY EXONERATE"

(a) Here we find that distinguished periodical already raising the cry of "suicide." "The Ethics of Hunger-Striking" is the title for the article we are reviewing. The entire purpose of the article, as indicated by its title, is to discuss and decide the complicated question whether Mayor MacSwiney's hunger-strike until death was suicidal or not, and if not suicidal, whether it was lawful or not. But to enter a "plea" for the Lord Mayor in the very first column of its article is to take his guilt for granted – to assume that his act was suicide. This fallacy of taking for granted, at the very beginning, the thing which the writer proposes to prove, and towards the close of his article claims to have proved – this fallacy is known to Logic as "petitio principii," or "begging the question." No man enters a plea for conduct which he judges to be in every way lawful. A plea has place only when an accused person has done something certainly unlawful and is convicted for it. A plea is an extenuating argument, and extenuation presupposes guilt. Such plea is directed to extenuate the guilt by modifying either the intention of the agent or the circumstances of his act. But the plea always takes for granted that the action itself is unlawful. And The Examiner, by introducing a "plea," ingeniously takes Mayor MacSwiney's guilt for granted, just when he sets out to establish it.

PLEAS CREATE PRESUMPTION OF GUILT

(b) "Two pleas which might possibly exonerate." This is heartless pleading! A master effort to exonerate Lord Mayor MacSwiney is not likely to follow that "might possibly" preamble. To say that the accused "might possibly" be innocent is to say that there is the strongest presumption of his guilt. If the presiding judge were to say, in open court, and before any testimony had been heard, that the prisoner might possibly be innocent, it would rightly be considered an effort to prejudice the jury against him. It is for the court to prove its charge against the accused, and not begin the trial by taking his guilt for granted and obliging him to prove his innocence. Now The Examiner has summoned Mayor MacSwiney into court. It is itself both presiding judge and prosecuting attorney; its readers are the jurors, and it tells them at the very beginning of the trial that "two pleas might possibly exonerate the Mayor from the guilt of suicide."

As to The Examiner's "two pleas," they are worthless. It claimed too much for them when it said that they "might possibly" exonerate. They could not exonerate nor even extenuate, if the Lord Mayor's conduct needed either exoneration or extenuation. Here are the "two pleas."

(4) "First came his hope and expectation that he would "not die, because the Government would yield and "order his release."

HOPE AND EXPECTATION NO PLEA, NO PROSPECT

(a) A plea can extenuate the guilt of an agent only by modifying one or more of the sources from which his unlawful act derives its morality. Imperfect deliberation makes an act of homicide, manslaughter instead of murder, and the circumstance of extreme necessity minimizes or entirely eliminates the guilt of taking what belongs to another. Now The Examiner's "hope and expectation," since they are only subjective mental states, could not modify the Lord Mayor's act or its circumstances. If they were to modify anything it could only be his intention to persevere in his hunger-strike even to death. Did they do so? The Lord Mayor's inflexible perseverance to the end shows that they did not. If, therefore, The Examiner's "hope and expectation" modified neither the Lord Mayor's act, its circumstances or his intention, it is in no sense a plea. The guilt or innocence of the Lord Mayor is unaffected by it.

(b) That "hope and expectation" could become a plea for the Lord Mayor, only by eliminating altogether his intention of persevering in hunger-strike until death. For, according to The Examiner's false assumption that the Lord Mayor's act was objectively suicidal, he contracted the entire guilt of suicide the very first instant that he intended hunger-strike until death, and before he had yet refused a single meal. But again the facts show that the Lord Mayor's intention was unaltered throughout, and that his "hope and expectation," if such existed, were entirely compatible with that unaltered determination. What then becomes of The Examiner's "plea" on the score of the Lord Mayor's "hope and expectation that he would not die?" The writer seems to use it **rather as a vehicle to insinuate his false assumption that Mayor MacSwiney's act was suicidal.** That it was no plea must have been very patent to him.

(c) From the very beginning the Lord Mayor was ready for the worst. Determination, not "hope and expectation," was then his master passion. He was well aware of the circumstances and surroundings in which he found himself, and he understood full well how scant were the grounds they held out to him for "hope and expectation." Did he not say to the Bishop of Cork, at the very beginning of his hunger-strike: "My death will be an example and an appeal for our young men to make every sacrifice for Ireland."

(5) "Secondly, even if he did die, **he might be imbued with a conviction that he was justified in doing so.**"

INVINCIBLE IGNORANCE IMPLIES EVIL ACTION

(a) "He might be imbued with a conviction." "Might be" and "might possibly" are conspicuous phrases in The Examiner's **affected effort to exonerate the Lord Mayor.** This is its nearest approach to a categorical affirmation of Mayor MacSwiney's innocence. But pleas are entered, **not on grounds of what might be or might possibly be,** but on the more realistic grounds of what **had been** or **has been or is.**

(b) The writer says that the Lord Mayor "might be imbued with a conviction that he was justified in doing so," and, by so saying, **implies that such a conviction, if it existed, was erroneous.** Thus he once more assumes the Lord Mayor's guilt, **even in the very act of pretended exculpation of him.** "It is suicide," says the writer, "**though the Mayor might be wrongly convinced that it is not.**" This is the plea of "invincible ignorance," a plea which does not fit the case at all. Invincible ignorance is invoked as a plea only where it is **certain and evident that the act is objectively wrong, and therefore forbidden, but the agent has no means of knowing that it is.** But this is the very point which the writer **implies and supposes** at every step, but does not, will not, cannot **prove.** His second plea does but reiterate **the false assumption insinuated in his first plea. He begs the question a second time.** Fortunately for the Irish hunger-strikers their conduct **needed no "pleas" from The Examiner or anyone else.** It was its own vindication.

(6) "It is not our intention to drift into a political con-
"troversy over the question whether Ireland is at
"war or in rebellion."

AFFECTS AVOIDING POLITICAL CONTROVERSY

Why does the writer avoid or evade this "political controversy?" Mayor MacSwiney's hunger-strike was part of the Revolution of the Irish people against the authority of England. If that Revolution was unlawful, so was the Lord Mayor's hunger-strike. And it was certainly unlawful if it was rebellion and not legitimate warfare.

But while professing to avoid political controversy, the writer enters it in the same paragraph. He writes:

(7) "Even a usurping power, unjustly annexing a coun-
"try, can acquire legitimate rulership by prescrip-
"tion, i.e. by a period of pacific possession. Outbreaks
"at frequent intervals prevented the English pos-
"session of Ireland from being altogether pacific.
"The question would have to be settled by historians
"combined with theologians whether these recurring
"revolts were sufficient to invalidate the English
"claim of prescriptive rights."

NO PEACEFUL ACQUIESCENCE IN ENGLISH RULE

Not every pacific possession over a lengthy period confers a legitimate title. If it sometimes does so, it is because it tacitly expresses the voluntary surrender of their exclusive rights by the previous possessors. And when does such undisputed occupancy express such voluntary surrender? Only where those previous possessors are free to contest the occupancy, yet do not choose to contest it. If, though wishing to challenge the occupation, they were, for some reason, unable to do so, such occupation, however long and peaceful, could never confer a lawful title. Compulsory acquiescence is far removed from voluntary surrender.

Only such pacific possession, then, as bespeaks voluntary surrender of exclusive rights, can ever confer a legitimate title. Did Irishmen ever voluntarily surrender to England their incontestable right to govern themselves? Did they ever freely acquiesce in England's government of their country? It can be demonstrated historically that they did not. "England," wrote George Creel, "holds title in Ireland only by armed occupation. Ireland never yielded the voluntary submission without which the sovereign independence of a nation does not and cannot pass." This the writer himself partially acknowledges when he says that "outbreaks occurring at frequent intervals prevented England's possession from being altogether pacific." The whole truth is that it was never pacific in any proper sense. Frequency or infrequency of revolt is not the sole test of whether a nation's submission to alien rule is voluntary or not. During the entire period between each revolt and the one succeeding it, the whole of Ireland was seething with discontent, living continually on the verge of revolt, and restrained from it only by military occupations, repressions and coercions. When The Examiner's "historians combined with theologians" come to settle this question of prescriptive rights, it is the measure of ineradicable discontent among the people of Ireland, and not his "revolts" or the absence of them that must decide the issue. They were prevented from revolting by rifles and bayonets.

> (8) "Speaking broadly, I think the consensus of civilized "humanity for at least a century back, would be "that Ireland had become and was an integral part "of the British dominions; that the English King "and Parliament was its legitimate ruler, and that "revolt against the existing authority was rebellion "and not war."

AFFECTS CONSENSUS OF CIVILIZED HUMANITY

What meaning has the writer's "speaking broadly"? Whatever he intended it to mean, in the present context it means "speaking incorrectly." A moment ago he said that "the question would have to be settled by historians combined with theologians." Now, within the same paragraph, he dispenses with the services of both, and settles the question himself – hands down to his readers his decision that the English King and Parliament are Ireland's legitimate rulers, and that this has been the consensus of civilized humanity for at least a century past.

Here is his way of avoiding political controversy and 'tis an easy way. When he would persuade his readers that something is true which, in reality, is false, he sets out by complacently assuming its truth. In the present question assuming is for him an easier task than proving. He began his article by falsely assuming that Mayor MacSwiney's hunger-strike was suicide, and then affected an effort to exonerate him. Now he falsely assumes that England's title to govern Ireland is legitimate, and follows, in quick succession, with another assumption equally false – that this has been the verdict of civilized humanity for at least a century past. But he does it by "speaking broadly."

MAKES NO ATTEMPT TO PROVE THAT CONSENSUS

Fortunate indeed is he who can rightly claim the consensus of civilized humanity for his side of any dispute. He has an ally that is irresistable. But the writer is not so fortunate. He claims for his contention the consensus of civilized humanity, but does nothing to establish his calim. He has at his disposal no machine that automatically registers the consensus of civilized humanity for the information of his readers. He gives no statistics, nor does he cite a single authority to substantiate his unprecedented contention. He simply says so. It was for him to prove the consensus he asserts and not for the friends of Ireland to disprove it, though their's were a much easier undertaking than his.

CONTRADICTED BY MANY ENGLISH AUTHORITIES

Omitting a goodly number of other reliable authorities on this subject, the writer's own countryman, **Gilbert Keith Chesterton** – a name and man of great weight – wrote this of Ireland's relation to England: "If Ireland is not a nation there is no such thing as a nation – France is not a nation, England is not a nation. Any Englishman of any party, with any proposal, may well clear his mind of cant about this preliminary question." ("Truth," New York, March, 1921.)

CHESTERTON, BELLOC, "LA VICTOIRE"

Again, Hilaire Belloc – another of the writer's enlightened countrymen and, like Mr. Chesterton, a historian – wrote in his "History of England" (11, 219): "Unless we understand Ireland's stern opposition to feudalism, we cannot understand the vigor of the Irish resistance to the Reformation; of the Irish national survival, active and aggressive, right into the Seventeenth Century; of the determination, in spite of massacre and wholesale dispossession, to re-arise, and, after three or four generations, in our own time, recover a nationhood which had been driven under the surface." And, on the death of Mayor MacSwiney, the French newspaper "La Victoire" said: "Can our English friends not pay too dearly for the defiance they are hurling at the Irish Nation, for the fact is clear today – there is an Irish Nation." How does all this harmonize with the writer's consensus of civilized humanity regarding England's prescriptive right to govern Ireland? There is a natural infallibility attaching to the verdict of civilized humanity, which protects it against rendering its consensus to things that are not so.

RIGHT ACQUIRED MAY AFTERWARDS BE LOST

But even if, contrary to fact, we suppose the prescriptive right in question, the writer, skilled in distinctions, is well aware that it is one thing to acquire a prescriptive right, and quite another to retain it. The legitimate right of a nation to rule a people which it has subjugated, **may be lost by a tyrannical exercise of that right**. In the article we are reviewing, the writer himself makes that admission in reference to England's method of governing Ireland. These are his words:

(9) "Rebellion, even against a legitimate ruler, **is justified when the government is absolutely unjust, tyrannical and intolerable to the nation as a whole**. . . . The English government of Ireland **in past centuries has been abominable**."

The writer here furnishes the major and minor propositions, and his readers may easily draw the conclusion. He distinguishes, however:

(10) "**It can be questioned** whether these epithets could be applied to the rule of the country **in recent generations**."

Unquestionably abominable in past centuries, in recent generations, **questionably abominable** – this is the writer's own summing up of English rule in Ireland, **and it is a terrible summary**. Questionably abominable "for at least a century back" is the utmost measure of endorsement which, even in his most daring mood, he dares demand for his country's behaviour toward Ireland. This is damning with faint praise.

"NO BLACKER, FOULER EPISODE IN HISTORY"

But, what is still worse, even the faint praise is undeserved. England's nineteenth century regime in Ireland was just as abominable as that of every other century. It opened with the notorious "Act of Union," which Lord Byron called "the union of the shark with its prey," and of which Gladstone said, that, "it has no moral force;" that "it rests on no moral basis;" that "there is no blacker or fouler transaction in the history of man." And what about **the Insurrection of 1803**, led by Robert Emmett, and the movement which, a quarter of a century later, **achieved Catholic Emancipation by the alternative of another revolution**? What about the "Repeal of the Union" movement which assembled two million men and women at a monster meeting on the Hill of Tara, on August 15, 1843, **to protest against the** "wholesale corruption," "wholesale bribery," "unblushing intimidation," "fraud and force"– these are Gladstone's epithets – by which the "Union" was achieved. What about the Insurrection of **the Young Irelanders in** "Forty-eight," under Smith O'Brien, and **the Fenian Insurrection in 1867?**

What about the "Black Famine" of 1846 which cost Ireland two millions of its people? G. K. Chesterton accuses the British Prime Minister of "publicly refusing to stop the famine by the use of British ships," and of positively spreading it "by making the half-starved population pay for the starved ones." And he adds that the well-known verdict of coroners' juries –"murder by Lord John Russell"– "was not only the verdict of Irish public opinion but is the verdict of history." ("The Crimes of England," pp. 58-60).

1855-1881 – FORTY-FOUR COERCION ACTS

And what about the forty-four coercion acts passed for Ireland by the Parliament of England during the twenty-six years intervening between 1855 and 1881? "There is no such instance in history," wrote Sir Thomas Wyse,– a Unionist Member of Parliament –"of a whole country standing for a series of years on the border of revolution." In the middle of this distracted period, Fr. Richard Clark, S.J., himself a loyal Englishman, wrote: "English Ministers point to the present calm which prevails in Ireland, as an argument in favor of their policy of repression. But it is the calm that forebodes the hurricane. It is the cessation of fevered restlessness, which betokens, not the restoration to health but the outbreak of a fiercer malady."

("My Visit To Distressed Ireland, p. 173.)

Again, David Lloyd George, speaking as Coalition Prime Minister of England said: "Centuries of brutal and often ruthless injustice, and, what is worse, centuries of insolence and insult, have driven hatred of British rule into the very marrow of the Irish race. The long records of oppression, proscription and expatriation, have formed the greatest blot on the British fame of equity and eminence in the realm of government. There remains the invincible fact that today she (Ireland) is no more reconciled to British rule than she was in the days of Cromwell."

(Speech in Parliament, March 7, 1917.)

Yet this is the century which The Examiner singles out as an instance of England's pacific possession and benevolent administration of Ireland, from which it would have its readers draw the conclusion that England has the right to govern Ireland, and Ireland's Revolution of 1916 was unlawful, and with it Mayor MacSwiney's hunger-strike in aid of it. It continues:

(11) "Whether the grievances and disabilities were so "grievous to the nation as a whole – apart from cer- "tain cliques of politicians, journalists and agitators "– as to justify rebellion, is a question which would "first require a close examination of the facts, and "then a close application of theological principles to "decide. We leave the question undiscussed."

SETTLES THE QUESTION BEFORE DISCUSSION

A moment ago, the writer said that, according to the consensus of civilized humanity, the English King and Parliament were Ireland's legitimate rulers. Now he says "the question whether the grievances and disabilities were so grievous to the nation as a whole as to justify rebellion, would first require a close examination of the facts, and then a close application of theological principles." This question-whether the English administration of Ireland was "absolutely unjust and intolerable to the nation as a whole"- he deals with exactly as he did with the question of pacific possession. His attitude towards these two questions is the same in seven particulars. First, he raises both questions; second, he declines to discuss either question, though both are fundamental to the morality of the Irish hunger-strike; third, he refers both questions to "historians combined with theologians;" fourth, he himself decides both questions; fifth, both decisions are in favor of his English claim; sixth in behalf of both decisions he appeals to the consensus of civilized humanity for at least a century past; seventh, in neither case does he attempt to establish that consensus. Of the true consensus of civilized humanity regarding England's right to govern Ireland, a painstaking and painful record is set forth in a long list of "verdicts" some of which are introduced into this volume. The writer gives no record. Unwilling as he was to concede Ireland's right to revolt, and unwilling to discuss that fundamental issue, he was unfitted to discuss the Irish hunger-strike at all. He says "we leave the question undiscussed." And he left the question undiscussed, but not undecided.

But although he will not concede that Ireland is legitimately at war with England, he is willing to "assume it" for the sake of discussion. "Dato sed non concesso" is his position,- an artful loophole to which he may still have recourse after every other avenue of escape from an undesirable conclusion has been closed against him.

* * * * *

And now he proceeds to formulate a method of his own for solving cases of "two effects"- a system which, by its contravention of fundamental morality, psychology and logic, forfeits all claim to be called Catholic. Anticipating, at the outset, the charge of ignoring standard authorities and departing from standard methods, he says apologetically:

(12) "We are not undertaking to prove a thesis, and therefore do not elaborate our article with the citation of authorities."

HIS THESIS THROUGHOUT –"MacSWINEY SUICIDE"

The writer says he was "not undertaking to prove a thesis." That is not true. He had a thesis to prove, and he labored with rare diligence and ingenuity to prove it. He began his article by admitting "two pleas which might possibly exonerate the Mayor from the guilt of suicide." Well aware that his "two pleas" were no pleas at all, he nevertheless, proposes them as the utmost limit of concession. Is not this a thesis! Is not his whole article directed to proving that thesis! Is not his "conclusion" merely a repetition of that thesis! At the close of his article he writes: "The conclusion we arrive at is that deliberate self-starvation contemplated as issuing in death, is an act of direct self-killing; and it is formal suicide, unless you can find some justifying reason for the act." He then denies "emphatically" that such justifying reason can be found in the case of Mayor MacSwiney.

AUTHORITIES MAY WELL BE CITED IN ESSAYS

In what, then, does his article fall short of a thesis? What did he set out to prove, and what is the burden of every page and paragraph of his article except the thesis that the Lord Mayor was a suicide? And still he claims that he is "not undertaking to prove a thesis," and assigns that manifest untruth as his entire reason for omitting from his article all "citation of authorities." In response to this claim of his, it may be asked, in the first place: Is it only a thesis that calls for or admits "citation of authorities?" Since he is unwilling that his article be called a thesis, if it be called instead an essay or dissertation, is the "citation of authorities" debarred from his composition? Secondly, when the reader has finished the present review of his article, he will have discovered the true reason why the writer did not, could not "elaborate his article with the citation of authorities." How was he to cite authorities where every Catholic author living and dead contradicted him! He adds:

(13) "We let our mind go its way, stating principles and "drawing conclusions according to our own judg-"ment."

NO UNLIMITED FREEDOM IN MORAL THEOLOGY

This, like his other numerous protestations, must be taken with a grain of salt. He did let his mind go its way stating principles as true which are absurdly false, and drawing conclusions as legitimate which are preposterously fallacious. And all this he did, not according to his own judgment, as he claims to have done, but according to his wildly partisan prepossessions. The principles, the conclusions and the prepossessions – all distinctively his – are in evidence on every page of his article. Instead of helping his readers to understand the subtle question of hunger-strike, he, like the Civilta writer, seems bent on preventing them from understanding it, or leading them to misunderstand it. He encumbers his article with issues that are altogether irrelevant, and certain to tire, confuse, bewilder and discourage his readers. And this is his apology for doing so.

(14) "The subject has its own interest as a study in ethics, "quite apart from the incident which has given rise "to the discussion. This is why we take a wide range "and cover diversified ground which includes other "questions as well."

"WIDE RANGE, DIVERSIFIED GROUND" IN WEEKLY

This further one of the writer's protestations is not a whit more plausible. The narrow limits of a weekly journal, when treating a subject so comprehensive as the theology of hunger-strike, can ill afford "wide range" and "diversified ground." His "wide range" and "diversified ground" had been used to better advantage in discussing prescriptive right and benevolent administration, instead of arbitrarily assuming them. Neither will the reader, after having concluded his study of that tangled question, have, for the time being, either leisure or inclination for "other questions" or further "study in ethics." All the same, the writer insists that his discussion of Mayor MacSwiney's hunger-strike begin "ab ovo" with the definition of a human act.

(15) "An 'actus humanus' is defined as 'actus deliberatus "cum cognitione finis'; and the 'finis' referred to is "the 'finis operis,' the effect issuing straight from the "act itself."

(a) Of the many who wrote on the MacSwiney hunger-strike, no one except the writer felt any need of defining a human act in order to settle that case. It is the science of Psychology that analyses and defines a human act. The ethical subtleties involved in the question of hunger-strike are sufficiently confusing, without superadded subtleties from Psychology.

EXPLAINS DEFINITION OF ST. THOMAS WRONGLY

Thus far the political side of MacSwiney's hunger-strike has been the subject of the author's prevarications. The remainder of his essay is made up of distortions and perversions of every fundamental principle of Ethics involved in the question he is discussing.

If a human act must be defined, why does the author tamper with its definition by St. Thomas, **to the extent of giving a wrong explanation of it?** Gury-Ballerini says that the "cum cognitione finis" of St. Thomas means "**with full advertence to the good or evil of the action,**" that is to say, with full advertence **to all three sources of its morality.*** And Sabetti-Barrett says, still more explicitly, that the "cum cognitione finis" of the definition means "**with full knowledge of the object, intention and circumstances**" of the action.** The Examiner says that the same "cum cognitione finis" means with knowledge of the action's morality **from object alone** – from the "finis operis" only. **Very falsely does he say:** "The 'finis' referred to (by St. Thomas) is the 'finis operis,' the effect issuing straight from the action itself." This is to say that knowledge of the finis operis alone – to the exclusion of intention and circumstances – **is sufficient for the imputability of any and every human act.**

Nor is he yet done with the excluding. He speaks of the "EFFECT" issuing straight from the action itself, though, in the case he is discussing, two EFFECTS issue straight from the action itself. He **disposes of its good effect by ignoring it.**

FINIS, OBJECT, SUBJECT, EXTERNAL ACT

Notice that "finis" may mean either (1) the **object – term**, **effect –** of an action, or (2) the **intention – aim, end, purpose, objective –** to which the agent ordains the action, or (3) the **external action itself**, as being **the effect of a previous internal act of willing it.**

Furthermore, "object" implies "subject." They are **correlatives.** An agent wanting something, and acting to attain it, is the "**subject.**" That something which the agent acts to attain, is the "**object.**" It is called "**object**" because it is **some good** or other to be **acquired by the agent.** It is called "**end**" because its possession **ends desiring and striving** for it. The action whereby the object is attained – the external act – is the **proximate object of the internal act of** willing it.

OBJECTIVE OF ACTION. OBJECTIVE OF AGENT

There are several kinds of "finis" or "objective," and the idea of a **good to be attained and satisfy,** runs through them all.

---

*"Actus humanus est actus procedens a voluntate libera, cum "advertentia ad bonitatem vel malitiam actus."

"Voluntarum est actus procedens a voluntate illuminata ab "intellectuali cognitone singulorum, **nempe objecti, finis et circumstantiarum."

I. "Finis operis" (the objective of an action) is the co-natural effect of the action itself. An act of almsgiving, by its nature relieves the poor, whether the objective of the donor be charity or pride or politics. The "finis operis" is not a "finis" proper, but only by analogy. An action cannot properly be said to have a "finis" or objective. The "finis operis," since it is not desirable for itself, is not strictly and properly a "finis" atall, but rather a means-medium ad finem. It is a "finis" only figuratively – by analogy with the "finis operantis," which is desirable for itself, and therefore strictly and properly a "finis." Only an intelligent agent is capable of conceiving an end, or purpose as such, and acting to attain it.

II. "Finis operantis" (the objective of the agent). It may be the same as the objective of the action, or different from it. The objective of the agent giving alms, may or may not be to relieve distress of the poor. It is ultimate or proximate according as it is an end itself or only a means to some end or other.

"OBJECT," "OBJECTIVE," "DIRECT," "INDIRECT"!

Readers should by this time be sufficiently warned regarding the terms "end," "object" and "objective." In one paragraph they may mean exactly the same thing, and in the next, things entirely different. It is unfortunate that the two principal sources of morality should ever have been called "object" and "end"–"objectum" et "finis"– which so often mean exactly the same obscure something, whereas the terms "end" and "means," bearing, as they do, a reciprocal relation to each other, clearly specify those same sources and distinguish them from each other.

"Caveat emptor" ("let the buyer beware") is a warning given to purchasers of such commodities as lend themselves more readily to deception. A parallel warning is in order to readers of The Examiner's pages on MacSwiney's hunger-strike. "Caveat lector"–"let the reader beware"– is the wholesome admonition. Beware of "end," "object," and "objective," with their many confusing applications. Beware, too, of "direct" and "indirect," with their more than ten different significations in different contexts. All this and much besides that first confuses and then misleads, will be handed out to you, dear reader, by the same writer in The Examiner, who opened his indictment of MacSwiney by assuming his guilt of suicide, and then presenting "two pleas" in extenuation of the Lord Mayor's "offense."

MAGNIFY ILL, IGNORE GOOD EFFECT AND PURPOSE

The Examiner does not revert to his definition of a human act in any succeeding part of his article. **What, then was his purpose in introducing it?** If he had intended to **obscure, confuse, bewilder, and mislead** his readers, he could not have hoped for better success. But his definition did more for him. He used it **to introduce the "finis operis"**—to inaugurate a process of **emphasizing the object** – the hunger-striker's action, with its ill effect of **self-killing, horrendum quid** – as a source of morality, **almost to the entire exclusion of the end** – the intention – the great legitimizing factor of actions producing an ill effect, and whose number is legion. Bravely does he assert that "the morality of the act is determined by its 'finis operis,' which must not be obscured by introducing the finis operantis." Again, he says that "an intention never makes the least difference to the objective morality of the act done;" that "it leaves the act objectively the same, with its objective effects and the full responsibility for them," and that moralists introduce it "only by way of corollary or appendix."

FALSE PARALLELS, EQUIVOCATIONS, ETC., ETC.

Each of these statements will afterwards receive separate consideration. They are given here **only to show the trend of the writer's ratiocination.** At one time he makes **the object count for everything and the intention for nothing.** At another he will use **absurd parallels** to make it appear that the hunger-striker **intends his own death,** though there is overwhelming evidence that he does not. Again, he will equivocate **on the word "direct,"** that he may seem to answer the solidly sound contention that hunger-strike is not direct self-killing. He will be found making assertions that are in **open contradiction with one another.** He will set down under the title of "conclusion," propositions **derived from no premises,** and which are, in many instances, **unqualifiedly false.** He will **industriously falsify the very principles that are fundamental** to all psychology and all morality, for the manifest purpose of deriving a final conclusion that will **appear to be true,** when, in reality it is **maliciously false.**

(16) "This definition has a corollary, namely that human "acts are acts for which the agent is **responsible.** "He is responsible for the 'actus' because it is 'de-"liberatus'; he is responsible for the 'finis,' that is, "for every result or consequence which is foreseen "(cognitione) to issue straight out of the act itself."

MacSWINEY NOT BOUND TO PREVENT HIS DEATH

It is false that the agent is "responsible for every result or consequence which is foreseen to issue straight out of the act itself." This contention is too absurd to call for refutation. The firemen are not responsible for the valuable merchandise destroyed by the streams of water poured by them on the burning building. The surgeon is not responsible for the pain he inflicts on the patient by probing, drilling, cutting and cauterizing. Yet, in the one case, the destruction of the merchandise, and in the other the pain inflicted on the patient, was "foreseen to issue straight out of the act itself." And the same is true of ten thousand other cases of daily occurrence. Under Principle I regarding cases of "two effects," Fr. Lehmkuhl says: "In order that I may be responsible for any ill effect of my action, I must be obliged to prevent that ill effect." And The Examiner does not prove nor attempt to prove, but only pretends to prove, that MacSwiney was obliged to prevent his own death. We have already proved that he was not.

ASSUMES, IMPLIES, SUGGESTS, INSINUATES

From the very outset, when he had admitted "two pleas" which might possibly exonerate the Mayor from the guilt of suicide, the writer has continued to assume and imply that all hunger-strike until death is objectively suicidal. Mindful of the old vulgar policy that if a good deal of mud be thrown, some of it will surely stick, he adopts the parallel policy that if the Lord Mayor's guilt be assumed and hinted and suggested and insinuated and reiterated, some, at least, of his readers will believe it. True, he does all this with scarce a single specific mention of the MacSwiney case. But in so doing he does worse than state mere falsehoods of fact. At each succeeding stage of his treatise, he formulates and enunciates a general ethical principle that is utterly false, leading his readers to make their own particular application of it to the MacSwiney case, and draw the false conclusion that the Lord Mayor was responsible for his own death.

MAKES ALL INDIRECT VOLUNTARY IMPOSSIBLE

If The Examiner's principle were true, it would be impossible that any action producing an ill effect foreseen but not intended, could ever be lawful, however many and great the good effects it might produce simultaneously. On this supposition, his indictment against Lord Mayor

MacSwiney would be already complete. His syllogism would run thus:

> Maj. Prop. Every agent is responsible for every result foreseen to issue straight from his act.
>
> Min. Prop. But Mayor MacSwiney foresaw that his death must result from his hunger-strike.
>
> Conclusion. Therefore, Mayor MacSwiney was responsible for his own death.

REPROBATED BY ALL MORAL THEOLOGIANS

The minor premise of this syllogism is true. No one denies or doubts that the Lord Mayor foresaw that his death must result from his persistent hunger-strike. The **conclusion** of the syllogism is **false** because the **major premise**, containing the writer's false principle – responsible for every result foreseen – is false. Every moral theologian who lives reprobates that principle, and every one of the dead ones, if they were living, would do the same. The writer is or ought to be well aware that it is one thing to be responsible for an act itself, and quite another to be responsible for its every foreseen effect. Nevertheless, from asserting responsibility for the act, he passes without hesitation, to asserting responsibility for every foreseen result or consequence of it. He would call it a "corollary."

(17) "When these definitions, which are axiomatic, have "been grasped, a further question arises: When is a "man justified in taking upon himself the responsi- "bility for the act, if some portion of the effect is "bad?"

(a) A definition can never be "axiomatic." A definition is a brief declaration of what a thing is. An axiom is a self-evident truth. A definition always needs some explanation in order that it may be understood. An axiom needs no explanation nor admits any. How then can a definition be axiomatic? And is it not the height of absurdity to complacently designate an unqualified falsehood of doctrine by the irreproachable titles of "definition" and "axiom?"

NEVER JUSTIFIED ACCORDING TO "EXAMINER"

(b) Waiving the difficulty of understanding how an axiom can be "grasped," The Examiner's "further question" had been answered by himself previous to his asking it. He had already answered his own question when he said that "the agent is responsible for every result or consequence which is foreseen to issue straight out of the act itself." If he wishes to be consistent, he must therefore say that a man is never "justified in taking upon himself the responsibility for the act, if some portion of the effect is bad." It follows as a corollary from his previous assertion. All the same, he writes a moment later: "It is my duty to obey orders in the army, **even though it means sacrifice of life.**" Here the act of obeying orders has an effect which is ill and foreseen, and yet, on the writer's own acknowledgment, **it is lawful and even obligatory.** His doctrine suffers alike from the twin defect of **falsehood and inconsistency.**

RESPONSIBILITY IRRELEVANT TO QUESTION

(c) Why drag in **responsibility** here! **It has nothing whatever to say as to whether any action is good or evil,** lawful or unlawful, whether the action of refusing all food until death in protest against proportionate injustice, **is lawful, or unlawful.** Recognition that the action is good or is evil, **precedes the action. Responsibility follows the action.** Moralists call it "imputability," and it follows upon every free action, either for **merit** or **demerit.** But **it is irrelevant to the present question.** His "man," laden with the heavy armor of responsibility, helps to solve the MacSwiney case no better than the bare "rational animal." Was his **responsibility introduced in order to confuse?** The "cognitio finis" does not inquire whether the agent is responsible or not, but whether the action is good or evil.

THEOLOGY'S SIMPLE QUESTION AND ANSWER

(d) The ponderous terminology of the writer's "question" makes it well nigh unintelligible. He knows that, in every text-book of Ethics and Moral Theology, the same question is asked in these few simple words: **"When is it lawful to place an act having an ill effect?"** The answer to this simple question is a complete solution of the MacSwiney hunger-strike, and the writer is well aware that Moral Theology answers it with like simplicity, clearness and brevity thus: **"It is always lawful to place an act having an ill effect, if (1) the action itself is either good or indifferent, if (2) the ill effect is not intended either as an end or as a means, and if (3) the good effect is in reasonable proportion to the ill effect."** This is an outstanding principle of morality, and, for that reason, is found, with scarcely a word of alteration, in every standard work on morals. It is the standard scales or yard-stick by which the morality of every act producing an ill effect is universally weighed or measured. But, somehow, it doesn't quite suit the writer. **His question is an acknowledgment that hunger-strike is a case of "two effects."** The reader must judge for himself why, with **measuring to do,** the writer pushes aside the yard-stick, why, with **weighing to do,** he dispenses with the scales. He seems bent on giving short measures! In the language of the underworld, he is taking his readers "for a ride." Here is his long labyrinth of foolish answers to the question he asked in No. 17.

(18) (1) "If there is only one outcome and that is bad, "the act must not be done."

(2) "If there is a good effect and a bad one, the "first question is whether the bad effect can be "separated and cancelled. If so, the difficulty "disappears."

(3) "If the bad outcome cannot be separated, the "action can nevertheless be justified for one or "more of these reasons: (1) a necessity; (2) a "duty; (3) a right."

ASKED NOT OF SOLE OR SEPARABLE BAD EFFECT

(1) Notice that The Examiner's "further question" was about an act "if some portion of its effect is bad." What place in the answer has an action having "only one outcome and that bad?" Besides, who needs to be told that "if there is only one outcome and that is bad, the act must not be done?" This is to enunciate a truism—the obvious and irrelevant.

(2) Again the obvious and irrelevant! It is all too evident that when the good effect can be obtained without an accompanying ill effect, the agent is obligated to so attain it. Such a case is no more a case of "two effects," and no more an answer to the writer's "further question" than the previous one. In every case of "duplex effectus," the ill effect flows essentially from the action, and hence is inseparable from it. Otherwise how could the ill effect be foreseen?

SUBSTITUTES FALSEHOODS FOR ETHICAL CANON

(3) In the third of the pronouncements we are now considering, the writer substitutes a chain or doctrinal falsehoods for the traditional canon of all moralists without exception—that any act producing an ill effect is lawful if the act and intention are good and the good effect proportionate. His terms "necessity," "duty" and "right," because they are abstract and of many varieties, are good materials for juggling. All theologians make man's moral relations to God, his neighbor and himself, consist of certain duties and corresponding rights. To these The Examiner adds another category of his own inventing, namely "necessity." And first he discusses absolute necessity positive and negative—the former a physical compulsion to place an action, the latter a physical compulsion to omit an action. Both of these kinds of necessity, the author rightly excludes from the domain of moral conduct, since each is incompatible with Free Choice—an excellent reason why he should not have introduced them at all.

HYPOTHETICAL NECESSITY BEWILDERING NAME!

The writer then passes to **relative** or **hypothetical** necessity – a term that would stagger a Doctor of Divinity.

His examples of "hypothetical necessity" show that it means only the NEED ("necessity") of certain actions as means, if corresponding non-obligatory ends would be attained. Here are some of the author's examples: "If I am to keep my appointment, I must either walk or ride." "If I have to ride, I must spend some money."

Note well that in these, and in all such examples, the term "MUST" does not connote any moral obligation, such, for instance, as it does when we say: "If you wish eternal salvation, you must keep the Commandments." This latter "MUST" expresses an absolute moral necessity. The "MUST" of hypothetical necessity merely expresses the NEED of certain specific actions as means, which agents are free to use or not use, because the corresponding ends are not of moral obligation. That NEED ("necessity") is not the action, nor is it the end or effect of the action. It is the relation between them. The end NEEDS the action.

Now it is this need or necessity that The Examiner proposes as justification of actions which agents have otherwise neither a duty nor a right to place. If an agent has not a right to place an action, it can only be because such action is evil from end, or means or circumstances. And it is just such actions that The Examiner would justify by his hypothetical necessity – by his NEED of such actions as means, if ends in nowise obligatory, would be attained. If the jurors are to be bribed, the necessity of stealing the money, with which to pay them, would, according to The Examiner, justify the plunder. Justification of any good or indifferent action producing an inseparable ill effect, is to be sought and found in the agent's good intention and right proportion of good effect. It is a far cry to look for it in the author's "hypothetical necessity." What have the writer's "absolute necessity," and his "relative or hypothetical necessity" done towards helping his readers to understand the Ethics of hunger-strike? They are more of the red herrings, which, from the very beginning, he has continued to drag across the trail of sound ethical doctrine!

NO ACT JUSTIFIED BY NECESSITY, DUTY, RIGHT

But not for "one or more" or all the writer's "reasons" can any act be justified. Every action that is justified is justified for one and the same reason – its intrinsic conformity with God's law, natural and revealed. It is from this intrinsic conformity that any action is good and lawful. And when is an action producing an ill effect intrinsically conformed to God's law? It is so conformed whenever the action and intention are good and the good effect proportionate. Such action is good from end, means and the circumstance of proportion – the only sources of all goodness and all lawfulness of all actions producing an ill effect.

Now, in this account of why an action is lawful, and why, in particular, an action producing an ill effect is, notwithstanding, lawful, The Examiner's "justifying reasons" have no place. Neither his "necessity" nor duty nor right contributes anything to the lawfulness (justification) of any action. How could they? They are all extrinsic to the act, and we have just seen that it is by their intrinsic conformity to the Divine Law, and not by any extrinsic denomination, that acts are lawful and justified. Justice and justification are not mere extrinsic denominations. They are intrinsic perfections. As it is by its own intrinsic entity ("tota rei realitas") that everything is individualized, so it is by its own intrinsic goodness, not by any extrinsic relation of necessity, duty, or right, that any act is justified.

NO ACT JUSTIFIED BY AGENT'S DUTY OR RIGHT

As to duty and right as "justifying reasons," it must be remarked that **no act is justified by the agent's duty or right to place it**. Since, as has just been said, all good actions derive their justification from their intrinsic conformity to the Divine Law, they are lawful and justified prior to being or becoming duties or rights. They are first objectively lawful and justified, and afterwards subjectively obligatory as duties or permissible as rights. Actions are by no means lawful or just simply because they are duties or rights. On the contrary, they are duties or rights because lawful and just. What then becomes the writer's "necessity," "duty" and "right" as justifying reasons for an action producing an ill effect? Is it overstepping the bounds of truth or moderation to call them a chain of doctrinal falsehoods – blind guides, leading their blind victims into the proverbial ditch!

But, as might be expected, the writer, a moment later, disowns his own "necessity" as a justifying reason. He writes:

(19) "In all such cases, where a bad effect is necessarily "tied up with an otherwise good action, I am justified "in performing the good act providing I have at my "back some reason of duty or right to perform the "act."

(a) Has not the writer just said that "necessity" is a justifying reason, **distinct from and independent of duty and right?** Was not his enumeration of justifying reasons **"a necessity, a duty, a right?"** Now, only a moment later, he cites several instances of necessity (hypothetical), and turns for the justification of them to "some reason of **duty or right.**" If his "necessity" cannot justify itself, then what can it justify!

ALL DUTIES, ALL RIGHTS NOT KNOWN TO ALL

(b) And what does he add to the science of Moral Theology, or to the solution of Mayor MacSwiney's hunger-strike when he tells his readers that an action is lawful **provided the agent has a duty or a right to perform it?** Everyone knows that it is lawful to do one's "duty," and lawful to place any act that one has a "right" to place. **Duty and right presuppose lawfulness.** But there is no tabulated prospectus of duties, and rights accessible to all. Moral theologians and spiritual directors are frequently asked to decide whether, in specific instances, a duty or a right exists or does not exist. The writer points to "**duty**" and "**right**" as guides to what is lawful, **as if all persons are at all times aware of all their duties and all their rights.** And in the case of hunger-strike in particular, his criterion of "duty" can be of no service, since, on his own acknowledgment, **no one is obliged to starve himself** to death from the motive of **patriotism as a duty.**

(c) The writer says likewise that hunger-strike is lawful if the hunger-striker **has a right** to perform the act. But this answer leaves the case just where it found it! "It is lawful," says he, "if the agent has a right to place the act, and unlawful if he has not." How is the agent to know when he has and when he has not a right to place an action? Is not this still the same "further question" which the writer asked and set out to answer? Every case of conscience that was ever discussed, or ever set down in print, was intended to be another lesson in the interminable ramifications of rights and duties!

(d) Duties and rights, **when known,** are signs that the corresponding actions are lawful. But the writer's claim is not that they are justifying signs, but that they are justifying "reasons"—constituents of the lawfulness of the actions that are duties and rights.

(20) "As regards rights to throw away my life, these are, "in every case, subject to the fundamental right and "duty of self-preservation. I have a right as well as "a duty to protect my life, my goods, my reputation "against unjust aggression."

RIGHT TO THROW AWAY MY LIFE. WHAT?

(a) What meaning has "rights to throw away my life." To "throw away" anything of value is to squander or otherwise destroy it, recklessly, wantonly – to throw away one's fortune, one's prospects, one's reputation, one's health, one's life. Hence we never say of the Christian martyrs or the patriot martyrs or the martyrs of charity or the martyrs in any worthy cause, that they "threw away" their lives. We invariably say that they "gave" their lives, "laid down" their lives, "sacrificed" their lives. And all these expressions are terms of praise. To "throw away" one's life, or anything that is precious, is, on the contrary, a term of reproach. This being so, "the right to throw away my life" and "the duty to throw away my life" are contradictions. It is the same as "the right to commit suicide" and "the duty to commit suicide." But none of it is too incongruous for the writer. He speaks repeatedly of "the right to throw away my life" and "the duty to throw away my life." Are his puzzling paradoxes aimed to bewilder his readers, to produce anesthesia of the reasoning faculty, making it passively receptive of conclusions that deserve to be rejected?

NOT ALWAYS BOUND TO DEFEND LIFE, GOODS, ETC.

(b) It is false that every man has the duty to protect all his goods against all unjust aggression; it is false that every man has the duty to protect his reputation against all unjust aggression; it is false that every man has the duty to protect his life against all unjust aggression. Where the victim of aggression has no dependents, and his spiritual interests are not jeopardized, he has no duty to protect his goods, his reputation or even his life. Heroic poverty and humility and charity might inspire him to surrender them all.

DUTY TO PRESERVE ONESELF NOT FUNDAMENTAL

(c) The writer speaks of "the fundamental right and duty of self-preservation." Neither the duty of self-preservation nor the right of self-preservation is fundamental. Man's fundamental duty is not to himself nor to any creature. His fundamental duty arises immediately out of his essential relations to God, as his Creator – the duty to love, reverence and serve God. Similarly, man's fundamental right is not the right of self-preservation, but the right to the means necessary to fulfill his duty to God, whether such means spell self-preservation, or self-immolation. Indeed that fundamental duty to God is sometimes discharged more effectively by sacrificing one's life than by preserving it. "Whoever would save his life will lose it: but he that shall lose his life for My sake, will find it." (Luc. ix, 24)

FUNDAMENTAL DUTY IS TO GOD, NOT TO SELF

And it is in that first, essential duty of man towards his Maker that all other duties originate. From it, as from a fountain-head, flows the coercive character of all other duties. All the obligations of all commandments and precepts, natural and supernatural – the obligation to be just and truthful and chaste and charitable, and patient and temperate and prudent and prayerful and penitent – all these, and all other duties, are binding only because that first of all duties is an absolute obligation from which no authority divine or human can dispense. Take that first duty away and the obligating power of every other duty goes with it. The word "duty" itself then ceases to have a meaning. That is why Atheism can have no code of morals. It cannot build a house without a foundation.

RIGHT TO NEEDED MEANS BASE OF ALL OTHERS

And similarly, all other rights originate in the first essential right to the means necessary to discharge that first, essential duty. They are, one and all, inviolable, simply because that first right, from which they derive their adequate title, is antecedently and absolutely inviolable – cannot be contravened by any authority of God or man. No system of rights which fails to duly recognize this primary right has any reason for its own existence.

Here, then, is the reason why the duty and the right to worship God are fundamental. It is also the reason why the right and duty of self-preservation are not fundamental. The writer's assertion that they are fundamental is false! If the duty of self-preservation were fundamental, it would admit of no exception, and he would have already established his case against Mayor MacSwiney. How many more fundamental principles of Ethics must he twist and wrench and falsify that he may appear to have found a verdict against the Lord Mayor!

PRIORITY OF SACRIFICE OVER PRESERVATION

(d) Since there is no such thing as a right or a duty to do what is evil, the writer, when he speaks of "the rights to throw away my life," cannot mean the right to criminally destroy my life, but rather the right to sacrifice my life in a good cause. But even when he is thus benevolently interpreted, it is false doctrine to say, as he does, that "the right to throw away (sacrifice) my life is, in every case, subject to the fundamental right and duty of self-preservation." According to this dictum of the writer, the duty of self-preservation is ever and always so dominant and urgent as to exclude all right ever to throw away (sacrifice) one's life in any cause however noble. Notice that he excludes every exception! He says that "the rights to throw away (sacrifice) my life are, in every case, subject to the fundamental right and duty of self-preservation." This is surely a vicious principle. It outlaws even an act which, according to the authority of Christ Himself, is the climax of Christian heroism and charity – the act of laying down one's life for one's friend. And this unhallowed principle the writer enunciates several times in the course of his article. By way of contradiction, however, he makes, within the same paragraph, the following partial retractation.

(21) "I have no right to throw away my life except in the "execution of my duty, or in defense of some neces-"sary virtue, such as faith, honesty, truthfulness, "chastity."

ADMITS EXCEPTIONS NOW THAT CONTRADICT HIM

(a) A moment ago he insisted that "the rights to throw away (sacrifice) my life are, in every case, subject to the fundamental right and duty of self-preservation." Now his canon does not extend to every case. He makes exception, first, for every "execution of duty," and secondly, for every "defense of some necessary virtue." He contradicts one of his own false principles by enunciating another equally false – and, like the former, characteristically his own.

(b) Besides the "execution of duty" and the "defense of some necessary virtue," there are cases without number in which a person may lawfully sacrifice his own life. A drowning man may lawfully give his life-buoy to another in like extremity, though certain that he himself will drown. Here his surrender of the life-buoy is neither the writer's "execution of duty," for it is manifest that no such duty exists, nor his "defense of some necessary virtue," since that drowning man is not then engaged in defending any virtue, necessary or unnecessary, but rather in practising, to a heroic degree, the virtue of charity, which does not oblige under grave inconvenience. Nevertheless, if the writer would avoid contradicting himself, he must hold, in opposition to Catholic Theology, and indeed in opposition to his own "consensus of civilized humanity," that the drowning man has no right to surrender his life-buoy. But consistency is the least of the writer's worries.

(c) An action good or indifferent in itself, a good intention regarding both end and means, and a good effect reasonably proportioned to the ill effect—these are the only requisites of Catholic Theology for the lawfulness of any act destructive of the agent's own life. To these the writer would add two further requirements of his own inventing—that, **outside of duty**, the act whereby the life of the agent is sacrificed must be (1) "defense" of some virtue, and (2) the virtue so defended must be a "**necessary virtue.**"

DEFENSE OF "NECESSARY" VIRTUE. WHAT? WHY?

On what grounds does he insist that the good effect, for whose attaining a person has the right, when not the duty, to sacrifice his life, **must be the defense of some virtue?** A defense is a reply by word or act to a challenge. Would not a single act of charity, **secretly performed in behalf of a beggar or a leper**, amply compensate for the sacrifice of a life? And it includes neither defense nor challenge.

(d) And what does he mean by a "necessary virtue?" Whenever theologians speak of a virtue as "necessary," they invariably specify either **the object** for whose attaining that virtue is necessary, or **the subject** for whose insufficiency it is necessary. They say that Supernatural Faith is necessary **for salvation**, and that the virtue of Evangelical Poverty is necessary **for perfection, but not necessary for salvation**. They say also that the virtue of Penance is necessary **for sinners, but not necessary for the just**. But theologians **never speak of any virtue as simply "necessary"** or **simply "unnecessary"**—"necessary" or "unnecessary" *sine addito*. A virtue that is simply "unnecessary" is not a very intelligible thing. Every virtue is ordained by God to satisfy some moral deficiency in man, and so every virtue is, in some sense, "necessary."

(e) If, according to the writer's classification, some virtues are "necessary" and others "unnecessary," how is it to be known which are the "necessary" virtues, in whose defense life may be sacrificed? He mentions only four—"faith, honesty, truthfulness, chastity,"—an enumeration evidently incomplete even according to his own rating of "necessary" virtues. The virtue of patriotism **he specifically excludes** from his category of "necessary" virtues. He writes:

(22) "No man is justified in sacrificing his life out of a "motive of patriotism merely as a right . . . It is "only patriotism as a duty that justifies such sacri-"fices."

NO RIGHT TO VOLUNTEER FOR "FORLORN HOPE"?

This assertion of the writer, like the one immediately preceding, is **unqualifiedly false**. It is not true in any sense in which the words can be taken. If it be lawful to sacrifice one's life out of a motive of honesty or of truthfulness, as a right, why not also for patriotism as a right? The act of sacrificing one's life for one's country is indifferent in itself, whether done as a duty or as a right. The intention of him who makes the sacrifice is generally good in regard to both end and means. And, in most instances of such sacrifice, the benefits to the nation abundantly compensate for the loss of life. What then are the grounds for the writer's sweeping injunction against every sacrifice of one's own life for patriotism as a right? He does not tell us. He is content to make the assertion and omit the reasons for it. Reasons for assertions that are utterly false cannot be very weighty or convincing! These, his own assertions, he flatly contradicts a moment later when he says:

(23) "A captain blows up his ship in order that it may "not be captured by the enemy. The blowing up in-"volves the death of himself and all who are under "him. The act is deliberate with knowledge of the "end. I do not think that any moral theologians would "condemn this act. They would justify it. The act "itself is justified by a combination of moral neces-"sity, duty and right. It must be acknowledged that, "by strict obligation, the captain is not bound to "blow up his ship. He would be fully justified in "yielding it up when fighting became useless."

CAPTAIN STAR WITNESS PROSECUTING AUTHOR

(1) The writer made a decided mistake of policy by introducing this case of the captain. That gallant gentleman will testify against The Examiner at every stage of the trial. Theologians are agreed that the captain **has the right but not the duty** to sink his ship – the right but not the duty to "throw away" (sacrifice) his life for the proportionate good which his country derives from depriving the enemy of his ship – for patriotism. We have just heard the writer agree with them – just heard him say that "the act is justified," though "the captain is not bound to blow up his ship" – has the right but not the duty to blow up his ship. But we have likewise seen him write on the same page (No. 22) that "no man is justified in sacrificing his life out of a motive of patriotism **merely as a right.**" Contradiction No. 1!

CONTRADICTIONS ONE, TWO, THREE, FOUR, FIVE, SIX, SEVEN, EIGHT, NINE, TEN!

(2) Moreover, we heard him say (No. 16) that "the agent is responsible for every result or consequence which is foreseen (cognitione) to issue straight out of the act itself." And now he admits that the captain's act "is deliberate with knowledge of the end." The inevitable conclu-

sion from these, the writer's own premises, is that the captain is responsible for his own death. Yet, the writer justifies the captain's act! Contradiction No. 2!

(3) Again, is the captain's right to throw away (sacrifice) his life "subject to the fundamental right and duty of self-preservation?" The writer says (No. 20) it is so in every case, none excepted. According to him, then, the captain, by blowing up his ship, failed to discharge his fundamental duty of preserving his own life. And the writer justifies his act! Contradiction No. 3!

(4) Furthermore, he says (No. 21) that no one has the right to throw away (sacrifice) his life "except in the execution of some duty or in defense of some necessary virtue." He moreover admits that the captain's act is not an act of duty. Neither is the captain's act in any sense "a defense of some necessary virtue," but rather an act of patriotism as a right. Therefore, according to the writer's principle, the captain has no right to throw away (sacrifice) his own life by blowing up his ship. But in the same breath he justifies the captain! Contradiction No. 4!

COMBINATION OF NECESSITY DUTY AND RIGHT?

(5) The writer adds that "the act (of sinking the ship) is justified by a combination of moral necessity, duty and right." What sort of commodity is "a combination of moral necessity, duty and right?" As a justifying source he now changes his "hypothetical necessity of No. 18 into "moral necessity," which differs in nothing from duty. He justifies the captain's act by "moral necessity" and "duty," while admitting that "the captain is not bound to blow up his ship" – has no moral necessity, no duty to do so! Contradiction No. 5! "Consistency thou art a jewel!"

NO RIGHT TO SACRIFICE LIFE TO SAVE RULER?

(6) And what about the private citizen who thrusts himself forward to receive, in his own heart, the dagger aimed by the assassin at the heart of the President? **The private citizen has ordinarily no duty to protect the person of the President.** That duty devolves on public officials. Would the writer say that the private citizen had no right to throw away (sacrifice) his life to save the life of the President? It is patriotism as a right but not as a duty, and The Examiner denies that life may be sacrificed for it – denies it by throwing away both **truth and consistency.**

(24) "Even so I am only allowed to throw away (sacri-
"fice) my life in a negative way. I am not allowed,
"deliberately and with foreseen results, to bring
"about my own death in order to preserve these vir-
"tues. I am only allowed to incur death at the hands

"of others through tenacity in adhering to them. I
"do not know any principle in Moral Theology which
"allows me to seek or incur death at my own hands
"or by my own act. Such an act can be allowed only
"where it is enforced by a duty."

CAPTAIN'S SACRIFICE NOT NEGATIVE – POSITIVE

(a) By "a negative way" of throwing away (sacrificing) one's life is meant the **omitting to use the ordinary means by which life is preserved**. The positive way would be actual violence to one's own life. Is it only in "a negative way" that the captain throws away (sacrifices) his own life? He explodes the powder – **a very positive, violent measure!** "Deliberately and with foreseen results," he brings about his own death – without, however, **directly intending** it either as **end** or **means** – in order to practice the natural virtue of patriotism as a right. Neither could he be said "to incur death merely at the hands of others." The hand that explodes the magazine is no other except his own. Contradiction No. 6!

(b) There is no principle in Moral Theology **which allows anyone to seek death at his own hands.** He who seeks death at his own hands intends it. But there is a principle which **allows one to incur death unintentionally at one's own hands, and by one's own act.** It is the very case of the captain. He incurs death at his own hands and by his own act, **without, however, seeking or intending it.** – Contradiction No. 7! – When the writer says he does not know any principle in Moral Theology which allows him to "seek" death at his own hands or by his own act, **he says what is true.** He does not know any such principle because there is none. It is only the same as saying he does not know any principle in Moral Theology which allows **anyone to commit suicide** – a veritable platitude.

DUTY TO "SEEK DEATH AT ONE'S OWN HANDS." WHAT?

(c) And what **duty** is it that allows anyone to "seek" death at his own hands or by his own act? "Such an act," says the writer, "can be allowed **only when it is enforced by a duty.**" The writer says "seek" or "incur" death, as if "seek" and "incur" mean exactly the same thing. An agent "seeking" his own death as a duty is another of the author's fictions and another of his contradictions! Every one of the assertions contained in the above citation is **false,** and, in addition, **inconsistent, contradictory.**

(25) "If this clear doctrine be accepted – and I do not see
"how, on our Catholic principles, it can be denied –
"it follows that no man has the right to kill himself

"or to expose himself to death because forsooth he "feels enthusiastic for the cause of his country, and "wants to externate his enthusiasm in an act of self-"sacrifice."

EXAMINER'S DOCTRINE NOT CLEAR, NOT CATHOLIC

It is false that The Examiner's doctrine is clear, and false that it is Catholic. We have seen that the writer's doctrine is not conspicuously clear, and, moreover, that much of it is untrue, and, therefore, opposed to Catholic principles, instead of being in accord with them. The already familiar case of the ship's captain shows that a person has the right, even when not the duty, to kill himself indirectly, provided some proportionate benefit accrues to his country from the action which deprives him of his life. And certainly the captain "feels enthusiastic for his country's cause, and wants to externate his enthusiasm in an act of self-sacrifice" directly beneficial to his country. Is it a crime, is it forbidden, by any law of God or man, to feel enthusiastic for the cause of one's country, and to want to externate that enthusiasm in an act of self-sacrifice? The Examiner would rewrite the Fifth Commandment in order to prove hunger-strike unlawful. Everything contained in his prohibitory mandate is verified in the lawful and laudable action of the ship's captain, whom the writer himself exonerates. The assertion we are now considering does but add another to his already lengthy list of contradictions. Contradiction No. 8!

(26) "Voluntary self-sacrifice of life cannot be justified "merely because it may serve the country indirectly. "For instance, soldiers would never be allowed to "shoot themselves in the presence of the enemy, "merely to make a demonstration of their heroism. "Nor would it be right for women and children to "stab themselves in the presence of the besieger in "order to excite the compassion of the enemy and "cause him to relax his rigor. Nor would it be allowed "for either soldiers or civilians to shoot themselves "rather than fall into the hands of the foe. These "actions could never be justified merely as an expres-"sion of enthusiasm for one's country, in order to "stir up zeal or fire the courage of others or to "create an impression on the minds of the foe."

SUICIDES! NO PARALLELS FOR HUNGER-STRIKE

(a) The general assertion with which this citation opens is false. Why should not voluntary self-sacrifice of life that serves the country indirectly be justified? An indirect service to one's country may be very great. It is not measured by directness or indirectness.

(b) The writer's **examples of "voluntary self-sacrifice of life" cannot be justified because they are all cases of directly intended self-killing** – suicide. Yet he implies, by presenting them to his readers, **that they are exact parallels to the case of the patriotic hunger-striker.** And when he says that these cases "could never be justified **merely because it may serve the country indirectly," he wrongly implies that it is only due proportion of good effect** that is lacking to them, and that therefore they could be justified in other circumstances. **He ignores the evil intention which vitiates them all, but is absent from every act of hunger-strike.** He says rightly that none of the cases cited by him can be justified, but he says wrongly – falsely – that "**no voluntary self-sacrifice of life can be justified merely because it may serve the country indirectly."** No such intended self-sacrifice can be justified on any grounds. Voluntary self-sacrifice of life which serves one's country even indirectly **can be, and often is justified aplenty.** Nothing prevents it from being a good action, done with good intention and due proportion of good effect. What examples he gives of "voluntary self-sacrifice of life"– **soldiers shooting themselves, and women and children stabbing themselves."**!!

(27) "A man, for the good of his country, may, in war, "run risks of death which amount to moral certain-"ties. But he can never deliberately kill himself or "bring about his own death."

AGAIN HE FLATLY CONTRADICTS HIMSELF

This is **false doctrine.** It is possible for a man to "deliberately kill himself or bring about his own death," and yet not intend his own death. It is the very case of the captain. He deliberately kills himself – deliberately brings about his own death. He foresees his own death, consents to it, precipitates it. And The Examiner says the captain's act is lawful. It is, moreover, laudable, though the writer does not say so. It is the perfection of devotion to a righteous cause. Again **he contradicts** himself. **Contradiction No. 9!**

(28) "Unless we are ready to open the door to moral an-"archy, we must limit the occasions of voluntary and "foreseen sacrifice of one's own life to cases where "patriotism involves **some clear and specific duty."**

ANOTHER FLAT CONTRADICTION

If this assertion were true, then the writer himself had already opened the door to moral anarchy. He had justified the captain's act of sinking his ship and thereby sacrificing his own life. The sacrifice was "voluntary and foreseen" and the motive was patriotism, but such patriotism as does not "involve some clear and specific duty." The writer says "by strict obligation, the captain is not bound to blow up his ship. He would be fully justified in yielding it." This, his latest declamatory assertion, is another piece of untruth and inconsistency, falsehood and contradiction. Contradiction No. 10!

(29) "Outside actual warfare or its equivalent, where "there is no specific duty to run risks, the normal "duty of self-preservation remains in possession."

YET ANOTHER FALSEHOOD AND CONTRADICTION!

(a) What about the man who, in extremity of hunger, gives his last crust to another in the same extremity and dies of hunger himself? What about the hero of the shipwreck, who gives his only life-buoy to another and drowns himself? Both of these happenings are "outside actual warfare or its equivalent," and, moreover, there exists in neither case any "specific duty to run risks." In these cases, does the writer's "normal duty of self-preservation remain in possession?" Here is another false principle that would ban the most heroic acts of charity – that would forbid a man to "lay down his life for his friend."

(b) Another passage from his essay directly contradicts the citation we are considering. Here it is:

"There is the case of two people and the plank in a "shipwreck. If I have got the plank, and it will only "support one, I am justified – by the right of self-"preservation – to thrust back another person who tries "to get hold of it. On the other hand, I have the right "(by virtue of charity) to relinquish my plank to the "other man, while I take to myself the risk of almost "certain death."

"The same with food which is not sufficient to keep "a whole party alive. I may refuse to take my share "because it means giving my share to save the life "of others."

Both these instances are cases in which "there is no specific duty to run risks," and they are "outside of actual warfare or its equivalent." Nevertheless, the writer admits that, in these cases, "the normal duty of self-preservation does not remain in possession." How consistent he is!

(30) "Any exception in the way of risk has to be justified "by the proved presence either of a duty or of a "right, and the burden of proof lies on the shoulders "of those who contemplate the action which involves "risk of life."

ONE MORE CONTRADICTION

(a) This assertion flatly contradicts what the author says in the preceding citation, No. 29. There he insisted that self-preservation is obligatory and risks of life forbidden except at the call of duty. Now he justifies the risk and dispenses from the self-preservation by the proved presence either of a duty or a right!

MacSWINEY'S HUNGER-STRIKE PROVED LAWFUL

(b) This is only a restricted statement of the more general principle in morals that it is never lawful for any one to place an action while in doubt about its lawfulness. But that is something which no instructed person denies or doubts. Why then does the writer state it with emphasis? His purpose is to say indirectly what he does not venture to say explicitly – that Mayor MacSwiney's hunger-strike has not been, and cannot be proved lawful. And this he asserts by implication, though proof abundant that the Lord Mayor's act was objectively lawful had been given long before by several theologians – notably by Fr. Kent, O.S.C., in the "London Tablet," and in "Studies," by Fr. Patrick Gannon, S.J., a professor of Theology! These defenses of the Lord Mayor – published in sundry Catholic periodicals during the progress of his hunger-strike – were at the writer's hand as exchanges, in his capacity of editor of The Examiner. Altogether they numbered thirty or more, and it is very certain that the writer read the bulk of them.

Nevertheless, when writing his treatise, "The Ethics of Hunger-Striking," nearly three months after the Lord Mayor's death – when the controversy was over, and the writer knew that his finding, both because it was the last word and because it was his word, was likely to be read more widely and longer remembered – he entirely ignores all the defenses and all the defenders, and tells his readers (1) that the burden of proving his hunger-strike lawful rested on the shoulders of the Lord Mayor; (2) that the Lord Mayor did not prove his conduct lawful; and (3) that, being unlawful, his hunger-strike could not be proved lawful. Of course the writer succeeds in saying all this without a single explicit mention of Mayor MacSwiney, well aware that the MacSwiney case will not be lost sight of for one moment by any of his readers. When he speaks about "risk of life" he is obviously not referring especially to the risk involved in aviation, mountain climbing or any enterprise save hunger-strike.

AUTHOR'S EFFORTS TO DISPROVE – BEST PROOF

Furthermore, for whose benefit and to whose satisfaction would the writer have Mayor MacSwiney prove his hunger-strike lawful beforehand? That, with the aid and under the direction of his spiritual adviser, Mayor MacSwiney **judged and judged correctly that his hunger-strike was lawful**, is shown by his words to the Bishop of Cork –"Your Lordship, my conscience is quite at ease about the course I am taking." Was the Lord Mayor in conscience bound **to prove**, even to those as unreceptive as the writer himself, **that his hunger-strike was lawful?** "Ad impossibilia nemo tenetur!" That **the lawfulness of his act admits of proof** is made manifest by the fact that it has been proved with the **evidence of certainty**. "Ab esse ad posse valet illatio." And **the proof is made much more evident and much more certain by the writer's helpless, hopeless efforts to impugn it and prove the contrary. Unintentionally, and even unwittingly, he has written an admirable defense of the lawfulness of the MacSwiney hunger-strike.**

(31) "If self-killing to escape imprisonment were justified, "every prisoner taken in the war would have been "justified in shooting himself if he could. For, as said "before, the self-killing is the same as to its finis "operis, no matter whether it is done by a revolver "in one second or by starvation in three months – "always assuming that the death is contemplated as "the de facto issue of the starvation, and the pur- "pose is to go on even if death results."

UNINTENDED SELF-KILLING TO ESCAPE PRISON

Neither the defenders of Mayor MacSwiney nor any other Catholic theologian ever asserted or even hinted that any "self-killing TO escape imprisonment"– or for any other purpose – could ever be justified. **In every such case, escape from imprisonment would be the end** – finis operantis – **and self-killing** (finis operis) **the means intended and used to attain it** – intended self-killing – suicide. Since, then, "self-killing TO escape imprisonment" has no application to the hunger-striker – inasmuch as he does not intend his own death – why does the writer introduce that case? For the same reason that he introduces **the prussic acid man, the revolver man, the sati woman, the bankrupt suicide, the sufferer, the biceps man.** For the same purpose that he will, later in his article, cite Origen, the cenobite, St. Pelagia, the prisoners of Kut, the general who finds his troops wavering. Parallels that converge, and general ethical principles that, in the present context, contain false implications – all this is the heart and soul of the writer's article.

INSINUATES INTENDED SELF-KILLING

Without expressly asserting that Mayor MacSwiney's act was "self-killing TO escape imprisonment," he says it implicitly — by what Logic calls a suppressed minor proposition — and concludes that it cannot be justified — that his escape from imprisonment was the end he aimed at, and his self-killing by starvation the means he intended and used to attain it. By way of proof of this, the writer says: "For the self-killing is the same as to its finis operis, no matter whether it is done by a revolver in one second or by starvation in three months"— no matter whether it is done by a prisoner who shoots himself because taken in the war, or by a hunger-striker who starves himself to death TO escape imprisonment. Notice the writer's implied acknowledgment that the finis operis — self-killing — is the only source of morality common to the prisoner of war and the hunger-striker. He will afterwards say, and say falsely, that the self-killing of the prisoner of war and that of the hunger-striker is the same also as to its finis operantis — in other words, that the hunger-striker, as well as the prisoner of war, intends his own death.

For the present, however, he does not venture to say so much openly. He omits all reference to intention and circumstances, and pronounces the act of hunger-strike to be as unlawful as the self-shooting of the prisoner of war, simply and solely because in both cases the self-killing is the same as to its finis operis — because both are self-killing. He must have forgotten the case of the sea captain whose act of sinking his ship and killing himself is also the same as to its finis operis (self-killing).

"TO BEHOLD DEATH AS ISSUE AND PURPOSE TO GO ON"

Finally, the writer's oracular insinuation that the hunger-striker intends his own death — TO escape imprisonment — is worthy of notice. Observe that "TO" here means "IN ORDER TO." "To contemplate death as the issue of self-starvation, and purpose to go on even if death results" — how much like INTENDING his own death this sounds to the average reader, though in reality it is very far removed from it. Translated into simple language, it means — "to recognize that death must finally result from self-starvation, and purpose to continue the self-starvation even if death results." Contemplation is an act of cognition, not of volition — an act of intellect not of will. Therefore not an act of intending atall. And "the purpose to go on even if death results" is only a purpose to continue the protest against injustice by refusing food. It is not the purpose to bring about his own death "TO escape imprisonment." The writer's captain contemplates his own death as the de facto issue of sinking his ship, and his purpose is to go on, though certain that his death must inevitably result. And the writer says that the captain does not intend his own death, but, by words chosen, carved and chiselled, insinuates that MacSwiney did.

> (32) "The morality of the act is determined by its finis operis, which must not be obscured by introducing the finis operantis. Fasting, if prolonged enough, is just as infallible (though gradual) a means of killing onself as taking prussic acid which acts instantaneously. This being the case, it is mere sophistry to say: 'Although I am acting in such a way as to encompass my own death, I do not intend my own death but only to promote the cause of my country.' One might as well argue: 'In taking prussic acid I do not intend my own death but only to demonstrate scientifically the effects of poison.' I might just as well argue: 'In putting a bullet through my brain I do not intend to kill myself. I merely want to prove the efficacy of my revolver.' The sati woman of India might just as well argue when she throws herself on the pyre: 'I do not intend to kill myself. I merely wish to add glory to my husband's funeral.' The bankrupt suicide might just as well argue: 'I do not mean to kill myself. I merely mean to shun disgrace.' A sufferer might argue: 'I do not mean to kill myself, but merely to relieve myself of intolerable pain and spare my relations the burden of nursing me'."

DOES THE END "OBSCURE" MORALITY OF ACTION?

This is shallow, hollow quibbling, unworthy of any Catholic editor, and unworthy of the grave theological question the writer is discussing. He says "the morality of the act is determined by the finis operis," and thus implies that the morality of the act is determined independently of the finis operantis, the intention of the agent. This, of course, is false. The morality of every act is determined by end, means, and circumstances—"finis operis," "finis operantis" et "circumstantiae."

Gury says: "There are three sources of morality—the object of the act, (the action), its circumstances, and the intention of the agent. In order that the act may be good, all three sources must be good. If any one of them be evil, it renders the act evil." ("De Actibus Humanis".) If then, the morality of every act is composed of the combined moralities from all three sources, why does the writer say that "the morality of the act is determined by its finis operis." Would he determine the morality of hunger-strike independently of the intention? Why is he so afraid that the object (finis operis) will be "obscured" by "introducing" the intention? The extent to which he bars the intention from the investigation, would lead his readers to suppose that it is not one of the sources of morality at all! He almost says so. "It is only by way of corollary or appendix that moral theologians add a caution – that you must direct your intention to the good which is in the act, and away from the evil which is in it." The writer is the only Catholic theologian living or dead who determines the morality of hunger-strike, or any other act, independently of the intention of the agent, and afterwards introduces that intention "by way of corollary or appendix."

CANONS OF THEOLOGY NOT SUITED TO AUTHOR

Somehow the reader feels that the doctrine of theologians generally, regarding the sources of morality, is not quite suited to the writer's purpose. He labors desperately to restate it, and, in doing so, sidetracks the intention – the saving feature of every lawful action having an ill effect. "The morality of the act," he says, "is determined by its finis operis." He further says that "fasting, if prolonged enough, is just as infallible (though gradual) a means of killing oneself as taking prussic acid which acts instantly." Granted, what follows? Blowing up his ship is just as infallible a means of killing the captain! Nothing follows, therefore, from the writer's infallible self-killing of the agent. It is present in the lawful case of the captain. All the same, he draws a long list of conclusions from it. "This being the case," etc., etc.

SELF-KILLING NEVER EVIL FROM ACTION ITSELF

Aside from the intention of the agent and the circumstances, infallible self-killing convicts no one. It may be laudable. Not even the self-killing by prussic acid, by a revolver, by the funeral pyre, is evil simply because of the "finis operis"– the object, self-killing. They are evil one and all, but it is either from intention or circumstances or both. Killing oneself with prussic acid is evil because the good effect – to demonstrate scientifically the effects of poison – is attained by means of the ill effect – which must therefore have been intended – and moreover lacks proportion to it. "You must intend the good and not intend the evil effect – an important service proportional to the gravity of the sacrifice," is the writer's own stating of these requirements. Would he forbid a doctor to inoculate himself with a deadly germ in order to describe the several stages of its development within his body, and leave a record of it as a valuable contribution to medical science? Like the captain, the doctor could truly say to himself: "Although, by inoculating myself, I encompass my own death, **I do not intend my own death, but only to demonstrate scientifically the effects of the death-producing germ.**" Notice that the writer's "finis operis"– self-killing – is the same in the germ inoculation case as in the prussic acid case. In the former case, however, the proportion of good is **manifestly present, and manifestly lacking to the latter case, in which, moreover, the ill effect was intended as a means.**

WRITER'S AGENTS ALL INTEND DEATH AS MEANS

In the case of the man who puts a bullet through his brain in order to test the efficiency of his revolver, the required proportion of good is also **manifestly wanting.** He does not survive the test. He "throws away" his life. In the case of the "sati woman," the "bankrupt" and the "sufferer," their own deaths were the means, chosen by themselves to attain their respective purposes, and **must therefore have been intended,** contrary to the writer's injunction –"you must direct your intention to the good that is in the act, and away from the evil which is in it."

It is of no avail therefore for the prussic acid man, the revolver man, the sati woman, the bankrupt or the sufferer to urge that **they did not intend their own deaths.** Whenever the proportion of good effect is decidedly lacking, it **must be concluded that the ill effect is intended.** Their **preposterous protestations** to the contrary, the writer **proposes as perfect parallels** for the sound theological reasoning of the hunger-striker, who rightly says to himself, with the captain who blows up his ship, and the doctor who inoculates himself with the deadly germ: "Although by fasting I am acting in such a way as to encompass my own death, **I do not intend my own death, but only to promote the cause of my country.**" "Sophistry!" exclaims The Examiner. "As well might I argue," etc. And the entire reason on account of which he rejects the ethically sound reasoning of the hunger-striker is because "**fasting if prolonged enough is just as infallible (though gradual) a means of killing oneself as taking prussic acid which acts instantaneously.**" "It is self-killing" says the writer, and the **popular mind reconciles itself with difficulty to the lawfulness of any self-killing.** Does he not instruct them accordingly when he says: "**The morality of the act is determined by its "finis operis," which must not be obscured by introducing the "finis operantis?**" "**It is only by way of corollary or appendix that theologians add a caution – that you must direct your intention to the good** which is in the act and away from the evil which is in it. The directing of the intention is **merely a secondary and personal matter.**" And this he says immediately after protesting that "in order to clear thinking on such points, we must first get our definitions and principles clear as a general background." Alas for the "definitions" and the "principles" and the "general background" and the "clear thinking!"

(33) "Still more sophistical would it be to make a verbal "distinction between 'self-killing' and 'suicide,' thus: "'I do not intend **suicide,** but I only mean **to kill** "**myself** in the interests of my country.' It would "be equally sophistical to say: 'I do nothing to kill "myself; I merely abstain from food which is an "indifferent and innocent action."

SOPHISTIC WHILE DENOUNCING SOPHISTRY

(a) The writer is unhappy in his example of a **verbal** distinction. The distinction between suicide and self-killing is more than verbal. The things are not the same. Contradictory predicates are one sign of a real distinction, and **self-killing may be lawful and laudable,** while **suicide never can be.**

Moreover, he makes his sophist say: "I do not intend suicide." This is neither sophistry **nor anything else that is right or wrong.** It is nothing. His sophist **predicates a contradiction** regarding himself. He says: "**I do not intend intended self-killing.**" But there is no such thing as an intended self-killing that was not intended. It is as veritable a paradox as **a black horse of another color.** His sophist would be guilty of **a mere verbal** distinction if he were to say: "I do not intend to kill myself; I only mean to end my life."

(b) Bent on making the position of the hunger-striker appear equally absurd, the writer makes him say: "I do nothing to kill myself; I merely abstain from food which is an indifferent and innocent action." The latter of those two assertions is **unqualifiedly true,** as has been already shown at considerable length. The first is artfully ambiguous. It may mean either (1) I do nothing **with the intention of** killing myself, or (2) I do **nothing positive** – shooting, drowning, poisoning – that would kill me, or (3) I do **nothing negative** – omit nothing – breathing, eating, sleeping – whose omission would kill me.

Plainly this last interpretation is not the mind of the hunger-striker. He could not say it truly. **He need not say it in order to justify himself.** Yet this is just the interpretation which the writer **wishes to convey to his readers as being the mind of the hunger-striker,** for it is the only interpretation that gives a handle for his "equally sophistical" verdict. This is like putting a falsehood on the hunger-striker's lips in order to have some grounds for calling him a liar. By saying what is correctly attributed to him in the first interpretation—"I do nothing with the intention of killing myself"—the hunger-striker says all that is needed to justify himself in the circumstances. But he says, moreover, though justified without it, all that is contained in the second interpretation—"I do nothing positive to kill myself." The writer's captain, whom he justifies, cannot say truly, "I do nothing positive that would kill me." He explodes the magazine.

Who then is it that is "equally sophistical" as when he was "still more sophistical" than when his argument was "mere sophistry?" Not the hunger-striker but the writer himself. He finds the hunger-striker guilty of sophistry only by sprinkling over every page and almost every paragraph of his own article the nauseating malodor of his own sophistry.

"All looks sophistic that the sophists spy,
"As all looks yellow to the jaundiced eye."

(34) "We have found people arguing that fasting, even "when it results in death, is not direct self-killing "but indirect. This is quite untrue. There is nothing "more direct than the relation between food and the "sustentation of life. To withhold food until a man "dies is just as direct killing as to administer a dose "of poison."

SOPHISTRY HUNG ON THE WORD "DIRECT"

The author here treats his readers to a piece of sophistry hung on the word "direct"—the most ambiguous word in the English language. The terms "direct" and "indirect" have more than a dozen different meanings, and therefore lend themselves readily to sophistry. Here are some of those different meanings:

1. A ROUTE is direct when NOT DETOURED.
2. An ANSWER is direct when NOT EVASIVE.
3. HEREDITY is direct when NOT COLLATERAL.
4. AUTHORITY is direct when NOT DELEGATED.
5. EXPRESSION is direct when NOT INVOLVED.
6. POLICY is direct when NOT VACILLATING.
7. ELECTRIC CURRENT is direct when NOT ALTERNATING.
8. TESTIMONY is direct when NOT BY CROSS-EXAMINATION.
9. NOMINATION is direct when done by popular vote, NOT BY CONVENTION.

10. FOOD is a direct sustainer of life, because its influx is IMMEDIATE, NOT REMOTE. (Notice that this directness is a MATERIAL quality of MATERIAL FOOD.)

11. KILLING is direct when INTENDED, indirect when NOT INTENDED. Notice (a) that this directness and indirectness are SPIRITUAL QUALITIES of the agent's will, in the one case wanting his own death FOR ITSELF, in the other MERELY TOLERATING his own death, for some good inseparable from his own death. Notice (b) that this is the only sense in which the word "direct" has any moral signification.

"It is never lawful to kill oneself **directly, that is, "intentionally,"** writes St. Alphonsus, "but it is some-"times lawful to compass one's own death by placing "an action from which death is certain to follow un-"**intentionally.**" (De Quinto Praecepto, No. 366.)

But when we say that food directly sustains life, the word "directly" no longer means intentionally, but immediately, that is, by its own immediate influx, not remotely, through the influx of some other proximate cause.

The vast variety of meanings here set forth should put readers on their guard whenever they meet the word "direct." A writer who wishes to lead his readers astray can readily do so by using the term "direct." Its meaning must always be cautiously gathered from the context in which it is used, and the average reader lacks ability to do the cautious gathering.

The sophist has therefore an asy task when he undertakes to make what he knows to be false, appear to be true. Juggler with words that he is, he passes unnoticed from one meaning of the word "direct" to an entirely different meaning, the unwary reader all the time concentrating on the first meaning.

HUNGER-STRIKER'S "DIRECT." SOPHIST'S "DIRECT"

And so when the hunger-striker rightly argues that fasting until death is not direct self-killing, this quibbler objects that "there is nothing more direct than the relation between food and the sustentation of life." Simply by using the word "direct," in any sense whatever, he makes it appear that he is meeting the hunger-striker's argument squarely, though, in reality, he shamelessly evades it. The hunger-striker's "direct" is an intention of his own will regarding his own death. (No. 11). The author's "direct" is a quality of all food whereby it immediately sustains llife. (No. 10). The hunger-striker argues a question in moral theology when he says that his own death is not intended – not direct – and therefore not suicide. The writer refutes him **by merely enunciating a principle in physiology** – that the action of food in sustaining life is **immediate, not remote.**

And, still using exactly the same tactics, **he delilvers what he considers a knockout blow to the hunger-striker** when he concludes that "to withhold food until a man dies is just as direct killing as to administer a dose of poison." He continues to lie like truth, in order to brand every hunger-striker until death with the infamy of "suicide." That hateful title must be pinned on every hunger-striker until death, even though, in doing so, theological truth has to be sacrificed to theological falsehood.

BASE QUIBBLE PIVOTED ON THE WORD "DIRECT"

And **the reason, the only reason** which the writer can give for crying "suicide" instead of "hero" is **the base quibble hinged on the word "direct."** The hunger-striker's self-killing is "direct," that is to say, essentially and immediately resulting, in the physical order, from his refusal of all food. "Therefore," says the writer, **it is also direct self-killing in the moral order** – in other words, intended. Just as reasonably might he have said: "Therefore the moon is made of green cheese." When hunger-strikers argue that fasting, even when it results in death, is not direct self-killing but indirect, **they argue quite truly.** When the writer in The Examiner argues that fasting, when it results in death, is intended self-killing, **he argues quite falsely.**

> "Oh what a tangled web we weave
> "Whene'er we labor to deceive!"

(35) "To withhold food until a man dies is just as direct "killing as applying a dose of poison. The only differ- "ence is that poison acts suddenly and starvation "acts gradually. But both are equally direct."

WRITER REPEATS THE BASE QUIBBLE

Here the performance of **juggling with the term "direct" is again repeated.** Physically there is the same essential **relation of cause and effect** between fasting and destruction of life that there is between a dose of poison and the destruction of life. Hence to withhold food is just as direct, **physical self-killing as applying a dose of poison. But in the moral order** – of which alone there is here any question – to withhold food from oneself, **in aid of one's country, is not direct self-killing at all,** – since death is not intended – whereas **death resulting from the dose of poison deliberately administered to oneself is intended.** Nevertheless, the writer asserts complacently that "both are equally direct." Both are equally direct in the physical order. In the moral order, the death by poison is direct, because intended; the death by fasting is not direct at all, because not intended. And it is of the moral order, and not of the merely physical, that the writer was supposed to be speaking, when he said that death from fasting and death from a dose of poison are "both equally direct." In the moral order, of which alone there should be any question, the statement is **unqualifiedly false and evidently so.**

(36) "Among several of the writers on this question we "have noticed another fallacy. They seem to think "that the 'directing of the intention' makes a differ-"ence to the morality of the act objectively con-"sidered: e.g. that if you kill yourself, intending "suicide, it is suicide; and if you kill yourself, in-"tending something else, it is not suicide. This is "just as good as saying: 'If you knock your neighbor "down, intending assault and battery, it is assault "and battery; but if you knock your neighbor down, "intending to test the strength of your biceps, it is "not assault and battery.' This kind of argumenta-"tion is muddle-headed to a degree."

OBJECTIVE *VERSUS* OBJECTIVELY CONSIDERED

The terms "subjective" and "objective," "subjectively" and "objectively," lend themselves readily to what Macbeth calls "the equivocation that lies like truth." "**Morality objectively considered**" is the **adequate morality** – from object, intention and circumstances – considered **apart from its subject** – the agent. It must not be confounded with "objective morality" – the **partial morality derived from the object alone.** Let this difference between "morality objectively considered" and "objective morality" be well understood and well remembered. Notice in particular that the **adequate morality of an act as it exists concretely in the agent as subject, is not diminished, does not become partial or inadequate when "objectively considered."** Objectively considered, it still retains the morality derived from object, intention and circumstances. "Morality objectively considered" merely disregards the subject – the agent. "Objective morality" – that derived from the object alone – **disregards the morality derived from intention and circumstances.***

---

*"It is obvious that some objects have an **objective** morality of "their own, and this causes the will which tends towards them to "be either good or bad, e.g. to blaspheme God, to love God."
(Slater, "Moral Theology," page 46.)

"Moralitas quae **ex objecto** desumitur appelatur moralitas "**objectiva**." (Gury-Ballerini, 1. page 21.)

DIRECTING INTENTION MAKES ALL DIFFERENCE

With this distinction well in mind, let us examine the argumentation cited by the writer, to see if it be as fallacious and "muddle-headed" as he claims it to be "The morality of the act, objectively considered," being the combined morality from **end, means** and **circumstances**, to say, as the writer does, that "directing the intention makes no difference to the morality of the act objectively considered," is the same as saying that the morality of the act, objectively considered, remains the same whether the intention be directed to the good effect or to the ill one. This is, of course, **absurdly untrue**, and is, besides, **contradicted** by **the writer himself**. A moment later he writes: "**You must direct your intention to the good** which is in the act, and **away from the evil** which is in it." Why does he urge directing the intention to the good effect, and, at the same time, **insist that it "makes no difference to the morality of the act, objectively considered?"** Of course it does not make a difference to the **objective** morality of the act – the morality from the object alone – but we cannot suppose this to have been the writer's meaning. In that case, he would only be saying that the morality from the object is a separate morality from that of the intention – a true truism.

NO FALLACY IN ETHICAL PRINCIPLE PROPOSED

And where, pray, is the fallacy in the ethical principle proposed by the writer: "If you kill yourself intending suicide, it is suicide; but if you kill yourself, intending something else, it is not suicide?" Is it not a fundamental principle of morals that no agent is credited with more than he intends? If he intends only good, he is credited only with merits, however much ill he may have done unintentionally, and, on the contrary, if he intends only evil, he receives only demerits, no matter how much good unintentionally results from his action. Hence, if he intends suicide, he is **guilty of suicide**, even when he does nothing to kill himself; and **if he doesn't intend suicide, he is not guilty of suicide**, even when he actually kills himself, as the writer's **captain** does. "Moral actions," says St. Thomas, "derive their species from the object intended, not from the object unintended or per accidens." (11-11-; q. 64. a. 7.)

FITS PERFECTLY THE CASE OF THE CAPTAIN

Notice how snugly the principle we are discussing **fits the case of the captain**. In justification of his behavior he says: "If – by blowing up my ship – I kill myself, **intending suicide, it is suicide**; but if – by blowing up my ship – I kill myself, intending only to benefit my country, it is not suicide." If the writer can discover a fallacy either in the general ethical principle enunciated by himself, or in the captain's application of it to his own case, then he is endowed with a special logical sense not granted to other mortals.

GENUINE DIRECTING MADE TO RESEMBLE BOGUS

All the same, he cries "fallacy" to his own fundamental ethical principle, and, in an attempt to demonstrate a fallacy where no fallacy exists, invokes the aid of a fallacy himself. He continues to wage war on the intention. At present his attack is directed against "the fallacy of directing the intention." To show the "fallacy," he has recourse to a parallel. Constructing parallels that are not parallel is an old practice, but not a very honest one. It is the role of the rhetorician rather than the philosopher or theologian. The writer elaborates several instances of counterfeit directing the intention, and from their manifest absurdity concludes that all directing the intention is equally absurd. In some of his examples, the intention is directed to the good effect as an end, but is also directed to the ill effect as a means, and thereby becomes evil. Of this kind of directing the intention, the sati woman, the bankrupt and the sufferer are specimens. In others of his cases – the prussic acid man and the revolver man – the utter disproportion of good effect points also to an evil intention. All these cases were deliberately chosen by the writer because the several agents profess to be directing their intentions to the good effect and away from the ill effect, when it is plain that, in reality they are doing the very opposite. And because, in their cases, it is evidently absurd to contend that directing the intention saves the morality of the act objectively considered, he asserts and insists that it is absurd in every case, none excepted – asserts and insists that it is absurd to say "if you kill yourself, intending suicide, it is suicide; but if you kill yourself, intending something else, it is not suicide."

ANOTHER OF AUTHOR'S UNPARALLEL PARALLELS

Of the simple theological axiom here correctly enunciated, the writer says: "This is just as good as saying: 'If you knock your neighbor down, intending assault and battery, it is assault and battery; but if you knock your neighbor down, intending to test the strength of your biceps, it is not assault and battery." This is another of his "parallels," made from exactly the same materials and cast in exactly the same mold as his previous ones. Like his "prussic acid" man and his "revolver" man, his "biceps" man perpetrates a grave injury, and while doing so, protests that he intends only the inconsiderable good of testing his biceps. The proportion of good, and also the good intention, necessary for the lawfulness of every act having an ill effect, are wanting. Another case of "knocking down," which has due proportion of good, as well as good intention, will exhibit the writer's own sophistry. A member of the coast-guard crew says: "If I stun a drowning man with a blow, intending assault and battery, it is assault and battery. But if I stun a drowning man with a blow, intending only to eliminate his frantic resistance and thereby save his life, it is not assault and battery." Will the writer venture to cry "fallacy" to the reasoning of the coast-guard? He will hardly be so rash. Yet the case of the coast-guard differs in nothing from the case of the biceps-man, except in the proportion of good, and the concomitant good intention.

DIRECTING INTENTION MAKES VAST DIFFERENCE

Directing the intention makes a vast difference to the morality of the act objectively considered, the writer to the contrary notwithstanding. Through directing the intention, the action of the coast-guard,—objectively considered—is made an act of heroic charity, instead of an act of assault and battery. By directing the intention, the actions of the captain and the hunger-striker—objectively considered—become acts of martyr-patriotism instead of acts of suicide. Quite a substantial difference, dear writer!

But there is more to come. He has not yet done with eliminating the intention.

> (37) "An intention never makes the least difference to "the objective morality of the act done. What the "intention does is merely to modify the subjective "attitude of the mind of the agent towards the act. "It leaves the act objectively the same, with its "objective effects and the full responsibility for "them."

"OBJECTIVE," "SUBJECTIVE," TO STATE A TRUISM!

Here again the writer serves up to his readers plenty of "subjective" and "objective," "subjectively" and "objectively"—terms that are strictly technical and therefore hardly understood by any except the metaphysician. Recall the difference between "objective morality" and "morality objectively considered." "Morality objectively considered" is the adequate morality—from end, means and circumstances—disregarding, for the time, its subject—the agent.

"Objective morality" is the inadequate morality **derived from the object alone**, disregarding, for the moment, **the further morality which the action must always derive from intention and circumstances.** With this distinction in mind, 'tis easy to agree with the writer's patent assertion that "an intention never makes the least difference to the **objective morality of the act done."** This statement only says that the morality from the end is not a component of the morality from the means, but something supervening upon it – the identical truism already called by the name it deserves.

INTENTION CHIEF COMPONENT OF ALL MORALITY

But though the end or intention does not make the least difference to the objective, inadequate morality of the act, it must not be concluded that the end or intention does not make the least difference to the adequate morality of the act. The intention is the chief constituent of all morality. Without it, there could never be any morality at all. Aside from the intention, adoration of God is not good, nor is blasphemy of Him evil. The act of intending, on the contrary, contracts, in addition to its own morality, the full morality of object and circumstances intended. Yet, the writer's version of it is that the intention "merely modifies the subjective attitude of the mind of the agent towards the act." (1) Why "merely," as if the changed attitude from not intending to intending, or from intending to not intending, counts for little or nothing? The intention to blaspheme, of itself, without act or circumstance, contracts "merely" the full guilt of blasphemy. (2) Is not the intention the attitude itself – of the agent towards the action – rather than a modifier of that attitude? (3) Is not intention an attitude of will rather than of mind – an act of appetition and not of cognition?

ALL RESPONSIBILITY FROM THE INTENTION

The writer's further assertion, that the intention "leaves the act objectively the same, with its objective effects and the full responsibility for them," seems to assert responsibility independently of the intention. If it means anything more than what he has already said several times – that the intention is not a component of the morality derived from the object and circumstances – it is false. He says the intention "leaves the act objectively the same." But the question at issue is not whether the intention does or does not leave the act objectively the same, but whether it does or does not leave the adequate morality of the act objectively the same. Will he say that the intention does leave the adequate morality of the act objectively the same – that it is not a component of that adequate morality? This would be equivalent to saying that the intention is not a source of morality at all – more than he will venture to say, at least in so many words, though he comes perilously near to saying so – and presumably hopes to be understood as saying so – when he says that the intention "leaves the act objectively the same, with its objective effects and the full responsibility for them." Is not this an attempt to say that, independently of the intention, there is full responsibility for the act and its objective effects; that agents are responsible for actions, and their effects, never intended; that there are deliberate acts which do not derive any of their morality from the intention of the agent; that the intention of the agent is not always one of the sources of morality at all. The intention "leaves the act objectively the same," but it leaves responsibility for the act where it found none.

And now, having expounded, as he thinks, or affects to think, the moral principles involved in every case of two effects, and rejected as "fallacy," "sophistry," "muddle-headed argumentation," legitimate inferences from first moral principles, he sets forth a method of his own for testing the lawfulness of every such action.

(38) "The right process in applying the 'principle of two "effects' is this. First, settle objectively whether the "act is morally allowed; whether it is permissible to "perform it as a good act in spite of the evil effects "which happen to be bound up with its performance."

"SETTLE OBJECTIVELY." "THE RIGHT PROCESS"?

Again the writer is harping on an old string. "Objectively" and "subjectively" are his special favorites. What does he mean by "settling objectively whether the act is morally allowed?" Does he mean that the objective standards of morality must determine whether the act is morally allowed? If so, this is the entire issue involved in all the controversy about hunger-strike. Moral Theology is not primarily concerned as to whether Mayor MacSwiney's hunger-strike was lawful or not, but whether any hunger-strike, prescending from every individual hunger-striker, be lawful or not. Moral Theology settles its questions "objectively."

But this can hardly be the writer's meaning, for he speaks of the "settling objectively" as the initial step in "the right process of applying the principle of two effects." By "settling objectively" he would therefore seem to mean determining whether the act is lawful **from its object—from the first of the three sources of morality.** If this be his meaning, it might have been expressed much more briefly, and certainly much more clearly, by the consecrated question—"is the act good in itself, or at least indifferent." This question should bring him immediately to consider the formal object whereby the act is specified. Yet he does not turn to the formal object of the act, but reverts to an old trail about "duty," "right" and so forth—"the right process."

(39) "The act is permissible if there is a duty to perform "it, and if this duty has precedence over the general "duty of avoiding evil effects as far as possible. It "may also be permissible if I have a strict right to "perform it—a right so strict as to override the gen-"eral duty of avoiding evil effects as far as possible. "It cannot, however, be performed if there lies on me "some specific duty of avoiding that particular bad "effect."

"PARTURIUNT MONTES, NASCETUR RIDICULUS MUS"

All this is beating the air. Instead of inquiring whether the action is lawful from **object, intention** and **circumstances**—whether the four requisite conditions are verified—he informs his readers that **"the act is permissible if there is a duty to perform it."** Does anyone need to be told that it is lawful for him to do his duty? And he adds the further meaningless proviso: "If this duty has precedence over the general duty of avoiding evil effects as far as possible." According to these words there can be a duty to perform an act, which duty, however, has **not precedence over the general duty of avoiding evil effects as far as possible.** Is the duty which has no such precedence a duty at all? Can there ever be such a duty?

"THE RIGHT PROCESS" CONTINUED

"The act is permissible," the writer says, "if there is a duty to perform it, and if this duty has precedence over the general duty of avoiding evil effects as far as possible." How much wiser are his readers now than before? They are now forced to ask themselves: (1) When is there a duty to place the act, and (2) how is it to be known that such duty "has precedence over the general duty of avoiding evil effects?" Again he says with as little meaning: "It may also be permissible if I have a strict right to perform it—a right so strict as to override the general duty of avoiding evil effects." As in the case of duty, no one needs to be told that it not merely **"may be"** but **IS permissible** to place an act which the agent has a strict right to perform, or that there can ever be a conflict between a strict right to perform an act having an ill effect, and an opposing general duty of avoiding ill effects. Moreover, as before, the author's readers are again thrown back on this twofold inquiry – first, how am I to know when I have a strict right to place the act, and, secondly, how am I to know whether that right is "so strict as to override the general duty of avoiding evil effects?" Non solvitur ambulando! "It cannot, however, be performed," continues the writer, "if there lies on me some specific duty of avoiding that particular bad effect." This again is but enunciating the obvious. The statement has all the solemn emptiness of Sir Roger de Coverley's pronouncement that "much might be said on both sides." Who is unaware that an action producing an ill effect is unlawful if the agent has a specific duty of avoiding that bad effect? And again the question recurs – How am I to know when I have such specific duty of avoiding ill effects, and when have I no such duty? How much light do the writer's rules throw on the lawfulness or unlawfulness of hunger-striking? His readers are now farther removed from the correct solution of this complicated case than when he introduced his method of solving it, with these pretentious words: "In order to clear thinking, we must first get our definitions and principles clear." "The right process in applying the principle of two effects is this," etc. The right process in catching wild fowl is to shake salt on their tails.

(40) "The good effect of the action must be inherent to "the action and the direct and immediate outcome of "it per se. The bad effect must not be inherent to "the action per se, but per accidens and concomitan- "ter, i.e. it happens to be inseparably attached on "this particular occasion. The act is not allowed if "the evil effect is the means by which the good effect "is obtained and without which it would not be ob- "tained. All this can be and must be settled without "the least reference to the intention. It is only by "way of corollary or appendix that moral theologians "add a caution ... You must direct your intention to "the good which is in the act and away from the evil "which is in it."

ACCIDENTAL ILL EFFECTS NOT IMPUTABLE

(a) The writer says truly that the good effect must always be "inherent" to the action – "the direct and immediate outcome of it per se." 'Tis evident, however, that he doesn't know why this must be so, for he says falsely, a moment later, that the ill effect must not be inherent, but accidental,—not per se but per accidens." But no case of contingent, accidental ill effect can ever be subject matter for a "duplex effectus." Why not? Because no action, however unlawful in itself, is unlawful **on account of any effect it produces** contingently.

The writer contends that, in every lawful case of two effects, the ill effect must be connected with the action, **not essentially and therefore necessarily and always, but accidentally, contingently and therefore rarely.** "The bad effect must not be inherent to the action **per se, but per accidens et concomitanter,** i.e. it happens to be inseparably attached on this particular occasion." Has he yet to learn what the essential requisites are for a case of "two effects!"

NOT IMPUTABLE BECAUSE NOT FORESEEN

And why is it that no act, however unlawful in itself, is ever unlawful **on account of any effect which it produces contingently?** Because contingent, accidental ill effects cannot be foreseen, and no agent is obliged to omit a good action on account of any effects which he in no way foresees. No one is obliged to do what is impossible, and it is impossible to prevent an ill effect that is unforeseen. **But not so the ill effect proper to every case of "duplex effectus." These are all foreseen effects—foreseen in the actions that produce them, because essentially, and not accidentally, necessarily, and not contingently, resulting from these actions.** In their act of pouring floods of water on the burning building, the firemen foresee the destruction of valuable merchandise. It is an inevitable result. The surgeon foresees, in his act of making an incision, the pain it must unavoidably inflict on his patient.

GOOD EFFECT MUST ALSO BE ESSENTIAL

And it is precisely because contingent, accidental ill effects have no place in any case of "duplex effectus," it is precisely because in every case of "two effects" **the ill effect follows essentially and necessarily and inevitably from the action, that the good effect must follow with the same necessity.** If the ill effect were to follow necessarily from the action, and the good effect only accidentally, it would always be certain that the ill effect would follow whenever the action was placed, **but only faintly probable that the good effect might follow.** Evidently such an action would be forbidden because of the ill effect. Yet, the author, when stating the essential requirements for every case of "two effects," says, unwittingly or otherwise, that "the bad effect must not be inherent to the action per se but per accidens, i.e. it happens to be inseparably attached on this particular occasion." How could the ill effect of any "duplex effectus" be foreseen if, as the writer claims, "it happens to be inseparably attached on this particular occasion" but not on every occasion? And if the ill effect "happens" only "on this particular occasion" and is recognized only after the action has been placed, and will probably never "happen" again, even when the same action is placed, why should such an action be ever forbidden on account of such accidental effect?

VERDICT AGAINST MacSWINEY

And what a complete verdict the writer would have secured against Mayor MacSwiney if this false as well as foolish principle of his were true. He would then reason, syllogistically as follows:

Maj. Prop. That an action producing an ill effect may nevertheless be lawful, the ill effect must be an accidental, not an essential effect of the action.

Min. Prop. But the ill effect of Mayor MacSwiney's hunger-strike until death is an essential, not an accidental effect of his action.

Conclusion Therefore his hunger-strike is unlawful.

Verily, the author, before he has finished, will have returned a verdict against the Lord Mayor on many counts!

"THE EXAMINER'S" SEA CAPTAIN CONTRADICTS

Let us see how the action of the author's captain squares with his doctrine that the ill effect "must not be inherent to the action per se, but only per accidens et concomitanter." The good effect of blowing up his ship is the aid rendered to his country by depriving the enemy of his ship. The ill effect is the death, or the imminent danger of death, to himself and his crew. Is it only accidentally and contingently and rarely that the crew incur death, or imminent danger of death, when their ship is dynamited and sunk? Death or imminent danger of death is as equally prompt and inevitable a consequence of the explosion as the destruction of the ship is. The explosion is, by its nature, essentially ordained to produce both effects.

ILL EFFECT LAWFUL MEDIATE MEANS

(b) A qualifying distinction is also needed for the writer's further assertion that "the act is not allowed if the evil effect is the means by which the good effect is obtained, and without which it would not be obtained." We are accustomed to speak of the good effect, and thus imply that there never is or can be more than a single good effect. This is not true. It is necessary to distinguish between immediate and mediate good effects of the action. The act is unlawful if the ill effect is the means by which the immediate, primary good effect, is obtained. The act is not rendered unlawful because the ill effect is the means by which a further mediate, secondary good effect is obtained. An example will make the distinction clear.* Whether that secondary good effect "would" or would not be obtained without the ill effect as a means, matters nothing. If de facto it is obtained by it, the principle is vindicated that secondary good effects, attained by means of the ill effect, are lawfully attained. Mayor MacSwiney's death helped enormously the cause for which he died – a good effect obtained by means of the ill effect, yet without rendering his act unlawful.

"WITHOUT LEAST REFERENCE TO INTENTION"?

(c) The writer says that "all this can and must be settled without the least reference to the intention." What is the "settling" and what is the "all this" to which he refers? What can it be except determining whether or not the action is lawful from object and circumstances? Nothing else, no other "settling" is done "without the least reference to the intention." This morality from object and circumstances the writer exaggerates, that the morality from the intention may seem to be a negligible factor. This is just what the author continues to do. He writes: "It is only by way of corollary or appendix that moral theologians add a caution ... You must direct your intention to the good which is in the act, and away from the evil which is in it." "The evil that is in it," says the writer. (a) There is no evil in the act when the conditions required for a lawful case of "two effects" are present. (b) The ill effect has no moral evil in it, since it is not intended but only permitted – tolerated.

GROSS CALUMNY OF MORAL THEOLOGIANS

(d) A corollary is an immediate inference from some evident truth, and an appendix is a supplementary discussion, subjoined to a treatise already substantially complete. How the caution of moral theologians about directing the intention to the good, and away from the evil, which is in

---

*Puella innupta, ex delicto gravida, lotione venenosa utitur ad morbum lethalem (cancer) depellendum. Veneno morbus eradicatur, foetus occiditur, bona fama puellae servatur **mediante effectu malo**.

the act, could, by any stretch of imagination, be called either an immediate inference or a supplementary discussion, is difficult to understand. Indeed the writer's "corollary or appendix" is a gross calumny of moral theologians. They will now speak for themselves in answer to this grave charge of treating the "directing" the intention as a "corollary" or "appendix."

BALLERINI-PALMIERI, S.J.

(1) "The intention, though listed among the circum-"stances, is the principal factor in morality, and so "receives a separate treatise. So important is its "place that it determines the morality of the means "whereby the end is attained, and since the object "('finis operis') is often such a means, the intention "frequently determines the morality of the object." (vol. 1, p. 79.)

LEHMKUHL, S.J.

(2) "Since the end of the agent is first in intention, and "according to the character of that end the agent "proceeds to seek the means, it is evident that the "morality of every action depends most of all on the "end or intention." (vol. 1, p. 32.)

VERMEERSCH, S.J.

(3) "Nothing is more the object of the will than the in-"tention – the good for which the will acts. The in-"tention is therefore the principal source of moral-"ity." (vol. 1, p. 105)

GENICOT, S.J.

(4) "The end or intention, though included among the "circumstances, is treated separately because it is "the principal source of morality. Occupying the "principal place among the circumstances, and often "determining the morality even of the object, the "intention is obviously the chief source of morality." (vol. 1, pp. 39-40.)

SLATER, S.J.

(5) "It is obvious that the end or motive which induces "the agent to act, holds a very prominent place "among the sources of the morality of an action . . . "It is the end or motive which sets the will in mo-"tion and gives its own moral quality to the action "which follows." (vol. 1, pp. 46-57.)

DE BOYLESVE, S.J.

(6) "The morality of human actions depends most of all "on the end or intention of the agent, for it is the "end or intention that principally arouses the agent "to action." ("Cursus Philosophiae," p. 367.)

RICKABY, S.J.

(7) "The end in view is what lies nearest to a man's "heart as he acts. On that his mind is chiefly bent. "On that his main purpose is fixed. Therefore the end "in view enters into morality more deeply than any "other element of the action." (Moral Philos. p. 32.)

POLAND, S.J.

(8) Question "Which is the chief determinant of the "morality of the act of the will?"

Answer "The final purpose, because it is the chief "thing on which the will is fixed, to which it "directs all else and without which it would "not act." ("Fundamental Ethics," p. 45.)

ST. THOMAS AQUINAS

(9) "Human actions are specified formally by the inten-"tion, materially by the object of the external act." ("Summa Theologiae," 1-11, Quaest, xviii, art. vi.)

"One and the same action may have two effects, the "one intended, the other not. Moral acts are specified, "not by the effect that is not intended, but by the "effect which is." (2a, 2ae, p. 64, a. 7.)

PRUMMER, O.P.

(10) "Though the subjective intention is also a circum-"stance of the act, nevertheless, since its influx into "the morality of every act is the greatest of all, the "Angelic Doctor, and after him theologians in general, "devote a special treatise to the purpose or intention." ("Manuale Theologiae Moralis," vol. 1, p. 65.)

FR. CRONIN, D.D.

(11) "The end aimed at ('finis operantis') is the original "source of the whole act, for the act, with its object "and circumstances, is nothing more than means to "the end aimed at. And as a man intends the end "more than the means, so the end is, in one sense, the "principal moral element in the act."
("The Science of Ethics," vol. 1.)

MENTIONS NO THEOLOGIAN. CITES NONE

Here is the answer of many most representative moralists to the author's unprecedented accusation that they refer to the intention only by way of "corollary or appendix." It is answer also to much besides that he says about the unimportance of the intention as a factor in morality. Whence and how he derived such novel principles regarding the intention, is known only to himself. He tells his readers nothing about it. It is worthy of remark that, in his entire discussion of hunger-strike, he does not make reference to a single individual theologian, nor give a single citation from the works of any standard author. It would be very interesting as well as instructive for his readers to be told which moral theologians in particular speak by way of "corollary or appendix" about directing the intention. He implies that all moral theologians do. But he does not cite a single author from among them, nor even refer his readers to the places in their writings in which they speak of the intention as a "corollary" or as an "appendix."

(41) "The proper lines of argument is to determine first "of all, whether a man is justified in starving himself to death, in the attempt to secure his release, "or, failing that, to give an example to his compatriots. When that point is settled, the dispute is "at an end. The direction of the intention is merely "a secondary and personal matter."

"RIGHT PROCESS." "PROPER LINES OF ARGUMENT"

(a) In No. 38 the author undertook to show "the right process in applying the principle of two effects." In the present citation, he again undertakes to show "the proper lines of argument" in the same matter. Which wrong process, which wrong lines of argument do these two pronouncements of his aim to correct? "The proper lines of argument," "the right process in applying the principle of two effects," is already outlined very accurately in every text-book on Moral Theology. The writer cannot add anything to it; he cannot subtract anything from it; he cannot substitute anything for it. That "process," that "lines of argument," is the only one Moral Theology has, and the only one it needs, to prove the lawfulness or unlawfulness of any case of indirect voluntary.

ARE CONDITIONS OF "TWO EFFECTS" REALIZED?

(b) Are all the conditions for a lawful case of two effects realized in the MacSwiney case or are they not? Is the action itself good? Is the intention good regarding both end and means? Is there due proportion of good effect?

When these questions are answered correctly, **then and not before**, is the MacSwiney case solved, and "the dispute at an end." But the case will never be solved by "The Examiner!" Not only does the writer not answer the above questions correctly, but he doesn't even ask them. Instead he tells his readers to "settle objectively whether the act is morally allowed," "whether a man is justified in starving himself to death in the attempt to secure his release." He tells his readers "the right process," "the right lines of argument," by barely stating the case in question. The test of **action, intention and circumstance of proportion** furnishes a **clear** and brief and simple way of solving the MacSwiney case. But we have long ago learned that the writer in "The Examiner" is not in quest of the clear, the brief or the simple. His purpose is better attained by shunning them.

(c) He says "when that point is settled **the dispute is at an end?**" What does he mean by "**that point?**" The dispute is at an end, only when it is found that all the requisites for a lawful case of two effects **are or are not realized**.

(d) He also says that "the directing of the intention is **merely a secondary and personal matter.**" This is but again turning the intention out of doors, notwithstanding that every theologian, none excepted, insists that the morality of every action depends most of all on the intention, even to the extent of sometimes determining the morality of the means, that is, of the action itself.

(42) "It is utterly inept to argue – as some have argued – "that the morality of self-killing depends on the in-"tention. Even though the act with a double effect "is allowed, this does not abolish the evil effect. It "still remains that the act is producing a bad effect, "which under other circumstances would be sinful. "Therefore (they say) you must not look on that "evil effect with complacency. You must still recog-"nize it as evil and dislike it, and wish you could "avoid it. You must feel that you are bringing it "about under a regrettable necessity, because it is "tacked on to an act which you have a duty or a "right to perform. If you could separate off the "evil effect and avoid it, you would be obliged to "do so."

HIS UNINTENDED KILLING SAME AS INTENDED!

(a) The writer here says expressly that the morality of self-killing does not depend on the intention. If this were true, then the morality of the self-killing that is intended would differ in nothing from that of the self-killing that is not intended. The self-killing of the captain, whom the writer **justifies,** and the self-killing of the **bankrupt suicide,** whom he **condemns,** differ in nothing except the intention. The **captain** intends, **as an end,** to aid his country, and intends the destruction of his ship **as a means** – both of **which intentions are lawful.** The bankrupt intends **as an end** to shun disgrace, and intends **his own death as a means** – the latter intention unlawful. "Malum ex quocumque defectu."

NO MORALITY DEPENDS ON INTENTION!

(b) Now since these totally opposite cases of self-killing **differ only in the intention,** if, as the writer contends, the morality of self-killing does not depend on the intention, neither does the morality of any other act. **Either all acts** – self-killing included – derive their partial morality from the intention, or no act does. The relation of the intention to the morality of the act is the same for **an act of self-killing as for an act of self-immolation, for an act of treason** as for an act of patriotism, for an act of burglary as for an act of charity. If, then the morality **of self-killing** does not depend on the intention, **neither does the** morality of self-immolation, or of treason, or of patriotism, or **of burglary or of charity.** In other words, the intention is not a source of morality at all – **a conclusion legitimately inferred several times already from other pronouncements of the writer,** in the course of his article on hunger-strike. Like the morality of every other action, **the morality of self-killing depends on object, intention and circumstances** – the only sources of morality.

NO INDIRECT VOLUNTARY MORE THAN ALLOWED

(c) Is no action producing an ill effect more than "allowed" – merely tolerated? The Christian martyrs, the martyrs of Charity, the martyrs of Patriotism, the martyrs in the cause of every virtue, one and all **merited and received their glorious crowns** by actions every one of which produced the ill effect of their own deaths. Does Moral Theology bestow on them **no higher rating than that of being merely "allowed"–"tolerated?"**

WAGES WAR ON PROPORTION OF GOOD EFFECT

(d) Having left the intention **all but dead,** the writer now proceeds **to similarly wrench and wreck the proportion of good effect.** That he accomplishes **by omitting every** word of commendation for the good effect, and pouring forth a Jeremiad of lamentation about the ill effect. **Imagine him delivering this homily to the firemen, as they** pour streams of water on the burning building! "You must not look with complacency on your drenching the merchandise! You must recognize it as evil and dislike it, and wish you could avoid it! You must feel that you are bringing it about as a regrettable necessity," etc., etc.!!

SORELY LAMENTS LOSS OF A SINGLE LIFE

(e) Remember that what the writer calls "evil effect," "bad effect," has in it no moral evil whatever – no sin and no approach to sin. It is only an inconvenience, and generally very small. Remember, too, that the inconvenience is abundantly, often superabundantly, compensated by the good effect, on account of which the action is, in most cases, placed without any compulsion. Why then all the lamentation about the ill effect, with never a word about the worth whileness of the good effect? The writer's distress about the ill effect will be better understood when we find him afterwards calling MacSwiney's death "the grave and irreparable evil of putting an end to one's own life." But he finds no "grave and irreparable evil" in his captain's action of sinking his ship and thereby putting an end to his own life and the lives of every one of his crew. He sheds a deluge of tears for a single life sacrificed for sorely persecuted Ireland, but he has neither tears nor pangs for the millions of human lives sacrificed on the battlefields of the world to the demons of international greed and political chicanery.

(43) "When it comes to persistent starvation wilfully "continued till it is foreseen to issue in death, this "cannot be justified even on the highest ascetical "grounds. 'Any cenobite who starved himself to "death in order to save his soul would be condemned "as a misguided fanatic."

STILL INSINUATING "INTENDED SELF-KILLING"

(a) This is rambling declamation instead of reasoning – a lengthy way of asserting, without proof or attempt at proof, that all hunger-strike until death is unlawful. It is but to reassert the question in debate. "Presistent starvation wilfully continued till it is foreseen to issue in death" – this sounds in the ear of the average reader like deliberately intended death. And apparently this is just how the writer intended it should sound. It was made to measure.

(b) Who ever undertook to justify hunger-strike, who ever said that it could be justified "on the highest ascetical grounds." It is not on ascetical but theological grounds that hunger-strike or any other act is justified. What have "ascetical grounds" to do with the justification of hunger-strike? "Even on the highest ascetical grounds" contains a false implication of **an a fortiori argument** against hunger-strike on **national grounds. If not justified for asceticism, surely not for patriotism! The fulfilment of the four requisite conditions are its adequate justification. The writer's cenobite was a suicide. He intended his own death and used it** to save his soul. Why compare him to the hunger-striker?

> (44) "By way of analogy we recall the fact that Origen "was condemned by a consentient voice for his mu-"tilation performed out of zeal for continency. In "like manner St. Palagia's throwing herself down "to save herself from outrage receives no satisfac-"tory objective solution."

AN ANALOGY THAT IS NOT ANALOGY

"By way of analogy" says the writer! But what **moral analogy is there between an ill effect unintended and an ill effect intended (an evil effect)?** What moral analogy is there between the **unintended** self-killing of the hunger-striker and the **intended** self-killing of St. Pelagia, or the **intended** self-mutilation of Origen? Yet the writer says equivalently: "Hunger-strike until death **is analogous to** the self-mutilation of Origen, to the self-starvation of the cenobite, to the death of St. Pelagia by leaping from a window. But all these acts are certainly unlawful, **and therefore hunger-strike until death is also unlawful."** This is but harping on the same string, **while making it appear to be another string.** The writer continues to **befog and belittle** the intention – the impregnable citadel of every lawful case of two effects and therefore of every hunger-strike. His present argument, **if sophistry may be dignified by that title,** might as well have been included under his "as well might I argue" series thus: "It is mere sophistry to say that the hunger-striker does not intend his own death, but only the benefit to his country. As well might I argue that the cenobite does not intend his own death, but only the salvation of his soul; that St. Pelagia did not intend her own death, but only the preservation of her chastity; that Origen did not intend his self-mutilation but only the preservation of continency." In each of those cases, which the writer calls "analogous" to hunger-strike, the ill effect was the **means intended and used** to attain the good effect. Analogy is partial similarity. But there is not even a partial moral similarity between **an ill effect intended and an ill effect that is not intended.** There is no moral analogy at all between an act that is lawful and an act that is unlawful.

(45) "Even though persistent fasting is ex **objecto direct** "self-killing **by** degrees, there always remains a "loophole **of escape** by stopping the fasting before "it becomes fatal."

"FASTING DIRECT SELF-KILLING BY DEGREES"

(a) Once again the writer trots out a pair of his old stalking-horses—"direct" and "ex objecto," working them this time in combination—team work. Here for a third time, he hangs the same miserable quibble on the word "direct." In Moral Theology direct self-killing always means intended self-killing. St. Alphonsus writes: "It is never lawful to kill oneself directly, that is intentionally." Persistent fasting is ex objecto physically direct, but by no means morally direct, or intended, self-killing. If he means only the former, the citation we are now considering has no more bearing on the morality of hunger-strike than a passage from Robinson Crusoe.

IRRELEVANT OR SELF-CONTRADICTORY

But if he means that persistent fasting is **ex objecto morally direct** (intended) self-killing, then he enunciates a paradox. Persistent fasting is certainly ex objecto, physical self-killing by degrees. That effect follows the act with physical necessity wherever a miracle does not interfere. But what meaning has the writer's "ex objecto intended" self-killing? "Ex objecto" refers only to the morality derived from the effect which persistent fasting does and must produce. It excludes, before all else, the further morality which the same act must always derive from the object of the agent—the intention. As sources of morality, there is an opposition between the object and the intention. There is direct physical self-killing "ex objecto," and there is direct, that is to say, intended, self-killing from the agent. But there is no such commodity as "ex objecto direct self-killing." It is a contradiction. "Direct" means "intended" and the intention is not from the object but from the subject—the agent. Moreover, the writer's "ex objecto intended" is contradicted by the already examined statement of his that "an intention never makes the least difference to the objective morality of th act done."

"LOOPHOLE OF ESCAPE" FROM WHAT?

(b) The assumption that "persistent fasting is 'ex objecto' direct self-killing" is, as we have just seen, either irrelevant or self-contradictory. Yet, on the strength of it, he says "there always remains a loophole of escape by stopping the fasting before it becomes fatal." A loophole of escape from what? From physical death? Not much theology is contained in that conclusion! A loophole of escape from the moral guilt of suicide? Not until Moral Theology declares – what it has not yet declared – that hunger-strike until death is suicide. It declares the very opposite. Furthermore, if hunger-strike until death were suicide –"dato sed non concesso"– the moral guilt of suicide would be incurred by every hunger-striker **the very instant that he intended hunger-strike**, even though he were to reverse his intention the very next moment. **What then becomes of the author's "loophole of escape by stopping the fasting before it becomes fatal"!** It sounds much like his "two pleas" at the beginning of his article.

(46) "There comes a point at which the hunger-striker "has either **to stop or determine to go on at all** "costs. What if he determines to go on, even if he "dies of it? In this case, his act, **by its objective** "**nature** (finis operis), becomes **an act of foreseen** "**and therefore intended** self-killing."

"FORESEEN AND HENCE INTENDED SELF-KILLING"

(a) Stopping and determining to go on are not contradictory attitudes. The hunger-striker may do both. It is stopping and **actually going on** – stopping and not stopping – that are contradictory positions.

(b) There are no "points" on the highway of hunger-strike. **The full morality** of hunger-strike is contracted the very first instant that the hunger-striker **decides on his hunger-strike. From the very beginning he "determines to go on at all costs, even if he dies of it."**

(c) "An act of foreseen and therefore intended self-killing," is the writer's **summing up** of the hunger-striker's behaviour. According to this proclamation, **all foreseen ill effects are intended. They are therefore morally evil,** and the actions which produce them **unlawful because of those evil effects.** "Foreseen and therefore intended"– **this is the grand climax** of all the false and vicious theology which the writer has been **invoking and appealing to** throughout his entire article. At a much earlier stage of his dissertation, we heard him enunciate the same principle in these words: "**The agent is responsible for every result or consequence which is foreseen** (cognitione) **to issue straight out of the act itself.**" (cf. No. 15).

The falsehood and the viciousness will be alike apparent as soon as we attempt to apply the writer's unheard of principle. **How does it fit the case of the captain?** Remember that the author, and all other theologians, justify and defend his action. Does the captain foresee his own death? He most certainly does! It is impossible for him to be blind to it. "The act is deliberate, with knowledge of the end," says the writer. (No. 22).

"EXAMINER" VERDICT AGAINST ALL HEROES

And now we have but to invoke his "foreseen and therefore intended" and we have the captain intending his own death, and therefore a suicide. And, according to the same principle, the same must be said of every martyr in every grandest cause of God and man. Every hero of the "forlorn hope" is a suicide; every hero of pestilence, dying from a disease contracted ministering to the sick and dying, is a suicide; every hero of the shipwreck, though resigning to others the available means of safety, is a suicide. The martyrs of the Coliseum, and the countless other Christian martyrs, notwithstanding that they gave their lives in testimony to Christ, are, every one of them, suicides. They all foresaw their own deaths, and the writter's verdict of "foreseen and therefore intended" stands against every one of them. But it is unfortunate for his ethical principle rather than for the martyrs. His principle stands discredited by their deeds – deeds which, notwithstanding that their deaths were foreseen, nay, for the very reason that their deaths were foreseen by them, will remain the greatest glory of the human race throughout Time and Eternity.

INSUPPORTABLE BURDENS FOR ALL CONSCIENCES

But the foregoing are not the only, nor indeed the worst, consequences of the writer's "foreseen and therefore intended." It would place insupportable burdens on the consciences of the entire human race, by making every act unlawful because it produces, however unintended, a foreseen ill effect. "Foreseen but not intended" is the rock-bottom foundation on which is raised the entire structure of "two effects." And The Examiner's "foreseen and therefore intended" utterly undermines that foundation.

SCIENCE OF PSYCHOLOGY ALSO OUTRAGED BY IT

Nor is it Moral Theology alone that is outraged by his "foreseen and therefore intended." The science of Psychology likewise cries out against it. It is nothing short of a denial of Free Will – the basic condition of all morality. It asserts a necessary, an essential connection between the act of the intellect foreseeing the ill effect, and the act of the will intending it. How can it be truly said that every ill effect foreseen by the intellect, is intended by the will, and, at the same time, be truly said that the will is free? Is it not to say that the will is necessitated, and,—what is worse—necessitated to evil? It matters nothing what, besides, the writer may have to say against Irish hunger-strike, or indeed against any other action having an ill effect. His "foreseen and therefore intended" hands down the same verdict of "guilty" against them all. He convicts the entire human race in order that MacSwineys' hunger-strike may be caught up in the condemnation. Thus does he reach the last, reckless limit in his perversion of Catholic moral teaching. Still he continues:

(47) "To foresee the sinful effect of an action and yet "go on with the action, involves internal guilt of "the sin contemplated and foreseen."

"AN ACT HAVING A SINFUL EFFECT IS SINFUL"!!

Here is smug satisfaction regarding a case which the writer affects to have proved sinful, though well aware that his twisting and wrenching of ethical principles has proved nothing. The present citation is another of his truisms. It merely says that to deliberately place an action having a sinful effect is sinful. Who doubts it! Psychology and Ethics alike say that actions are specified by their formal objects. In the citation we are considering—together with the one immediately preceding it—the writer presents what he would have his readers consider the premises of his final argument. What he proposes as their ungainsayable consequent and consequence, he sets forth under the title "Our Conclusion." And here is the "conclusion."

(48) "The conclusion we arrive at is that deliberate self-"starvation contemplated as issuing in death is an "act of direct self-killing—formal suicide, unless "you can find some justifying reason for the act."

HENCE FAST UNTO DEATH IS "FORMAL SUICIDE"

"Deliberate self-starvation contemplated as issuing in death is direct self-killing—formal suicide," says the author. Here, if never before, he uses the term "direct" in the strictly theological sense of intended—morally direct, not physically direct, as when he said (No. 34) that "there is nothing more direct than the relation between food and the sustentation of life."

"The conclusion we arrive at," says the writer! The conclusion from what antecedent premises? He doesn't dare to present his rambling disquisition in the form of syllogisms. The multiplicity of fallacies it contains would then be all too evident. The nearest approach of his final argumentation to the appearance of a syllogism would be as follows:

Maj. Prop. To foresee the sinful effect of an action and nevertheless place the action is sinful.
Min. Prop. But hunger-strike until death is an act of foreseen and therefore intended self-killing.
Conclusion Therefore deliberate self-starvation is an act of direct self-killing – formal suicide, unless, etc.

First – The major proposition of this "reasoning" says nothing. It is tautological – the same as to say that to place a sinful act is sinful. Second – The minor premise is, as we have just seen, absurdly, outrageously false. Third – What the author calls his "conclusion"–"the conclusion we arrive at"– is not a conclusion at all. It is but a repetition, with scarcely a word changed, of what is falsely asserted in the so-called minor premise. Indeed it may be said with all truth that his entire discussion of hunger-strike scarcely contains a single valid inference. It is rather made up of a series of dogmatic assertions, some of them ambiguous, others utterly false, and not a few vicious.

JUSTIFYING REASON FOR DIRECT SELF-KILLING!

Of this latter sort is his statement that "self-starvation" is direct self-killing, formal suicide, unless you can find some justifying reason for the act." This is "muddle-headed argumentation," to use his own words. It assumes wrongly that an act of intended self-killing – already intrinsically evil from the intention – still admits of "a justifying reason." The writer seems not to realize that the evil intention has already placed the act outside of all justification. "Malum ex quocumque defectu." In other words, the "justifying reason" of every act having an ill effect, is the proportion of good on account of which it is lawful, notwithstanding its ill effect. But this proportion, this justifying reason (always a circumstance of the act) presupposes the act lawful from object and intention. The author speaks of a "justifying reason" for an act already evil from the evil intention!! Here, as on many other occasions, he loses himself in a labyrinth of his own constructing. He might with as much meaning speak of a justifying reason for blasphemy or perjury.

JUSTIFIED AFTER REMOVING EVIL INTENTION

There can be no "justifying reason" for intended self-killing. Before the question of a justifying reason can ever be raised, the intended self-killing must give place to unintended. Such justifying reason obtains in the unintended self-killing of **his sea captain,** but not in the intended self-killing of his "revolver-man," or of his "sati woman" or of his "bankrupt-man" or of his "sufferer." In every one of these cases, **justifying is at an end,** because, in every one of them, **the intention is evil** – the intention which he calls **"merely secondary,"** a **"corollary,"** an **"appendix."** "Formal suicide **unless you can find some justifying reason,"** says the writer. There is only one **"unless"** that can have any meaning in this context – **unless you can eliminate the evil intention.** Let him not urge that his **"justifying reason" always indicates a good intention.** He wrote (in No. 46): **"An act of foreseen and therefore intended self-killing."** Only a moment before, he had used **another "unless" that is equally meaningless and for the same reason.** Here it is:

(49) "The will must exclude sin and must therefore re-
"pudiate any act **which is seen to issue in a sinful
"result, unless some justifying cause of necessity,
"duty or right intervenes to alter the case."**

JUSTIFYING AN ACT HAVING SINFUL EFFECT!!

"A justifying cause for an act which is seen to issue in a sinful result" – this is new theology! It is certainly not the theology of the "standard theological schools," with which the author claims so much familiarity! **A justifying cause for an act forbidden on account of its sinful effect, would, if it existed, be a theological curiosity. The idea of such an ethical monstrosity could originate only from cerebral bewilderment** similar to that which brought Bishop Vaughan to ask Fr. Patrick Gannon, S.J. "is it ever lawful to commit a sin." "No, unless there be some justifying cause," is The Examiner's answer. Fr. Gannon exclaimed – "what a question!" Can any "justifying cause" undo the evil intention of an agent who places an action seen to issue in a sinful effect? Is there any way in which it can "alter the case?" Yet, immediately, and with the same inconsistency that pervades his entire article, the author adds:

(50) "My memory may be defective, but I cannot remem-
"ber any single case in moral theology in which
"direct self-killing, deliberately contemplated as the
"'finis operis' of the act performed, is defended or
"allowed for any cause whatever."

STILL JUGGLING WITH THE TERM "DIRECT"

(a) The writer keeps on assuming that his juggling with theological terms has effectively proved that all hunger-strike unto death is direct self-killing. "Direct self-killing" has now grown to be a favorite expression for him. Does he now mean mere **physically direct self-killing,** as when he said that "nothing is more **direct** than the relation between food and the sustentation of life?"

(b) Only a moment ago he wrote (1) "Direct self-killing – formal suicide, unless you can find some justifying cause," (No. 48) and (2) "the will must repudiate any act which is seen to issue in a sinful result, unless some justifying cause intervenes." (No. 49). Now (No. 50) he abandons his first assertion – that formal suicide may admit of a justifying cause – while his second more general statement of the same principle – that an act seen to issue in a sinful effect may yet have a justifying cause (No. 49) – he allows to stand.

(c) Assuming that here at least the writer means by "direct" self-killing, intended self-killing – as Moral Theology always does – his memory is defective. The case is cited in Moral Theology of a man **justly sentenced to death**. Theologians say that **the State may lawfully authorize him to execute his own death-sentence, and that he may lawfully do it**. They insist, however, that **the State has not the right to compel him to execute himself**, if he is unwilling to do so. This is a case of "directly intended self-killing, deliberately contemplated as the 'finis operis' of the act performed." Yet it is defended and allowed by theologians.

(51) "I have never found theologians justifying any case "analogous to that of a man who, being put in "prison, sets about **gradually but persistently killing** "himself in order to **force** his own release, or – failing "this – persevering even to death for the sake of "setting an example to his countrymen of heroic "resistance and tenacity of purpose."

HE HAS NOT FOUND THEOLOGIANS JUSTIFYING

(a) In this and the previous citation, the writer guilelessly asserts his own intimate acquaintance with moral theologians and their unanimous verdict in his favor. Notice, however, that **he does not quote a single theologian, nor even name one**, throughout his entire article.

(b) Why does he inquire whether or not theologians justify **analogous** cases, and disregard the justification given by several theologians and professors of theology, of the MacSwiney case itself?

Fr. Patrick H. Casey, S.J., Fr. Patrick Gannon, S.J. and Fr. Peter Finlay, S.J., – all professors of theology at Jesuit Scholasticates – had written in defense of Mayor Mac-Swiney's hunger-strike, several months before the author took up his pen. So too had the scholarly **Fr. Kent, O.S.C.,** many other priests, and not a few Catholic bishops. The Catholic press was also well nigh unanimous in its defense of the Lord Mayor's conduct. And all these verdicts, and a hundred similar verdicts, were at the writer's hand, on the pages of his editorial "exchanges." Why should he turn away from them all – to the extreme of not mentioning a single one of them even by a passing reference – and tell his readers that all moral theologians condemn hunger-strike, since he has "never found theologians justifying any case analogous?" His knowledge of Catholic Theology does little credit to him. Theologians mention numerous cases that are analogous to hunger-strike – the besieged garrison refusing food offered on condition of surrender; the Christians refusing food previously offered to idols; the Carthusian monk refusing meat – when only meat can sustain him – in order to honor his rule. Will the author deny the analogy? If so, this judgment of Fr. Peter Finlay, S.J. – a judgment not to be set aside lightly – stands against him: "What the dying Carthusian monk did, and did lawfully, for religion and his Order, the dying patriot does, and may do lawfully, for his country's service. But it is self-murder? He kills himself? Only as the Carthusian did ... A hunger-strike is as lawful in a prison as in a Carthusian cell."

So much for what the writer has found, and also what he has failed to find, among moral theologians. Neither the one nor the other entitles him to claim their authority against hunger-strike.

(52) "If a hunger-strike is carried on for a time, with "some risk, but not an imminent risk of death, I "should be prepared to take a lenient view of the "case, first on objective grounds, because the death "is not contemplated or intended or expected. Sec- "ondly, on subjective grounds, because passionate "zeal and sanguine hope can blind a man to the "seriousness of the risk and the sinfulness of it."

"LENIENT" VIEW RECALLS WRITER'S "TWO PLEAS"

(1) The morality of hunger-strike in which death is neither "contemplated," "intended" nor "expected," is irrelevant to the subject which the writer set out to discuss. (2) Moral Theology knows nothing of "lenient views." "Lex dubia non obligat" – a doubtful law is not binding – is the utmost limit to which it may go in the direction of leniency. (3) And that is a universal principle of morals, not a personal concession by any individual theologian. (4) How does the "contemplation" or "expectation" of death make the act unlawful? The captain contemplates and expects his death, but this does not make his act unlawful. (5) The writer is "lenient" towards hunger-strike

for a time, "first, on **objective** grounds, because the death is not intended." Besides falsely implying that every hunger-striker until death intends his own death, this latest citation is a change of front on the part of the writer towards the intention. When he would seek some justification or mitigation of the act, he immediately turns to the intention. This can only be because he regards the intention as the principal source of morality. Notice too that he includes the intention among the objective grounds for being "lenient." It is, in fact, the only source of morality to which he appeals. It is no longer "a merely secondary and personal matter," a "corollary" or "appendix." (6) The hunger-striker until death no more intends his own death than the hunger-striker for a time. Where then are the objective grounds for leniency? (7) "The sinfulness of it," says the writer!

(53) "But when anyone comes forward to justify the hunger-striker on the grounds of patriotism, and allows him deliberately to contemplate and work towards his own death by starvation, I feel that all ground of principle is taken from under my feet."

RHETORIC – NOT THEOLOGY

This passage, like the one immediately preceding, is all declamation and no theology. It is part of the peroration of the writer's rhetorical rather than theological masterpiece. He is simply giving expression to his distress for not being able to justify Mayor MacSwiney!

(54) "If the ground of justification be patriotism as a right, I say emphatically that no citizen has a right to sacrifice his life by a deliberate act of self-killing, in order merely to defy what he regards as an unjust Government, nor has he any right to sacrifice his life on the additional reflex motive of stimulating his fellow-citizens to resist that Government with greater pertinacity."

THE "EXAMINER" SAYS EMPHATICALLY, FALSELY

(a) Is it because it happens to be a "deliberate act of self-killing" (that manner of self-killing) that the citizen has not the right to so sacrifice his life, or is it because the motives for doing so are insufficient? The writer has already rejected patriotism as a right, independently of any and all motive. "No man is justified in sacrificing his life out of a motive of patriotism merely as a right." The absurdity of his efforts increases as he goes on. "Crescit agendo." He has already pronounced hunger-strike suicide pure and simple, and yet turns, with seeming seriousness, to its "justifying reasons"– the good effects of the Irish hunger-strike. And he is unfair even in his statement of these good effects. He introduces them with the word "merely"—his favorite expression when he wishes to belittle. As may be seen from the proof of our thesis, in which these good effects are enumerated, he does not mention all the good effects, nor even the principal ones. He says the purpose of Mayor MacSwiney was "to defy what he regards as an unjust Government." Why does he not rather say "to resist"? Resistance of injustice enlists public sympathy; defiance tends to alienate it.

(b) On what grounds has the captain the right to sacrifice his life, but the Irish hunger-strikers have not such a right? Both are cases of **patriotism as a right, but not as a duty**? "The Examiner" has already said that the "captain is not bound to blow up his ship."

(c) The statement we are considering is not made true by saying it "emphatically." Moral Theology knows no emphasis. It aims only to say what it is that is lawful and what it is that is unlawful. In the present case it is proof and not emphasis that is needed but not forthcoming. The writer **merely asserts and reasserts**, to the end of the chapter, the very question in dispute from the beginning. The very opposite has been proved without flaw or fallacy in previous chapters.

> (55) "If self-killing could be justified for such reasons, "(patriotism as a right) then any captives, say the "prisoners of Kut, would be justified in doing the "same, if thereby they thought their fellow-soldiers "would be stimulated to prosecute the war with "greater vigor."

INFERENCE FALSE. ANOTHER BOGUS PARALLEL

The prisoners of Kut or any other captives would be justified in doing the same self-killing, provided the conditions requisite for the lawfulness of an action having an ill effect were verified in their case, as they were verified in the Irish hunger-strikers. But according to the writer's statement of their case, they would be intending and using their own deaths **as a means to stimulate their fellow soldiers**.

> (56) "Similarly, a general, finding his troops wavering "with fear, would be justified in shooting himself "in their presence, if he thought that such an act "of bravery would galvanize them into courage and "help them to win a battle. No theologian would "justify such an action on any grounds either of "duty or right."

"SIMILARLY"–THAT IS TO SAY "DISSIMILARLY"

Amid the writer's many inconsistencies in the article we have been reviewing, he displays one outstanding consistency. He is a consistent sophist. His reputation for making honest parallels has not survived his discussion of hunger-strike. And so when he says "similarly," it is fairly certain that the cases he presents as similar are dissimilar. Very truly does he say that "no theologian would justify such action." All theologians would condemn it, not because it is similar to the Irish hunger-strike, but because it is not similar to it. The general intends his own death as the means by which to help his wavering soldiers to win a battle. He says to them –"I am not afraid to die! Why should you be!" This case of the general is the case over again of the writer's "revolver-man," "sati woman," "bankrupt," "sufferer."

JUGGLING RHETORIC. NOT CAUTIOUS THEOLOGY!

On the very onerous and very complicated matter of proportion of the good effect, he bestows scant scrutiny. He dismisses it with a gesture. The ill effect he calls "grave and irreparable," the good effects "dubious and problematical." Both these epithets are borrowed. And these pronouncements of his were published in the middle of January, 1921 – nearly three months after Mayor MacSwiney's death, and after the writer had read in his "exchanges," secular no less than religious, more than one hundred glowing tributes to the Lord Mayor's behavior, and to his unparalleled achievement for the cause of Ireland. A subject so subtle, confused rather than clarified by much that had been written about it prior to his article, called for clear exposition and convincing proof. Yet he gave neither! He began with a grand profession of impartiality, and how impartial he has been! Every page,– and, for the most part, every paragraph – of his article bears abundant traces of the juggling rhetorician, but few traces of the cautious, conservative moralist.

ASSUMES SUICIDE. "POSSIBLE" EXONERATION!

He began his task by conveniently assuming that Mayor MacSwiney's hunger-strike was suicide – assuming the point denied vehemently by many theologians. Two "pleas" occurred to him, however, "which might possibly exonerate the Mayor from the guilt of suicide." It has been already shown that neither of the two is any plea at all. Purporting to set forth what he calls "the proper lines of argument"– as if the proper lines of argument had not been already handed down with minute detail – **he emphasizes the object** (self-killing) as a source of morality, and **confuses and minimizes the intention**. "Suicide" is what he is bent on predicating of Mayor MacSwiney, and **suicide is intended self-killing, direct self-killing**. That hunger-strike until death is self-killing is patent to all. But self-killing is far removed from intended self-killing, and the writer is called to **bridge the gap over**. An equivocation hinged **on the word "direct"** solves his problem. Outside a miracle, food is necessary, directly necessary to sustain life, and therefore hunger-strike until death, is **physically direct self-killing**. Hence, the writer, speaking in the **physical and physiological**, but not in the **theological sense** of the word "direct," says truly that "there is nothing **more direct than the relation between food and the sustentation of life.**" Here, however, he is using the word "direct" in the sense just explained – of essential, **necessary relation of physical cause to physical effect** – a sense far removed from "intended." Direct causation of food in **sustaining** life is had in brute animals as well as in humans; – intending belongs exclusively to intelligent beings. Intending is a **free act**; direct action of food in sustaining life is **not a free but a necessary act**. But while the things are very different, they are called by the same name ("direct") and he uses that name to span the chasm between mere physical self-killing and intended (moral) self-killing. He writes:

> "We have found people arguing that fasting, **even** "when it results in death is not direct self-killing but "indirect. **This is quite untrue. There is nothing more** "**direct than the relation between food and the sus-** "**tentation of life.**"

UNDIGNIFIED TRICK OF DIALECTICS

Here, by an undignified trick of dialectics – **a mental slight-of-hand** – he denies a theological truth, and makes it appear a theological falsehood. He would lead the incautious reader to believe that because fasting is **direct physical** self-killing, it is also direct moral self-killing. "This is quite untrue. There is nothing more direct," etc. And since "direct" is a synonym for "intended," he is able to say with apparent truth that hunger-strike until death **is intended self-killing**, in other words, "suicide." To this longer formula he now adds another and shorter one – "foreseen and therefore intended self-killing."

CHAINS OF CONFUSED CONFUSING DISCUSSION

And this is the very best the masterful editor of "**The Examiner**" can do to accomplish what he wanted to do, set out to do, and strove mightily to do! That he taxed his ingenuity to its utmost capacity is evidenced by every page he wrote. At the very beginning he professed to have waited until "feeling has died away and people are in a condition to think impartially." But much time and labor also were required to construct the labyrinths of confused and confusing discussion he has erected. After the Lord Mayor's death, nearly three months elapsed before the publication of "The Examiner's" article.

(57) "Even if direct self-killing could be justified for "serious reasons, in a great cause, which, as far as "I can see, has never been done by the standard "theological schools, at least some proportion would "be required between the benefit accruing to the "cause and the grave and irreparable evil of putting "an end to one's own life."

"DIRECT SELF-KILLING"–"IRREPARABLE EVIL"!

(a) Now, if never before, the writer means by direct self-killing, intended self-killing. He is nearing the end of his article, and Mayor MacSwiney's doom cannot be further deferred. From the very beginning he wanted this verdict of direct self-killing, notwithstanding his protest that he was "not undertaking to prove a thesis." He wriggled into it by degrees as his article progressed. He is now established in it. But the track which he traced remains as evidence against him.

AGAIN HIS "STANDARD THEOLOGICAL SCHOOLS"!

(b) For a second time, on the same closing page of his article, he would impress on his readers that his entire doctrine on hunger-strike is in complete accord with the teaching of "standard theological schools." But, which one of those "standard theological schools," when treating the question of "two effects," speaks of the ill effect as "foreseen and therefore intended"? Which standard theological school deals with the intention "by way of corollary or appendix"? Which of the "standard theological schools" teaches that in every case of "two effects"–"duplex effectus"– the ill effect must not follow essentially from the act but only contingently? Which school is it that teaches that the agent is "responsible for every result or consequence which is foreseen to issue straight out of the act itself"? The article on hunger-strike contains very little that accords with the teaching of "standard theological schools," but very much that does not.

"STATING PRINCIPLES," "DRAWING CONCLUSIONS"

Though the composition we are reviewing occupies not more than five pages of "The Examiner," and contains little more than five thousand words, the author succeeded in introducing into it FIFTEEN FALSE IMPLICATIONS,(a) NINE FALSE PROTESTATIONS,(b) FOUR FALSE INFERENCES,(c) THREE FALSE ASSUMPTIONS,(d) ONE FALSE EXPLANATION,(e) TWO SOPHISMS,(f) TWO PRACTICAL INCONSISTENCIES,(g) THIRTY-SIX FALSE PRINCIPLES,(h) EIGHTEEN TRUISMS,(i) SEVEN AMBIGUITIES,(j) FOURTEEN FALSE PARALLELS,(k) SIX FALSE STATEMENTS OF FACT,(l) ONE EVASION,(m) ONE OBSCURITY,(n) TWO ABSURDITIES,(o) AND SIXTEEN CONTRADICTIONS.(p)

Behold the sequel to the author's protestation at the beginning: "Keeping silence until feeling has died away and people are in a position to think impartially." (No. 1). "We let our mind go its way, stating principles and drawing conclusions **according to our own judgment.**" (No. 13).

GHASTLY LOGICAL AND THEOLOGICAL SPECTRES!

And yet, notwithstanding this **long array of ghastly logical and theological spectres,** he freely speaks of what he **finds** and what he **does not find** in "the standard theological schools," and closes his article with this solemn manifesto:

> "The **conclusion** we arrive at is that deliberate self-
> "starvation, contemplated as issuing in death, **is an**
> "**act of direct self-killing – formal suicide, unless you**
> "can find some justifying reason for the act."

(c) Minimize the good effects,—"merely to defy what he regards as an unjust Government," etc.— exaggerate the ill effect,—"the grave and irreparable evil of putting an end to one's own life"— thus destroying the proportion of good, and the act is made unlawful and the case won. Is such procedure sanctioned by "standard theological schools?" "Grave and irreparable evil" is the saying of another, and

---

(a) See Nos.	26. 30. 31. 32. 42 43. 49. 50. 51. 52 . 53. 55. 57. 58	
(b) " "	1. 12. 13. 14. 25. 53	
(c) " "	. 12. 16. 25. 28	
(d) " "	. . . 3. 4. 5	
(e) " "	 15	
(f) " "	. . . 34. 35	
(g) " "	. . . 1&2. 6&7	
(h) " "	15. 16. 17. 18. 20 21. 22. 26. 27. 28 29. 32. 33. 34. 35 40. 41. 46. 48. 54	
(i) See Nos.	19. 27. 31. 32. 35. 37 39. 41. 44. 45. 47	
(j) " "	31. 36. 38. 44. 45. 50	
(k) " "	26. 32. 33. 36. 44. 56	
(l) " "	8. 10. 11. 57 . .	
(m) " "	6.	
(n) " "	37.	
(o) " "	48. 49.	
(p) " "	16&17. 18&19. 20&21 16&23. 20&23. 21&23 22&23. 23&23. 23&24 23&25. 23&27. 23&28	

merely adopted by "The Examiner." Perhaps the expression was originally used to denounce the vicious victimizing of Irish troops at Gallipoli, during the first World War, or to condemn the Croke Park massacre, or the savage murder, by the Black and Tans, of Mayor MacCurtain, Fr. Griffin, or Mrs. Quinn - a prospective mother. Each one of these murders was a "grave and irreparable evil"- as grave and irreparable as the death of Mayor MacSwiney. And yet the author never expressed any regret for any of them, either in "The Examiner" or anywhere else. But he weeps over the "grave and irreparable evil" of Mayor MacSwiney's death - the evil for which no one was responsible except the British Government.

WHAT "GRAVE AND IRREPARABLE EVIL"?

And what is the "grave and irreparable evil" for which he "cannot find compensating reason" or "proportionate beneficial effects?" Is it the physical death of the Lord Mayor, or is it the spiritual and eternal death of his soul by suicide? If the writer means only the ill effect of physical death, let him remember that it is sweet as well as noble to die for one's country. "Dulce et decorum est pro patria mori." If by "grave and irreparable evil" he means the eternal loss of the suicide hunger-striker's soul, let him remember that he has not proved suicide of any hunger-striker, but merely assumes and exclaims it. And he assumes "suicide" even in his very efforts to prove it.

(58) "In none of these cases can I find such compensating "reason. The beneficial effects are "dubious and "problematical." They are only remotely and in-"directly connected with the death. In short, the "plan fails altogether to provide a valid justification "either on ground of necessity, duty or right, for "making an exception to the fundamental duty of "self-preservation, and the laws of God's reserved "dominion over life and death."

GOOD EFFECTS "DUBIOUS AND PROBLEMATICAL"

This is "The Examiner's" grand finale. It but prolongs the flourish of trumpets inaugurated at the very beginning of his article.

The "cases" he refers to are those just set forth by him under the title "similarly." They are hunger-strikers, the prisoners of Kut, and the general who shoots himself to inspire his wavering troops. Each of these cases is dissimilar from every other instead of similar. Yet the author puts them all in the same category.

NO COMPENSATION FOR MacSWINEY'S DEATH!

He puts the poor hunger-striker in bad company, and then bewails his misfortune. "In none of these cases can I find such a compensating reason." He can find a compensating reason for the captain, who kills himself by sinking his ship; for him who gives his last crust to another in extremity of hunger, and dies of hunger himself; for the Carthusian monk, who dies rather than depart from his rule by eating meat; for him who drowns, because he yielded to another the plank or the life-buoy that would have saved him; for the garrison, who die of hunger rather than surrender the fortress. For a hundred like cases of "grave and irreparable evil," the author can find "compensating reasons," but none, none, absolutely none for the Irish hunger-strikers!

FALSEHOODS, FALLACIES, CONTRADICTIONS, ETC.

Nor has he proved Mayor MacSwiney a suicide or even a sinner, except by the aid of falsehoods, fallacies self-contradictions and suchlike subterfuges. A single falsehood or a single fallacy is enough to invalidate an argument. The author's argument – if it deserves to be called an argument – abounds in falsehoods, fallacies and contradictions. And he makes them serve a most ignoble, ungodly purpose – to persuade the world that those of Ireland's sons who, in this her latest struggle to be free, had behaved the very bravest, were, in reality, her very basest.

CONSOLED BY ENDURING IN FREEDOM'S CAUSE

Throughout their days and nights, weeks, months, years of unspeakable cruelty and outrage, terror, horror, crucifixion, at the hands of England's hardened, heartless, hireling Black and Tans, the people of Ireland were consoled by the grand reflexion that they were enduring and resisting in Freedom's cause and in Freedom's name. The writer would rob them of even this well-merited consolation. The world is well aware and ever mindful that Freedom's cause can never be advanced, nor Freedom's name ever glorified by any conduct that is base and criminal – least of all by the foul crime of suicide. Yet "suicide" is the writer's verdict against the bravest of Ireland's brave, the noblest of her noble. In the course of his article he acknowledges that, in past centuries, England's rule of Ireland had been "abominable." To that long list of abominations he would, nevertheless, add a further abomination of his own invention. He would filch from the living the soothing solace which even the extremest agony finds in the consciousness of right and brave and noble endeavor. And he would, in addition, taint the memory of their noblest dead. Under cover of a smoke-screen of cunning misrepresentation, he steals unobserved to the grave of Mayor MacSwiney, erases from his tombstone the well-earned inscription, "MacSwiney-Martyr," written in the Lord Mayor's lifeblood, and inscribes in its stead the opprobrious, calumnious, murderous substitute – "MacSwiney-Suicide." With protests of impartiality on his lips, he surreptitiously snatches from the Lord Mayor's head his crown of immortal glory, and substitutes in its place a crown of immortal infamy.

MEANS HE USES AS IGNOBLE AS HIS PURPOSE

And the means he used to attain this inglorious purpose are as ignoble as the purpose itself. They are nothing better than obscurities, ambiguities, truisms, evasions, implications, inconsistencies, fallacies, sophisms and falsehoods. These reach the climax of distortion and perversion in his "foreseen and therefore intended self-killing." "Confusion now hath made his masterpiece!" And – strangest of all his inconsistencies – protests against the use of these vicious practices by the defenders of Mayor MacSwiney, were freely dropping from his pen while he himself was actually using them. "All looks yellow to the jaundiced eye."

PROOF PATENT THAT MAYOR'S ACT WAS LAWFUL

"The Examiner's" article is a most convincing proof of the lawfulness of Mayor MacSwiney's hunger-strike. He ransacked all creation for an argument against it, and found only transparent equivocations. Furthermore, the contributions of many others who wrote against hunger-strike showed that their authors were groping in the dark. "The Examiner's" contribution shows all too plainly that the writer was not. Though in reality proving nothing, the incautious reader, inexperienced in dialectical manoeuvering, will carry away from it the conviction that it proves all it proposed to prove. It "lies like truth and yet most truly lies." And it is too ingeniously elaborated to admit of any extenuation on the score of inadvertence.

SLAVISH SERVING BLIND NATIONAL PREJUDICE

This review of that labored composition may well close with a reiteration of the regret expressed at its opening – the regret that its distinguished author should have prostituted his head and heart, his pen and his periodical, all of which had served the cause of Catholic truth long and well, to the slavish service of a blind national prejudice.

Goldsmith condensed into a single line an immortal eulogy of Edmund Burke, when he said that the great Irishman was "too fond of the right to pursue the expedient." The writer reverses the formula. He is too fond of the expedient to pursue the right — so fond of his country that he sacrifices on its altar the principles of morality, the ideals of patriotism, the laws of inference, and even the claims of consistency. He fights his country's battles by foul tactics when they cannot be successfully fought by fair. For Lord Mayor MacSwiney, whom he finds guilty of suicide, "a fight that is not clean-handed will make victory more disgraceful than any defeat."* For the writer, as for the witches in "Macbeth," "fair is foul and foul is fair." At the degrading task of manufacturing and broadcasting fallacies and sophisms, and perverting fundamental principles of Moral Theology, in order to make what is absurdly false in doctrine appear true, in order to make what is entirely lawful in conduct appear criminal; in order to make what is most courageous and noble in human nature appear most cowardly and dishonorable — in this sinister occupation, the widely known and highly respected editor of "The Bombay Examiner" is a painfully pathetic figure.

NO DEPOSIT OF TRUTH. NO STANDARD THEOLOGY

It is very certain that his contribution to the theology of hunger-strike is no part of the deposit of Truth, which he, as a Catholic priest and Catholic editor, is commissioned to "teach all nations." Equally certain is it that, of the many theological absurdities contained in his unlogical as well as untheological dissertation on hunger-strike, not a single one was taught him in the "standard theological school" of the Society of Jesus. And it is deplorably certain that his readers, almost without exception, make the crucial mistake of accepting, without challenge, on the authority of that "standard theological school," vagaries and extravagances in logic, psychology and theology which were entirely private and personal to himself. If these vagaries, with their wealth of serpentine writhings, have exhausted the patience of readers of this our review, let them remember that it was he who constructed the labyrinths. The present writer did no more than furnish the threads wherewith to escape from them.

*"Principles of Freedom." (Chap. I.)

CAN THE WRITER'S FRIENDS EXONERATE HIM?

Two worthless "pleas" were the best the author was capable of, towards "exonerating" Mayor MacSwiney from the guilt of suicide. Let the author's friends do more, if they can, to exonerate him from the multiplicity of guilt attaching to his article on the hunger-strike of Lord Mayor MacSwiney.

"TABLET," "CIVILTA," "EXAMINER," VERY SIMILAR

The article in "The Tablet" by the "Professor of Morals," and the articles in "The Civilta" and "The Examiner," have much in common – so much in common that the reader thinks it no hazardous conjecture to surmise that all three articles were excogitated in the same brain, and dropped from the same pen. All the articles have the same trade mark – an unmistakable purpose to mislead and deceive their readers. And, as might be expected, each of the writers makes use of practically the same means to attain that same sinister purpose.

In the first place, each writer tampers with the hunger-striker's intention. The "Professor" says falsely that intending his own death even indirectly, is sufficient for responsibility for his own death. The Civilta writer says very falsely that Mayor MacSwiney intended the impossible good effect of Ireland's independence, and that his hunger-strike was unlawful because unable to attain that good effect intended. The editor of "The Examiner" wrote most falsely that MacSwiney's action was a case of "foreseen and therefore intended self-killing."

Secondly, the "Professor" says that hunger-striking is "morally wrong ex objecto or as a means;" "The Examiner" says that persistent fasting is "ex objecto direct self-killing by degrees;" the Civilta writer says that "voluntary fast even until death is not an act intrinsically bad." Finally, the circumstance of proportion is played up by "The Examiner" thus: "The beneficial effects are dubious and problematical," compared to "the grave and irreparable evil of putting an end to one's own life." That question of proportion is counted out by The Civilta writer when he misrepresents MacSwiney's aim and object. And proportion or disproportion is entirely ignored by the "Professor."

The articles – here reproduced in full (in Appendixes A, B and C) and examined in detail in Chapters Sixteen, Seventeen and Eighteen – present three of the most competent among the Catholic clergy, discussing, in three standard Catholic periodicals, the morality of hunger-strike from **object, intention** and **circumstances**. In applying each of these three sources of morality to hunger-strike until death, no two of the writers agree about Mayor MacSwiney's act or about his intention or about the circumstances of his fast until death. Every one of the three writers disagrees with every other about every one of the three sources of the morality of the Lord Mayor's action. Once again – as in the case of Fr. Tanquerey, Fr. Wouters, Fr. Merkelbach and Fr. Daman – their testimony does not agree – another convincing proof that none of them was right, that they were all wrong.

MACSWINEY'S PHILOSOPHY

"In a physical contest on the field of battle, it is allowable to use tactics and strategy, to retreat as well as advance, to have recourse to a ruse as well as open attack; but in matters of principle there can be no tactics, there is one straightforward course to follow, and that course must be found and followed without swerving to the end."

"A fight that is not clean-handed will make victory more disgraceful than any defeat."

Chapter Twenty Three

THE CHURCH AND THE QUESTION OF HUNGER-STRIKE

HUNGER-STRIKE AN INTRICATE QUESTION

As to the assertion of The Review's correspondent – that "it cannot be said that the question needs no teaching, being so clear in itself" – it will be readily acquiesced in by anyone who understands the theology of hunger-strike, as well as by all who read the torrents of controversy which the MacSwiney hunger-strike called forth. Indeed the persons who would contend that "the question needs no teaching, being so clear in itself," would, by the very contention, show that they know nothing about it. If Fr. Patrick Gannon, S.J., whose article, already referred to, was by far the most complete discussion of the MacSwiney case, and the most ungainsayable vindication of the Lord Mayor that the entire controversy produced – if the author of that excellent contribution called the MacSwiney hunger-strike "that vexed subject that is exercising the best casuists of the Church," then all who have not understood the theological principles involved and the difficulty of applying them correctly to the very exceptional case of hunger-strike, may well accept both on the authority of Fr. Gannon.

REFERENCE TO THE CHURCH UNWARRANTED

It appears altogether unfortunate that your correspondent should make any comment whatever **on the attitude of the Church** regarding hunger-strike or any other question. By doing so he makes **an unwarranted encroachment on a sacred domain.** It is often very difficult to decide when it is for the best interests of the faithful that the Church should speak, and when it is that those same interests are better consulted by silence. But there is no precipitate haste and no impatience in the behavior of the Church. Her existence is not measured by years or decades of years, or hundreds of years. A thousand years is a small unit when measuring the duration of the Church which "is to last until the end of time." Thus the Church can afford to wait where merely human institutions cannot. And the Church does wait. It waited for more than eighteen centuries before defining the dogma of the Immaculate Conception, and still longer to define the dogma of the infallibility of the Sovereign Pontiff. **Why then should it**

hasten to pronounce on hunger-strike – a doctrine with which the welfare of the faithful is much less inseparably bound up?

And who is to guide the Church in determining when to speak and when to remain silent, which subjects to pronounce on and which to reserve for more opportune times and circumstances? Neither the responsibility for making such momentous decisions nor the ability to make them belongs to any subordinate members of the Church, lay or clerical. Their horizon is all too narrow, the range of their observation and their experience is all too restricted to encompass all the faithful and guide them all in the ways of truth and righteousness. The Vicar of Christ, and he alone, stands on the position of eminence from which he may look out upon all the nations. He alone is commissioned to teach them all, and therefore to him alone have been given the resources adequate for the fulfillment of that universal mission. The unique prerogative of divine inerrancy is bestowed on him alone. Who else "hath known the mind of the Lord"! Who besides "hath been His counsellor"!

CHURCH ALWAYS FEARLESS, ALWAYS PRUDENT

Nor should the correspondent of The Ecclesiastical Review need to have it impressed on him that the Church is as fearless today as it ever was. Like its divine Founder, it is "yesterday and today and the same fore ever." (Hebrews, xiii, 8.) The continually recurring encroachments on its rights, notably the encroachments of the civil power, it resists today even as it did in the days of the Apostles and the Martyrs. Then it "resisted unto blood." Today it does the same. At different periods of the never-ending struggle, that resistance had to take a different form to meet the varying conditions with which the Church was confronted. It is unthinkable, for instance, that the Spain of Ferdinand V or Charles V or Philip II should persecute the Church, as the Spain of today is doing. If it had attempted to do so, the entire nation would have been placed under immediate interdict. But those were the ages of faith. Practical prudence dictates a different policy in present circumstances.

Thus we see that, at one period, the resistance of the Church is eminently active, at another, it is, for the most part, passive. Now it is vigorously militant, and again it is patient and long-suffering. "We are reviled and we bless: we are persecuted and we suffer it; we are blasphemed and we entreat." (I Cor. iv, 12.) At one time, the excommunication hurled against the Emperor of a powerful nation brings him to Canossa in the garb of a penitent.

At another, the Catholic ruler of a Catholic people subjects the Sovereign Pontiff to the outrage of arrest and imprisonment, while yet another despot deprives him of all his temporal possessions by armed invasion. But at all times, and amid all the vicissitudes of the Church, its spirit has been the fearless spirit of the Apostles, the Martyrs, the Crusaders. That fearless spirit lives and glows today no less than when the Apostles and Martyrs "went from the presence of the Council rejoicing because they were accounted worthy to suffer reproach for the name of Jesus," or when the Christian warriors marched to the rescue of the Holy Places with the holy cry upon their lips—"God wills it."

ITS MODERN WEAPONS

In this twentieth century the battle has to be fought by other methods and other weapons. The Church substitutes today a crusade of prayers in the place of a crusade of arms. During this month of February 1933, the faithful the world over were recommended by the Holy Father to pray for the Rulers of Nations, that they may faithfully discharge the grave responsibility of ruling their peoples according to the dictates of eternal justice and eternal charity.

Negotiations too with civil governments have always been and must always be a very essential factor in the administration of the Church. It is in the successful conduct of such negotiation that the long rule of Pope Leo XIII was conspicuous. At his death, Theodore Roosevelt, then President of the United States, asserted that the history of no country could be complete without a reference to Pope Leo. Now, all such diplomatic negotiation involves conciliation, concession and compromise. The good will of Rulers and other influential personages who may greatly promote or hamper the work of the Church must be secured and maintained. And this must be done without any sacrifice of the popular confidence. Commissioned to teach and sanctify all, the Church is called to champion the interests of all. The eternal salvation of galley-slave or savage is as precious an achievement in her estimation as that of king or emperor. Like St. Paul, she makes herself all things to all men that she might save all. (I Cor. ix, 22.)

CHURCH IMPARTIAL, THEOLOGIANS SILENT

And this being so, the Church is called to rise superior to every partisan policy and every suspicion of partisanship. At the very beginning of the World War, Pope Benedict XV proclaimed to the entire world that the attitude of the Catholic Church towards the nations in conflict **was one of neutrality.** Amid the multiplicity of violent clashings that are constantly arising out of party, political, national and international disputes, **the Church is, and must always remain the friend of all, in the hope that she may one day heal the wounds of all with the sweet balm of her Christian Charity.**

These reflections may suggest to your correspondent that the Church perhaps "keeps silence and avoids committing herself" regarding the morality of hunger-strike, **rather because she refuses to consider** the **rival claims** of political or national parties than on account of her consideration for them. **She may not with propriety be asked why she does not pronounce on hunger-strike.** But professors of Moral Theology and authors of treatises on Moral Theology, may very reasonably be asked why they do not discuss it in their lectures and writings – why Moral Theology continues to maintain silence regarding the morality of hunger-strike. The Church, certainly, has not forbidden the discussion or imposed the silence. Neither may the theologians urge that the morality of hunger-strike is a dead issue.

THE EDITOR OF THE REVIEW

The Editor of The Ecclesiastical Review refused to publish the foregoing comments, and gave the following reasons for his refusal.

> "Our theologian – who answered the question about "hunger-strike – and myself, noticed that the question 'was specific, and that it related exclusively to moral "theologians and not to the argument for or against "the hunger-strike.
>
> "We both felt that it would be futile to take up the "problem itself, since endless discussions, some years "ago, led at best to a negative outcome. The answer "published, therefore, was restricted to the single point "raised. In view of this, I return your manuscript . . . "You may be interested in knowing that our theologian "personally believes that the hunger-strike is licit."

THE REVIEW'S ANSWER IS THE ISSUE

Certainly **the inquiry of The Review's correspondent** did not call for any presentation and discussion of the arguments for or against hunger-strike, and therefore there is no ground for complaint that The Review did not present and discuss those arguments. The Reverend Editor says very correctly that the correspondent's inquiry related exclusively to the attitude of authors on Moral Theology towards "the question of death brought on by wilful fast."

The one and only question asked The Review was "whether there is any manual of Moral Theology taught in seminaries which treats that question."

But the answer given by The Review to that single question calls for comment, and it is with that answer that the present article is exclusively concerned. If, occasionally, it makes passing reference to arguments for or against hunger-strike, it is only by way of either completeness or illustration. The substance of the article is occupied with The Review's answer. It examines that answer at considerable length, and fairly demonstrates its incorrectness. That answer assures the readers of The Review that manuals generally of Moral Theology treat the question of hunger-strike, though the truth is there is not a single manual of Moral Theology in existence that does so. The Review mentions Fr. Tanquerey in particular, and says that he treats the question of hunger-strike "briefly yet adequately." The present article has examined Fr. Tanquerey's treatment, and has shown that it is neither adequate nor inadequate, since it does not touch the question of hunger-strike at all. Let the reader now judge for himself whether this answer of The Review deserves to pass unchallenged. Is it not to be regretted that the clergy who come to seek theological information at this foundation head of theological learning in America should go away misinformed?

ANSWER RESTRICTED AND WRONG

The reason given by the Editor for declining the present article is that The Review's answer "was restricted to the single point raised." The answer was restricted, very restricted indeed. But we respectfully submit that the examination to which it has been subjected in the foregoing pages, shows that, in addition to being "restricted to the single point raised," other qualifications, which The Review's answer does not possess, are necessary in order that that answer may be correct and adequate.

THE REVIEW'S THEOLOGIAN

The Editor of The Review assures the present writer that The Review's Theologian "considers hunger-strike licit." But which hunger-strike does he consider licit? In this generation, there have been hunger-strikes aplenty, some of them licit, others illicit. His reasons for considering hunger-strike licit would prove interesting and instructive, even if his readers should find it difficult to forget that he is the same who referred the readers of The Review to Fr. Tanquerey's Synopsis, and assured them that the treatment of hunger-strike contained therein is "**adequate**." And if he is convinced that hunger-strike may sometimes be lawful, why does he not give to **a misinformed clergy and laity** the benefit of his conviction and of the reasons on which it rests?

The fact urged by the Editor – **that the endless discussions, some years ago, led at best to a negative outcome instead of militating against renewed discussion of hunger-strikefi should**, on the contrary, be an added motive in its favor. The fact that mountain climbers fail to reach the pinnacle they had aspired to is not considered an argument against renewed effort **but rather a further incentive to it**.

THEOLOGY OF HUNGER-STRIKE NOT KNOWN

The chief reason why the theology of hunger-strike is not more generally understood is because the great majority of those who profess an interest in it **are unwilling to bestow on it the time and effort it demands**. Let no one undertake to learn the theology of hunger-strike by a single hour's study of it. Whoever is, for any reason, unable to grasp the real question at issue, and the meaning of the general moral principles bearing upon it; whoever is unable to proceed, with caution and correctness, from these general principles, through the winding ways of distinction and subdistinction, down to a final and safe conclusion; whoever lacks the time or the patience or the logic for all this, must be content to accept that conclusion on the authority of others. **A casual hour spent in a casual study of the theology of hunger-strike were "love's labor lost."**

NOT IMPOSSIBLE TO UNDERSTAND

Will any one venture to say that this searching scrutiny is impossible? What prevents the precise question involved being clearly understood and clearly stated? Why cannot the terms employed throughout be defined with rigorous accuracy? Why cannot the irrelevant issues that lie outside the last border of the question – and whose name is "legion" – be left and kept where they belong? Why may not the study proceed, step by step, with logical precision, from the widest of all moral principles – that good is to be done and evil avoided – down to the last ungainsayable conclusion that hunger-strike **is** or **is not** suicidal, **is** or **is not** lawful?

SHOULD BE TAUGHT AND STUDIED

Several years have now passed since Mayor MacSwiney's death, and with the years have passed many of the aggravating circumstances that induced his hunger-strike. It is therefore possible now to pass more deliberate, dispassionate judgment on the theological character of his act, and to determine more clearly whether and why it was lawful or unlawful. The present writer, when presenting the present article to the Editor of The Review, offered to undertake this task in its pages. The Editor, however, declined the article and the offer, though priests and people alike are manifestly lacking in knowledge of the morality of hunger-strike, and desire to acquire it. If The Reviewer's correspondent asked only about "death brought on by wilful fast" when he evidently meant to ask about hunger-strike; if The Review's theologian believed that the inquiry was about hunger-strike, and answered that inquiry by an answer entitled "Morality of The Hunger-Strike," in which he told his readers that Fr. Tanquerey treats that question adequately, when in reality he does not treat it at all; if the Editor of The Review writes that Fr. Wouters discusses the question of hunger-strike, when in reality he does not; if, in fine, Fr. Tanquerey, Fr. Wouters, Fr. Merkelbach and Fr. Daman believed that they were discussing hunger-strike when they were not; if all these "teachers of the Law," "doctors in Israel," are unaware what is hunger-strike and what is not hunger-strike, it is high time that the deposit of theological truth be enlarged by the solution of that question, in the interests alike of laity, clergy, theologians, professors of theology and authors of theological manuals. And what vehicle is as well suited to convey this not inappreciable knowledge as "The Ecclesiastical Review"?

It is no commendation then that The Review – published especially for the Clergy, by The Catholic University of America – should refuse to publish explanation and discussion of a current question in Morals, involving the sacrifice of many human lives. In the year nineteen hundred and twenty, five Irish Catholic young men continued their hunger-strike until their deaths at the end of two months or more. The lawfulness of their act was discussed the world over – in the Catholic Press, and even in the Secular Press. American periodicals took considerable part in the discussions. The American Clergy looked, before all else, to The Review, for professional pronouncements and professional verdicts on that burning question. But no verdict and no pronouncement, and no discussion, ever came. The word "hunger-strike" was never seen in the pages of The Ecclesiastical Review before January of 1933 – thirteen years later – and then only to give it a wrong meaning, and give wrong information as to whether and where correct and adequate treatment of it might be found. Was The Review party to the conspiracy of silence?

HUNGER STRIKE HAS RETURNED TO STAY

When the twentieth century opened, hunger-strike as a weapon of defense, had long been obsolete, nothwithstanding that its appeal to justice is more in accord with the rational and moral nature of human beings than the appeal of revolver or battleship. With the advent of new and improved methods of destruction, however, the moral appeal of right and wrong was unhappily supplanted by the savage appeal of superior brute force.

But the moral appeal of hunger-strike has returned and returned to stay. Hunger-striking did not end forever with the deaths of MacSwiney, Fitzgerald, Murphy, Sullivan and Barry. Intolerable provocation will induce hunger-strike again as it has done in the past. Recently the question and answer regarding its morality had their application in Ireland and India. Tomorrow it may be necessary to ask the question and give the answer for Germany or France or England or the United States. More than ten thousand hunger-strikes have been staged in this twentieth century, the very latest for a period of twenty-one days, by the champion hunger-striker, Mahatma Gandhi, in protest against his arrest and imprisonment by the English Government.

In the supreme interest of theological doctrine, then, let the truth, the whole truth about hunger-strike be told "though the heavens were to fall." Sentiment, favorable or unfavorable to the cause which any particular hunger-striker may be advocating, should have no place in determining whether his action is lawful or not. The question is one not of sentiment but of cold, impartial reason. It is before all else a question of Moral Theology, and therefore bigger than the issues involved in any national or political controversy. It is bigger than the Nations at war or in peace, in freedom or in fetters. Kingdoms, empires and republics rise and fall, but "the truth of the Lord remaineth forever." "If you continue in my word you shall be my disciples indeed, and you shall know the truth, and the truth shall make you free." (John, viii, 32.)

Chapter Twenty Four

THE ACTIONS OF THE IRISH HUNGER-STRIKERS WERE MORE THAN LAWFUL

NO SUICIDES, NO SINNERS. HEROES, HEROES ALL!

What a meagre boon the theologians bestow on Mac-Swiney, Fitzgerald and Murphy when they tell them that their hunger-strike until death was not suicide, nor anything else that is unlawful! In the littleness of their souls, and, indeed, in the littleness of their Theology, several of them began by suspecting the hunger-strikers of lawless fanaticism. Next they were summarily summoned into court on the charge of suicide, as if their guilt was apparent to all. A long array of professional witnesses, mostly fellow Irishmen and members of the Roman Catholic clergy, turned States evidence and gave expert testimony against them, after the manner of spies and informers. But, as in all such cases, their testimony did not agree. It is worthy of special notice that, of those who exclaimed "suicide," some gave no reason at all for the faith that was in them. They simply declared that Mayor MacSwiney was a suicide whether he knew it or not. Others who returned the same verdict attempted to prove it, but without much success. Fr. Lawless, P.P., of Faughart, Dundalk, Ireland, unwittingly summed up the case for Mayor MacSwiney, though intending to sum it up against him. "No two writers, in all the correspondence," said Fr. Lawless, "gave the same reasons for the Lord Mayor's hunger-strike. So it was plain that they could not all be right. Now I know they were all wrong." "Mutato nomine, de te fabula narratur." No two of those who called hunger-strike suicide, gave the same reasons for saying so. This is not surprising. There is, as has been shown, no such reason, no theological or philosophical reason, and therefore all who wanted a reason had to invent one. Their position was analogous to that of the man who gave reasons why a fish is heavier in the water than out of it. Reasons for what is not so, cannot be very convincing. In the words of Fr. Nicholas Lawless, "they could not all be right. Now we know that they were all wrong."

NOBLEST OF THE NOBLE, BRAVEST OF THE BRAVE!

So much for the theologians. When they had pronounced the Irish hunger-strike lawful, they had reached their highest limit of appreciation. The heroism of it all scarcely called forth from them a word of admiration. They would say, with reason, that admiration is not their specialty. Indeed, any true appreciation of heroism calls for another kind of genius – that of the orator and the poet. Had there been, at the time of the Irish hunger-strike, a modern Demosthenes, what burning philippics he would have hurled at King George and Lloyd George for their policy of systematic persecution of Ireland and its heroes. Even if the wrathful Achilles of Homer, and the good Aeneas of Virgil, had been real instead of imaginary heroes, what sickly heroes they would have been by comparison with Lord Mayor MacSwiney!

PROUD PAGANS OF ANTIQUITY NO HEROES AT ALL

In truth, the heroes of pagan antiquity were not heroes at all. They were, every one of them, filled with pride and selfishness, and the proud, selfish man can never be a hero. The more proud and selfish, the less heroic. Achilles frequently gave himself up to fitful sulking and Aeneas to fitful weeping – neither of which becomes a hero. A hero is one who is constant above ordinary mortals in doing what is right and noble. Now to be noble it is necessary to be unselfish – self-sacrificing, and the most perfect form of self-sacrifice is suffering endured with patience and resignation and courage. Everyone who will pay that price may own the most perfect brand of heroism, nor can anyone purchase it for any lesser price. It is a market that has no fluctuations. This the poets understood with almost inspired insight.

> "Sweet source of every virtue, O sacred Sorrow! he "who knows not thee, knows not the best emotions of "the heart." (Thomson)

> "Affliction is the good man's shining scene. Pros-"perity conceals his brightest ray." (Young)

> "Sorrow and silence are strong, and patient endur-"ance is godlike." (Longfellow)

> "Know how sublime a thing it is to suffer and be "strong." (Goldsmith)

> "Adversity! Thou tamer of the human breast." (Gray)

> "Sweet are the uses of adversity." (Shakespeare)

HUMILITY, PATIENCE – CHRISTIAN, NOT PAGAN

Now, humility, self-sacrifice, patience, resignation and courage in suffering – these are all Christian virtues, entirely unknown even to the philosophers of pagan antiquity. For them meekness was weakness, and the meek man a weak man, though, in truth, meekness is strength, and the meek man the strong, if not the only strong man. "Pride goeth before destruction and the spirit is lifted up before a fall. It is better to be humbled with the meek than to divide spoils with the proud." (Prov. xvi, 18). The meekness of the Christian martyrs in every age has been the secret source of their heroic strength. It is what St. Paul calls "the weakness of God." (I Cor., i-25).

IGNORANT OF SELF-SACRIFICE AND RESIGNATION

Equally unintelligible to the pagan were self-sacrifice and resignation to suffering. The holy folly of the Cross was still a hidden mystery to the entire pagan world. It is not surprising then that the pagan heroes failed ingloriously when tried by this test. Brutus is a typical specimen. The tragic Muse and the epic Muse, and, indeed, all the Muses have conspired to glorify him. The great master of tragedy tells us that

> "His life was gentle and the elements
> "So mixed in him that Nature might stand up
> "And say to all the world: 'This was a man'!"

Yet this "noblest Roman of them all" lacked the courage to bear up under his defeat at Philippi by the armies of Octavius and Mark Antony. His weak soul, crushed by what Hamlet calls "the slings and arrows of outrageous fortune," "the noble Brutus," with consummate cowardice, pierced his own body through with his own sword. He was no hero. He utterly lacked the courage of patient endurance.

MacSWINEY'S PRUDENCE, FEARLESS COURAGE

Let us now turn from a typical pagan hero to a truly Christian hero. Let us turn to Lord Mayor MacSwiney and estimate his character by the same identical standards by which we tested the character of Brutus. It has been already remarked that one of the chief requisites for heroism is courage – the ready will to make sacrifices in spite of selfishness. The race from which Mayor MacSwiney sprang has always been recognized as a fearless race. But fearlessness, of itself, can never rise to the dignity of courage. Divorced from prudence, fearlessness is nothing better than recklessness. And so we find Shakespeare making prudence a part of the character of Banquo. Macbeth says of him:

> " 'Tis much he dares,
> "And, to that dauntless temper of his mind,
> "He hath a wisdom that doth guide his valor
> "To act in safety. And under him
> "My genius is rebuked, as it is said
> "Mark Antony's was by Caesar."

NO DREAMY IDEALS, NO IMPRACTICAL VISIONS

Few men in public life, few leaders of men have united in their character the same measure of sound, practical prudence, unflinching courage, and lofty integrity that Lord Mayor MacSwiney did. And, first of all, his solid, practical judgment. He was no dreamy idealist, no wild, unpractical visionary. He recognized the necessity of prudence and stressed its importance. "You among us who have no vision," he said in his **Inaugural Address**, "have been led astray by false prophets." In his **Principles of Freedom** he wrote:

> "Now, and in every phase of the coming struggle, "the strong mind is a greater need than the strong "hand. We must be passionate, but the mind must "guide and govern our passion. In the aberrations of "the weak mind decrying resistance, let us not lose our "balance and defy brute strength."

KNEW THE DIFFICULTIES AND DANGERS AHEAD

From the very beginning he understood full well the ruthless policy of the Government he was resisting, the difficulties and dangers that had to be reckoned with in proclaiming the Irish Republic, in projecting the Revolution, and in continuing the intermittent warfare of the years that followed, until that day of triumph for Ireland when England's Prime Minister officially asked for a truce. In the inaugural address already referred to, he said:

> "Mayor McCurtain and myself, discussed, in an "intimate way, everything touching our common work "together, since that hour in Easter week when we "lay under the enemy's guns. We discussed what ought "to be done and what could be done, keeping in mind, "as in duty bound, not only the ideal line of action "but the line practicable at the moment as well."

MORAL NOT PHYSICAL POWER HOPE OF VICTORY

Well too did the Lord Mayor understand the practical policies by which these incidental difficulties and dangers were to be combated. The power on which he relied to vindicate Ireland's claim to independence, and overcome the many obstacles to its realization, was not a physical but a moral power – the power of right, on whose side he saw ultimately arrayed the forces of Earth and Heaven. Here are his words:

> "It is not those who can inflict the most but those "who can suffer the most who will conquer. The civil"ized world dare not look on indifferent, while new "tortures are being prepared for our country, or they "will see undermined the pillars of their own govern"ments and the world involved in unimaginable an"archy. But if the rulers of Earth fail us, we still have "refuge in the Ruler of Heaven."

SOUGHT COURAGE, ENDURANCE FROM HEAVEN

Finally, the Lord Mayor had the fullest understanding of the sources from which himself and his fellow revolutionists might hope to derive their needed courage and endurance.

> "God is over us. In His divine intervention we must have perfect trust. To the divine Author of Mercy we appeal for strength to sustain us in our battle, whatever the persecution, that we may bring our people to victory in the end. Those who are strong in faith will endure to the end in triumph. The shining hope of our time is that so many of our people are now strong in faith."

MORE EVIDENCE OF HIS PRACTICAL PRUDENCE

"Further evidence of the Lord Mayor's eminently prudent, practical bent is found is the following extracts from his "Principles of Freedom." They enunciate great fundamental truths, suited alike to the citizen in private life, the ruler steering the ship of state, and the soldier marching to battle. Indeed many of them apply no less to the religious in the cloister – to every man and woman whose life would be regulated by the loftiest principles of conduct.

(1) "Our philosophy is valueless unless we bring it into life. With sufficient ingenuity we might frame theory after theory, but if they could not be put to the test of a work-a-day existence, we but add another to the many dead theories that litter the History of Philosophy. Our principles are not to argue about, or write about, or hold meetings about, but primarily to give us a rule of life. To ignore this is to waste time and energy."

(2) "An idea you hold as true is not to be professed only where it is proclaimed. It will whisper and you must be its prophet in strange places. You must glory in it or deny it. There is no middle way. Wherever your path lies it will cross you and you must choose."

(3) "Wherever an appeal for the flag is calling us, the snare of the enemy is in wait. Priests will get more patronage if they discourage the national idea; professors will get more emoluments and honours if they ban it; public men will receive places and titles if they betray it; the professional man will be promised more aggrandisement, the business man more commerce, the tradesman more traffic if he put by the flag."

(4) "In places there is a dangerous idea that sometime in the future we may be called on to strike a blow for freedom, but, in the meantime, there is little to do but watch and wait. This is a fatal error. We have to forge our strength in the interval."

(5) "In whatever sphere a man finds himself, his acts "must be in relation to and consistent with every "other sphere. He will be the best patriot and the "best soldier who is the best friend and the best "citizen. **One cannot be an honest man in one sphere "and a rascal in another.** Everything that crosses "a man's path in his day's round of little or great "moment, requires of him an attitude towards it, "and the conscious or unconscious shaping of his "attitude is determining how he will proceed in other "spheres not now in view."

(6) "**Every act of personal discipline is contributing to "a subconscious reservoir, whence our nobler ener-"gies are supplied for ever.** Little things lead to "great. In an office wrangle or a social squabble "there is need for developing those very qualities "of judgment, courage and patience, which equip a "man for the trials of the battlefield or the ruling "of the State." (Chap. 5 and 6.)

Thus far Mayor MacSwiney's practical prudence. His was the loftiest idealism known to man, yet mingled, at every stage, with the most practical realism.

"Keeping in mind not only the ideal line of action "but the line practicable at the moment as well."

THE UNDAUNTED COURAGE OF THE LORD MAYOR

Let us now devote a paragraph to considering his undaunted courage. Listen to one brave though seemingly helpless man, as he flings thunderbolts of defiance in the face of a mighty empire! Boldly accepting the post of Mayor McCurtain – recently assassinated by Black and Tan soldiers, in his own home, at the midnight hour, in the presence of his wife and children – Mayor MacSwiney said:

"I came here more as a soldier stepping into the "breach than as an administrator to fill my post in the "municipality. Facing our enemy we must declare our "attitude simply. We see in their regime a thing of "evil incarnate. With it there can be no parley any "more than with the powers of Hell. **This is our simple "resolution. We ask no mercy, and we will accept no "compromise.**"

FIRST TO ANSWER HIS OWN CALL TO ACTION

Bold, brave words these – a bugle call to brave action; a call which the Lord Mayor was himself the first to answer, acting out his bold defiance in bravest deeds, down to the last gruesome, harrowing detail of Brixton Prison. Worn and weakened in body at the end of sixty-four days of absolute fast, his message to his eleven fellow hunger-strikers in Cork jail holds up to the gaze of an astonished and admiring world, his spirit still unbroken, still unbending.

> "I offer my sufferings here for our martyred people to withstand the present terror in Ireland, not only for two months but for two years if need be."

HIS DYING WORDS THE SAME BOLD DEFIANCE

And, when, ten days later, after an agony of seventy-four days and nights, the kindly Angel of Death at last claimed his emaciated body, the Lord Mayor's last recorded words, spoken to his sister just before he sank into his final unconsciousness, breathed the same bold defiance.

> "I want you to bear witness that I die a soldier of the Irish Republic. God save Ireland."

VERDICT OF CLERGY, CATHOLIC, SECULAR PRESS

Does history furnish any record of sublimer courage, more inflexible constancy or nobler endurance? If, in addition to Mayor MacSwiney's own words and deeds, further corroborative evidence of this claim be necessary, the reader will find it, to his heart's content, in the verdicts of Archbishops, Bishops, Priests, and laymen; in the verdict of the Catholic Press, and, most of all, in the verdict of the Secular Press. Writers of editorials usually approach their subject in a coldly judicial mood, feeling, as they do, in duty bound to exclude from their inquiry every prejudice likely to modify their verdict or its presentation. And so when an editorial writer in THE LONDON TIMES or in the NEW YORK TIMES or in the CHICAGO TRIBUNE – all of them proverbally pro-English and anti-Irish – when an editorial writer in any of these papers, or indeed in any one of the many other papers of similar policy – calls an Irishman a hero, it is safe to agree that he is a hero. If, at any time in the world's history, the secular press of every nation – putting aside every prepossession, racial, religious and national – conspired to bestow on any other hero as large a measure of immortal eulogy as it conferred on Mayor MacSwiney, the present writer is not aware of it. "There are few persons," said the BALTIMORE SUN, "who will not agree that this prison tragedy is one of the most pathetic as well as one of the most extraordinary known to modern civilized history." THE NATION (New York) said: "Once more, passive resistance, most deadly of weapons, has triumphed. Once more, the whole world is quickened and inspired and glorified by the example of one who placed his cause above his existence. Who today is more certain of immortality? And the roots of British Government in Ireland are loosened."

The MORNING POST (London, Eng.) wrote: "To defy to the death the right of jurisdiction of a powerful State, without hope of reprieve, is, in the abstract, a brave action."

THE WESTMINSTER GAZETTE: "It is a tragedy that will fill Irishmen the world over, with the proud conviction that the race which can produce a martyr like Terence MacSwiney can never be subdued by might. He has won his battle."

And THE MANCHESTER GUARDIAN: "There was almost as large a muster of foreign journalists at Southwark Cathedral as there was of English. Some saw the service only as a sign of England's disgrace, and that is the story that will mainly go to the world."

THE TIMES (London): "The Lord Mayor of Cork is dead. His sincerity and his courage are now, at all events, vindicated beyond all question."

"He has won his battle," exclaimed THE WESTMINSTER GAZETTE.

The EVENING NEWS (London): "MacSwiney's death has made a deep impression the whole world over."

THE TIMES (London – Editorial): "The death of MacSwiney will have an effect which will not be confined to the British Isles alone."

The DAILY NEWS (London – Editorial): "Irish Nationalism will be given a stimulus almost incalculably effective by MacSwiney's death."

THE HERALD (London – Editorial): "The murder of MacSwiney by the government was accomplished after slow torture for seventy-four days."

THE EVENING SUN (Baltimore, Md.): "There is not the slightest doubt that public sentiment runs high in favor of the Mayor of Cork. Practically all shades of public opinion join in condemning England."

THE STANDARD UNION (Brooklyn, N. Y.– Editorial): "MasSwiney's death was at once a tragedy and a triumph."

THE POST (New York – Editorial): "The result is a strengthening of the Irish will to resist, and an immense propaganda for Sinn Fein."

THE WORLD (New York – Editorial): "The status of the Irish problem is not the same. The subtlest change of the past two-months is the growing conviction, even of

British Conservatives, that there must be a settlement. To this change MacSwiney's story powerfully contributed."

THE HERALD (New York – Editorial): "Unfortunately for the people of the British Isles, nothing is over except MacSwiney's pain. The agony of the Irish problem grows worse. Starving, MacSwiney fed his own cause."

THE TIMES (Brooklyn – Editorial): "MacSwiney is dead, but his death is a triumph. He has left his impress on history. He has done more for the cause for which he fought than a thousand rifles."

THE SUN (Baltimore – Editorial): "The death of the Lord Mayor of Cork has deeply saddened part of the vast audience upon which it was thrust, and maddened a large proportion."

SPRINGFIELD REPUBLICAN (Editorial): "MacSwiney's renunciation of life will inspire Irish patriots to increased zeal and fortitude for the cause to which he dedicated his life."

BRANN'S ICONOCLAST (Editorial): "Terence MacSwiney is dead, but the faith that was his, the unbending spirit of the man, will continue to work for Irish independence until victory for right ends British rule."

THE MILWAUKEE JOURNAL (Editorial): "Irish independence is measurably nearer today, for Terence MacSwiney is dead in Brixton Gaol."

ECHO DE PARIS: "The sacrifice of MacSwiney has had the entire world as spectator, and it will resound throughout the whole universe as the heart-rending appeal of a suffering nation."

LA CROIX: "When the claims of a people can induce such sacrifices as that of the Lord Mayor, it is very difficult not to listen to them."

L'ERE NOUVELLE: "When the death of MacSwiney took place, all humanity shuddered, with emotion. The regime of egoism, of barbarism, in which the war had nearly buried us, is about to end."

LA PETITE JOURNAL: "The death of the Lord Mayor of Cork is going to interest humanity as a whole in the independence of Ireland."

L'HUMANITE: "The death of the Lord Mayor opens a new chapter in the bloody and tormented history of contemporary Ireland."

LE RAPPEL: "A ruder blow to England than the loss of a whole battalion."

LA LIBERTE: "Ireland will count one legendary hero the more, and England has not rid herself of an enemy. On the contrary, the dead are more dangerous than the living."

LIBRE PAROLE: "The act of the Lord Mayor has a symbolic force and there lies its greatness. He wished to show the world that, in this twentieth century, a nation that piques itself on its liberalism, and claims to erect into a system the right of people to dispose of themselves, **keeps a neighboring race under the rudest yoke.**"

LA BATAILLE: "Rarely has death of Emperor or King had an influence more profound on the destiny of a people, than that which we expect the death of Terence MacSwiney, simple Mayor of Cork, will have on the future of England."

LE BONSOIR: "England finds itself now **before a corpse more formidable** than the living body. The cause that gives its supporters such force of character and will **is assured of inevitable triumph.**"

PETIT PARISIEN: "The cortege was the largest seen since the death of King Edward."

"Yes! MacSwiney, thou hast triumphed," was the despairing cry of England, even as, of old, the apostate Roman Emperor cried out in despair: "Thou hast triumphed, O Galilean!"

"A MAN OF DARING, ENERGY, INFLEXIBILITY"

Truly and well might we say of the Lord Mayor of Cork all that Macbeth says of Banquo: "'Tis much he dares, and to that dauntless temper of his mind, he hath a wisdom that doth guide his valor to act in safety." More truly, far more truly than of Brutus, might it be said of Lord Mayor MacSwiney that "the elements were so mixed in him that Nature might stand up and say to all the world: 'This was a man'!" And indeed that is exactly what men said and continue to say about him. ROBERT LYND, Literary Editor of the London Daily News, briefly described Lord Mayor MacSwiney thus:

> "He is at the same time meditative and a man of "action. He gives the impression at once of daring, "energy and inflexibility,—a man in whose presence "men stand up straighter."

IDEAS ON LIBERTY, PATRIOTISM, GOVERNMENT

The noble integrity of the Lord Mayor's character is admirably exhibited both in his "Principles of Freedom" and in his "Inaugural Address." The lofty conceptions of liberty, patriotism and government there set forth, show him to have been a man whose ideals were the very highest, who continually strove, with all his might, to realize these ideals, and who shrank from ever falling below them in anything. He upbraids his followers who allow themselves to lose sight of the grand ideal.

"Most of us lose faith in the ideal. We are apathetic. "We have powers and let them be fallow. Our minds "should be restless for noble and beautiful things. "In the destruction of the spirit entailed, lies the "deeper significance of our claim to freedom. When "foolish people make a sacred thing seem silly, let us "at least be sane. The man who cries out for the sacred "thing, but voices a universal need. To exist, the "healthy mind must have beautiful things. It is noth-"ing but love of country that rouses us to make our "land full-blooded and beautiful, where now she is "pallid and wasted." (Prin. of Freedom, Chap. 1.)

FURTHER EXAMPLES OF HIS SUBLIME IDEALIZING

Here are several other specimens of the Lord Mayor's grand idealizing. Remember that Terence MacSwiney was an educated Catholic gentleman, an author of distinction, chief magistrate of a capital city, a patriot without peer, now sacrificing his young life, with all its ties and prospects, in order to cooperate with his compatriots in ending the long dark night of his country's thraldom. Those bent on finding him guilty were prompt to insist that he was willing to attain his lofty purpose by means fair or foul. How little they knew, how little they cared to know, of his incomparable ideals, savoring, as they do, of an apostle and an evangelist, pleading for universal peace and love. These ideals are met with on every page of his "Principles of Freedom," and in every paragraph of his "Inaugural Address." There is space here for only a few of them.

I. HIS IDEA OF IDEALS

"Let the cultivation of a brave, high spirit be our "great task. It will make each man's soul an unassail-"able fortress. It is only in the light of a perfect ideal "that we can come near to perfection. We may reach "the mountaintops in aspiring to the stars."

II. HIS IDEAL OF MANHOOD

"Forbearance is the final test of men. A true soldier "of liberty will always remember that restraint is the "great attribute that separates man from beast; that "retaliation is the vicious resource of the tyrant and "the slave; that magnanimity is the splendor of man-"hood."

III. HIS IDEAL REGARDING CIVIL LIBERTY

"The liberty for which we strive today is a sacred thing, inseparably entwined with that spiritual liberty for which the Saviour of men died, and which is the foundation of all just government. Because it is sacred, and death for it is akin to the sacrifice of Calvary, following afar off, but constant to that example, in every generation our best and bravest have died."

IV. HIS IDEAL REGARDING THE AIMS OF FREEDOM

"The end of freedom is to realize the salvation and happiness of all peoples, to make the world, and not any selfish corner of it, a more beautiful dwelling place for men."

V. HIS IDEAL REGARDING WAR

"War must be faced and blood must be shed, not gleefully but as a terrible necessity, because there are moral evils much worse than any physical horror, because freedom is indispensable for a soul erect, and freedom must be had at any cost of suffering. But a true soldier of liberty will remember that he strikes, not at his enemy's life but at his misdeed, and that, in destroying the misdeed, he makes not only for his own freedom but even for his enemy's regeneration."*

VI. HIS IDEAL ABOUT THE ETHICS OF WARFARE

"A fight that is not clean-handed will make victory more disgraceful than any defeat. It is possible for Ireland to win her independence by base methods. But I stand for this principle – no physical victory can compensate for spiritual surrender. Whatever side denies this is not my side."

"It is love of country that inspires us, and not hate of the enemy, and desire for full satisfaction for the past. Our enemies are brothers from whom we are estranged. Neither kingdom, republic or commune can regenerate us. If the world is to be regenerated, we must have world-wide unity, not of government but of brotherhood."

VIII. HIS IDEAL REGARDING PRINCIPLES

"In a physical contest on the field of battle, it is allowed to use tactics and strategy – to have recourse to a ruse as well as to an open attack. But in matters of principle there can be no tactics. There is one straightforward course to follow, and that course must be found and followed unswervingly to the end."

IX. HIS IDEAL OF BROTHERHOOD

"If, then, beyond individual and national freedom, there is this great dream of international brotherhood to be striven for, let us not decry it as something too sublime for earth. It must be our guiding star to lead us rightly as far as we may go."

---

*Thus does the Lord Mayor apply to warfare the "servato moderamine" condition, necessary that personal self-defense may be lawful.

X. HIS IDEAL REGARDING SPIRITUAL VALUES

"The soul is greater than the body. The body is a "passing phase. The spirit is immortal, and the de-"gradation of that immortal part of man is the great "tragedy of life."

XI. HIS IDEAL ON THE POWER OF SUFFERING

"It is not those who can inflict the most, but those "who can suffer the most, who will conquer. The civil-"ized world dare not look on indifferent while new "tortures are being prepared for our country, or they "will see undermined the pillars of their own govern-"ments, and the world involved in unimaginable "anarchy. But if the rulers of earth fail us, we still "have refuge in the Ruler of Heaven."

XII. HIS IDEAL OF COMRADESHIP

"While the meanness and tyranny of our enemies "stand forward against our argument for universal "brotherhood, and leave our reasoning cold, we can "find a more subtle appeal in a play of Shakespeare, "a song of Shelley, or a picture of Turner. From the "heart of the enemy, genius cries, bearing witness to "our common humanity, and the yearning for high "comradeship is alive, and the dream survives to light "us on our onward path."

(1) "We are no longer boys. We have had years of ex-"perience, keen struggles, not a little bitterness, "and we are steadied. We feel a heart-beat for "deeper things. It is no longer sufficient that they "sound bravely. They must ring true. The school-"boy's dream is more of a Roman triumph – tramp-"ing armies, shouting multitudes, waving banners – "all good enough in their way. But the dream of "men is something beyond all this show. If it were "not, it could hardly claim a sacrifice."

(2) "If there are tyrannies on earth, one nation cannot "set things right. But it is still bound so to order "its own affairs as to be consistent with universal "freedom and friendship . . . Freedom rightly con-"sidered is not a mere setting up of a number of in-"dependent units. It makes for harmony among na-"tions and good fellowship on earth." (Chap. 1.)

(3) "It is a truism of Philosophy and Science that the "world is a harmonious whole, and that, with the "increase of knowledge, laws can be discovered to "explain the order and the unity of the universe. "Accordingly, if we are to justify our position as "separatists, we must show that it will harmonize, "unify and develop our national life, that it will re-"store us to a place among the nations – a destiny "which, through all our struggles, we ever believe "is great, and waiting for us. A great doctrine that "dominates our lives, that lays down a rigid course "of action, that involves self-denial, hard struggles,

"endurance for years, and possibly death before the goal is reached – any such doctrine must be capable of having its truth demonstrated by the discovery of principles that govern and justify it. Otherwise we cannot yield it our allegiance."

(4) "We will find courage in moving forward, and will triumph in the end, by keeping in mind at all times that the end of freedom is to realize the salvation and happiness of all peoples – to make the world, and not any selfish corner of it, a more beautiful dwelling place for men."

(5) "There is a common error that a man's work for his country should be based on the assumption that it should bear full effect in his own time. This is most certainly false. A man's life is counted by years, a nation's by centuries. And as work for the nation should be directed to bringing her to full maturity in the coming time, a man must be prepared to labour for an end that may be realized only in another generation. A man's prime is great as his earlier years have been well directed and concentrated. In the early years the ground is prepared and the seed is sown for the splendid period of full development. So it is with the nation. Bearing in mind that the maturity of the nation will come, not in one generation but after many generations, we must be prepared to work, in the knowledge that we prepare for a future which only other generations will enjoy." (Chap. 2.)

NO PHYSICAL VICTORY BY MORAL SURRENDER

The ideals here enunciated are surely nothing short of the loftiest. It was characters of this type that Edmund Burke had before his mind when he spoke of "that chastity of principle, that delicate sensibility of honor that felt a stain like a wound." When, at the beginning of the first World War, it was suggested that Ireland's cause could be promoted by an alliance with Germany, Mayor MacSwiney made this answer:

"It is possible for Ireland to win her independence by base methods. But I stand by this principle – no physical victory can compensate for spiritual surrender. Whatever side denies this is not my side. If Ireland were to win her freedom by helping, directly or indirectly, to crush another people, she would earn the execration she herself poured out on tyranny for ages. A fight that is not clean-handed will make victory more disgraceful than any defeat."

NATIONAL INDEPENDENCE A SACRED THING

The Lord Mayor likewise sets forth his conception of national independence, and again it is the loftiest conception. In his Address of Inauguration, he shows how precious a thing he held it to be. Neither is he, in the least mistaken regarding the price that must be paid for it.

> "The liberty for which we strive today is a sacred thing, inseparably entwined with that spiritual liberty for which the Saviour of men died and which is the foundation of all just government. Because it is sacred, and death for it is akin to the sacrifice of Calvary, following far off but constant to that Divine example, in every generation our best and bravest have died. But it is because they were our best and bravest that they had to die. No lesser sacrifice would save us. Because of it our struggle is holy. Our battle is sanctified by their blood. Our victory is assured by their martyrdom."

MUST SECURE AND SAFEGUARD IT AT ANY COST

Again, he states the great fundamental reason why this national independence should be secured and safeguarded at any cost.

> "We fight for freedom, not for the vanity of the world, not to have a fine conceit of ourselves, not to be as big as our neighbours. The inspiration is drawn from a deeper element of our being. A spiritual necessity makes the true significance of our claim to freedom. We stifle for self-development, individually and as a nation. If we don't go forward we must go down. It is a matter of life and death. It is of vital importance to himself and the community that each man be given a full opportunity to develop his powers and to fill his place worthily ... It is love of country that inspires us, not hate of the enemy, or desire for full satisfaction for the past. We stand for a right that is inalienable. A majority has no right to annul it, and no power to destroy it. Tyrannies may persecute, slay or banish those who defend it. The thing is indestructible. One man, alone, may vindicate it, and because that one man has never failed, it has never died."
> (Prin. of Freedom, Chap. 1.)

HIS REFUSAL TO RESENT – CAPACITY TO FORGIVE

There remains yet another standard by which the Lord Mayor's character may be judged – unwillingness to resent injuries, and capacity to forgive them. This is the supreme test of true nobility. It is shown by abundant experience that very many who come forth triumphant from other tests, fail ingloriously under the ordeal of forgiving and forgetting. The splendid superiority that refuses to resent an injury, is, alas, all too rare among frail mortals.

But even under a test so crucial, Mayor MacSwiney is equal to the emergency. Indeed it is here that he soars to his sublimest heights, fulfilling the letter and the spirit of Christ's precept to forgive and to love even our enemies.

It is needless to remark that he had much to forgive. The unending agonies of his country were for him a perpetual nightmore. Her literature – her histories, her songs and ballads, her dramas and her works of fiction – tells the story, a story written red on every page, with the lifeblood of millions of her best and bravest sons and daughters. Of this the Lord Mayor had read aplenty. But he had also heard it aplenty. Even as recently as his generation, plenty of old men and old women survived, to tell their children's children anecdotes of suffering in the evil days of the "Great Famine"– England's most cruel contrivance, that collected from Ireland a toll of two millions of her people – to kindle in their hearts undying hatred, thirst for revenge, and hope of one day wresting the soil which their ancestors had reclaimed and cultivated, from the grasp of the usurping and tyrannical stranger. **This is some of what the Lord Mayor was called to forgive, and he forgave it all.** Again we quote his own words at considerable length.

(1) "Our enemies are brothers from whom we are estranged. . . . If the world is to be regenerated, we must have world-wide unity, not of government but of brotherhood."

(2) "It is love of country that inspires us, and not hate of the enemy, and desire for full satisfaction for the past. If we want full revenge for the past, the best way to get it is to remain as we are – a menace to England. The opportunity will come, but it would hardly make us happy."

(3) "Forbearance is the final test of men. By those who cling to prejudice and extol enmity, the counter plea for forbearance is always scorned as the enervating gospel of weakness and despair. Though we like to call ourselves Christian, we have no desire for that outstanding Christian virtue. Yet men not held by Christian dogma have joyously surrendered to the sublimity of that divine idea. We shall receive every provocation to acknowledge ancient bitterness, but then is the time to stand firm. Then shall we need to practise the divine forbearance that is the secret of strength."

(4) "Happily, it is nothing new to plead for brotherhood among Irishmen now. Unhappily, it is not so generally recognised that the same reason exists for the reestablishing of friendship with England. Friendliness between neighbours is one of the natural things of life. . . . There is one honest fear that our independence would threaten their security. It will be replaced by the conviction that there is a surer safe-guard in our freedom than in our suppression."

(5) "But if, in the gross materialism and greed of em-
"pire that is now the ruling passion with the enemy,
"there is apparently little hope for a transformation
"that will make them spiritual, high-minded and
"generous, we must not abandon our ideal. From the
"heart of the enemy Genius cries, bearing witness
"to our common humanity."

(6) "If the greatness and beauty of life, that ought to
"be the dream of all nations, is denied by all but
"one, that one may keep alive the dream within her
"own frontier, till its fascination will arrest and
"inspire the world. If this ultimate dream is still
"floating far off, in its pursuit there is for us
"achievement on achievement, and each brave thing
"done is, in itself, a beauty and a joy for ever. For
"the good fighter there is always fine recompense –
"a clear mind, warm blood, quick imagination, grasp
"of life, joy in action, and, at the end of the day,
"always an eminence won. Yes, and from the height
"of that eminence will come ringing down to the
"last doubter a last word – we may reach the moun-
"tain-tops in aspiring to the stars."

("Principles of Freedom," Chap. 3 and 4.)

HIS SUBLIME PRINCIPLES OF CIVIL POLITY

Where besides, in the world of statesmanship, do we meet with such sublime principles of civil polity internal and international? Whoever desires more exalted principles of civil government must seek them outside of this terrestrial orb. Neither can it be urged that such principles are too ideal to admit of being put in practice by men and nations in their ordinary relations one with another. The Lord Mayor anticipated and denied the objection.

"If then, beyond individual and national freedom,
"there is this great dream – of international brother-
"hood – to be striven for, let us not decry it as some-
"thing too sublime for earth. It must be our guiding
"star to lead us rightly as far as we may go. We can
"travel rightly that part of the road we now tread on,
"only by shaping it true to the great end that ought
"to inspire us all. We shall have many temptations to
"swerve aside, but the power of mind that keeps our
"position clear and firm, will react against every
"destroying influence."

SUPERNATURAL FAITH HIS CONSPICUOUS TRAIT

The truth is, no line of conduct was too sublime for the sublime faith of Lord Mayor MacSwiney. Beyond question, the most conspicuous – because most fundamental and most energizing – trait of his very exceptional character was his rare gift of supernatural faith. It was always burning – flaming. It kept him ever mindful of God and of His merciful Providence, that often overrules the decrees of merciless men. "God is over us. To the divine Author of Mercy we appeal for strength." The same glowing faith brought him to view man and all that pertains to him in the light of man's spiritual nature, and his immortal and supernatural destiny. "A spiritual necessity makes the true significance of our claim to freedom. The material aspect is only a secondary consideration." From this he passed to the divine Redeemer and the Redemption which He wrought for the human race by His passion and death. When an English official in Ireland would asperse the Republican Army, saying "there is no beauty in liberty that comes to us dripping in innocent blood," the Lord Mayor replied:

"At one stroke this judge would shatter the foundations of Christianity, by denying beauty to that spiritual liberty that comes to us dripping in the blood of Christ crucified, Who, by His voluntary sacrifice on Calvary, delivered us from the domination of the devil, when the pall of evil was closing down and darkening the world."

CIVIL AND SPIRITUAL LIBERTY INSEPARABLE

With the spiritual liberty which Christ restored to the human race, the Lord Mayor saw, inseparably connected, the national liberty for which his countrymen have never ceased to struggle, and which likewise demanded a holocaust in every generation. And he adds that, in imitation of the Saviour, the willing victim was always to be found.

"The liberty for which we strive today is a sacred thing, inseparably entwined with that spiritual liberty for which the Saviour of men died. Because it is sacred, and death for it is akin to the sacrifice of Calvary, following far off but constant to that Divine example, in every generation our best and bravest have died."*

NATIONAL LIBERTY DEVOTED TO SACRED CAUSE

And since national independence is "a sacred thing inseparably entwined with spiritual liberty," the Lord Mayor is at pains to insist that the cause to which it is to be devoted, the end to which it is to be directed, should be equally sacred. He wrote:

"The end of freedom is to realize the salvation and happiness of all peoples, to make the world, and not any selfish corner of it, a more beautiful dwelling place for men."

KINSHIP OF NATIONS VS. NARROW PROVINCIALISM

Human mind has never conceived nor has human tongue ever expressed a more exalted notion of national liberty and the purpose it should be made to serve. Could anything be further removed from the narrow provincialism which, in our times more than ever before, has become the poison of all international relations. Witness the nations in conference at Geneva. They are in a deadlock. The conference is threatened with disruption. They are "looking for a formula." Why the deadlock? Why the threatened disruption? Why the formula? Because of national selfishness! Because each nation is bent on consulting its own best interests, and refuses to sacrifice even a reasonable measure of them for the sake of international harmony. Because, in the words of Lord Mayor MacSwiney, each nation aims to make, not the whole world, but some selfish corner of it, a more beautiful dwelling place for itself. If, on other occasions, individual nations accept and profess Mayor MacSwiney's eternal principle that "the end of freedom is to realize the salvation and happiness of all peoples," they accord that principle but scant recognition when they assemble in international session. And yet that principle should be the pivot on which all their deliberations revolve – the goal to which all their striving should be directed, since it is God's own purpose, in bestowing liberty on the individual, the nation, the entire human race.

MINGLED LANGUAGE OF APOSTLE AND PATRIOT

Having always in his mind the exalted conception of national independence that would make it minister, in due measure, to the salvation and happiness of all nations, it is not surprising that Mayor MacSwiney, when he spoke and wrote, should be found mingling the language of the Apostle with the language of the patriot. When, for instance, he insists that "a fight that is not clean-handed will make victory more disgraceful than any defeat," he but says what St. Paul wrote to Timothy: "He that striveth for the mastery is not crowned unless he strive lawfully." (ii, 2-5). Again the Lord Mayor, in his Inaugural Address, speaks of "that spiritual liberty which comes to us dripping in the blood of Christ crucified"– a paraphrase of St. Peter's words in his First Epistle: "You were not redeemed with

---

*This conception of inseparable union between spiritual liberty and national liberty, did not originate with Mayor MacSwiney. It was shared by all Irish patriots of all times. Dr. Drennan, himself an Irish revolutionary leader, in his poem—"The Wake of William Orr"—identifies the two liberties, and parallels the two victims.

"Here we watch our brother's sleep;
"Watch with us but do not weep;
"Watch with us through dead of night,
"But expect the morning light."
"Why cut off in palmy youth?
"Truth he spoke and acted truth;
"'Countrymen, unite!' he cried,
"And died for what our Saviour died."

corruptible things as gold or silver, but with the precious blood of Christ." (i, 1, 9). Once more, when the Lord Mayor asserts that "those whose faith is strong will endure to the end in triumph," he is but repeating Christ's own assurance: "Amen I say to you if you have faith you shall say to this mountain: 'Remove from hence hither,' and it shall remove, and nothing shall be impossible to you."
(Matt. xiii, 19.)

WISDOM OF HEAVEN IN HIS POLITICAL POLICIES

And as the Lord Mayor's principles savored more of heavenly than of earthly wisdom, so too did his political policies. "It is not those who can inflict the most, but those who can suffer the most who will conquer." Where, in this world of strife – social strife, political strife, economic strife, religious strife, national strife, international strife – where do we find individuals, organizations or nations hoping to triumph by mere endurance? True, the greatest of all triumphs – the triumph that wrought the Redemption of the entire human race – was accomplished rather by endurance than by active, energetic measures. But, of those shaping national policies, who has ever borne in mind the lessons of wisdom contained in the endurance of Bethlehem and Nazareth and Calvary? Unfortunately, the wisdom of this world looks for its triumphs not so much from the justice of its cause and the overruling Providence of God, as from its armaments and ammunition. "In God we trust but keep your powder dry," is its well known motto.

SUPERIOR ARMAMENTS MAKE RIGHT OF MIGHT

Undue attention to the development of superior armies and navies has brought the nations to the unethical conviction that might makes right. The nations assembled at Versailles, at the end of the first World War, to negotiate a world peace, furnish a classic example. After the manner of bandits, they unceremoniously wrested the province of Shangtung from China, and bestowed it on Japan. The daring international plunder would long since have been a fait accompli, had not the United States Senate, to its everlasting credit, raised a cry of protest and refused to ratify the transaction. If China had been a strong military nation, the monstrous injustice would never have been attempted. But China had no powder, and the nations were unmoved either by fundamental justice or by Mayor MacSwiney's grand ideal of "universal brotherhood" founded on the "common humanity" of all nations and peoples. Theirs were the big battalions and big battleships, and that was all that mattered.

MAYOR HOLDS TRULY THAT RIGHT MAKES MIGHT

Lord Mayor MacSwiney reverses the formula. For him right makes might.

> "Freedom is an individual right that is inalienable. One man, alone may vindicate it, and because that one man has never failed, it has never died."

He does not, by any means, decry armed force. He himself invoked armed force, not, however, to perpetuate scandalous injustice but to defend an inalienable right. This is the Lord Mayor's own statement of the case.

> "But war must be faced and blood must be shed, not gleefully but as a terrible necessity, because there are moral horrors much worse than any physical horror, because freedom is indispensable for a soul erect, and freedom must be had at any cost of suffering. The soul is greater than the body.... The moral plague that eats up a people whose independece is lost, is more calamitous than any physical rending of limb from limb. The body is a passing phase; the spirit is immortal. And the degradation of that immortal part of man is the great tragedy of life."

HE INSISTS RIGHTEOUS WAR MUST BE CHRISTIAN

Neither may the war for national independence be, according to the Lord Mayor's code, a round of ruthless and unreserved destructiveness. We have already seen him insist that the fight must be "clean-handed." He now further insists that it should be a humane warfare, and points out how even righteous war must be waged in a truly Christian spirit.

> "When the time demands and the occasion offers, it is imperative to have recourse to arms, but in that terrible crisis we must preserve our balance. If we leap forward for our enemies' blood, glorifying brute force, we set up the standard of the tyrant, and heap up infamy for ourselves.... A true soldier of liberty will always remember that restraint is the great attribute that separates man from beast; that retaliation is the vicious resource of the tyrant and the slave; that magnanimity is the splendour of manhood. He will remember that he strikes, not at his enemy's life but at his misdeed, and that, in destroying the misdeed, he makes not only for his own freedom but even for his enemy's regeneration."

CIVIL LIBERTY'S TEMPORAL, ETERNAL BLESSINGS

Here again we see the apostle mingling with and dominating the patriot. Among the great patriotic leaders of all the ages, where do we find a single one who stresses the distinction between the temporal blessings of national independence and the eternal blessings that flow from them.

But, for Mayor MacSwiney the eternal is everything. Freedom, liberty, independence, not in order to indulge a destructive national pride or even to inaugurate and promote a laudable national glory; not for the sake of the passing things that minister to the needs and conveniences of the body – which is only "a passing phase" – but freedom, liberty, independence, for the sake of the spirit, and because it is immortal – for the eternal salvation and happiness of men's immortal souls.

ABHORS ETERNAL EFFECTS OF CIVIL OPPRESSION

And as the Lord Mayor's passionate love of national freedom is principally on account of the eternal freedom which it inspires and fosters, so his passionate abhorrence of slavish oppression is chiefly because of its eternal consequences. "The degradation of that immortal part of man is the great tragedy of life." He enumerates and deplores the terrible consequences of national servitude:

(1) "Consider all the mean things and debasing tendencies that wither up a people in a state of slavery. There are the bribes of those in power to maintain their ascendency; the barter of every principle by time-servers; the corruption of public life, and the apathy of private life; the hard struggle of those with high ideals; the conflict with all ignoble practices; the general gloom, depression and despair – everywhere a land decaying. Viciousness, meanness, cowardice, intolerance – every bad thing arises like a weed in the night and blights the land where freedom is dead. And the aspect of that land, and the soul of that people become spectacles of disgust, revolting and terrible – terrible for the high things degraded and the great destinies imperilled." (Chap. iii.)

(2) "It is the duty of the rightful power to develop the best in its subjects; it is the practice of the usurping power to develop the basest. Our history affords many examples. When our rulers visit Ireland they bestow favours and titles on the supporters of their regime. But it is always seen that the greatest favours and highest titles are for him who has betrayed the national cause that he entered public life to support. The men who should be respected are passed over for him who ought to be despised. In this corrupt politician there was surely a better nature. A free state would have encouraged and developed it. The usurping state titled him for the use of his baser instincts. Such allurement must mean demoralization. We are none of us angels, and under the best circumstances find it hard to do worthy things. When all the temptation is to do unworthy things, we are demoralized." (Chap. 1.)

"CIVIL LIBERTY ABOVE NATION, RACE, RELIGION"

Once again the patriot but still more the apostle! How circumscribed the soul and scope of even the noblest patriot when compared with that of Mayor MacSwiney! The highest aspirations, hopes and efforts of the great patriots of history were aimed at vindicating the liberties of their own countries and peoples. To this and this alone they, with an unselfishness truly admirable, dedicated their genius, their energies and frequently their lives. But Mayor MacSwiney's gospel of freedom rose superior to all boundaries – national, racial, religious, geographical. It encompassed the entire human race.

> "While the meanness and tyranny of contemporary "England stand forward against our argument – for "universal brotherhood – and leave our reasoning cold, "we can find a more subtle appeal in spirit – such an "appeal as comes to us in a play of Shakespeare's, a "song of Shelley's, or a picture of Turner's. From the "heart of the enemy Genius cries, bearing witness to "our common humanity, and the yearning for such "high comradeship is alive, and the dream survives to "light us on our forward path." (Chap. iv.)

COMMON HUMANITY. UNIVERSAL BROTHERHOOD

"Universal brotherhood" and "high comradeship," because of "our common humanity"– this is the world-freedom which Mayor MacSwiney lived and died to champion. The red man – a brother and a comrade; the yellow man – a brother and a comrade; the black man – a brother and a comrade. Is this not Christ's gospel of universal charity, rather than a charter of any mere provincial nationalism? That "above all nations is humanity" was the cold creed of Goethe and the master passion of MacSwiney.

Furthermore, the ambitions and strivings of patriotic men seldom aspire to more than the temporal blessings of national independence. To procure and preserve to their countrymen the precious boon of civil liberty, is, generally speaking, the very highest achievement they propose to themselves. There have been, it is true, some grand exceptions, among whom may be specially mentioned the great champion of Catholic Emancipation. But patriots, for the most part, regard the spiritual and eternal as pertaining exclusively to the domain of religion, and therefore altogether outside the realm of civil policy. This palpable misconception is nowhere more apparent than in the flagrant unconcern of civil authorities with regard to the religious education of the people. Pope Benedict XV, in his Encyclical,

"AD BEATISSIMI," administers this salutary admonition to them.

> "Let princes and rulers of the people seriously consider whether it be the part of political wisdom to exclude from the ordinance of the State and from public instruction, the teaching of the Gospel and of the Church. Only too well does experience show that when religion is banished, human authority totters to its fall."

"BELIEF TRUE, IN ETERNAL SENSE PRACTICAL"

Civil authority is incapable of teaching religion, nor has it any commission to do so. But it can and ought to minister, in sundry ways, to the needs of those delegated by the Church to teach religious doctrine and practice. As the temporal should be subordinate to the eternal, so the State, whose scope is restricted to the temporal, should be subordinate and subsidiary to the Church, which reaches out to the things of Eternity. Here as always, Mayor MacSwiney is admirably orthodox. For him the spiritual and eternal are everywhere supreme.

(1) "The liberty for which we strive today is a sacred thing, inseparably entwined with that spiritual liberty for which the Saviour of men died, and which is the foundation of all just government. And because it is sacred, death for it is akin to the sacrifice of Calvary." (Inaugural Address)

(2) "We can always be prepared by understanding that the vital hour is the hour at hand. Let the brave choice now be made, and let the life around be governed by it. In all the vicissitudes of the fight, let us not be distracted by the meanness of the mere time-server, nor the treachery of the enemy, and, remembering the many who are not with us from honest motives, show our belief beautiful and true, and, in the eternal sense, practical. Then shall those who are worth convincing come to realize that he who maintains a great faith unshaken will make more things possible than the opportunist of the hour; they will have a vision of the goal, and with that vision will be born a steady enthusiasm, a clear purpose and a resolute soul." (Chap. vi)

SUSTAINED BY GRAND DOMINATING PATRIOTISM

Before concluding the estimate of Mayor MacSwiney's character and conduct undertaken in this chapter, it may well be asked what it was that principally sustained his courage and resolution throughout the fierce ordeal of seventy-four days and nights of ever increasing exhaustion and prostration. The answer is not far to seek. The Lord Mayor was principally sustained by the grand, dominating passion of patriotism, a ruling passion elevated and enlightened, fortified and exalted in him by ever new inspiration drawn from his strong, living, supernatural faith. Thus heightened, brightened and strengthened, that grand master passion possessed and permeated his whole being, until it made him the grand master patriot of all the ages — unless indeed we regard as rivals, his comrade hunger-strikers, no less courageous, no less patriotic than himself. It kindled in his soul an unquenchable love for national liberty, and an undying hope of being instrumental in restoring it to the land of his love.

GRAND MASTER PATRIOT OF ALL THE AGES

From the pursuit of that grand ideal neither threats nor caresses could ever divert him, nor could any reverses or any disasters ever make him despair about it. It was therefore an inevitable consequence that he should be constantly seeing new opportunities and new prospects, where they who lacked the vision of the patriot could discern neither. It was inevitable, too, that he should be continually feeling the joyful pulsations of anticipated triumph, while weak, wavering, cowardly spirits experienced only the depression of prospective defeat. National freedom was for him the complement and completion of spiritual freedom, and, like it, deserving to be secured "at any cost of suffering" – "a sacred thing" for which it is glory to die – a sacrifice "akin to the sacrifice of Calvary."

(1) "Some will never survive to celebrate the great victory that will establish our independence. Yet they shall not go without reward; for to them will come a vision of soul of the future triumph; an exaltation of soul in the consciousness of laboring for that future; an exultation of soul in the knowledge that the destiny of our country is assured and her dominion will endure for ever."

(2) "Where now are the empires of antiquity? The peoples have endured; the empires perished. And the nations of the earth of this day will survive in posterity when the empires that now contend for mastery are gathered into the dust with all dead, bad things .We shall endure, and the measure of our faith will be the measure of our achievement and of the greatness of our future place."

(3) "If, with our freedom to win, our country to open up, our future to develop, we learn no lesson from the mistakes of nations, and live no better life than the great Powers, we shall have missed a golden opportunity and shall be one of the failures of history. So far, on superficial judgment, we have been accounted a failure, although the simple maintenance of our fight for centuries has been in itself

"a splendid triumph. But then only would we have "failed in the great sense, when we had got our field "and wasted it, as the nations around us waste theirs "today."

(4) "Let us beware of the delusion that if we can scram- "ble through anyhow to freedom, we can then begin "to live worthily, but that in the interval we cannot "be too particular. Everyone should realize the duty "to be high-minded and honourable in action; to re- "gard his fellow, not as a man to be circumvented, "but as a brother to be sympathized with and up- "lifted. Neither kingdom, republic nor commune can "regenerate us. It is in a beautiful mind and a great "ideal that we shall find the charter of our freedom. "We must not ignore it now, for how we work today "will decide how we shall live tomorrow."

(5) "That we shall win our freedom I have no doubt. "That we shall use it well I am not so certain. We "shall look for prosperity no doubt, but let our en- "enthusiasm be for beautiful living. We shall build "up our strength, yet not for conquest but as a "pledge of brotherhood and a defense for the weaker "ones of the earth. We shall rouse the world from a "wicked dream of material greed, of tyrannical "power, of corrupt and callous politics, to the wonder "of a regenerated spirit."

(6) "Everything that crosses a man's path in his day's "round of little or great moment, requires of him an "attitude towards it, and the conscious or uncon- "scious shaping of his attitude is determining how "he will proceed in other spheres not now in view. "Every act of personal discipline is contributing to "a subconscious reservoir whence our nobler ener- "gies are supplied for ever."

(7) "It is harder to live a consistent life than to die a "brave death. Most men of generous instincts would "rouse all their courage to a supreme moment and "die for the Cause. But to rise to that supreme mo- "ment frequently, and without warning, is the bur- "den of life for the Cause. We must get men to "realize that to live is as daring as to die. To slip "apologetically through existence is not life."

(8) "There are two great resting-places in our historic "survey – the generation of the living flame, and the "generation of despair. It is for us to decide – for "the decision rests with us – whether we shall, in "our time, merely mark time, or write another lumi- "nous chapter in the splendid history of our race. "Seeing the futility, in other years, of every pa- "thetic makeshift to annoy or circumvent the enemy, "let us put by futilities and do a great work to jus- "tify our time."

(9) "You may weaken and yield or you may stand your "ground, refuse the bribe, uphold the flag, and be "rated a fool and a failure. But they who rate you

"so will not understand that you have won a battle
"greater than all the triumphs of empires. You will
"keep alive in your soul true light and enduring
"beauty. You will hear the music eternally in the
"heart of the high enthusiast, and have vision of
"ultimate victory that has sustained all the world
"over the efforts of centuries."

(10) "It may well be that in the hour of depression you
"may feel that your voice, pleading for the Old
"Cause, is indeed a voice crying in the wilderness.
"But it may serve till your blood warms again and
"your imagination recover its glow, to think how a
"Voice that cried in the wilderness, thousands of
"years ago, is potent and inspiring now."

INDOMITABLE AS INSPIRED BY PATRIOT'S VISION

If the Lord Mayor's character were to be summed up in a single word, it would have to be the word "indomitable." The contest between the British Empire and himself was an unequal contest, with the odds decidedly in his favor. "He has won his battle," says the Westminster Gazette. And what, before all else, was it that made him indomitable? Again the answer is contained in what Mayor MacSwiney himself frequently calls "vision." He was indomitable because he was possessed and inspired by the patriot's vision – the vision vouchsafed to the chosen few who are predestined to be heroes. For the Lord Mayor, that vision was neither more nor less than intimate knowledge and appreciation of God's eternal truths, and of the beauty incomparable of every life lived in harmony with them. Thus we see him speaking of the "vision of the goal;" "the vision of soul of the future triumph"; "the vision of a future victory that has sustained all the world over the efforts of centuries." And we know that he is speaking only of a goal, a triumph, a victory, won by methods "clean-handed" and beautiful. The subjoined citations would seem to have been penned by the Lord Mayor while he was under the spell of the vision to which he there makes repeated reference. He unconsciously wrote the story of his own mind and heart and life and death in these glowing paragraphs.

(1) "Let the cultivation of a brave, high spirit be our
"great task. It will make of each man's soul an un-
"assailable fortress. Armies may fail, but it resists
"for ever. The body it informs may be crushed. The
"spirit, in passing, breathes on other souls, and
"other hearts are fired to action, and the fight goes
"on to victory. To the man whose mind is true and
"resolute, ultimate victory is assured. No sophistry
"can sap his resistance. In every issue he is justified.
"In every crisis he is steadfast. Hold we our heads

"high, then, and we shall bear our flag bravely
"through every fight. Persistent, consistent, straight-
"forward and fearless, so shall we discipline the soul
"to great deeds and make it indomitable. In the in-
"domitable soul lies the assurance of our ultimate
"victory."

(2) "We all recognise that great virtue of mind and
"heart that keeps a man unconquerable above every
"power of brute strength. I call it moral force.
"A man of moral force is he who, seeing a thing to
"be right and essential, and claiming his allegiance,
"stands for it unheeding any consequence. It is a
"first principle of his that a true thing is a good
"thing, and from a good thing rightly pursued can
"follow no bad consequence. And he faces every pos-
"sible development with conscience at rest. This it
"is that explains the strange and wonderful buoy-
"ancy of men standing for great ideals so little
"understood by others of weaker mould."

(3) "A man who will be brave only if tramping with a
"legion, will fail in courage if called to stand in the
"breach alone. 'Tis the bravest test, the noblest
"test, the test that offers the surest and greatest
"victory. For one armed man cannot resist a multi-
"tude, nor one army conquer countless legions. But
"not all the armies of all the Empires of the earth
"can crush the spirit of one true man. That one man
"will prevail."

(4) "One day the consciousness of the country will be
"electrified by a great deed or a great sacrifice, and
"the multitude will break from lethargy or prejudice
"and march with a shout for freedom in a true, a
"brave and a beautiful sense. We must work and
"prepare for that hour."

(5) "Ultimately the work of the pioneer patriot opens
"out, matures and bears fruit a hundred fold. It
"may not be in a day. But when his hand falls his
"glory becomes quickly manifest. He has lived a
"beautiful life and has left a beautiful field. He has
"sacrificed the hour to give service for all time. He
"has entered the company of the great, and with
"them he will be remembered for ever. He is the
"practical man in the true sense."

(6) "A body of principles is primarily of value, not as
"affording a case that can be argued with ingenuity,
"but as inspiring one great principle that shines
"through and informs the rest; that illumines the
"mind of the individual; that warms, clarifies and
"invigorates; that, so to speak, puts the mind in
"focus, gets the facts of existence into perspective,
"and gives the individual everything in its true place
"and right proportion. It brings a man to the point
"where he does not dispute but believes."

(7) "There is a power of vision latent in us, clouded by
"error. The true philosophy dissipates the cloud and
"leaves the vision clear, wonderful and inspiring.
"He who has acquired that vision is impervious to
"argument. It is not that he despises argument. On
"the contrary, he always uses it to its full length.
"But he has had awakened within him something
"which the mere logician can never deduce, and that
"mysterious something is the explanation of his
"transformed life. He was a doubter, a falterer, a
"failure. He has become a believer, a fighter, a
"conqueror."

(8) "You miss the significance of the philosopher com-
"pletely when you take him for a theorist. The theo-
"rist propounds a view to which he must convert the
"world; the philosopher has a rule of life to imme-
"diately put in practice. His spirit flashes with a
"swiftness that can be encircled by no theory. It is
"his glory to have – over and above a new penetrat-
"ing argument in the mind – a new and wonderful
"vitality in the blood. Dialectic is a trick of the mind.
"Philosophy the wine of the spirit. Philosophy gives
"its believer vision and grasp of life as a whole. It
"warms and quickens his heart and makes him in
"spirit buoyant, beautiful, wise and daring."

(9) "He is called to a grave charge who is called to re-
"sist the majority. But he will resist, knowing that
"his victory will lead them to a dearer dream than
"they had ever known. He will fight for that ideal in
"obscurity, little heeded; in the open, misunder-
"stood; in humble places, still undaunted; in high
"places, seizing every vantage point; never crushed,
"never silent, never despairing; cheering a few com-
"rades with hope for the morrow. And should these
"few sink in the struggle, the greatness of the ideal
"is proven in their last hour. As they fall their
"country awakens to their dream, and he who in-
"spired and sustained them is justified – justified
"against the whole race, he who once stood alone
"against them. In the hour that he falls he is the
"saviour of his race."

"WHO TODAY IS MORE CERTAIN OF IMMORTALITY"

Our purpose to discover and lay bare the innermost soul of Mayor MacSwiney must be our justification for introducing so unprecedented a list of citations. He was an unknown man the day he began his hunger-strike. Ten weeks later he was the admiration of all the world. "Who today is more certain of immortality," said 'The Nation' (New York). His career, brief but meteoric, surely calls for a biography. Till then, the world, spell-bound by his unprecedented sincerity, courage, constancy and endurance, must be content with such further knowledge of his fascinating character as may be gathered from his words spoken and written.

The passages here reproduced admirably reflect the profound, penetrating insight of his mind, nor less the fiery, frenzied ardor of his high resolve. At one time he discriminates with the calm, academic subtlety of a philosopher; at another his emotions burn and blaze like the flame of a furnace.

LIFE, DEATH STORY ADD FORCE TO HIS WORDS

And it is needless to remark that the Lord Mayor's own life and death story give an added significance to his words. He did not merely think lofty thoughts and express them in lofty language. He lived it all and died for it all.

(1) "The true antithesis is not between moral force and "physical force, but between moral force and moral "weakness."

(2) "When men revolt against an established evil, it is "their loyalty to the outraged truth we honour. "We do not extol a rebel who rebels for rebellion's "sake."

(3) "Literature is the Shrine of Freedom, its fortress, "its banner, its charter. Whatever state prevails, "passionate men can pour their passion through "Literature to the nation's soul, and make it burn "and move and fight."

(4) "What if we are held up occasionally by the cold "cries shot at every high aim –'dreamer,' 'Utopia'! "Let who will deride us, but let us prepare. We may "not guide our steps with the certainty of prophets, "nor hope by our beautiful schemes to make a per-"fect state. But it is only in the Light of a perfect "ideal that we can come near to perfection, and "however far below it we may remain, we can, at "least, under its inspiration, reach an existence ra-"tional and human, whereas the governments of this "time are neither the one nor the other."

(5) "It is the distinguishing glory of our soldiers of the "forlorn hope that the defeats of common men were "for them but incentives to further battle. They "knew they stood for the Truth, against which noth-"ing can prevail, and if they had to endure struggle, "suffering and pain, they had the finer knowledge "born of these things – that if it is a good thing to "live, it is a good thing also to die. And when one "or more of them had to stand in the darkest gen-"eration and endure all penalties to the extreme "penalty, they knew that they had had the best of "life and did not count it a terrible thing if called "by a little to anticipate death. Yes, and when the "reawakened people will have massed into armies "and marched to freedom, they will know, in the "greatest hour of triumph, that the success of their "conquering arms was made possible by those who "held the breach."

WITHERING DENUNCIATIONS, SOLEMN WARNINGS

Of the many things relating to the Lord Mayor which might be of general interest, his mentality during the ordeal of Brixton Prison surely holds the foremost place. His words of those tragic days and nights received a multiplied significance from the unprecedented situation in which they were spoken. It is therefore regrettable that neither his chaplain nor any member of his family has given to an admiring and expectant world any record of those precious sayings. It is easy however to picture him rousing himself from the stupor of his exhaustion, at one time to utter a withering denunciation; at another to administer a solemn warning with the fire of an inspired prophet; at yet another, to deplore the disloyalty, the indifference, the cowardice, the blindness of the multitude - "men dull of apprehension and cold of heart"- or again to send forth a rallying cry to the chosen few, exhorting them to hold the breach with a heroism worthy of their noble tradition, and confidently await the fair dawn of Freedom's day.

(1) "In paying a fitting tribute to those great men who "have been our exemplars, it would be fitting also "to remember ourselves as the inheritors of a great "tradition. And it would well become us not only to "show the splendor of the banner that is handed on "to us, but to show that this banner we too are "worthy to bear. For how often it shall be victorious and how high it shall be planted will depend "on the conception we have of its supreme greatness; "the knowledge that it can be fought for in all times "and places; the conviction that we may, when we "least expect, be challenged to deny it."

(2) "Let us, with the old high confidence, blend the old "high courtesy of the Gael. Let us grow big with "our cause. Shall we honor the flag we bear, by a "mean, apologetic front? No! Wherever it is down, "lift it; wherever it is challenged, wave it; wherever it is high, salute it; wherever it is victorious, "glorify and exult in it. At all times and for ever, "be for it proud, passionate, persistent, jubilant, "defiant; stirring hidden memories, kindling old fires, "wakening the finer instincts of men, till all are one "in the old spirit, the spirit that will not admit defeat, the spirit that is noblest in Emmett's one line "setting the time for his epitaph."

WHENCE THE CLEARER VISION INSPIRING HIM?

This effort to analyse the character of Mayor MacSwiney may well end with such an answer as can be given to the very difficult question - whence the clearer vision that enabled the Lord Mayor to triumph over all the difficulties, dangers and sufferings that confronted him. That his keen perception of what is true and good and beautiful in human life was supernatural – and not such exceptional natural insight as surprises us in pagans like Socrates and Aristotle, Seneca and Marcus Aurelius – is all too plain. There is, however, no evidence that he was directly and immediately inspired by God regarding his hunger-strike, as St. Joan of Arc was, respecting her campaign for the freedom of France. But there is, in the Lord Mayor's own words and deeds, abundant evidence that his mind was illuminated and his will inspired to a career of very extraordinary political as well as personal rectitude.

> "We think of some hazy hour in the future when we
> "may get a call to great things. We realize not that
> "the call is now. If we are to be fit for the heroic to-
> "morrow, we must arise and be men today."

LIGHT ABUNDANT. MORE FAITHFUL RESPONSE

And why, it may be further asked, did God bestow on Mayor MacSwiney supernatural light and strength such as He does not grant to ordinary mortals? The question is easier to ask than to answer. God's dealings with individual souls will always have some mystery attaching to it, at least on this side of Eternity. This much however is certain – that God bestows His graces more abundantly on all who are more faithful in corresponding with them. In accordance with this principle then, the Lord Mayor received choicer favors from God because he made himself a fitter subject for them; because he harkened with exceptional fidelity to God's whispering in his soul; because he listened to God's call to higher and ever higher things, while ordinary mortals refuse to listen. "Lord I have never sinned against the Light," was Cardinal Newman's prayer of protest, when in danger of death, but still outside the Catholic Fold. Rev. Joseph Farrell, in his "Lectures of a Certain Professor," speaks of "the sweetness of that inner song that is borne upon ears that know how to listen." And the author of "Paradise Lost" introduces the same idea into his eulogy of Chastity.

> "So dear to Heaven is saintly chastity
> "That when a soul is found sincerely so,
> "A thousand liveried angels lackey her;
> "Driving far off each thing of sin and guilt;
> "And in clear dream and solemn vision
> "Tell her of things that no gross ear can hear."

GOD'S CHOICER FAVORS FOR FITTER SUBJECT

We see, therefore, that there are some who sin against the Light, and others who see the Light and walk faithfully in the splendor of its brightness; that there are ears which know how to listen to Heaven's inspirations and ears that do not; that there are truths proportioned to the capacity of gross ears, and other truths too exalted for their low grade of hearing. And evidence superabundant has already been presented in these pages that Mayor MacSwiney's was not the "gross ear," unfitted to hear the whisperings of divine grace, but rather the ear that knew how to listen to the high – the very highest message that God's messengers had to communicate to him. His was not the soul to sin against the Light.

(1) "In a physical contest on the field of battle, it is allowable to use tactics and strategy – to retreat as well as to advance, to have recourse to a ruse as well as an open attack. But in matters of principle, there can be no tactics. There is one straightforward course to follow, and that course must be found and followed without swerving, to the end."

(2) "Everything that crosses a man's path in his daily round of little or great moment requires of him an attitude towards it, and the conscious or unconscious shaping of his attitude is determining how he will proceed in other spheres not now in view. Every act of personal discipline is contributing to a subconscious reservoir whence our nobler energies are supplied forever."

HOW PSYCHOLOGIC, THEOLOGIC, ASCETIC VISION?

The Lord Mayor here states several fundamental truths, tersely yet elegantly. It is a psychological truth that, by our "attitude towards the daily round of little or great moment," lifelong habits are formed for better or worse – habits of neglect or fidelity, habits of vice or virtue. "Ex repetitis fit habitus." It is also a theological truth that in every faithful soul not dead by mortal sin, there exists a treasury of supernatural grace – "a subconscious reservoir" – augmented by every meritorious act "of personal discipline," itself in turn securing new inspiration of "our nobler energies," for other deeds high and holy. Finally, the Lord Mayor's assertion regarding our "attitude towards the daily round of little or great moment," is backed by the authority of all escetical writers, and even by the authority of Christ Himself. "He that is faithful in that which is least, is faithful also in that which is greater: and he that is unjust in that which is little, is unjust also in that which is greater." (Luke, xvi, 10.)

SPOKE LIKE ST. PAUL SINCE HE LIVED LIKE HIM

But whence the psychology, the theology and the asceticism, hardly to be expected in one who was by profession neither a psychologist, a theologian or an ascetic? It would seem that the Lord Mayor derived his intimate knowledge of these very technical subjects, not by the deductive but by the inductible method – not so much from any study of their fundamental principles, but rather from the corresponding practice of the virtues they inculcate. The intense conviction, so noticeable in his speeches and writings alike, could never have been acquired by any amount of mere speculative study, nor indeed in any other way except by living, in his daily life, the truths he spoke and wrote. He spoke and wrote like St. Paul because he lived his life like St. Paul. And he also died like him – a martyr's death.

SPOKE LIKE ST. PAUL. PRAYED LIKE KING DAVID

But if he spoke and wrote like St. Paul, he prayed like King David. The saint, canonized or uncanonized, is made by the combined influence of suffering and prayer.

> "And one is the dark mount of sorrow,
> "And one the bright mountain of prayer."

Blessed, then, is the man who had learned to utter the prayer of sweet resignation when his body writhes with pain, or his soul is laden with anguish. And Mayor MacSwiney was well versed in both of these heavenly arts. The extent of his sufferings for Ireland during his maturer years, and most of all during his prolonged hunger-strike, is known only to God. And the same must be said of the number and intensity of his prayers. These were not mere recitals of prayers that other minds and hearts and lips had previously prayed. Like the Psalmist, he poured forth his heart to his Maker in language of his own composing. Think of it! At the end of fifty-seven consecutive days and nights of absolute, unmitigated fasting, when he would address his fellow hunger-strikers in Cork jail, his address was neither more nor less than a request that they join with him in offering a prayer for Ireland. And this was the prayer he proposed to them:

> "Oh, my God, I offer my pain for Ireland! She is on
> "the rack. My God, Thou knowest how many times her
> "enemies have put her there to break her spirit, but
> "by Thy mercy they have always failed! I offer my
> "sufferings here for our martyred people, to with-
> "stand the present terror in Ireland, not only for two

"months but for two years, if need be, that by Thy "all-powerful aid the persecution may end in our time, "and Ireland arise at last triumphant! God save, bless "and guard the Irish Republic, to live and flourish and "be a model Government of truth and justice to all "nations! May the liberty of the Irish People shine "with Thy glory, O my God, for ever and ever. Amen!"

ONE OF HIS MANY PRISON PRAYERS FOR IRELAND

It has just been remarked that this prayer was Mayor MacSwiney's own composition. It cannot be called **an inspired prayer**, except in the very general sense in which every prayer is inspired. But it breathes, none the less, the soul and spirit of a perfect prayer. And think you, dear reader, that the Lord Mayor recited this prayer **only on this occasion?** Do you think it was **the only prayer** he offered to God during those seventy-four agonizing days and nights? He loved Ireland and the liberty of its people with a passionate love, yet not altogether or principally for the sake of Ireland or its people, **but primarily and principally that both may redound to God's glory.** "May the liberty of the Irish people shine with Thy glory for ever and ever. Amen." And this is he of whom some of the Catholic heirarchy and clergy of England, America, and his own Ireland cried "suicide." Arthur Griffith summed up the Lord Mayor perfectly when he called him **"a fit companion for Joan of Arc in Heaven."**

BURNED AS WITCH. NOW ST. JOAN OF ARC

In the year 1431, the "Maid of Orleans" was burned at the stake, by order of the Inquisition, on the charge of being "a relapsed heretic." Twenty-four years later, a court of appeal, appointed by Pope Callistus III, annulled and reversed the verdict. Those who had put St. Joan to death were helpless to undo or even obscure her heroic deeds of virtue. These, after having been left to smoulder for five hundred years, burst at last into a heavenly flame and Joan of Arc was beatified by Pope Pius X and canonized by the present Pontiff, Pius XI.

SUFFERED NO LESS. MOTIVES AS HOLY. MARTYR!

And who will say that Mayor MacSwiney sacrificed less or suffered less, or that the motives which animated him were less exalted? His young life and the alluring prospects it held out to him, he laid upon the altar of his country's liberty, because he believed it to be "inseparably entwined with the spiritual liberty for which the Saviour of men died," and therefore "death for it is akin to the sacrifice of Calvary." Is any deed more heroic? Is any purpose more supernatural? Is it stretching the meaning of the word "martyr" to predicate it of Mayor MacSwiney? Everyone who suffers death for any Christian virtue is a martyr, in the strict, technical, theological sense of the word "martyr."

GAVE LIFE FOR MOTIVE OF CHRISTIAN CHARITY

And what Christian virtue was it for which Mayor MacSwiney sacrificed his life? Patriotism is not a Christian virtue. It was practiced in its highest perfection by pagan heroes on the plains of Marathon and at the pass of Thermopylae. A distinction is needed. Every act of virtue is made up of two essential elements – the act itself – the matter – and the impelling motive (the form). Now the act of sacrificing his life for his country must be the same for the Christian that it is for the pagan. But, in the case of the pagan, the motive which prompts the sacrifice can never be more than a purely natural motive, whereas the motive which inspires the Christian patriot is generally, if not always, the supernatural motive of charity. Thus is Christian patriotism seen to be an incomparably higher and holier thing than pagan patriots could ever attain, or ever aspire to. And will any one say that, in the sacrifice of Brixton Prison, the voluntary victim was actuated by any motive short of supernatural love for God and for the oppressed and persecuted millions of his countrymen?

The Lord Mayor may never be canonized. But he is, on that account, none the less "a fit companion for St. Joan of Arc in Heaven." And as much must be said of his hero comrades of the hunger-strike – Michael Fitzgerald and Joseph Murphy.

MACSWINEY'S PHILOSOPHY

"If the world is to be regenerated, we must have worldwide unity – not of government but of brotherhood."

"From the heart of the enemy Genius cries, bearing witness to our common humanity."

"Our principles are not to argue about, or write about, or hold meetings about, but primarily to give us a rule of life."

SECULAR PRESS OF ENTIRE WORLD CRIES "ALL GLORY TO MacSWINEY"

Terence James MacSwiney

"He is not dead. Such men never die. Their souls "go to God, their bodies into the earth, but the memory "of them lives forever. Freed at last, he cries out with "a voice that the whole world hears: 'Be brave, be "true! Serve your country, love your God, commit your "ways to Him, and in the evil day He will not forget "you'!"

>............At his name
>We sorrow, not with shame,
>But proudly; for his soul is as the snow.

"The sod of his own dear Ireland lies light today "upon MacSwiney. Nay, not even the soft bosom of "the Little Dark Rose is his grave. For him there is "no grave beneath the earth, but over all the world a "shrine. For wherever beats an Irish heart, or a heart "that hates oppression, there is a heart that enshrines "for ever with love and veneration this man who to the "end loved nobly the things that are just and true. He "loved us, he fought for us, he gave his life for us, for "us who believe, in the presence of the most high God, "that liberty is too precious a gift to be given over "into the hands of tyrants.

"Therefore with tears and gratitude will all good "men make intercession for him with God the Father "of Our Lord Jesus Christ, that even as Terence James "MacSwiney hath not denied the faith, but hath ever "believed in God and hoped in Him, so, cleansed by the "saving blood of Calvary, and freed from all stain of "human frailty, he may be counted worthy to enter "forthwith into happiness without end.

"Now may Michael and Patrick and Columcille and "Bride, with the Angels that guard the four seas of "holy Ireland, bear him into Paradise. May Mary, his "sweet Mother, greet him, a child come home, with a "mother's kiss. May Jesus Christ, with whose Sacred "Body he was daily nourished, receive him into the "place of light and refreshment and quiet everlasting. "Pie Jesu, Domine, dona ei requiem. Gentle Jesus, "Lord, give him peace."

"AMERICA" (NEW YORK) EDITORIAL

Fitzgerald and Murphy

"As the glorious MacSwiney lies in the solemn
"majesty of death, with the laurels of victory upon
"his brow, the world must not forget that others are
"dying as heroically as he died for the cause of liberty.

"But a few days before the hand of God touched the
"eyelids of the sweet poet of Cork into sleep, Michael
"Fitzgerald won his victory for freedom, and went to
"meet his King, the only King he acknowledged on
"earth, in his eternal home in Heaven. A few hours
"after the stainless spirit of the immortal leader
"passed from earth, Joseph Murphy was at last re-
"leased from the chains of his cruel jailors and he
"went to join the thousands of patriots who have died
"upon the battlefields of Holy Ireland.

"In this very hour when all the world is watching
"with surpassing wonder the struggle of a heroic
"people for their freedom, other men are slowly dying
"the deaths which only saints can die. As the great
"leader of his people, Terence MacSwiney must and
"shall be given the place of honor, as that place is his
"by right. But the humbler patriots shall not be for-
"gotten. These men are dying for a land whose ground
"has been made holy by the blood of saints and martyrs.
"To be a martyr in that land is not remarkable. For
"centuries, its men, women and little children have
"suffered the torments of an earthly hell, established
"by the most monstrous government that the world
"has ever known, because they have dared to be loyal
"to their country. Until the chains of tyrants of Eng-
"land are forever removed from the bodies of these
"heroic people, they will continue to struggle for lib-
"erty, and will die as the men within the walls of
"British prisons are dying.

"Fitzgerald and Murphy have received their reward.
"Their names will live when the empire which per-
"mitted them to die as slaves, shall crumble under
"the wrath of the Almighty."

"The Charleston-American," (Editorial),
Charleston, S. C., Oct. 27, 1920

MacSWINEY, FITZGERALD AND MURPHY

In Freedom's name three sacred altars rise —
One hallowed shrine extending to the skies;
The sacrifice, **three noble lives** must be,
For cruel power still slays with cruel glee.
The victims all were **soldiers young and brave;**
Their lives they gave, their Country's life to save.
Free are they now and safe from tyrant rage,
And tyrant war — the scourge of every age.

* * *

MacSwiney — magic name that far hath sped!
In every land thy deeds are heard and read;
Thy fervid faith and hope for Ireland's cause,
Thy burning love that gave the tyrant pause;
For greater love than this hath no man shown —
That for his Country's life he yield his own.

* * *

Fitzgerald too — thy name, through endless time,
Shall live immortal as thy soul sublime!
While Murphy shares the same immortal lot —
Three all too valiant e'er to be forgot!
In every clime free men your trophies raise;
Till end of time their bards will chant your praise;
To swell that praise let voice with voice combine,
Let every pen record its glowing line,
Till praising echoes ring through every land —
A tribute worthy of that peerless band.

* * *

Hail, worthy sons of Ireland and of God!
You trod the winepress as your Master trod!
You died your people's birthright to restore,
That they might live in Freedom evermore.
Good fight you fought for Country and for Creed!
For both combined all Ireland's bravest bleed.
If they their ancient Faith did but betray,
Their freedom were achieved that very day.

* * *

But Freedom robbed of Faith, though Freedom still,
Too weakly bends to do the Master's will.
Those choicest gifts of Heaven to mankind,
In erring man should never be disjoined;
**For Freedom, blind, forsakes man's lofty goal
When frenzied passion inundates the soul;**
And thus, where blessings should from Freedom flow,
Too oft 'tis made a heritage of woe.

What crimes untold licentious freedom brings!
Things best, corrupted, prove the basest things.
But Faith to Freedom holds its beacon rays,
To steer it safe through life's encumbered maze;
Its strength it lends to Freedom's feebler pace,
Which else must falter in Life's weary race;
Faith's light and strength thus aiding to the last,
Faith's crown is won and Freedom's shallows past.

* * *

May notes thus loud, now struck on Freedom's lyre,
All slaves, all traitors and all weaklings fire!
Who while men die to set their Country free,
Nor strive nor long that blessed boon to see.
May Ireland's brave still lead in Freedom's fight!
Forever mindful that their cause is right;
That in good time right will, right must prevail,
The more where wrongs most cruel long assail;
For curst is might that would make free men slaves,
And blest is right that counts its martyrs' graves.

* * *

O God of right! Thou wilt not now disdain
To heal poor Ireland's wounds, to soothe her pain,
To end at last her crucifixion sore,
And make her grand as she was grand of yore!
Thy Word her children sought without delay;
They challenged not, but hastened to obey.
Thy Faith they kept, and spread to every shore,
Adored, and taught the nations to adore.

* * *

And when fierce storms of persecution raged,
And powers of darkness with Thy powers engaged;
With naught of flinch or fear they fought and died,
And dying gloried in the Crucified!
And now these martyrs in High Heaven pray
That, in Thy mercy, Thou wouldst speed the day
That rights the wrongs of countless torturing years,
Till Ireland cease to be a land of tears.

* * *

Or must it be that they who love Thee well,
And still Thy glory to the nations tell —
Must they their freedom to the end forego,
And only serve the tyrant here below?
Must they base serfdom to the end endure,
The better Heaven's freedom to secure?
Must they behold their ancient glory die,
Nor glory hence, except in Thee, Most High?
Must all their aims henceforward seek one goal —
To make Thee known and blessed from pole to pole?

If that accords with Heaven's high decree,
Then Ireland, though in fetters, thou art free!
Thy children, bondsmen on their native sod,
Are truly free for they are sons of God!
And if God's sons, then heirs to God's Estate,
Where Heaven's Kingdom on His blessed wait;
There! there! O God, will Ireland's sons be free,
And Ireland's glory be restored – in Thee!

* * *

Her glory wrought by deeds of glory done.
They have no equal underneath the sun!
Her children – actors on life's tragic stage –
Have played the heroes' role in every age.
But noblest drama mortal e'er essayed,
MacSwiney, Murphy and Fitzgerald played!
To pray God's mercy on their souls were vain,
Who mercy show, God's mercy ever gain;
And greater mercy man can never give
Than yield his life that other men may live;
'Tis perfect love, and potent to efface
All sin, all stain, and clothe the soul with grace.

* * *

Such perfect love those Irish heroes felt,
As they on England's altars meekly knelt;
They prayed and suffered, blessed and bade adieu
To home and country, friends and chosen few
Who stood beneath their crosses while they died,
As stood His own close by the Saviour's side.

* * *

And as the Saviour, with His parting breath,
Forgave the fiends who foully wrought His death;
So they, in perfect charity, forgave
Foul foes who hewed for each a martyr's grave.
Then, like their Master, prayerful to the end,
Their souls to Heaven's keeping they commend.
What land like martyr patriots can toast!
What age like Christian chivalry can boast!
Their deeds will live with men while men will dare be free;
Their glory lives with God throughout Eternity.

THESE VERSES ARE DEDICATED

TO IRELAND'S BRAVE MEN AND BRAVER WOMEN

TO THE MEMORY OF

TERENCE MACSWINEY-MICHAEL FITZGERALD-JOSEPH MURPHY

BRAVEST OF THE BRAVE

Appendix A*

"THE TABLET," LONDON, ENGLAND
(Dec. 4, 1920)

"A PROFESSOR OF MORALS IN AN IRISH ECCLESIASTICAL COLLEGE"

"The true view of the ethical character of the hunger-strike can best be stated, I submit, in terms of the section in our ordinary manuals of Moral Theology entitled, "De Fontibus Moralitatis." An action to be morally good must conform to the Moral Law – or at least must not deflect therefrom – in regard to the **object** of the act, the **circumstances** in which it is performed, and the end in view. The whole voluntary act is analyzed, so to speak, into these three elements, and the relation of each to the Moral Law is separately considered. If each is found to be in conformity with the Moral Law, the whole act is pronounced to be good; if even one is discovered to be at variance therewith, the act is condemned as bad. **Bonum ex integra causa, malum ex quovis defectu.** 'Whoever knows this principle,' writes Father Rickaby, S.J., 'does not thereby know the right and wrong of every action, but he knows how to go about the inquiry. It is a rule of diagnosis.'

"Now my thesis, briefly, is: Hunger-striking fails on the first score. It is morally wrong by reason of the **object**. Wonderful endurance and heroism may accompany it, excellent ends may be attained by it, but **in itself** it is at variance with the Moral Law.

"It becomes necessary, therefore, for the purpose of our diagnosis, to examine carefully what is the **object** (in the technical sense) as distinct from the **end** and **circumstances** in the case of hunger-striking. By the **object** of a voluntary act – that is, the proximate object of the will – theologians mean **the action** – usually of a faculty other than the will itself – which the will commands, looked upon, however, in the abstract, and apart from the circumstances with which, when done, it will be clothed. 'The object, writes Lehmkuhl (Theol. Mor., vol. i, 95), **'is the action itself . . . considered in the abstract, as, to walk to write, to worship God, to honour parents, etc., all of which are assumed by the will as an object, before they are put into execution or exercised externally.'** Similarly Dr. Walsh 'De Act. Hum.,' (p. 163): 'It (the object) is taken in the stricter sense to mean only the substance of the act, for instance, to give alms, to steal, etc., putting aside all the circumstances and the end in view of the agent.'

---

*NOTE. In this appendix and the following ones, the Arabic numerals [in brackets] indicate the extracts on which comments have been made in the corresponding numbers of the text.

"These definitions become clearer from the distinc-"tion made by St. Thomas: 'In a voluntary act there is "found a twofold act, namely, the interior act of the "will, and the exterior act. This exterior act – as to "its substance and apart from the circumstances – is "the proximate object of the will. If I propose to my-"self to steal a sum of money in order to give an alms, "to steal the money is the object in the technical sense; "to give an alms is the purpose or end in view; while "the precise amount stolen is a circumstance, as also "the time, place, manner, etc., of stealing. In the case "of an omission, the object is to be understood in the "very same sense – at least in that form of omission "with which alone we are here concerned, which is "commanded by a positive act of the will. The omission "takes place of the exterior act. And the very same "principles of morality apply.

"What, then, is the object in the case of the hunger-"strike? **It is precisely the whole series of abstentions "from food – leading up to and including the last fatal "abstentions – physically many, but to be regarded as "a moral unit.** This is the object in the case of the only "form of hunger-striking which I am contemplating, "that in which one is determined to carry the strike "even to the point of death, or actually does so. This "is the exterior act – or omission – which is commanded "by the will, which when carried out, is found to be "clothed with many circumstances. But, for our present "purpose, it is to be considered apart from the circum-"stances, as also from the end in view to which it is "directed. We must further note that it is manifestly "insufficient to consider the physical abstentions sepa-"rately, for **they are clearly made into one by the "unifying determination of the will.** Nor is it the "abstentions **for a day or a week** that are to be so "considered, but the series which one is determined to "carry on **to the point of death.**

"We are now in a position to put the critical ques-"tion: How does the object so described – to abstain "from food to the point of death – stand in relation to "reason and the moral law? To propose the question is "surely to compel the only possible answer. (1) Such an "object clearly militates against reason and the moral "law. It has only one intrinsic, natural and necessary "effect – the finis operis – namely, death; to this, and "to this only – to borrow the language of St. Thomas – "it has a proportion; and by this its intrinsic charac-"ter is determined. For one, therefore, to freely adopt "a course, which of its own nature has only the one "effect of death, is to sin against the law of self-"preservation and to violate God's dominion over life.

"The conclusion we have come to becomes all the "clearer when we consider that whatever good accrues "from hunger-striking is entirely referable to the cir-"cumstances or the end in view. It is a protest against "injustice, and a powerful one to boot, because of the "supreme test of sincerity accompanying it; but it is "not a protest of itself or or its own nature, but only in the circumstances and because it is extrinsically directed to this end. Such an accompanying feature, therefore, however impressive, is powerless to change the intrinsic nature of the act or omission, and therefore leaves the essential morality – that arising from the object – untouched.

"Nor, again, can the morality arising from the object be changed or affected by the consideration that the protest has powerfully moved the world, and has brought opprobrium, and even defeat, on what the hunger-strikers regard as a tyrranical Government. Such an effect, however desirable, is quite extrinsic and accidental; it may be present or absent, or may vary, while the hunger-strike in itself and in its own nature remains the same. For instance, consider an hypothesis which is not at all fanciful in the present unhappy state of affairs. If, for instance, a prisoner were spirited away without the knowledge of his friends, and confined unjustly in some English prison, without the knowledge of the public, and if he went on hunger-strike, the substance or nature of the act – or omission – would be precisely the same, and yet it would have no effect on public opinion. This shows conclusively that the effect on public opinion is quite an accidental effect, not following from hunger-striking of its own nature, and therefore not a determinant of its intrinsic morality at all.

(2) "And here it is to be observed that the conclusion we have come to is not invalidated in the least by the fact that 'no hunger-striker aims at death . . . not even as a means.' This is true, but it is really only a half-truth. It is sufficient for the voluntariety and imputability of an evil effect that it be willed implicity and indirectly. The hunger-striker wills directly not only the end in view, but also the means, namely, the continued abstention from food even to its fatal conclusion. Death, therefore, the finis operis of the means, is imputed to him even though he may not will it directly and explicitly; he wills it at least implicitly and indirectly, precisely because of the obligation he is under to avoid it.

"We conclude, therefore, that hunger-striking in the sense explained is morally wrong **ex objecto** or as a means, and therefore may not be employed as a political weapon."

MACSWINEY'S PHILOSOPHY

"He who maintains a great faith unshaken, will make more things possible than the opportunist of the hour."

"Forbearance is the final test of men. Though we like to call ourselves Christian, we have no desire for that outstanding Christian virtue."

Appendix B

"LA CIVILTA CATTOLICA," ROME, ITALY
(Dec. 18, 1920)

THE CASE OF THE MAYOR OF CORK —
A MUCH DISCUSSED MORAL QUESTION

(1) "The case of MacSwiney, Mayor of Cork, who, "to vindicate the independence of Ireland against Eng- "land, had recourse to hunger-strike or voluntary fast, "and died after seventy-four days, has aroused, in the "field of Physiology, Medicine and Theology, many dis- "cussions. Physiologists and Physicians have treated "the question of the longest extent of time a man can "exist without food. Theologians have discussed the "lawfulness of the act,— whether it be lawful to under- "take, of one's own will, a fast which must of necessity "bring on death — whether or not an act of this kind, "constitutes suicide as understood by moralists."

(2) "We think it useful to briefly examine this ques- "tion in its theological aspect, because some news- "papers and reviews have treated it, in our opinion, "very superficially, and without that impartiality and "serenity of judgment which is indispensable in all "theological discussions. (3) We shall do no more than "present in clear and precise terms the Catholic doctrine "of direct and indirect suicide — suicidio diretto e "indiretto."

I

(4) "An action, as all know, may be directly or in- "directly voluntary, that is, voluntary in se or in causa. "('Un'azione, come tutti sanno, puo essere volontaria "direttamente o indirettamente, cico volontaria in se "oppure in causa.') Applying this general notion to "our case, killing may be direct or indirect. It is direct "when death is willed either as an end or as a means, "that is, when one places the action with the intention "of procuring the death of oneself or another. (5) It is "indirect when death is neither meant nor willed, but "only permitted, inasmuch as it occurs praeter inten- "tionem as a consequence of a human act which is not "directed to cause death, but only to obtain some good "end. (6) In order to have direct killing, in the strict "sense of the word, it is necessary that of its nature, "immediately and exclusively, or at least by the inten- "tion of the agent, the action aim at the destruction "of life."

(7) "If, on the contrary, the action, even though "necessarily causing death, aims, by its very nature — "and not merely by the intention or declaration of the "agent, nor by accidental or purely extrinsic circum- "stances,— to produce some other effect, the formal in- "tention of death is excluded, and we have indirect

"killing. (8) In the former case life is destroyed; in
"the latter it is not preserved. In the former, death is
"inflicted; in the latter it is only permitted. (9) Note
"well that while the intention of the agent can change
"into direct voluntary that which otherwise had been
"only indirect, it cannot, on the contrary, change into
"indirect what, by its own nature, is direct."

(10) "The reason is manifest. When an action is, by
"its own nature, ordained to immediately and ex-
"clusively produce an effect, he who places such action
"wills also the effect, and wills it directly, even though
"he protests by words that he does not will it. Since
"there is not another immediate and direct effect of
"the action, the will – which necessarily must have its
"own proper object or end – directly and immediately
"wills the action, and, by it and in it, wills also the
"contained effect. (11) Let us explain this by an
"example. Titius is affected with a grave and incur-
"able disease. The thought of the sufferings which will
"torment him for a long time, without any hope what-
"soever of recovering, arouses in his heart, which is
"not comforted by the sweet balm of religion, a senti-
"ment of profound sadness. Giving himself up to
"despair, he conceives the insane determination of
"poisoning himself. Yet he formally protests and de-
"clares that he does not will death, but only the cessa-
"tion of his sufferings. What shall we say? Despite his
"declarations and protests, death is voluntary in itself,
"that is, directly voluntary. The same is to be said of
"an unmarried woman arrived at motherhood, who, to
"avoid infamy, procures abortion, protesting that she
"does not will the death of her innocent babe, but solely
"the guarding of her own reputation.

"This doctrine concerning direct and indirect volun-
"tary, applies not only to positive acts, but also to
"negative acts, i.e. omissions, when effects flow from
"them as causes."

II

(12) "Suicide properly so-called (autochiria) is de-
"fined by moralists: 'Directa et proprio voluntatis motu
"suscepta sui ipsius occisio,' that is, 'the direct killing
"of oneself, by one's own will and authority.' That
"suicide is an intrinsically unlawful act, a grave sin, is
"beyond all doubt. It is repugnant to nature's right;
"the Fifth Precept of the Decalogue, which confirms the
"Natural Law, openly forbids it; Holy Writ, in many
"places, condemns it; the Church deprives of ecclesias-
"tical burial those who deliberately kill themselves and
"die without any sign of repentance.

(Can 1240, No. 1, 3.)

"St. Thomas, with his usual depth and precision of
"language, thus demonstrates the unlawfulness of
"suicide: 'I answer by saying, that killing of oneself
"is absolutely unlawful for three reasons. In the first

"place, because everything naturally loves itself; and as a consequence, naturally preserves itself in its own being, and resists, as far as possible, corruptive influences. Therefore that anyone should kill himself, is against natural inclination, and against charity whereby everyone is obliged to love himself. From this it follows that suicide is always a mortal sin, because it is opposed to the Natural Law and to charity. In the second place, because every part – as such – belongs to the whole. Now, every man is part of the community, and therefore, as such belongs to the community, as we learn from the Philosopher in V. Eth. In the third place, because life is a gift bestowed on men by God, and therefore subject to Him who 'kills and makes live.' (Deut. xxii, 39). Therefore, he who deprives himself of life sins against God, as he who kills the servant sins against the servant's master, and as he sins who arrogates to himself the disposal of a thing which does not belong to him. It belongs only to God to determine the duration of human life, according to the words of Deut., xxxii, 29 – 'Ego occidam et ego vivere faciam'.

"It is clear that suicide properly so-called, being an intrinsically evil action, cannot, in any case or for any reason whatsoever, become lawful. It is not allowed, e.g., to take one's own life to abbreviate the sufferings of this valley of tears, or in order to escape shame and infamy, nor even in order to avoid offending God any more, or to hasten the possession of the celestial kingdom.

"Some facts which we read in ecclesiastical history and in the lives of Saints, i.e. those who voluntarily gave themselves up to death either for desire of martyrdom or for other motives honest and excellent in themselves, must be explained by ascribing them to divine inspiration or inculpable ignorance.

"Life may certainly be taken by divine authority, because God is Absolute Lord of life as well as of death, according to the foregoing expression of Holy Writ. Some authors say it is lawful also by public authority – that as the judge may commit the execution of capital punishment to Titius, to Caius, to any one, so he may commit it to the culprit himself. Therefore, by the consent or command of the judge, he who has been justly condemned to death, may, according to this opinion, lawfully bring about his own death. However, the contrary opinion, which denies the lawfulness in such case, is common among theologians,– according to St. Alphonsus, Lessius, De Lugo, Ballerini, Lehmkuhl, Berardi and others – or we say it is at least the more common."

III

(13) "Suicide improperly so-called, that is, indirect self-killing, is also unlawful (e' illecita). It is permitted only in some cases, that is, in the cases in

"which the conditions of indirect voluntary are verified. "It is lawful to place a cause good or indifferent in it-"self, from which follows immediately a double effect – "one good, the other ill-provided the ill effect, although "foreseen, be not intended, and there is a just and pro-"portionately grave reason for permitting such ill "effect. In this case the ill effect, i.e. death, as we men-"tioned before, is per accidens and praeter intentionem. "For instance, it is lawful for the soldier, in war-time, "to explode a munition warehouse, in order that it "should not fall into the hands of the enemy, although "he foresees he shall die in the wreck of the explosion. "The naval officer may sink the ship, rather than sur-"render it into the hands of the enemy. It is lawful to "administer to a child-bearing woman suffering from a "serious malady, a medicine necessary for her recovery, "although abortion be foreseen.

"Four conditions, according to the common and cer-"tain doctrine of authors, are required in order that "an ill effect be permitted: 1st. It is necessary that the "cause or action be good or at least indifferent. If, for "instance, it were intrinsically bad, it could not be "placed, even prescinding from its evil effect. 2nd. In "addition to the ill effect, it is necessary that the cause "produce a good effect, which must be independent of "the ill effect and not subordinate to, or dependent on it. "It must proceed from the cause or action as immedi-"ately as the ill effect. 3rd. The ill effect must not be "'willed' either as an end or as a means to obtain "something else, and moreover must not be approved. "If the agent intends it when placing the cause, or ap-"proves of it when it happens, he is always guilty of a "sin. 4th. There is required a just and proportionate "cause both to the seriousness of the ill effect and to "the **greater or lesser** influx, as well as the **more or** "**less certain** influx which the cause exercises in pro-"ducing it.

"Someone might ask: Why is it that when the men-"tioned conditions are fulfilled, the action becomes law-"ful? The answer is obvious. The malice of an act is "derived from the object, the end, and the circum-"stances. An act placed in the mentioned conditions, is "neither bad on account of the object, the end or the "circumstances. The object is good, or at least indiffer-"ent; the end is right; the circumstance of the ill effect "is compensated and eliminated, so to say, by the cir-"cumstance of the good effect."

(14) "To eliminate every doubt and throw further "light on the above mentioned conditions, we call the "attention of our readers to the following indisputable "considerations, which determine whether an affirma-"tive or negative answer must be given to the present "question.

"1st. The good effect must be certain. It might be "doubtful only when the ill effect would also be doubt-"ful. (Allora solo potrebbe esser dubbio quando fosse "dubbio anche l'effetto cattivo) .2nd. The cause – the

"action – must be capable of producing the good effect.
"St. Thomas, speaking specifically of killing praeter
"intentionem, says: 'An action placed with a good inten-
"tion may become unlawful from its incapacity to pro-
"duce the good effect intended.' 3d. The cause must, by
"its own nature, produce the good effect, and not merely
"by the intention or protest of the agent or by purely
"extrinsic circumstances. 4th. It is necessary that the
"good effect be not otherwise obtainable – that is, with-
"out the ill effect. In other words, it is necessary that
"the ill effect be inevitable. 'It is certainly necessary,'
"says Suarez, 'that the ill effect be unavoidable.' The
"reason is manifest. If the soldier, for instance who
"explodes a powder-magazine so that it might not fall
"into the enemy's hands, can nevertheless save his own
"life, he is obliged to do so. Otherwise he sins, and
"sins gravely.

IV

(15) "The doctrine of direct and indirect killing
"being set down, let us pass to examine the proposed
"question of the so-called hunger-strike or voluntary
"fast. It is superfluous to say that our examination is
"purely objective, and that we do not intend to either
"directly or indirectly deny or call in question the
"formal or subjective lawfulness of the conduct of the
"Mayor of Cork.

"First of all, in order that our study, although
"brief, be complete, let us see what value the argu-
"ments adduced by the defenders of the lawfulness may
"have. The only argument, if so it may be called, which
"has any value as proof is the accurate exposition and
"application of the Catholic doctrine of indirect volun-
"tary. The other arguments, so called by the said de-
"fenders, either do not prove anything, or prove very
"little. They are the following: 1st. The example of
"Jesus Christ and of Elias who fasted forty days; 2nd.
"The fact of Samson, who pulled down the columns
"which supported the building, and perished with the
"others under the ruins; 3rd. The fact of St. Eusebius,
"(A.D. 356) told by Baronius in his 'Annals'; 4th. The
"doctrine of Suarez, 'De Legibus,' book iii, chap. 30,
"n. 1, and book vi, chap. 7, n. 9; 5th. The doctrine of
"Lessius, 'De Justitia et Jure,' book ii, chap. 9 Dubit.
"6, n. 29; 6th. The example of the soldier who explodes
"the powder-magazine; the case of the shipwrecked
"person who gives to another the plank of safety;
"the case of the Religious who, in order to be faithful
"to his Rules, abstains from those foods which are
"necessary for his health, etc."

(16) "1st, In regard to the first argument we remark
"that it has no value, and it is, to say the least, the
"very height of irreverence to make a comparison be-
"tween the fast of the Mayor of Cork and that of Elias
"or of the Divine Master."

(17) "2nd, As to the second, we may answer with the Angelic Doctor in the words of St. Augustine: 'Sampson is excused for killing himself and his enemies by presuming that he did so under the inspiration of the Holy Spirit, Who wrought many miracles through him'."

(18) "3rd, The words which St. Eusebius of Vercelli, while imprisoned for the faith, addressed to the heretic Patrofilus, do not apply. They are an open profession of faith, a generous protest of preferring rather to die than receive food from the hands of heretics, instead of from his own brothers, so that it might not seem that he made common cause with the heretics. The following is, in fact, how Baronius himself explains the conduct of the holy Bishop: 'Patrofilus, when all his wiles failed to induce Eusebius to hold communication with him, planned to compel him, when detained in prison, to accept the food he sent him. If he accepted it, Patrofilus could boast,—however vainly—that Eusebius made common lot with him in food and drink. But if, on the other hand, he refused the food, and thus died of hunger, Patrofilus would proclaim to the whole world the calumny that Eusebius, to his shame, had voluntarily put an end to his own life.'

"It is necessary,—using the words of Suarez—to incur even death—and nobody can doubt it—'when violation of the law would result in contempt or injury to religion or give scandal to the weaker ones. In such cases the interests of the community and of religion must be consulted in preference to the private good even of one's own life'."

(19) "4th, Suarez (De Legibus, book iii, chap. 30, nn. 1-11) does no more than expound the true doctrine of the obligation to sometimes observe the law even at the risk of one's own life. Here is the title of the chapter: 'Can the civil law oblige its subjects to its observance at the risk of every temporal evil and even of death?' And he answers affirmatively, adding that this opinion is 'common and, to my mind, certain.' (l.c.n. 4) And undoubtedly it is certain. But in our case there is no human law which imposes the hunger-strike."

(20) "In book vi, chap. 7, n. 9, Suarez says, 'So too, a person justly sentenced to death by starvation is not obliged in conscience to abstain from food if he can get it. He may, however, abstain from the food if he chooses to do so.' This case, as one may see, is altogether different from ours. It is the case of someone who has been justly condemned to the penalty of death and that by starvation."

(21) "5th, The doctrine of Lessius in the place cited (De Justitia et Jure, book ii, chap. 9, Dubit. 6, n. 29) is the same as that of Suarez. Here are his precise

"words: 'A person condemned to death by starvation "may lawfully abstain from food surreptitiously "brought to him . . . For this he has a just reason "namely that he may conform to a just sentence'."

(22) "6th, The case of the soldier who explodes the "powder-magazine, even though he foresees that he "will be the victim of the explosion; the case of the "shipwrecked person who gives the life-preserver to "another; the case of the Religious who, to be faithful "to his Rules, does the heroic act of refusing those "foods which are necessary for his health – these and "similar examples aptly illustrate the doctrine of in-"direct voluntary, in its practical applications."

V

"Let us, in fine, conclude this study, and express "our opinion about the proposed question."

(23) "Voluntary fast is not an act intrinsically bad. "That is certain. So, if voluntary fast is not intrinsi-"cally bad, and therefore may even be good, or at least "indifferent, (e quindi puo' essere anche buono o al-"meno indifferente), it evidently follows that the doc-"trine of the indirect voluntary is applicable to it. "Therefore, according to the expounded principles, to "abstain from food is not unlawful, even if some in-"jury results from this voluntary fast, provided that "the injury be not intended, and there is a just and "proportionate reason to permit it. (24) Neither can "it be said that voluntary fast is, within certain limits, "good or at least indifferent, but becomes unlawful if "prolonged until it causes death. Undoubtedly a time "comes when it necessarily produces death. But not for "this, and this alone, does it become bad. If, at the "beginning, it was not bad, it cannot become such as "time advances. Moreover, it cannot become bad as "long as a right intention remains in the agent, and a "just reason continues. (25) This only must be added, "that the ill effects of the fast increasing, and the fast "becoming the proximate cause of inevitable death, "the motive (the good effect) which, at the beginning, "could make it lawful, now perhaps, does not any "longer do so. For, according to the principles before "mentioned, the reason for placing the action must be "proportionate to the gravity of the ill effect, and to "the greater or lesser influx which the cause exerts "in producing it."

(26) "Therefore the whole question, objectively "speaking, resolves itself into inquiring whether he "who has recourse to a voluntary fast producing death, "has a reason just in itself, and if that reason is suffici-"ent (27) Even the defenders of the lawfulness of the "Cork case admit that the desire of shortening impri-"sonment in order to regain liberty, the wish to place "an act of protest against the sentence pronounced by

"the judges, the wish to excite public opinion in one's "own favor, would not be just and sufficient reasons. "(28) These reasons are grave, it is true, but pertain to "private, individual welfare, and, as such, are not "sufficient to render lawful an act which brings about "the loss of a good supreme in the natural order – the "loss of life."

(29) "In our case, the good effect which is desired "through the voluntary fast is the autonomy, the "liberty of Ireland,– the public welfare of the Nation. "(30) This reason is certainly just in itself. Nobody "can doubt it. But is it just and sufficient also when all "the circumstances of this case are considered? In "other words, are there verified in this case, all the "before mentioned conditions of an indirect voluntary?"

"Is it true, 1st, that the good effect is certain?"

"Is it true, 2nd, that the cause is adapted to producing that effect?"

"Is it true, 3rd, that the good end cannot be otherwise obtained, i.e., without the bad effect?"

"THIS WE DO NOT SEE (Non lo vediamo.)"

(31) "Therefore we cannot admit, that the so-called "hunger-strike is a means sure, of its nature efficacious, "necessary, proportionate to obtaining national liberty "and independence, and that there are no other and "more efficacious means to assert and vindicate the one "and the other. How many are the means to secure "public opinion, to safeguard one's own rights, to uphold the cause of one's own Nation? Is it really necessary to have recourse to a voluntary fast and die of "hunger?"

(32) "Then only could and should the lawfulness of "this fast, resulting in death, be admitted, when it "could be demonstrated that it is the means certain, "efficacious, necessary, proportionate to attaining national freedom and independence – in other words, "only when there are verified each and all the conditions of the indirect voluntary. (33) Until this be "shown, we shall, in concluding, say with St. Thomas "(l.c.): 'An action placed with a good intention may "nevertheless be unlawful if it be incapable of producing the good effect intended'."

— MACSWINEY'S PHILOSOPHY —

"That we shall win our freedom I have no doubt. That we shall use it well, I am not so certain."

Appendix C

"THE EXAMINER," BOMBAY, INDIA
(Editorials, Jan. 8 and 15, 1921)

THE ETHICS OF HUNGER-STRIKING
A POST-FACTUM SURVEY

(1) "The Examiner has a rather irritating way of "keeping silence on a current controversy while excite-"ment is on, and tackling it only after feeling has died "away, and people are in a condition to think impar-"tially. In regard to that hunger-striking business, we "followed this policy almost to the end, but yielded to "the pressure of many correspondents just before the "event reached its denouement. Shortly afterwards, we "were informed of the death of the Mayor of Cork, and "of ecclesiastical ceremonies calculated to cause in-"dignation and scandal to some, and pleasure and "triumph to others. It is reported that Rome has under-"taken to sit in judgment on the question, and every-"body is waiting eagerly for the result. Meantime this, "if true, is no reason why people should not discuss "the ethics of the question according to their lights. "This we have already done in two short articles, and "now we propose to supplement these articles by an-"other of a more comprehensive kind."

THE MOOT QUESTION

(2) "MacSwiney died, and was buried amidst scenes "of enthusiasm. He had pitted his determination "against the Government, and almost 'praeter spem,' "the Government bucked up and stood firm and held "its own. The defeat of MacSwiney is then converted "into a vctory by calling MacSwiney a martyr – not "for his faith but for his country. This was the atti-"tude adopted by the decreased himself. He officially, "and in writing, declared this attitude, and this there-"fore is the moot question to be discussed.

"After our first article appeared, we received a long "letter which took up a line diametrically opposite to "ours on this point. (3) We had admitted two pleas "which might possibly exonerate the Mayor from the "guilt of suicide. (4) First came the hope and expecta-"tion that he would not die, because Government would "yield and order his release. (5) Secondly, even if he "did die, he might be imbued with a conviction that he "was justified in doing so, as an act of patriotic serv-"ice to his country. The correspondent, in embracing "these concessions, presses the second one further than "we should allow. He considers that the idea about "dying for his country as a martyr is not only a sub-"jective conviction but also an objective verity. He "repeats the contention, often heard, that Ireland is "not in rebellion against a legitimate Government, but

"is fighting for its rights against an illegitimate Gov-
"ernment, and is therefore acting in self-defense
"against an unjust aggressor. All the conditions of
"war are there, he considers. But in the state of
"war it is legitimate for citizens to die for the cause
"of their country, even if the death is brought on by
"deliberate self-starvation. There is much else in the
"letter which we have already dealt with, and need
"not say the same thing over again. But the above
"point is one not hitherto handled, and it has now be-
"come the moot-point of the discussion."

WAR VS. REBELLION

(6) "It is not our intention to drift into a political
"controversy over the question whether Ireland is at
"war or in rebellion. We will merely offer the follow-
"ing points, and leave our readers to apply them for
"themselves:

(7) (a) "Even a usurping power, unjustly annex-
"ing a country, can acquire legitimate rulership by
"prescription, i.e., by a period of pacific possession.
"England first invaded Ireland seven hundred years
"ago, in the 12th century, and gradually acquired
"possession piece-meal till the occupation was com-
"pleted after the coming of William of Orange about
"1688. Since then, the complete possession has been
"continuous, but marked by local revolts, some of them
"widely spread, occurring at frequent intervals – per-
"haps a couple in a century – ever since. These out-
"breaks prevented the English possession from being
"altogether pacific. But the question would have to be
"settled by historians combined with theologians,
"whether these recurring revolts, which certainly re-
"vealed discontent among a section, were sufficient to
"invalidate the English claim of prescriptive rights.
"(8) Speaking broadly, I think the consensus of civil-
"ized humanity, for at least a century back, would be
"that Ireland had become, and was, an integral part of
"the British dominions, that the English king and par-
"liament was its legitimate ruler; and that revolt
"against the existing authority was rebellion and not
"war."

(9) (b) "Theologians lay down certain rules under
"which rebellion, even against a legitimate ruler, is
"justified, namely, when the government is absolutely
"unjust, tyrannical and intolerable to the nation as a
"whole; when no remedy is possible except deposition,
"and where revolution will achieve the desired remedy,
"and will probably not make matters worse. Granted
"that the English government of Ireland in past cen-
"turies has been abominable – a fact acknowledged by
"the greatest English statesmen and historians times
"out of number – (10) it can be questioned whether
"these epithets could be applied to the rule of the
"country during recent generations. Grievances still
"remained, disabilities still remained, both clamouring

"for a remedy. (11) But whether these were so grievous
"to the nation as a whole – apart from certain cliques
"of politicians, journalists and agitators – as to justify
"rebellion, is a question which would first require a
"close examination of the facts, and then a close ap-
"plication of theological principles, to decide. We leave
"the question undiscussed."

OUR PRESENT SCOPE

"In what follows, so far as we touch on the question
"of patriotism, we treat of it in the abstract only.
"Even assuming that Ireland is legitimately at war
"with an illegitimate government, we have still to ask
"what kind of exposure to death in the name of pa-
"triotism is justified by principle in such a state of
"war. In particular we have to ask whether among
"legitimate acts of sacrifice of life, is to be included
"the act of a citizen in prison deliberately starving
"himself with a view of securing his release, or fail-
"ing that, of exhibiting enthusiasm for his country, and
"persevering in his act, even while contemplating his
"own death as the natural and perhaps inevitable con-
"sequence of his persistency. (12) We are not under-
"taking to prove a thesis, and therefore do not elabo-
"rate our article with the citation of authorities. (13)
"We let our mind go its way ruminating and reasoning,
"stating principles and drawing conclusions according
"to our own judgment.

(14) "The subject has its own interest as a study
"in Ethics, quite apart from the incident which has
"given rise to the discussion. This is why we take quite
"a wide range, and cover diversified ground which in-
"cludes other questions as well."

THE BASIS OF RESPONSIBILITY

"The whole foundation of moral responsibility lies
"in the definition of an 'actus humanus' or human act.
"(15) An 'actus humanus' is defined as 'actus delibera-
"tus cum cognitione finis;' and the 'finis' referred to is
"the 'finis operis,' the effect issuing straight from the
"act itself. (16) This definition has a corrollary, namely
"that human acts are acts for which the agent is re-
"sponsible. He is responsible for the 'actus' because it
"is 'deliberatus;' he is responsible for the 'finis,' that is
"for every result or consequence which is foreseen
"('cognitione') to issue straight out of the act itself."

(17) "When these definitions, which are axiomatic,
"have been grasped, a further question arises: When
"is a man justified in taking upon himself the respon-
"sibility of the act, if some part of its effect is bad?"

(18) (a) "If there is only one outcome, and that is
"bad, the act must not be done.

(b) "If there is a good effect and a bad one, the first "question is, whether the bad effect can be separated "off and cancelled. If so, the difficulty disappears.

(c) "If the bad outcome cannot be separated, the "action can nevertheless be justified for one or more "of these reasons: (1) a necessity; (2) a duty; (3) a "right.

"Take these three in turn:"

NECESSITY, DUTY, RIGHT

(a) "It is difficult to think of any positive act which "is absolutely or physcially necessary, and at the same "time deliberate. One can only think of absolute neces-"sities of the negative order. Thus, being unable to get "to church in time, I must miss Mass. Being unable "to carry a load, I have to leave it behind. In such "cases the omission of the act is involuntary.

"But there can be cases of relative or hypothetical "necessity; for example: If I am to preserve my life, "I must breathe and eat. If I am to keep my appoint-"ment, I must either walk or ride. If I have to ride, I "must spend some money. If a soldier has to be present "at parade, he cannot also be present at Mass. If a "general has to blow up a fort, he has to destroy every "life that is in it, more or less. If an admiral has to "clear the decks of a warship for action, he has to "throw some wounded overboard. If I want to save my "life from snakebite, I must have my arm cut off. If "I want to escape from a ship on fire, I have to throw "myself helpless into the sea. If I want to defend my "country, I have to run imminent risk of losing my "life; and so on through a thousand instances."

(19) "In all such cases, where a bad effect is neces-"sarily tied up with an otherwise good action, I am "justified in performing the good act, provided I have "at my back some reason of duty or right to perform "that act."

(b) "The duty in question may be to God, my neigh-"bor or myself. It is my duty to adhere to the pro-"fession of the faith, even though this brings death on "myself or my family. It is my duty to obey orders "in the army, even though it means sacrifice of life. "A magistrate is bound to pass a sentence of death, "even though the criminal be his own father, etc., etc. "In such cases the act is justified by duty, in spite of "the concomitant and unavoidable bad outcome."

(20) (c) "As regards rights to throw away my life, "these are, in every case, subject to the fundamental "right and duty of self-preservation. I have a right as "well as a duty to protect my life, my goods, my reputa-"tion, against unjust aggression, and this justifies me "in the action of self-defense –'moderamine inculpatae

"tutelae'- even though it involves damage to the ag-
"gressor. (21) But I have no right to throw away my
"own life except in execution of my duty, or in defense
"of some necessary virtue such as faith, honesty, truth-
"fulness, chastity."

(24) "Even so, I am only allowed to throw away my
"life in a negative way. I am not allowed, deliberately,
"and with foreseen results, to bring about my own
"death, in order to preserve these virtues. I am only
"allowed to incur death at the hands of others, through
"my tenacity in adhering to them. I do not know of any
"principle in Moral Theology which allows me to seek
"or incur death at my own hands or by my own act.
"Such an action can be allowed only when it is en-
"forced by a duty, and this duty must be a higher and
"stronger duty than that of self-preservation — for it
"is an axiom that where two duties clash, the higher
"or more imperative duty must have the preference."

RIGHTS OF PATRIOTISM

(22) "If this clear doctrine be accepted — and I do
"not see how, on our Catholic principles, it can be
"denied — it follows that no man is justified in sacrific-
"ing his life out of a motive of patriotism merely as a
"right. (25) No man has a right to kill himself, or to
"expose himself to death, because forsooth he feels
"enthusiastic for the cause of his country, and wants
"to externate his enthusiasm in an act of self-sacrifice.
"It is only patriotism as a duty that justifies such
"sacrifices. This duty is limited to acts of war by those
"who are enlisted in the belligerent army. It can at
"most be extended to those who are incidentally thrust
"into a position of having to defend their community or
"their city — in which case the citizens can be regarded
"as enlisting in a voluntary and temporary emergency."

(26) "Voluntary self-sacrifice of life cannot be justi-
"fied merely because it may serve the country in-
"directly. For instance, soldiers would never be allowed
"to shoot themselves in the presence of the enemy,
"merely to make a demonstration of their heroism and
"determination to resist. Nor would it be right for
"women and children to come to the ramparts and stab
"themselves in the presence of the besieger, in order to
"excite the compassion of the enemy and cause him to
"relax his rigour. Nor would it be allowed for either
"soldiers or civilians to shoot themselves rather than
"fall into the hands of the foe, or in order to escape the
"cruelties of capture, or the hardships of imprison-
"ment. These actions, whether of self-killing or killing
"of others, could never be justified merely as an ex-
"pression of enthusiasm for one's country, in order to
"stir up the zeal or fire the courage of others or to
"create an impression on the mind of the foe."

DUTIES OF PATRIOTISM

(28) "No, unless we are ready to open the door to "moral anarchy, we must limit the occasions of voluntary and foreseen sacrifice of one's own life to cases "where patriotism involves some clear and specific duty. "Thus it is a duty for the soldier to risk his life in "battle under orders. It is his duty to place himself in "special danger in order to secure an advantage in the "battle. He has a right to offer himself to undertake "to expose himself to such dangers voluntarily, where "some important service needs to be done by somebody. He may rush forward to spike a gun, knowing "full well that even if he manages to do it, he cannot "possibly get back alive. He may try to race across a "field of battle with a message in the hope of getting "through, even though the chances of getting through "may seem infinitesimal. (27) In short, **a man for the "good of his country may in war run risks of death "which amount to moral certainties. But he can never "deliberately kill himself, or bring about his own death "even in battle. He is allowed to expose himself to "death at the hands of the enemy, and that is all.**

(29) "Outside actual warfare or its equivalent, "where there is no specific duty to run risks, the normal duty of self-preservation remains in possession. "(30) Any exception in the way of risk has to be justified by the proved presence either of a duty or of a "right; and the burden of proof lies on the shoulders "of those who contemplate the action which involves "risk of life."

KILLING OTHERS

"So far as regards the sacrifice of one's own life. A "kindred question arises about causing the death of "others. Even when shooting an enemy in battle, the "only sound mental attitude of the army is this: 'We "are defending our country against an unjust aggression, and our whole objective is to put a stop to this "aggression. The war must be defensive throughout "in its ethos, even though the action is sometimes aggressive, e.g., in trying to recover rights which have "been usurped. The real object of our warfare is to "stop the enemy who is attacking us, and bring his "aggression to an end. If the enemy perseveres in his "intention to attack us, a status belli is established in "which sometimes one side attacks and sometimes the "other. But even when we are attacking, our attacks "must have fundamentally the nature of a defense. We "are only killing the enemy because he is bent on killing us, and because we can only defeat his intention "of killing us by killing him.

"It is clearly recognized that this killing is confined "strictly to belligerents officially organized as such. If "civilians, not enlisted, acquire the same right to kill, "this is only on the principle of self-defense either of "an individual or a community which is actually suffer-

"ing from an attack. It is recognized that no citizen "(nor even a soldier) is justified in a private or unofficial "killing of a pacific enemy-subject. He might be "arrested and delivered over to the authorities by way "of precaution, and that is all."

PECULIAR CASES

(23) "Peculiar cases arise in which a warlike act in-"volves the destruction of lives (one's own and others) "by an act deliberately performed. Thus **a captain "blows up his ship in order that it may not be cap-"tured by the enemy, and thus be added to the enemy "fleet. The blowing up involves the death of himself "and all who are under him. The act is deliberate with "knowledge of the end.** The formal object is to destroy "the ship, and thus deprive the enemy of a material "object which will strengthen his resources. But this "carries with it the death of the crew, including the "leader who orders the explosion. I do not think any "moral theologian would condemn this act. They would "justify it by saying that the destruction of the ship "is a legitimate act of war, because it deprives the "enemy of a serious advantage. It is merely a regret-"table accident that the crew cannot escape from the "explosion. If they could escape, they would be bound "on the ground of self-preservation to do so. They "cannot, and so are involved in the destruction. This "evil aspect of the case has to be regretfully ignored, "just because **the act itself is justified by a combina-"tion of moral necessity, duty and right.**

"I do not think, however, that a captain would be "allowed morally to blow up his ship merely out of "bravado or enthusiasm, or to escape capture, if the "taking of the ship would be of no use to the enemy. "No captain would be considered guilty of a breach of "duty by yielding himself and his crew when nothing "was to be gained by holding out. Nor has he any right "to take his own life or that of his crew merely to "escape imprisonment.

"It must be acknowledged that by strict obligation "the captain is not bound to blow up his ship. He would "be fully justified in yielding it up when fighting be-"came useless. But I think it is feasible to answer that "idealism conceives a higher notion of duty than that "of minimal obligation. There is a certain generosity "which leads a man to throw himself wholly into the "cause, and put his noblest and best into it regardless "of sacrifice. This ideal is considered not only legiti-"mate but praiseworthy and admirable. Such enthusi-"astic ideals seem to carry with them justification for "running risks to life and facing morally certain death "even though not obliged strictly to do so. Many such "voluntary self-sacrifices have been glorified in song, "and I do not think that theologians have deemed it "necessary to condemn them as immoral. They would, "however, insist on a cause or reason, an important "service to the cause proportional to the gravity of the

"sacrifice; and this is realized only if the blowing up of
"the ship deprives the enemy of some serious ad-
"vantage in acquiring it for himself."

WHAT IS NOT ALLOWED

"It is this margin of zeal and enthusiasm, outside
"the range of strict obligation, that makes our moral
"judgments somewhat elastic. It enables us to con-
"done on subjective grounds acts which perhaps ob-
"jectively one would find it difficult to justify. Still
"while making such allowances, it is important always
"to bear in mind the objective principles and standards,
"and not drift into loose doctrine, because forsooth we
"are filled with enthusiastic admiration for persons and
"actions heroic. Thus we find numerous examples in
"romances of people killing themselves rather than
"fall into the hands of their enemies – not out of
"cowardice but out of noble pride. We read of men
"arranging to stab the women of their party in case
"they fall into the hands of a hoarde of lecherous
"savages. In real life we have been told of cases where
"soldiers in Mesopotamia shot themselves and, at spe-
"cial request, shot each other in order to avoid the
"brutalities and mutilations apprehended from the
"Arabs. Whatever sentiments of respect, charity and
"pity may invade our minds on such occasions, and
"whatever subjective condonations we may be able to
"frame, still it will never do to justify such actions
"objectively. For if we begin thus, the foundations of
"the moral law will be undermined, and there is no
"telling what lengths we shall go by degrees."

OTHER CASES

"Other cases occur to the mind. A captain sticks to
"his ship and goes down with her; and the newspapers
"are full of praises for his heroic devotion to duty.
"But here a distinction is wanted. It is truly heroic for
"a captain to be the last to leave his ship, in order to
"set an example of self-control, to calm the passengers
"and crew, to give preference to others, and to take
"the greatest risks on himself for their sake. But when
"remaining on the ship is of no further use, either to
"the owner of the ship or to the crew or passengers,
"there is no intelligible reason why he should remain.
"Duty does not require it either in the way of justice
"or of charity. When all useful purposes have been
"served, the fundamental duty of self-preservation
"emerges in full force, and the captain is bound to
"take all means available to save his own life, pro-
"vided it does not endanger the life of others by over-
"crowding a boat, etc. To go down with his ship under
"such circumstances is heroism of the false melo-
"dramatic order, and has no justification in moral
"theology.

"Again there is the case of two people and the
"plank in a shipwreck. If I have got the plank, and it
"will only support one, I am justified – by the right of

"self preservation – to thrust back another person who "tries to get hold of it. If I thrust him off he will be "drowned; but if he gets on we shall both of us be "drowned. In any case one must be drowned; and in "equal dangers I have a right to prefer myself to "others. On the other hand, I have a right – by virtue "of charity – to relinquish my plank to the other man, "thus giving him the preference of certain safety, "while I take to myself the risk of almost certain death "– I say almost certain, for something may turn up and "save me after all.

"The same with food which is not sufficient to keep "a whole party alive. I may refuse to take my share, "because it means giving my share to save the life of "others. Again I may throw myself into the water to "save a drowning man, even though my chances of sav-"ing him are problematical. But if it is certain that I "cannot save the life, I ought to remain on the bank "and helplessly witness the death. The jumping in "under such hopeless circumstances might secure me "the acclamations of an admiring nation and a glorious "epitaph on my grave. But my credit would be a hol-"low one. It would testify to my spirit of self-sacrifice, "but the self-sacrifice itself would remain unjustified, "just because it was futile. No one is justified in throw-"ing away his own life when the loss is futile.

"The noble feeling that a man has under such cir-"cumstances is expressible thus: 'I cannot stand by and "witness this horror! I must be doing what I can.' The "instinct is good. But instincts, even good ones, have "to be controlled by reason. If 'doing my best' means "achieving nothing, what is the good of it? And if "doing my futile best involves the loss of my own life, "neither duty impels me, nor right justifies me, in "performing the act, which is not only futile but mis-"chievous. According to the foregoing method of an-"alysis, such an act produces no good effect, but only "a bad effect; and an act which produces only a bad "effect must never be done.

"But you will urge, it produces at least the good "effect of an example of heroism stimulating the ad-"miration and imitation of others. I answer: The ad-"miration thus stimulated is an indiscriminate one. A "judicious mind would admire the subjective heroism, "while condemning the futile act, and he would judge "the heroism misapplied. As to imitation, if the act "is a mistaken one and objectively wrong, it ought "not to be imitated.

"Other cases occur in connection with imprisonment. "Moral theologians allow simple attempts to escape "from prison on the ground that the State does not "put the prisoner on his conscience to submit to con-"finement, but confines him by force, with fetters and "bars, and, rather expects him to escape, if he can. "He is allowed to file away the bars, or even break "the door, and to trick the guards, but not to bribe "or corrupt them in their duty. They would allow him "to struggle with his guards, but not to do them a

"serious injury in the struggle; still less to kill them.
"They would allow him to run some risk in jumping
"out of a window. But they do not justify him in bring-
"ing himself to certain death as an escape from im-
"prisonment into the next world. (31) If self-killing
"to escape imprisonment were justified, every prisoner
"taken in war would have been justified in shooting
"himself if he could. For, as said before, the self-killing
"is the same as to its finis operis, no matter whether
"it is done by revolver in one second, or by self-starva-
"tion in three months – always assuming that the death
"is contemplated as the de facto issue of the starva-
"tion, and the purpose is to go on even if death results."

SOME FALLACIES

"In order to clear thinking on such points, we must
"first get our definitions clear as a general background.
"To confine ourselves to self-killing by starvation, we
"must first of all realize the following principles:

(32) "The morality of the act is determined by its
"finis operis, which must not be obscured by introduc-
"ing the finis operantis. Thus abstention from food has
"for its finis operis gradually to weaken the body; and
"if prolonged, this weakness will issue in death. Fast-
"ing, if prolonged enough is just as infallible – though
"gradual – a means of killing oneself as taking prussic
"acid which acts instantaneously. This being the case,
"it is mere sophistry to say: 'Although I am acting in
"such a way as to encompass my own death, I do not
"intend my own death, but only to promote the cause
"of my country.' One might as well argue: 'In taking
"prussic acid I do not intend my own death, but only to
"demonstrate scientifically the effects of poison.' I
"might as well argue: 'In putting a bullet through my
"brain I do not intend to kill myself; I merely intend
"to prove the efficacy of my revolver.' The sati wo-
"man in India might just as well argue, when she
"throws herself on the pyre: 'I do not intend to kill
"myself; I merely wish to add glory to my husband's
"funeral.' The bankrupt suicide might just as well
"argue: 'I do not mean to kill myself, I merely mean
"to shun disgrace.' A sufferer might argue: 'I do not
"mean to kill myself, but merely to relieve myself of
"intolerable pain and spare my relations the burden of
"nursing me'."

(33) "Still more sophistical would it be to make a
"verbal distinction between 'self-killing' and 'suicide'
"thus: 'I do not intend suicide, but I only mean to kill
"myself in the interests of my country.' It would be
"equally sophistical to say: 'I do not kill myself; I
"merely die' or 'I do nothing to kill myself; I merely
"abstain from food, which is an indifferent and inno-
"cent action.' (34) We have found people arguing that
"fasting, even when it results in death, is not direct
"self-killing but indirect. This is quite untrue. There
"is nothing more direct than the relation between food
"and the sustentation of life; and to withhold food till

"a man dies is just as direct killing as applying a dose
"of poison. (35) The only difference is that poison acts
"suddenly and starvation acts gradually; but both are
"equally direct."

A FALLACY ABOUT INTENTION

(36) "Amongst several of the writers on this question we have noticed another fallacy. They seem to
"think that the 'directing of the intention' makes a
"difference to the morality of the act objectively considered, e.g., that if you kill yourself intending suicide
"it is suicide, and if you kill yourself intending something else, it is not suicide. This is just as good as
"saying: 'If you knock your neighbor down intending
"assault and battery, it is assault and battery; but if
"you knock your neighbor down intending to test the
"strength of your biceps, it is not assault and battery.
"This kind of argumentation is muddle-headed to a
"degree."

(37) "An intention never makes the least difference
"to the objective morality of the act done. What the
"intention does is merely to modify the subjective
"attitude of the mind of the agent towards the act.
"It leaves the act objectively the same, with its objective effects and the full responsibility for them."

(38) "No, the right process in applying the 'principle of two effects' is this: First settle objectively
"whether the act is morally allowed; whether it is
"permissible to perform it as a good act, in spite of
"the evil effect which happens to be bound up with
"its performance. (39) The act let us say is permissible if there is a duty to perform it, and if this duty
"has precedence of the general duty of avoiding evil
"effects as far as possible. It may also be permissible
"if I have a strict right to perform it; a right so strict
"as to override the general duty of avoiding evil effects
"as far as possible. It cannot however be performed
"if there lies on me some specific duty of avoiding that
"particular bad effect. Then again other conditions are
"added."

(40) "The good of the action must be inherent to
"the action, and the direct and immediate outcome of it
"per se. The bad effect must not be inherent to the
"action per se, but per accidens et concomitanter, i.e.,
"it happens to be inseparably attached on this particular occasion, etc. The act is not allowed if the evil
"effect is the means by which the good effect is obtained
"and without which it would not be obtained – and
"so on."

"All this can be, and must be, settled without the
"least reference to intention. It is only by way of corrollary or appendix, that moral theologians add a
"caution. Even though the act with a double effect is
"allowed, this does not abolish the evil effect. It still
"remains that the act is producing a bad effect, which,
"under other circumstances would be sinful. Therefore
"(they say) you must not look upon that evil effect with

"complacency, as if it were not evil. You must still recognize it as evil, and dislike it, and wish you could avoid it. You must feel that you are bringing it about only under a regrettable necessity, because it happens to be tacked on to an act which you have a duty or a right to perform. If you could separate off the evil effect and avoid it you would be obliged to do so. Therefore (they conclude) you must direct your intention to the good which is in the act, and away from the evil which is in it. You must intend the good, and not intend, but merely allow or tolerate, the evil effect."

(42) "Hence it is utterly inept to argue (as some have argued) that the morality of self-killing depends on the intention. 'If he intends to commit suicide, it is suicide; if he does not intend suicide but something else, it is not suicide.' (41) To come back to the concrete case, the proper lines of argument is to determine first of all whether a man is justified in starving himself to death in the attempt to secure his release, or failing that, to give an example to his compatriots under such and such circumstances. When that point is settled the dispute is at an end; and the direction of the intention is merely a secondary and personal matter."

FOOD AND LIFE

"It is true that scanty feeding (or underfeeding) even though it weakens the system, is an indifferent act; and if through such weakening the body falls into a poor condition and thus opens the way to the contracting of a disease of which the man dies, this is an indirect result of abstention. Total abstention from food for a certain time, on the principle of the 'fasting cure,' is again an indifferent act. Fasting and abstinence practised on the principle of penance and mortification is a virtue. (43) But when it comes to persistent starvation wilfully continued till it is foreseen to issue in death, this cannot be justified even on the highest ascetical grounds, unless on the strength of a divine inspiration in a particular case; of which however we never came across an instance recorded in history."

(44) "By way of analogy we recall the fact that Origen was condemned by a consentient voice for his mutilation performed out of zeal for continency; and any cenobite who starved himself to death in order to save his soul, would be similarly condemned as a misguided fanatic. In like manner St. Pelagia's throwing herself down to save herself from outrage, receives no satisfactory objective solution. Except under the hypothesis 'Deo inspirante,' she could not be justified objectively in throwing herself down from an upper window, when the act, in human estimate, meant certain death. The only other excuse would be the subjective one, namely, that her mind was so filled with

"the one idea of escape, that she simply jumped by impulse without reflecting on the consequences of her act."

STOPPING SHORT

(45) "Even though persistent fasting is ex objecto direct self-killing by degrees, there always remains a loophole of escape by stopping the fasting before it becomes fatal. Hence arises the question of hopes and uncertainties. 'It is certain that if I fast long enough I shall infallibly die. But I hope and expect that this will not be necessary. Before it comes to that, my perseverance will conquer, and they will let me out.'

"This expectation might justify fasting for a short time, even if it was calculated to weaken health, provided the intention was to stop as soon as the risk of permanent ruin to health, and the risk of dying by starvation became threatening. But as soon as the risk becomes imminent, and perseverance in fasting makes death likely, then the hunger-striker is confronted with a clear issue."

(46) "There comes a point at which he has either to stop or determine to go on at all costs. What if he determines to go on even if he dies of it? In this case his act by its objective nature (finis operis) becomes an act of foreseen and therefore intended self-killing. (47) To foresee a sinful effect of an action and yet to go on with the action, involves internal guilt of the sin contemplated and foreseen. St. Ignatius points out in his Exercises that to deliberate about a mortal sin is in itself a mortal sin. (49) The will must exclude sin, and must therefore repudiate any act which is seen to issue in a sinful result, unless some justifying cause of necessity, duty or right intervenes to alter the case."

OUR CONCLUSION

(48) "The conclusion we arrive at is that deliberate starvation, contemplated as issuing in death, is an act of direct self-killing; and it is formal suicide unless you can find some justifying reason for the act. Can such justification be found?"

(50) "My memory may be defective, but I cannot remember any single case in moral theology, in which direct self-killing, deliberately contemplated as the finis operis of the act performed, is defended or allowed for any cause whatever. All the causes are of the negative type, namely, of facing death threatened by some external cause, in the performance of a duty, or in the right of self-defense, or in the maintenance of a virtue. For such reasons a man may expose himself to serious risk, and even what is called morally certain death from some external cause. (51) But I have never found theologians justifying any case analogous to that of a man who being put in prison sets about gradually but persistently kill-

why propose to "do no more than state Catholic doctrine"? cases solved by applying doctrine, not by stating; author neither clear, concise nor correct; tautology and contradiction, 125-7; his "indirect suicide" never sinful, often heroic virtue; it is effects of actions, not actions themselves, that are willed directly or indirectly, 127-129; effect willed (a) for itself, or (b) for another inseparable effect, 130; his "effects neither intended nor willed" have no morality; three flaring falsehoods; direct killing explained away; more explaining away; two further false exlanations, 131-4; direct killing defined without mention of intention; tampering with technical theological terms; speaks of "changing indirect voluntary into direct," 135; protest against injustice the immediate and essential good effect of hunger-strike, 136; his examples no parallel for hunger-strike, 137; false implications by false parallels, 138; his Latin definition of suicide correct, his translation of it wrong; his "suicide improperly so called" an ugly phrase, 139; his "unlawful but permitted sometimes," approaches contradiction; "merely permitted," "merely tolerated" he predicates of most heroic actions, 140; his wrong defining and explaining led his readers into many errors; states conditions for lawful indirect voluntary, but makes no effort to apply them; turns instead to his own four "indisputable considerations," two of them truisms, other two false, one copied from Irish "Professor of Morals" who insisted, as we have seen (page 111), that hunger-strike is made protest by intention and circumstances, 141-5; pretends to state and refute arguments of defenders; states them wrongly at every step; his refutations a comedy; palpable proofs and their authors, slyly ignored; "altogether different" his chief rejoinder where difference is only partial; evades proofs of Suarez and Lessius by another "altogether different"; suppressions and evasions; says of some proofs of defenders that they "aptly illustrate doctrine of indirect voluntary"; but our question is, do they, or do they not, prove something for lawfulness of hunger-strike, 141-158; writer says "hunger-strike not an act intrinsically bad and therefore a case of indirect voluntary." Non sequitur; he admits it to be indirect voluntary; why then not solve it by the four familiar conditions, and not by his own "indisputable considerations"? 159; he assumes act itself lawful; why not prove it lawful? why hide defenders' proof? he excogitates different moralities for different refusals of the series; all refusals made one by intention to continue, 160-161; varying proximities to death irrelevant, 162; puzzle copied later in "The Tablet" by Irish "Student of Morals"; writer says "therefore the whole question resolves itself into inquiring" whether the hunger-striker "has a reason just in itself and sufficient"; he should have said "resolves itself into inquiring whether the four conditions of lawful indirect voluntary are verified or not," 160-163; defenders have made no admissions of sufficient or insufficient reasons; writer substitutes fictitious reasons for MacSwiney's real reasons; he discounts all reasons of private welfare, 164-5; says unblushingly that good effect desired by MacSwiney was "the liberty of Ireland"; thus far he only says "desired"; now he adds "desired and necessary," and by necessary he means necessary for the lawfulness of MacSwiney's hunger-strike until death; "reasons grave but not grave enough, just in themselves, but not in the circumstances," 166-7; note writer's "practical application" of indirect voluntary, mixed with his "indisputable considerations," 168-9; more of his "accurate application," 170; asserts and denies indirect voluntary of hunger-strike, 171; does not see because he does not look; recklessly asserts good effect of Irish hunger-strike to be otherwise attainable, 172-3; demands demonstration that is neither necessary nor sufficient, 174; thus far his "proportion of good desired"; now it is desired and necessary for lawfulness, 175; still more of his "altogether different," 176; makes false statement of MacSwiney's purpose, 177; returns to his "indisputable considerations"; began by falsely attributing to MacSwiney a purpose impossible to attain; sums up and solves MacSwiney case, 178; states, "with St. Thomas," the fatal verdict; cooperates with other adversaries in their pretense of orthodoxy, 179; arrives at fatal verdict "with St. Thomas," after twenty-six wrong explanations, five contradictory explanations, four absurdities, two false parallels, three tautologies, twelve evasions, eighteen false statements of fact, nine false denials, seven false assumptions, two false protestations, five wrong conclusions and eleven wrong definitions—a long list of crimes against Catholic theology and also against pagan justice, 181-2.

COMMANDMENT, FIFTH: Forbids always, commands sometimes; entirely negative in form, in substance negative and positive; expressly says what must not be done, implies what must be done; wanton destruction of life forbidden; generous sacrifice of one's own life approved and commended (Suarez, Lessius, St. Alphonsus), 45-47.

DAMAN, FR. C. S. S. R.: Another retailer of contradictions; says that hunger-strike until death is contrary to the law of self-preservation, 101; goes on to admit exceptions to that law, but only by contradicting himself, 102; he writes: "From this it seems to follow," and his false consequent follows from his false antecedent, 103; "hunger-strike inaugurated until death," he writes, "by some in good faith"; this assumes that hunger-strike is morally evil; again, it is not what any agent professes to intend, but what he actually does intend that is a determinant of the morality of his act, 104; he too omits all mention of injustice and protest against it; concludes with an ugly insinuation of suicide, without any proof whatever, 105.

"ECCLESIASTICAL REVIEW, THE": Published correspondent's inquiry, 10; Review's theologian gave wrong answer to correspondent's inquiry; Editor of The Review wrongly informed present writer that Fr. Wouters, C. S. S. R., "discusses that problem, 11; The Review refused to publish strictures, by the present writer, on its answer to the inquiry of its correspondent, 266, 269; refusal to publish explanation and discussion of current question in Moral Theology is no commendation of The Review, 269.

END OR INTENTION: Its exact meaning not known; chief source of morality; if good, action is good, if evil, action is evil; suicide defined and objections answered, 33-5, 48; subject, object of intention; intending one effect, merely permitting another inseparable effect, 36-37; intention of hunger-striker is to continue refusals of all food, either for some fixed period or until death, 15.

"EXAMINER, THE," BOMBAY, INDIA: Article on hunger-strike a synthesis of all previous fallacies of all adversaries; like Civilta writer, the author professes to want impartial thinking; how impartial!, 183; author begins with "two pleas" in MacSwiney's favor, and pleas presuppose guilt, 184; author's first "plea" of "hope and expectation" groundless, 185; his second "plea" assumes MacSwiney's invincible ignorance that hunger-strike is objectively evil, 186; refuses to discuss whether Irish Revolution was rebellion or war; but assumes rebellion by unproved "consensus of civilized humanity for past hundred years"; contradicted by many English historians and by forty-four Coercion Acts, between the years 1855 and 1881, 188-192; author disclaims undertaking to prove a thesis, yet concludes his article with these words: "The conclusion we arrive at is that deliberate self-starvation, contemplated as issuing in death, is an act of direct self-killing — formal suicide unless" etc.; his pretended reason for not citing authorities, 193; affects unlimited scope of discussion — "wide range," diversified ground"; why define human act, and unintelligibly, 194; "finis," "subject," "object," "external act"; "objective," "direct," "indirect," 195-6; magnifies ill effect, ignores good effect and intention which legitimizes it; false parallels, equivocations, etc., etc., 197; assumes, implies, suggests, insinuates; makes any indirect voluntary impossible, 198; he writes: "The agent is responsible for every foreseen effect"; this reprobated by all moralists living and dead; standing on this dictum of the Editor of "The Examiner," no action producing an ill effect could ever be justified, 199; his "responsibility" irrelevant and confusing; theologians' simple question and answer, 200; requirements all his own for lawful indirect voluntary; he wantonly substitutes and continues to substitute his concoction of "necessity, duty and right" for the sacred ethical Canon, 201; his "necessity," obsolute and hypothetical, irrelevant and confusing; no act justified by his "necessity" or by duty or by right, 202-3; all duties, all rights not known to all agents, 204; his "right to throw away my life" means what? not always obliged to preserve life, reputation, or possessions, 205; fundamental duty is to God not to self; confers fundamental right to necessary means; priority of self-sacrifice over self-preservation, 206; admits here an exception that contradicts him, 207; he writes: "No man is justified insacrificing his life for patriotism as a right," 208; author, with all theologians, defends the captain who sinks his ship and perishes with it; immediately after, the captain contradicts the author ten times, 209-214; "combination of moral necessity, duty and right," what is it?; how does his "moral necessity" differ from duty? 210; captain's sacrifice not negative — very positive; "duty to SEEK death at one's own hands," what is it? 211; Examiner doctrine neither clear nor Catholic; suicides no parallels for hunger-striker, 212; two further contradictions of the author, 213-214; demands proofs, having received proofs aplenty; his feeble objections and numerous contradictions are best proof, 215; his self-killing "TO" escape imprisonment means with the intention of escaping imprisonment; assumes that every hunger-striker intends his own death, 216; he writes: "To behold death as issue and purpose to go on" — another miserable quibbling with words, 217; why and how is the "finis operis" "OBSCURED" by introducing the "finis operantis"? 218; "sources of morality" not suited to author; self-killing never evil from act itself, 219; author's pawns all intend their own deaths as means, 220; author copiously sophistic while accusing defenders of sophistry, 221; his sophistry hung on the term "direct," 222; his "direct" versus the hunger-striker's direct, 223-4; he repeats base quibble, 224; "objective" versus "objectively considered," 225; directing intention makes vast difference; no fallacy in saying "if I intend suicide, it is suicide, if not, it is not suicide"; it is the exact case of the captain, 226;

author makes hunger-striker's genuine directing intention resemble bogus directing of his pawns — another of his unparallel parallels, 227; more of his "objective" and "subjective" in stating a truism; again, directing intention makes a vast difference, 228; intention chief component of all morality; all responsibility derived from it, 229; author says: "First settle objectively"; "the right process is," 230; many words, no reasoning, more of "the right process"; accidental ill effect not imputable because not foreseen; good effect must also be essential, 231-3; author's verdict against MacSwiney; his sea captain contradicts him for the eleventh time; ill effect lawful, mediate unintended means, 234; author writes: "All this can and must be settled without least reference to intention; only by way of corollary or appendix do moral theologians add a caution — you must direct your intention to the good," etc.; "by way of corollary or appendix"!! gross calumny of all moral theologians, 235; verdict of eleven standard moral theologians against "The Examiner's" "corollary or appendix," 236-7; author cites no theologian, mentions none; more of his "right process," "proper lines of argument"; are the four familiar conditions realized or not? 238; his unintended self-killing morally same as intended, hence no morality from intention; turns now to warring on hunger-striker's proportion of good effect, 239-240; sorely laments loss of a single life; continues to insinuate intended self-killing, 241; his "analogy" not an analogy, 242; his "fasting is direct self-killing by degrees" plays up the same old quibble; his "loophole of escape" is on a par with his "two pleas," 243; he writes: "An act of foreseen and therefore intended, self-killing" — an appalling verdict against all heroes, even the martyrs; spells insupportable burdens for all consciences; outrages even the science of Psychology, 244-5; listen to his solemn platitude: "To foresee the sinful effect of an action, and yet go on with the action, involves internal guilt of sin contemplated and foreseen." In other words, an act having a sinful effect is sinful — not very profound theology! Again he writes: "The conclusion we arrive at is that deliberate self-starvation contemplated as issuing in death is an act of direct self-killing — formal suicide, unless you can find some justifying reason"; intended self-killing unless his justifying reason makes the hunger-striker's death unintended instead. And the author finds no such "justifying reason" in the case of MacSwiney. See his thesis and its proof, 246; has not found theology justifying any analogous cases, 248-250; his "lenient view" is like his "loophole" and his "two pleas" — rhetoric, not theology; he says emphatically and falsely; his inference false; another bogus parallel, 250-52; he says "similarly," that is to say "dissimilarly"; more juggling rhetoric; he assumes suicide instead of proving it, and then turns to "possible" exoneration, 253; undignified trick of dialectics, strings of discussion confused and confusing, direct self-killing "irreparable evil," more of his "standard theological schools," 254-5; he writes: "Stating principles, drawing conclusions"; here are some of them — fifteen false implications, nine false protestations, four false inferences, three false assumptions, one false explanation, two sophisms, two practical inconsistencies, thirty-six false principles, eighteen truisms, seven ambiguities, fourteen false parallels, six false statements of fact, one evasion, one obscurity, two absurdities, and sixteen contradictions, 256.

Ghastly logical and theological spectres these of the Editor's "stating principles and drawing conclusions." Why was MacSwiney's death "a grave and irreparable evil"? No compensation for it? "He has won his battle," said the "Westminster Gazette"; "Irish Nationalism will be given a stimulus almost incomparably effective by his death" was the verdict of the editorial writer in the Daily News, London, Eng.; author's falsehoods, fallacies and contradictions forged to serve a most ignoble purpose; Irish people meanwhile consoled by enduring in Freedom's cause, 258; author's slavish serving a blind national prejudice; his treatment of hunger-strike no part of the sacred deposit of theological truth; two worthless pleas presented by him in mock defense of MacSwiney; not even so much remains in extenuation of his own many crimes against Moral

On Morality of Hunger-Strike   345

Theology, and also against the memory of those noblest and bravest champions of eternal justice the world has ever known, 259-60; articles in "The Tablet," "Civilta Cattolica" and "The Examiner" so much alike as to create suspicion of having been composed by the same author, 261.

HUNGER-STRIKE: Correspondent's inquiry from "The Ecclesiastical Review" whether any textbooks on Moral Theology treat of its morality, 10; Catholic Clergy unaware thirteen years after the MacSwiney controversy that hunger-strike is essentially a protest against injustice, 10; correspondent's inquiry wrong, 10; The Review's answer to correspondent's inquiry wrong, 11; question not treated by any theologian, 12; Fr. Tanquerey brief and wrong, 12, 13; "vexed question exercising best casuists of the Church," (Fr. Gannon, S.J.), 12; true doctrine obscured by two-fold conspiracy of equivocation and silence, 13; no definition of hunger-strike ever given by any author, 13; hunger-strike defined and explained; all refusals of food are morally one, by unrevoked intention to continue either for limited period or until death, 14; actual continuance not essential, for the intention is never absolute, but always conditioned, 15; protest against injustice distinguishes hunger-strike from every other fast, 16; proved essentially (i.e. necessarily) protest against injustice; originally instituted as such by conventional usage; of human institution; practised (always in protest) by hierarchy, clergy, by St. Patrick himself, by "the twelve Apostles of Ireland," and by many other holy ones long since canonized by the Church. They fasted, sometimes separately, sometimes conjointly, 17-25; twentieth century hunger-strikes, 23-24; typical case of two effects, 24-5; good effect, protest against injustice; ill effect, physical weakness with probable death; acts producing ill effects sometimes lawful; conditions necessary and sufficient for lawfulness, 26-8; is hunger-strike intil death suicide? sometimes suicidal, never suicide; if not suicide, is it ever lawful? 29; lawful for hunger-striker to desire his death, 33; hunger-strike until death never suicide; he never intends his death either as end or as means; intended death would hinder not help his cause; justice not championed by suicide, 61-3; hunger-strike until death against proportionate injustice always lawful; it is killing oneself, intending only protest; other lawful refusals of food until death, 65-7; other lawful self-killings (1) by positive acts, not by mere omissions; (2) with death certain, sudden and violent, not merely probable, slow, and almost natural, as in hunger-strike, 68; authority of Fr. Patrick Gannon, S.J., Fr. Patrick Casey, S.J., and Fr. Peter Finlay, S.J., 69-71; our conclusions about hunger-strike and its morality are true, evident and certain; our appeal is to the tribunal of all mankind, 74-6; the objections urged against our conclusions have no foundation; they consist of false assumptions, parallels not parallel, false principles aplenty and proofs that prove nothing, 87-90; act not intrinsically evil, 91; theology of hunger-strike not known, nor yet difficult to understand; should be taught, and studied by intelligent lay persons, 268-9; has come to stay; Gandhi, 270.

IRISH "PROFESSOR OF MORALS": States case of hunger-strike briefly, clearly, correctly, 111; solves case of every hunger-strike incorrectly and dishonestly; conceals and minimizes good effect; falsely calls it accidental, not essential, 112; explains protest by extrinsic directing, 113; no circumstance makes hunger-strike protest, 114; absurd conclusions from "Professor's" false principle, 115; infers imputability from every indirect voluntary — unintended as well as intended; his falsified statement of fundamental principle of "two effects"; how enunciated by all moralists, 116; he says "implicitly willed, therefore imputable"; inadvertence cannot excuse him, 117; false! falser!! falsest!!! essentially good effect of protest again sidetracked; concludes indictment, omits intention and urges intrinsic evil of fast itself as means, 118-119; his spurious substitute for moralists' proviso — "provided there is an obligation"; must be credited with enuntiating, in the course of his brief article, thirteen false moral principles, 120-121.

LIFE, HUMAN: Its value; God's own evaluation of it should be man's guide in estimating its value; man's sense of horror at its destruction; need not be preserved in all circumstances; God's dominion over it is absolute; man may sacrifice his own life in any proportionately good cause; he may not arbitrarily destroy it; this doctrine avoids both unreasonable extremes, 54-6.

MacSWINEY, LORD MAYOR: Hunger-strikers no suicides, no sinners, heroes all, noblest of the noble, bravest of the brave, 271; proud pagans of antiquity no heroes; humility, self-sacrifice, resignation in suffering, patience — all Christian virtues of which pagans knew nothing, 272; MacSwiney's prudence and courage, 273; no dreamy ideals, no unpractical visions; knew difficulties and dangers before him; his hope lay in moral rather than physical power, 274; sought prudence, courage, endurance, from Heaven; more evidence of his practical prudence, 275; hurls thunderbolts of defiance at a mighty Empire; first to answer his own call to action; his dying words the same bold defiance, 276; verdict of hierarchy, clergy, Catholic press, secular press; a man of daring, energy, inflexibility; his ideals of liberty, patriotism, government, 277-8; his sublime idealizing about ideals, manhood, freedom, war, ethics of warfare, principles, brotherhood, comradeship, spiritual values, 281-3; no physical victory through moral surrender; national independence a sacred thing; must be secured and safeguarded at any cost; his refusal to resent; his capacity to forgive, 284-6; his sublime principles of civil polity; supernatural faith his conspicuous trait; civil and spiritual liberty inseparable for him; national liberty should be devoted to sacred cause; kinship of nations, not narrow provincialism, 287-8; mingled language of apostle and patriot; wisdom of Heaven in his political policies; "superior armaments make right out of might," 289-90; he reverses the formula; insists righteous war must be Christian; civil liberty's blessings temporal and eternal, 291; abhors eternal effects of civil oppression, 292; civil liberty above nation, race, religion; common humanity, universal brotherhood, 293; let us show our belief beautiful and true, and, in the eternal sense, practical; he was sustained by grand dominating patriotism, 294; grand master patriot of all the ages, 295-6; indomitable because of that master patriotism; "who today is more certain of Immortality"! (The Nation, New York) 297-9; life story and death story added power and force to his words, 300; withering denunciations, solemn warnings, 301; whence the clearer vision that inspired him? 301-2; response more faithful, light more abundant; God's choicer favors for worthier subjects; whence psychologic, theologic, ascetic vision? 302-303; spoke like St. Paul because he lived like him; spoke like St. Paul, prayed like King David, 304; one of his many prison prayers for Ireland; Maid of Orleans, burned as a witch, now St. Joan of Arc; MacSwiney suffered no less, motives as holy — martyr, 305; gave life for motive of supernatural charity towards all his countrymen, 306; "Terence James MacSwiney," 307; "Fitzgerald and Murphy," 308; MacSwiney, Fitzgerald and Murphy, (Poem) 309-311.

MEANS: Actions themselves are the direct and essential means used by agents to attain the ends they have in view, 38, 39.

MERKELBACH, FR. O. P.: Contradicts himself twice on the same page; argues against all hunger-strike until death "for greater reasons," when he not only had not given an "a fortiori" reason nor an "a pari" reason, but had not given any reason at all, 99-100; he says nothing about injustice or protest against it.

MORALITY: Defined; derived from end, means and circumstances — object, intention and circumstances, 30; actions intrinsically good, evil, indifferent, 30-32, 38.

PHILOSOPHY, MacSWINEY'S: 13, 25, 29, 32, 37, 40, 44, 47, 53, 56, 59, 63, 100, 105, 122, 262, 306, 314, 322.

PROPORTION, CIRCUMSTANCE OF: The only circumstance involved in the question of hunger-strike; it is the moral equality of the good effect of protest against injustice, with the life sacrificed to vindicate justice, 64.

SUICIDE: Defined, 35; the suicide essentially a coward; attains most selfish end by most selfish means, 48-50; things that look like suicide but are not, 51-3; ignorance of the doctrine has brought some hunger-strikers to suicidal deaths but not to suicide; justice is not vindicated nor is injustice overthrown by any action of a suicide, 62-3.

TANQUEREY, FR. S.S.: Does not treat question of hunger-strike at all; it is essentially a protest against injustice, and he says nothing whatever about injustice or protest against it, 12; his entire treatment consists of two cases, neither of them a case of hunger-strike at all, and both of which he solves wrongly; his proofs have no value; his first case has no good effect and contradicts itself; his second case doubly wrong, 77-82; wrongly cites "L'Ami du Clergé" as holding with him; contradiction and ethical paradox, 82-85; another of his contradictions, another of his untruths, 86-87.

VERMEERSCH, FR. S.J.: Wrongly cited by adversaries as being in opposition to hunger-strike; neither condemns nor disapproves of any hunger-strike even though it be unto death; merely enunciates three propositions, each of them true, but none of them applicable to hunger-strike at all, 106-7; Tanquerey, Wouters, Merkelbach and Daman alike; each first says what is false, and then asserts the contradictory truth, not by way of retractation, but in self-contradiction; each assents to a true proposition and a false contradictory proposition, at the same time and in the same context, 107-8; note well that each of them has a different indictment of hunger-strike from all the others. At the beginning of the MacSwiney controversy, that was true only of amateur moralists. Now it is true of professionals, 109-10.

VOLUNTARY: Means wished, willed, wanted; actions alone properly voluntary; their effects denominated voluntary — in their causes; direct voluntary is effect willed for itself; indirect voluntary is effect willed (permitted) because inseparable from the direct voluntary, 40.

WOUTERS, FR. C.S.S.R.: Like Frs. Tanquerey, Daman and Merkelbach, he does not treat hunger-strike at all; says nothing about injustice or protest against it, 12; his contribution to the controversy is not discussion; merely a single paragraph full of false principles, ambiguities, errors and contradictions, 94-98.

IRISH WORLD EDITORIAL, MAY 20th, 1933
MORALITY OF HUNGER-STRIKE

THE IRISH WORLD this week presents its readers with a treatise entitled "The Morality of the Hunger-Strike" by the Rev. Michael Hogan, S.J., one of the most vitally important contributions to this subject which has been made in over twelve years of controversy.

The heroic sacrifice of Terence MacSwiney in the cause of Irish freedom was responsible for bringing to public attention the question as to whether it was lawful for a man to die by self-imposed hunger as a protest against injustice. In journals, theological and lay, this question was discussed pro and con by many whose training and mental equipment should have fitted them for a clear and definite exposition of the underlying principles. Yet it is a curious fact that this "clear and definite exposition" was not forthcoming.

Theologians, well-versed in their studies, otherwise capable of logical reasoning, seemed to go sadly astray when they began the consideration of hunger-strike. One of the first and even elementary principles of discussion is the laying down of an accurate definition of the terms we use. Those who discussed this subject seemed averse to defining hunger-strike. It cannot have been that such definition was impossible. Father Hogan, in his treatise, makes this definition his first business. He says:

"Hunger-strike is refusal of all food, intended until "death, in protest against injustice."

Here is the crux of the entire question. For lack of this definition, incalculable confusion has reigned, a question of vital importance has been muddled and messed, and "clear and definite exposition" so much to be desired, has been delayed until Father Hogan produced this present treatise.

Here, at last, we have this subject set forth in its proper terms, without which it is impossible for any intelligent discussion to follow. The world is indebted to Father Hogan for lifting this question out of the quagmire of confused controversy and placing it in a position where it is viewed in its true perspective.

Now that we have the definition, to what conclusion does Father Hogan arrive?

"He points out, in striking and memorable words, "that hunger-strike until death is lawful for propor- "tionate grievance; that it is lawful for a man to "declare he will fast until death in protest against "injustice. In other words, he furnishes clear and con- "vincing theological proof that Mayor MacSwiney and "his heroic comrades, who gave their lives for Ireland in "1920, were not suicides, as some have sought to de- "clare. He shows them for what the people of Ireland "recognize them – martyrs to a cause rendered sacred "by their sacrifice and the sacrifice of countless others "who gave their lives for Ireland before and after "them."

From an Irish point of view this will doubtless be the most significant feature of Father Hogan's treatise. All who remember the death of MacSwiney will recall, also, the furious controversy which raged in theological circles regarding the morality of his hunger-strike; will recall the many who insisted that MacSwiney was a suicide, the few who had the vision to declare that his was a lawful sacrifice.

This discussion, as Father Hogan recalls, continued for months, and, when it did end, it was without any definite decision emerging from one side or the other – so far as the theologians were concerned. It then happened that, recently, the Ecclesiastical Review, in a reply to a question, declared that the manuals of theology had settled the dispute. It is in response to this declaration that Father Hogan prepared his treatise on the subject which The Irish World this week presents to its readers.

Apart, however, from the interest which Irish men and women will take in this question, it has an even wider significance.

The teaching of theological truth is, and must be, a primary consideration. Students preparing for the priestly vocation must be presented with the truth at whatever cost. Due to misunderstanding and misinterpretations, the morality of the hunger-strike has, until now, been left in an ambiguous position. The tendency, in fact, has been, as Father Hogan points out, to leave the impression that hunger-strike was either unlawful or doubtfully lawful, whereas, as a matter of fact, the manuals do not discuss actual hunger-strike at all. A question which, at any time, in any part of the world, may cry out for decision should be made clear in the minds of all who may have to make such decision.

Father Hogan's treatise, therefore, will be welcomed by the Catholic priesthood throughout the world. Not merely does it shed much needed light upon a matter that has for too long stirred controversy to the dregs. It is presented with a definiteness and conclusiveness which makes seemingly impossible any further discussion. It sounds very like the final word on the morality of the hunger-strike.

We need not dwell on the scholarly and literary qualities of the treatise. These will be apparent to all with an eye to what is best in the presentation of the written word. There is a classical simplicity about some of Father Hogan's lines which cannot but be appreciated, while the clarity of his logic will be a delight to all who believe in straight thinking.